Decolonizing
International Relations

Decolonizing International Relations

Edited by
Branwen Gruffydd Jones

ROWMAN & LITTLEFIELD PUBLISHERS, INC.
Lanham • Boulder • New York • Toronto • Plymouth, UK

ROWMAN & LITTLEFIELD PUBLISHERS, INC.

Published in the United States of America
by Rowman & Littlefield Publishers, Inc.
A wholly owned subsidiary of The Rowman & Littlefield Publishing Group, Inc.
4501 Forbes Boulevard, Suite 200, Lanham, Maryland 20706
www.rowmanlittlefield.com

Estover Road
Plymouth PL6 7PY
United Kingdom

British Library Cataloguing in Publication Information Available

Library of Congress Cataloguing-in-Publication Data

Decolonizing international relations / edited by Branwen Gruffydd Jones.
    p. cm.
    Includes bibliographical references and index.
    ISBN-13: 978-0-7425-4023-1 (cloth : alk. paper)
    ISBN-10: 0-7425-4023-5 (cloth : alk. paper)
    ISBN-13: 978-0-7425-4024-8 (pbk : alk. paper)
    ISBN-10: 0-7425-4024-3 (pbk. : alk. paper)
    1. International relations—Congresses. I. Gruffydd Jones, Branwen, 1972–
JZ43.D43 2006
327.101—dc22

                         2006009987

Printed in the United States of America

For my parents

Contents

Acknowledgments   ix

List of Acronyms   xi

Introduction: International Relations, Eurocentrism, and
Imperialism   1
Branwen Gruffydd Jones

PART I EUROCENTRIC ORIGINS AND LIMITS

1 International Relations as the Imperial Illusion; or, the
   Need to Decolonize IR   23
   Julian Saurin

2 International Relations Theory and the Hegemony of Western
   Conceptions of Modernity   43
   Sandra Halperin

3 Liberalism, Islam, and International Relations   65
   Mustapha Kamal Pasha

**PART II THE COLONIAL AND RACIAL CONSTITUTION
           OF THE INTERNATIONAL**

4 Race, Amnesia, and the Education of International Relations   89
   Sankaran Krishna

5 Decolonizing the Concept of "Good Governance"   109
   Antony Anghie

6 Dispossession through International Law: Iraq in Historical and
   Comparative Context   131
   James Thuo Gathii

**PART III TOWARD DECOLONIZED KNOWLEDGE
          OF THE WORLD AND THE INTERNATIONAL**

7 Beyond the Imperial Narrative: African Political
   Historiography Revisited   155
   Alison J. Ayers

8 Mind, Body, and Gut! Elements of a Postcolonial Human
   Rights Discourse   179
   Siba N'Zatioula Grovogui

9 Retrieving "Other" Visions of the Future: Sri Aurobindo and the
   Ideal of Human Unity   197
   B. S. Chimni

   Conclusion: Imperatives, Possibilities, and Limitations   219
   Branwen Gruffydd Jones

Bibliography   243

Index   265

About the Contributors   273

Acknowledgments

The origins of this project lie in a panel organized at the 2003 International Studies Association conference in Portland, called International Relations and "The Rest of the World," which included papers by Mustapha Kamal Pasha, Sandra Halperin, and Branwen Gruffydd Jones, with Siba Grovogui as discussant. The panel was organized while I was holding an ESRC postdoctoral fellowship (no. T026271069) at the University of Sussex, the support of which is gratefully acknowledged. Thanks to Marc Williams, Cate Eschle, Sandra Halperin, Julian Saurin, Alison Ayers, Mustapha Pasha, Mike Sheehan, Martin Mills, Burak Ülman, and Muhammed A. Ağcan for helpful discussions, encouragement, and contributions at various stages of the book project.

The papers contributing to the book were presented at a workshop on Decolonizing International Relations held at the University of Aberdeen in April 2005. The workshop was made possible by a grant from the British Academy, with additional financial support from the University of Aberdeen Visiting Scholars Fund, which were greatly appreciated. I thank Peter Wilkin and Marc Williams for their encouragement and support at that stage of the project. I also thank Grant Jordan and Steve Bruce in the Department of Politics and International Relations, Aberdeen, for their advice and support.

Two of the chapters in this book are revised versions of already published articles. Sankaran Krishna's chapter is revised from "Race, Amnesia and the Education of International Relations," originally published in *Alternatives: Global, Local, Political* (vol. 26, no. 4, October–December 2001). Copyright

I wish to express warm thanks to Renée Legatt at Rowman & Littlefield. From her initial enthusiastic reception of the book proposal to her enduring patience through various delays and extended deadlines, she has provided a close interest in the project and friendly, helpful support. Thanks to Jessica Gribble and Jehanne Schweitzer for seeing the book to completion. Thanks also to the anonymous reviewer for constructive and encouraging comments.

I offer thanks and also apologies to my family and friends who have had to put up with endless responses of the form "I'm sorry I haven't called for a while, I've been so busy" and who, regardless, have continued to provide invaluable support, which is deeply appreciated. Finally, thanks as ever to Elly Omondi for his loving support and solidarity.

Acronyms

AAPS	African Association of Political Science
AAWORD	Association of African Women for Research and Development
AIDS	acquired immune deficiency syndrome
BBC	British Broadcasting Corporation
CIDA	Canadian International Development Agency
CODESRIA	Council for the Development of Social Science Research in Africa
DAC	Development Assistance Committee
GATS	General Agreement on Trade in Services
GNP	gross national product
IFIs	international financial institutions
IMF	International Monetary Fund
IPE	international political economy
IR	international relations
ICZs	Islamic cultural zones
NGO	nongovernmental organization
NIEO	new international economic order
OECD	Organization for Economic Cooperation and Development
OED	Oxford English Dictionary
OSSREA	Organization for Social Science Research in Eastern and Southern Africa

CPA	Coalitional Provisional Authority
SAPES	Southern Africa Political Economy Series
TWAIL	Third World approaches to international law
UK	United Kingdom
UN	United Nations
UNDP	United Nations Development Program
US	United States
USA	United States of America

Introduction: International Relations, Eurocentrism, and Imperialism

Branwen Gruffydd Jones

> We are at a point in our work when we can no longer ignore the empires
> and the imperial context in our studies.
>
> —Edward Said[1]

"Education was so arranged that the young learned not necessarily the truth, but that aspect and interpretation of the truth which the rulers of the world wished them to know and follow."[2] These words were written by W. E. Burghardt Du Bois in 1946, about European society in the early twentieth century. His concern was to understand the reasons for the collapse of Europe in the first decades of the twentieth century. His inquiry focused on the history of European expansion, slavery and colonialism, and the devastating implications, for Europe and the whole world, of the contradictions of Europe's global imperial "civilization." His concern to emphasize these histories was in part because "certain suppressions in the historical record current in our day will lead to a tragic failure in assessing causes." These suppressions arise from "the habit, long fostered, of forgetting and detracting from the thought and acts of the people of Africa."[3]

Has the education of international relations improved since then? This volume is concerned with the education of international relations and world history today. It seeks to expose enduring suppressions in the historical record, to break out of long-fostered habits of distorted Eurocentric thought. International Relations (IR) scholarship and teaching, over the decades since Du Bois was writing, has remained concerned predominantly with relations between and issues of concern to the great powers, the hegemons, the large and powerful in the global political economy. The standard historical reference points of the discipline's rendering of international relations are drawn almost exclusively from Europe's "internal" history. The acknowledged disciplinary canon of modern IR consists of European classical thought. For much of the twentieth century and into the twenty-first, the field of IR has been dominated by North American, European, and, to a lesser extent, Australian scholars. Thus, the majority of literature in the discipline of IR is written by and about only some of the peoples of the world—predominantly Americans and Europeans. IR remains guilty of forgetting and detracting from the thought and acts of not only the people of Africa but also "the rest" of the non-Western world.

The modern discipline of IR and its twentieth-century trajectory is presented to the newcomer in a huge number of textbooks and compilations. What is remarkably *absent* from IR's self-presentation—so starkly apparent to Du Bois—is awareness of its colonial and imperial roots and context. A number of surveys, histories, and genealogies of developments and debates in the discipline have been produced in recent years. Such accounts routinely observe that IR was formally established in the aftermath of World War I, often pinpointing the moment to the establishment of the first chair in International Politics at the University of Wales, Aberystwyth, in 1919.[4] This was at the height of imperialism, when the European powers were occupying and controlling vast areas of the world through direct colonial rule. At this time, a whole set of profoundly ideological and racist notions were held by the colonizers about colonized peoples, lands, and histories. The belief in a hierarchy of peoples—in the superiority of Europeans or people with European ancestry and the inferiority of non-Europeans or "people of color"—was widespread and routine, a generally unquestioned assumption embedded both in the public and personal European imagination and in the formal institutions of European and international order. As Edward Said noted, "There was virtual unanimity that subject races should be ruled, that they *are* subject races, that one race deserves and has consistently earned the right to be considered the race whose main mission is to expand beyond its own domain."[5]

Thus, a discipline that claims to be *international*, of relevance to all peoples and states, traces its modern origins without embarrassment to a place and moment at the heart and height of imperialism. Imperialism is characterized by relations, doctrines, and practices of exclusion; imperialism is the very antithesis of universal international recognition. It is therefore imperative to examine critically the effect of this historical context on the understanding of international relations and history that emerged. The discipline of anthropology was similarly born in and of colonialism, and anthropologists have engaged in major efforts to rethink the discipline and shed the legacy of its colonial origins.[6] Yet most recent surveys of twentieth-century IR have little to say about the implications for the discipline of one of the most important historical processes of that century—the political liberation from colonial rule of formerly colonized peoples. IR has generally accommodated this historical process in terms of "the expansion of international society." Existing theories about the international system, international society, international law, sovereignty, security, and state formation remained in place, used to address the effects of the inclusion of a significant number of "new states," most of which were smaller and weaker than the original members of international society. A more fundamental questioning of core assumptions about world history and the central conceptual tools of IR has rarely been deemed necessary.

The architects of IR's self-construction not only have ignored the imperial context of the discipline's modern origins but also have self-consciously located IR's heritage or canon in classical European thought from ancient Greece through to the Enlightenment—Thucydides, Machiavelli, Bodin, Grotius, Hobbes, Rousseau, Kant, Hegel, and so on.[7] These thinkers lived during the context of, and in part helped to legitimize, European violence against non-European peoples through conquest, enslavement, slave trade, colonization, dispossession, and extermination over more than five centuries. Of course, the content of classical European thought cannot be wholly *reduced* to this historical context and thereby dismissed. Nor should it be *abstracted* from this context and thereby sanitized.[8] Yet, for the most part, the discipline of IR has engaged in precisely such abstraction and sanitization, willfully ignoring the relationship between its own intellectual canon and European imperialism. In this way, IR has remained unembarrassed; it has not developed, in Said's words, "an acute and embarrassed awareness of the all-pervasive, unavoidable imperial setting."[9]

While a lot of writing in IR seems strangely more interested in the discipline itself than the world around us, even the substantive concerns that are recognized as defining IR's field of enquiry have remained stubbornly narrow. The themes and preoccupations of IR largely reflect the history of the West (in idealized form) and the interests of the powerful. For example, theorization of the interstate system has been central to the self-definition of the discipline. The history of modern international relations is widely accepted to be rooted in the European state system, which was born at the Peace of Westphalia: "The present-day structure of world international relations is a structure between Great Powers, and it has come down in unbroken descent from the days when such a structure first materialised in Europe."[10] "Our present international society is directly descended from [the] universalized European system."[11] This, in Siba Grovogui's words, is IR's "Westphalian common-sense."[12]

Yet for most of the world, over the past few centuries *and still today*, the major defining forms of international relation, structure, and historical experience were and are colonialism and imperialism. The long history of imperialism—in its economic, political, institutional, cultural, and legal dimensions—is arguably more significant to the form of the current international system and the states that make it up than Europe's internal political developments. Imperialism is foundational to the origins, form, and normative basis of international organizations and international law,[13] to the prevailing inequalities in power relations between states and the position of states in the highly uneven and exploitative international system, as well as to national and regional structures and relations, cultures, and languages, in all regions, formerly colonized and metropolitan. It appears then that imperialism is inextricable from the very foundations of modern international relations and world order.

IR is largely silent on the imperial foundations and constitution of modern international relations, however. According to IR common sense, the "expansion of international society" has entailed the spread of European forms of state, sovereignty, democracy, law, and rights to non-European areas and peoples. But Europe's legacy to most of the rest of the world has been one of authoritarianism, theft, racism, and, in significant cases, massacre and genocide. For most of the world, it is arguably the history of the colonial state and political economy rather than European sovereignty and liberal democracy that is central to understanding modern international relations. To diminish the significance of colonialism to the study of international relations—for understanding international relations both past and present—is nothing less than to diminish the significance and worth of all peoples who have suffered colonialism. This, truly, is the massive "collateral damage" of modern IR.

To the extent that political institutions and norms of liberal democracy and sovereignty did emerge, slowly and partially, in Western Europe in the centuries after Westphalia, these developments unfolded during the same centuries as European expansion, slave trade, and formal colonial occupation and rule of most of the world. That such very different forms of political and international interaction took place during the same period in time is not a coincidence, and they cannot be understood in isolation. However, the modern intellectual division of labor conveniently separates these processes. Europe's internal history is treated as pristine and the source of Enlightenment, modernity, democracy, sovereignty and rights, and taken as the basis for theorizing modern international relations. Meanwhile, it is more specialized scholars of history or area studies who might focus on topics such as slavery and colonialism, combined with a regional specialism in, say, West Africa, South Asia, or the Caribbean. This habitual bracketing through the institutionalized division of intellectual labor does not merely allocate contemporaneous developments as a matter of convenience, but also severs relations of *cause and conditions of possibility* that are central to both. This severing through division of labor prevents social inquiry from ever asking, for example, what the historical and causal relationship is between the rise and form of liberalism in Europe and the structures and practices of colonialism. Few treatments of liberal democracy care to unravel its internal relationship with imperialism.

DECOLONIZING IR

In any social context where relations of unequal power prevail, knowledge and ideas can serve either to mystify or reveal those unequal relations. For many centuries, the international order has been characterized by profoundly unequal power relations. There are a myriad of ways in which such power is mystified in everyday life, and the Eurocentric form of the modern discipline of IR is one of these. This volume rests ultimately on a belief in the importance and necessity of critical social inquiry as one means of better understanding the world. It seeks to contribute to a better understanding of international relations, history, and world order by confronting the colonial heritage that modern IR has failed to shed. In this regard, the project joins others who have sought to expose and overcome the many omissions and biases of mainstream IR. Feminist scholarship has worked hard over three decades to expose and overcome the entrenched gender biases inscribed in the core of IR that define and limit what can be said and thought. Much work has been done to insist that the environment is not simply one among many topics or issues within IR but integral to the very practice, structures, and reproduction of international relations. This volume confronts the Eurocentric nature of IR and its status as effectively a form of modern imperial ideology. In doing so, it joins effort with an emerging strand of critical literature that is gradually enlarging the scope for such discussions within the formal settings—the journals and conferences—of the discipline.[14] There has been a welcome advance from earlier observations regarding the dominance of Anglo-American scholarship in IR[15]—which was met, for example, by responses from continental Europe and Australia[16]—to critical explorations of the relationship between IR, Eurocentrism, colonialism, and imperialism.[17]

What has been termed the "self-images" of the discipline, its self-consciousness or self-construction, take shape and are reproduced in part through the imperatives of teaching.[18] Communicating to large numbers of newcomers produces a need for textbooks, increasingly so as student numbers and student-to-staff ratios rise. Introducing an area of inquiry to newcomers leads inevitably to packaging and summarizing and, with the help of textbooks,

a level of standardization. The Western or Eurocentric bias of IR is thus reproduced as the discipline is repeatedly packaged and presented. Eurocentrism
is not the *product* of such dynamics, however. It is rooted far deeper in the
consciousness of the discipline and the scholarship that dominates and is embedded in the very structures of international order. The routine reproduction
of Eurocentric forms of social inquiry is parasitic on widespread ignorance of
world history, including the histories of colonialism and imperialism and, even
more so, the histories of non-European peoples. These structures of ideology
and ignorance are deeply embedded in historical process, in actual international relations. This volume, then, is not simply yet another book about the
discipline of IR. It explores what forms of knowledge have come to dominate
the field and why, what problems arise, and what can be done to escape and
move beyond Eurocentrism or the imperial imagination. It is motivated more
by a concern to consider how to research and produce knowledge about the
international—how we can and should study international relations—than by
a wish to produce a comprehensive if critical survey of recognized IR.

As such, this volume could be situated within postcolonial literature in a
broad sense in that certain themes and concerns are shared. However, this volume does not set out specifically to elaborate a postcolonial approach to or theory of IR, with specific reference to existing frameworks of postcolonial theory.
It does not begin with postcolonial theory as such, nor does it seek to improve
on selected existing approaches in IR by adding postcolonial theory, as some
others have.[19] Much postcolonial theory seems to operate with or be framed
by unhelpful dichotomies between political economy and materialism on the
one hand and poststructural inflections of power/identity/culture/knowledge
on the other. Such dichotomies suggest an inaccurate or artificial distance between positions and approaches that have actually been far richer in concerns
and method. For example, much contemporary postcolonial theory distances
itself from historical materialism and political economy while in the process
misappropriating iconic figures such as Fanon into a cultural studies shorn
of political economy.[20] So the aim here is not to develop a new postcolonial
perspective in IR that can slot in among existing critical perspectives, a new
"-ism" alongside feminism, environmentalism, and poststructuralism on the
one hand and against liberalism, Marxism, and realism on the other. What is
needed is a broader and deeper form of critique that encompasses the discipline
as a whole—its underlying assumptions, modes of thought and analysis, and
its consciousness and very *attitude*—and that, moreover, is committed not only
to critique but also to elaboration of more adequate accounts and explanations
of international relations. Only by doing so can we hope to free the imagination of social inquiry from the narrow blinkers of Eurocentrism and enable the
study of international relations "from the perspective of the world."[21]

EUROCENTRIC ORIGINS AND LIMITS

The first step for IR must be to develop greater recognition and self-awareness of its own origins and reproduction in the imperial (colonial and neocolonial) metropolis and to acknowledge and account for the consequent problem of Eurocentrism in the development of IR knowledge.

Concerns about the relationship between power and knowledge and the legacy of colonialism on this "nexus" have long been debated across the social sciences. It would therefore seem that the critique of Eurocentric IR can follow paths already established by postcolonial theory and subaltern studies. Julian Saurin questions this starting assumption, however. In the opening chapter, he sets up the terrain of the rest of the volume by examining the methodological and political imperatives of confronting Eurocentric IR. While making a strong argument regarding the necessity of decolonizing knowledge, Saurin's discussion raises difficult questions that subsequent chapters might resolve in differing ways. He explores the question of not only why it is necessary to subject IR scholarship to critique but also *how* this should be done, considering what is at stake in different possible responses. He argues that the imperative to decolonize IR arises from its colonial and imperial character: IR theory *misrepresents* the current world order as essentially a postcolonial, international order. But imperialism remains in neocolonial forms; we do not live in a postcolonial world. Therefore, we cannot turn to postcolonial theory in order to decolonize IR. Rather, we need to recognize international relations *as imperial relations*—to reject IR theory in its entirety and instead explain the imperial production of world order.

Why has IR scholarship remained so little concerned to rethink its foundations in the wake of formal decolonization? The self-confidence of IR is rooted to some extent in a general sense of progress and achievement that enables the almost triumphal embrace of what is seen as an expansion of European or Western international society. The sense of progress and civilization that pervades the mainstream study and practice of international relations is mirrored by an equally confident belief in the *need for* progress and civilization. According to IR, the "rest of the world" has benefited and continues to benefit from the spread of the West's civilizing values and institutions, through development, modernization, state building, foreign assistance, and the construction and maintenance of international order and security. The evolution of international relations is a story of progress that has entailed the birth and spread of democracy, human rights, sovereignty, and good governance. Thus, the fact that central forms of international relations—democratization, development, the promotion of good governance, security, protection of human rights, and even invasion, war, and military occupation—are conducted by some for the supposed benefit of others is not considered to be a problem. IR scholarship remains for the most part convinced by the good intentions that have cloaked international relations for centuries.

It is necessary to turn to history in order to disrupt this self-confidence in the tale of Western progress and civilization, to bring evidence to bear that exposes this story to be fundamentally characterized by *myth*. IR's self-confidence is possible because it believes its own myths, its construction of a "privileged, genealogically useful past, a past in which we exclude unwanted elements, vestiges, narratives."[22] A superficial understanding of the problem of Euro-centrism would suggest that what is required is filling in the gaps, restoring the excluded narratives from beyond the confines of Europe. The decolonization of IR cannot be construed only in terms of seeking non-Western narratives and elements, however. IR's imagination and mythological foundation involves a double maneuver of silencing or denying the historicity of non-Western soci-eties *and* idealizing a distorted history of the West—more specifically, Europe. Sandra Halperin therefore begins the critique of mainstream IR with a system-atic exposure of foundational myths about European history and the Western origins of modernity, which both mainstream and critical scholarship tend to assume. She argues that telling other histories cannot be enough while IR's basic "myths of origin" remain intact: "what is needed is to confront the hege-monic perspective with an unassimilable difference, one that cannot be ren-dered compatible or incorporated but that, if accepted, makes it impossible to retain the dominant account." It might seem literally Euro-centric to place a reconstruction of important elements of Europe's own history at the beginning of this collection. However, the aim in doing so is to strike at the foundations of Eurocentrism and imperial ideology. As subsequent chapters by Anghie, Gathii, Grovogui, and Ayers discuss, a central feature of imperial ideology, international law, and Eurocentric method of social inquiry is the assumption of a European ideal against which all else—all other societies, histories, tradi-tions, value systems, and institutions—are compared and measured, an ideal to which all the rest should aspire to conform. The very self-evident, assumed quality of the European ideal saturates not only academic discourse but also the public sphere more broadly, certainly but not only in the West. It is nec-essary to puncture this myth of Europe, to reveal its idealized and distorted quality, and thereby dismantle a central foundation of all imperial ideologies. Telling the real history of Europe has an important place in the broader project of decolonizing IR and the Western imagination.

The twin of IR's myths of modernity is the simultaneous construction of the barbaric Other whose being is fundamentally different, at the limit of or beyond comprehension. Self-confidence in progress is mirrored by fear of its lack. Today this dialectic of self-confidence-in-ignorance is manifest above all in IR's fearful apprehension of the specter of Islam. Mustapha Kamal Pasha provides a sustained reflection and critique of the limits of IR that arise from its dependence on a culturally specific Western imaginary of progress, modernity, and secularism. His discussion makes an important contribution to revealing the historicity of the form and content of IR as a first step toward decolonizing knowledge. He characterizes IR knowledge—with its central assumptions regarding the Westphalian sovereign system, a narrative of progress, commitment to the individual over society, and the logic of capitalist organization of social life—as a "particular realization of the liberal-modernist imaginary" that has accompanied the expansion of capitalism. However, there are fault lines inherent to this liberal-modernist imaginary that are deeply rooted in history. IR has inherited the orientalist mentality generated through the long history of European encounters with non-European peoples and cultures. With its originary orientalism, it has been impossible for IR to approach and understand politics, international relations, and social process in Islamic cultural zones on their own terms. When turning to the question of Islam, then, we immediately confront the cultural limits of the IR discipline: Islam is beyond IR's field of apprehension as anything other than caricature. The discipline of IR claims boldly to understand the world and offer universal knowledge. Yet in the face of Islam, IR is paralyzed; it retreats to the apparently firm ground of old assumptions of essential difference and the barbarity of the Other, offering empty stereotypes and paranoia as substitute for analysis, explanation, and reflection. Pasha explores further the dialectic of liberalism and illiberalism, tolerance and exclusion, by examining the necessary role and response of securitization as an essential feature of global liberal modernity. The confrontation with Islam thus reveals another limit inherent to IR: the limits of liberal tolerance.

THE COLONIAL AND RACIAL CONSTITUTION OF THE INTERNATIONAL

One of the central effects of Eurocentrism has been to quietly remove the massive world history of imperialism from the theories and substantive concerns of the disciplines of both IR and international law. A second step toward decolonizing knowledge is therefore to reveal the imperial and racialized constitution of international relations. This entails moving imperialism from its bracketed location in specialist studies and the distant chronological past and demonstrating the unbroken centrality of imperialism to international relations from the fifteenth century to the twenty-first. The recent popularity of the term "postcolonial" has diverted attention from the persistence of imperialism in its neocolonial forms. Similarly, the twentieth-century discourse about development—and its most recent agenda of "good governance"—has naturalized the structures of global inequality and exploitation that were the product of European expansion and formal colonialism. This naturalization serves to depoliticize and dehistoricize present inequalities, thus occluding the routine reality and effects of imperialism in the neocolonial era, and to close off colonialism, bracketing colonial relations and practices into a discrete, earlier chronological period. The changing nature of imperialism into forms that go widely unrecognized must be exposed. In the words of Issa Shivji,

> The central question we need to address is how did imperialism rehabilitate and legitimise itself to the extent that the former British Secretary of State, Douglas Hurd, could say with satisfaction in 1990 that "we are slowly putting behind us a period of history when the West was unable to express a legitimate interest in the developing world without being accused of neo-colonialism."[23]

Over the past five years, critical IR scholars have suddenly discovered imperialism: since September 2001, there has been a surge in publications about empire and "the new imperialism." It is a major mistake to think of the present conjuncture in terms of a "return" of imperialism, however. This suggests a shallow understanding of imperialism in terms of obvious visible features of military invasion and occupation and overt racism. But imperialism and racism never went away despite the formally decolonized appearance of the modern international system. Neocolonialism has been suffered and recognized as such by non-Europeans throughout the twentieth century, yet only when its effects suddenly reverberate in the West does IR take notice. Decolonizing IR thus requires exposing the unobvious imperial qualities of international relations, qualities that are not new and that are central to international order and have endured in changing form over five centuries.

How is it possible that IR has paid so little attention to race, colonialism, and imperialism, to the intertwined nature of the histories of the West and "the rest"? This question is important because the silences and omissions of IR do not arise from mere oversight or forgetfulness. It is not that IR knowledge is *incomplete*, and what is required is to fill in the gaps. Rather, there are systematic absences that are the product, Sankaran Krishna argues, of a *willful amnesia*. Krishna exposes the methodological underpinnings of IR's amnesia, the manner in which particular modes of abstraction serve to systematically tear or isolate the West from world history and its racialized structures. In response, it is necessary to develop a different mode of abstraction that reveals and remembers that which IR is unembarrassed to forget. Krishna demonstrates the power of contrapuntal analysis, which, as Halperin has advocated, produces knowledge of international relations that cannot be assimilated to the mainstream.

One of the achievements of IR's strategies of containment and the resultant amnesia on questions of race, as examined by Krishna, is the routine misrecognition of contemporary manifestations of imperialism. The current international order is premised on the equality of all peoples, while relations between richer and poorer countries take the form of aid and humanitarian assistance. It is ignorance of the history of imperialism that enables the embrace of contemporary expressions of Western humanitarian concern and technical assistance in the Third World. Antony Anghie shares Krishna's concern to expose the racialized nature of modes of international relations that appear to be innocent of racism. His account of the long history of international law in the service of colonialism serves to demolish the "good governance" agenda's surface appearance of benign technocratic assistance. He reveals instead the consistency and continuity of changing discourses of international law across centuries and continents in facilitating the reordering of non-European societies in the interest of Western commerce and capital.

James Thuo Gathii similarly turns to history and international law in order to develop a broader framework within which to situate the current occupation of Iraq. His starting point is the principle in customary international law that prohibits the confiscation of private property during wartime, conquest, and occupation. That the Anglo-American conquest of Iraq has led not only to the confiscation of private property but also to the wholesale transformation of Iraq's economy, legal system, and property regime is, Gathii argues, contrary to international law but consistent with the long history of imperial international relations. Gathii sets this in context by examining the uneven and inconsistent application of international law regarding property rights in situations of conquest and war. He demonstrates—through examination of cases from the Spanish conquest of the Americas, British colonial occupation and war in Africa, and the postwar occupation of Italy, Japan, and Germany—that the rules and practice of international law over centuries and across continents have favored the interests of powerful Western states at the expense of conquered states, especially in the conquest of non-European states. International law has thus systematically facilitated the dispossession of non-European peoples.

Certain themes reappear across each of the chapters in part II of this volume, which together provide a richer understanding of imperialism than is found in some of the recent "presentist" preoccupations with current U.S. military unilateralism. Central themes include property and dispossession, the imposition of modes of governance, and the varied discourses of humanitarianism, civilization, and liberalism that accompany European conquest and rule of non-European peoples. All three identify salient dimensions of the administration, rationalization, and regulation of imperial practices, for example, through the standardization of language and the formalization of property relations. But in each case, the necessary violence and brutality of imperialism, however much the colonial encounter is governed and managed, is also apparent.

TOWARD DECOLONIZED KNOWLEDGE OF THE WORLD AND THE INTERNATIONAL

The success of mainstream IR in appearing to be sufficient with regard to understanding the world poses a heavy burden of critique and exposure, and the chapters in the first two parts of this volume make important contributions to this broader imperative. However, elaborating such critique must only be the beginning and is incomplete without confronting the moment of construction and reconstruction. How can the Eurocentrism of IR be overcome and transcended? In light of the preceding chapters, it is clear that Eurocentrism cannot be overcome by simply applying existing IR knowledge to the rest of the world, "bringing the regions in." Any attempt to decolonize IR must confront the substantive, methodological and political distortions embedded within the mainstream in order to reconstruct non-Eurocentric, historically adequate knowledge about the global constitution of all regions of the world and the global constitution of the international itself.

One of the major characteristics of the imperial imagination of IR and social inquiry more generally is the simple but often massive failure to mention or remember events, processes, and scholarship of the non-Western world. In this way, IR contributes systematically—and indeed arrogantly—to the reproduction of ignorance. In all sorts of substantive areas, the capacity to ignore non-Western histories and scholarship is sometimes staggering. For example, even critical IR, which claims to be centrally concerned with questions of emancipation and social transformation, has turned almost exclusively to Europe's heritage of critical thought (Kant, Hegel, Marx, Gramsci, Adorno, Horkheimer, and Habermas).[24] Critical IR has overlooked the histories and thought of anticolonial struggles—which surely constitute major historical struggles for emancipation and social transformation in the context of international relations. It seems remarkable that few of IR's self-identified critical theorists have sought to learn from Fanon, Cabral, or Gandhi alongside Gramsci, Adorno, and Habermas.

The reason for this Eurocentric omission is not just narrow ethnic or regional parochialism but a deeply rooted, almost subconscious tendency to deny the very legitimacy and worth of non-Western values, traditions, practices, struggles, discourses, and thought. Through intent or lazy habit, the IR mainstream reproduces today a process central to colonialism, which was never

> simply content to impose its rule upon the present and the future of a dominated country. Colonialism is not satisfied merely with holding a people in its grip and emptying the native's brain of all form and content. By a kind of perverted logic, it turns to the past of the oppressed people, and distorts, disfigures and destroys it.[25]

So, too, the reasons for transcending Eurocentrism go beyond the need for regional or sociological inclusivity, important though this is in itself given current inequalities in the production and focus of knowledge in IR. What can or should be the relationship between decolonizing knowledge and decolonizing international relations? Just as one can be critical in various ways, so too anticolonial struggle and critique can take various forms that can be but are not necessarily progressive. The imperial quality of European and Western international relations revealed in part II has implications for thinking about the necessity for non-Eurocentric knowledge about international relations. What is important about decolonized knowledge is not simply that it might be about or written by non-European peoples. It is the possibility of revealing nonimperial and anti-imperial histories, values, struggles, ideas, and ways of being. This is both a possibility and an imperative.

The methodological and substantive challenges of decolonizing the international imagination through positive reconstruction are enormous, and this volume can do no more than illuminate some possibilities. The three chapters in part III contribute in different ways to the broader project. All three address questions that are central to international relations thinking and practice and to the organization of social life throughout the world: forms and practices of democracy, ideas about and struggles for human rights, and the historical necessity and possibilities of human unity on a world scale. They do so, however, by turning first not to the standard IR canon of democratic, normative, and cosmopolitan theory (Kant et al.) but to histories and scholarship that have been almost wholly ignored by IR.

Alison Ayers's examination of political systems in nineteenth-century Africa addresses a number of tasks. First, the recovery of histories routinely denied by imperial historiography and IR discourse is, as Ayers underlines, an intrinsically radical endeavor. The detailed analysis of different forms of African polity and modes of production in itself affirms the historicality and legitimacy of Africa's history and Africa's own experiences of democracy and political community, which have been systematically excluded from Western imagination over centuries. Ayers rightly refuses to engage in the very question of the legitimacy of African history in itself—to do so "only confers gratuitous respectability to the suggestion that Africa and its people are required to justify admittance in the concert of humanity." Nevertheless, it is unfortunate that the importance of her chapter in the current context goes beyond the substantive account of democratic traditions in nineteenth-century Africa to the very *recognition* of such traditions. In popular and academic discourse, it is the case not only that the standard reference point for any discussion of democracy is Western liberal democracy but also that the very existence of *any* non-European history of democracy is simply and massively denied. Thus, a recent Open

University television program exploring questions of democracy and citizenship in postapartheid South Africa turns, with predictable instinct, to Rousseau, only reaffirming once again the imperial conceit that Africa has no history of democratic tradition, thought and scholarship.[26] Second, her account contributes to the critique of the imperial narrative by undermining the false promotion of European history to the realm of universal History. Halperin's chapter began to undermine this narrative by destroying the mythological version of Europe that is falsely universalized. Ayers advances the critique from the other side by refusing to treat the European myth as a universal standard. In contrast to most discussions of democracy in Africa—in IR, comparative politics, and the various realms of Africanist scholarship—Ayers acknowledges the specificity of Africa's own history of democratic forms, institutions, and values. In other words, she analyzes African political systems *in their own right* rather than by comparing them to the European touchstone, which invariably leads to judging non-European social forms as deviant—forms that might approximate but fail to fully realize the "universal" standard. Third, her analysis recovers alternative values and institutions regulating social life and social order that are important in themselves. She provides detailed evidence of the importance of values of reciprocity and egalitarianism, power and authority rooted in popular legitimacy, and deliberate measures to retain a decentralized, *antistate* form of social order. It is arguably liberal democracy that is to be found wanting in light of African democratic traditions.

Siba Grovogui similarly refutes the assumption that the West holds a monopoly of virtue regarding notions of democracy, human rights, or any other category of normative discourse and political community. Western histories of human rights, through the French and American revolutions, are certainly acknowledged. However, any claim that these constitute *the origin and standard* of human rights is, quite simply, historically wrong. Such claims of origination are not simply historically wrong but also integral to the ideological privileging of the West over all other societies and histories. Just as Ayers has demonstrated that norms and practices of democracy are not foreign to African societies, as the imperial narrative assumes, so too Grovogui reveals that authoritative discourses that seek to ennoble human existence are not foreign to non-Western regions and cultures. Moreover, his discussion reveals that the ideas articulated in the context of the Haitian Revolution embodied a broader and more widely encompassing basis on which to build a moral discourse to ennoble human existence than that contained in the discourses of the European enlightenment. That recognition of the Haitian Revolution's contribution to the world-historical development of human rights discourses is routinely absent from the human rights literature thus not only is one more instance of the silencing of non-Western histories but moreover leaves an impoverished understanding of human rights discourse itself.

In the final chapter, B. S. Chimni brings to the attention of IR scholars the thought of Sri Aurobindo. His discussion of Sri Aurobindo's work makes a vital contribution to this volume for several reasons, and it is suitable that this should conclude part III. First, Chimni offers another avenue of retrieval: retrieving scholarship that has simply been ignored by IR. This is important because of the near-total failure of the discipline of IR to acknowledge the scholarship of the non-Western world with regard to central themes of international relations, world history, world order, and political philosophy. IR leaves the impression that only Western scholars, from the days of Hegel and Kant through to our own times, have reflected on questions of concern to humanity. Second, Sri Aurobindo's thought regarding humanity, history, social change and progress, and the possibility of human unity provides a unique and important emphasis on both material and spiritual dimensions of human being in the world and the mutually dependent relationship between individual and collective or social fulfillment. This serves as a basis for a critique of Western imperial states and civilization as well as for thinking about possibilities and imperatives of overcoming the alienation of the current global condition and realizing human unity on a world scale. Third, the very fact that Sri Aurobindo, a key figure in India's anticolonial struggle, placed such importance on the ideal, possibility, and indeed necessity of human *unity* provides a very significant instance of a particular form of anticolonial thought and struggle. His work offers an example and inspiration for a form of struggle that seeks not to mirror but to transcend logics of exclusion, to struggle against domination in a way that seeks the unity of all rather than only the liberation of the oppressed.

There is both a political and a substantive import to these accounts in part III. The imperial denial of legitimacy and recognition of non-Western forms, discourses, histories, and scholarship demands a political response because, as Pasha argues, the "rigidity of commitment" to the ideal and idealized benchmark of the West accounts for "the enormous difficulty of according legitimacy to alternative modes of thinking and behavior." It ought not to be necessary to have to insist on such legitimacy—as Ayers objects, to do so in some sense descends to the base level of imperial mentality. Yet so pervasive and insidious is the universalization of an idealized Western History and Political Thought, at the expense of all other history and political thought, that such acknowledgment remains intrinsically radical in itself. However, beyond the necessary politics of recognition and affirmation, the response cannot rest with questions of authenticity. What is required, as presented variously in these three chapters, is not an essentialist return to the past or a celebration of the authenticity of the indigenous for its own sake but a *critical* engagement with alternatives, both past and present.

This volume brings together the work of scholars in both IR and international law. The themes of these two fields of social inquiry and practice share many core concerns—with sovereignty, international order, international organization, questions of justice, legitimacy, political community—and yet to date there has been insufficient interdisciplinary communication among scholars with related concerns in the two disciplines. In particular, the Third World Approaches to International Law (TWAIL) scholarship has made pioneering contributions to the critique and reconstruction of themes that are central not only to international law but also to IR. IR needs to learn from and incorporate such work. In the effort to address the challenges of decolonizing IR, this volume brings critical IR scholars together with founding TWAIL members— Antony Anghie, James Thuo Gathii, and B. S. Chimni.

The concluding chapter addresses two tasks. First, central themes and concerns raised across the chapters are drawn together through reflection on the imperatives, possibilities, and limitations of the objectives of this volume and the broader problems it seeks to address. Second, the conclusion finishes by considering how international material inequalities affect the very conditions of academic teaching and research, with particular reference to Africa. This is an important problem of international relations as such and constitutes a major constraint against a truly international production of IR scholarship. Yet the material inequality underlying international inequalities in scholarship is rarely given sufficient attention when calls are made to broaden the scope of the IR field and incorporate marginalized voices. Until such conditions are transcended, the project of decolonizing IR will necessarily remain partial and fragmentary.

NOTES

1. Edward W. Said, *Culture and Imperialism* (London: Vintage, 1994), 5.

2. William Edward Burghardt Du Bois, *The World and Africa: An Inquiry into the Part Which Africa Has Played in World History* (1946; reprint, New York: International Publishers, 1996), 24.

3. Du Bois, *The World and Africa*, 2.

4. For example, Chris Brown, *Understanding International Relations* (Basingstoke: Palgrave, 2001), 24; John A. Vasquez, *The Power of Power Politics: From Classical Realism to Neotraditionalism* (Cambridge: Cambridge University Press, 1998), 32; Steve Smith, "The Self-Images of a Discipline: A Genealogy of International Relations Theory," in *International Relations Theory Today*, ed. Ken Booth and Steve Smith (Cambridge: Polity Press, 1995), 14; and Scott Burchill,

"Introduction," in *Theories of International Relations*, ed. Scott Burchill, Richard Devetak, Andrew Linklater, Matthew Paterson, Christian Reus-Smit, and Jacqui True (Basingstoke: Palgrave, 2001), 4.

5. Edward W. Said, "Secular Interpretation, the Geographical Element and the Methodology of Imperialism," in *After Colonialism: Imperial Histories and Postcolonial Displacements*, ed. Gyan Prakash (Princeton, N.J.: Princeton University Press, 1995), 30.

6. See Talal Asad, *Anthropology and the Colonial Encounter* (London: Ithaca Press, 1975); Kathleen Gough, "Anthropology and Imperialism," *Current Anthropology* 9, no. 5 (1968): 403–7; and Dell H. Hymes, ed., *Reinventing Anthropology* (New York: Random House, 1972).

7. For specific works on what is often termed international relations in political theory, see, for example, Chris Brown, Terry Nardin, and Nicholas Rengger, eds., *International Relations in Political Thought: Texts from the Ancient Greeks to the First World War* (Cambridge: Cambridge University Press, 2002); Howard Williams, *International Relations in Political Thought* (Milton Keynes: Open University Press, 1992); and Torbjörn L. Knutsen, *A History of International Relations Theory: An Introduction* (Manchester: Manchester University Press, 1992).

8. Works that explore the relationships between classical European thinkers and imperialism include Emmanuel Chukwudi Eze, ed., *Race and the Enlightenment: A Reader* (Oxford: Blackwell, 1997); Peter Hulme and Ludmilla Jordanova, eds., *The Enlightenment and Its Shadows* (London: Routledge, 1990); Uday Singh Mehta, *Liberalism and Empire: A Study in Nineteenth-Century British Liberal Thought* (Chicago: University of Chicago Press, 1999); and Beate Jahn, *The Cultural Construction of International Relations: The Invention of the State of Nature* (Basingstoke: Palgrave, 2000).

9. Said, "Secular Interpretation," 34.

10. F. H. Hinsley, *Power and the Pursuit of Peace: Theory and Practice in the History of Relations between States* (Cambridge: Cambridge University Press, 1963), 153.

11. Adam Watson, *The Evolution of International Society: A Comparative Historical Analysis* (London: Routledge, 1992), 214. This foundational narrative has recently been challenged by Benno Teschke, who provides a historical materialist analysis of changing geopolitical dynamics and relations in Europe and the significance of the rise of capitalism. He identifies the period from 1688 to World War I as the period of "modernizing" international relations, with the expansion of capitalism from its endogenous origins in England throughout Europe, modernizing international relations finally expanding beyond Europe in the twentieth century. See Benno Teschke, *The Myth of 1648: Class, Geopolitics and the Making of Modern International Relations* (London: Verso, 2003). Thus, while revising the analysis of European state formation, Teschke remains resolute that the origin of modern international relations arises from inter-European developments within Europe.

12. Siba N'Zatioula Grovogui, "Regimes of Sovereignty: International Morality and the African Condition," *European Journal of International Relations* 8, no. 3 (2002): 315–38.

13. See Antony Anghie, *Imperialism, Sovereignty and the Making of International Law* (Cambridge: Cambridge University Press, 2005).

14. See Arlene Tickner, "Seeing IR Differently: Notes from the Third World," *Millennium: Journal of International Studies* 32, no. 2 (2003): 295–324. Notably, the theme of the International Studies Association annual convention in 2006 was *The North-South Divide and International Studies*, while that of 2004 was *"Hegemony and Its Discontents": Power, Ideology and Knowledge in the Study and Practice of International Relations.* Panels included "Reading Race in International Relations"; "Beyond Power/Knowledge" (seven panels); "The Burden of American IR Theory" (three panels as follows: "Intellectual Hegemony in International Studies," "Second-Order Hegemony and Dissenting Voices," and "Challenging Intellectual Hegemony in International Studies: Strategies for Resistance and Change"); "Geo-Cultural Epistemologies in IR" (seven panels as follows: "Peripheral Thinking and Its Role in Constructing a Post-Western Discipline," "Who or What Is Hegemonic in International Relations?," "Thinking Theory Differently," "Thinking Authority Differently," "Thinking Security Differently," and "The State of International Relations around the World" I and II); and "Epistemic Violence: The Future of World Politics." No doubt several important publications are forthcoming from these many contributions.

15. Stanley Hoffman, "International Relations: An American Social Science," *Daedalus* 106 (1977): 41–59; Ekkehart Krippendorf, "The Dominance of American Approaches in International Relations," *Millennium: Journal of International Studies* 16, no. 2 (1987): 207–14; Steve Smith, "The Discipline of International Relations: Still an American Social Science?" *British Journal of Politics and International Relations* 2, no. 3 (2000): 374–402; Robert M. A. Crawford and Darryl S. L. Jarvis, eds., *International Relations—Still an American Social Science? Toward Diversity in International Thought* (New York: State University of New York Press, 2001).

16. Ole Wæver, "The Sociology of a Not So International Discipline: American and European Developments in International Relations," *International Organization* 52 (1998): 687–727; Knud E. Jørgensen, "Continental IR Theory: The Best Kept Secret," *European Journal of International Relations* 6, no. 1 (2000): 9–42; Richard Higgott and Jim Richardson, eds., *International Relations: Global and Australian Perspectives on an Evolving Discipline* (Canberra: Australian National University, 1992).

17. See, for example, Philip Darby, ed., *At the Edge of International Relations: Postcolonialism, Gender and Dependency* (London: Pinter, 1997); Albert J. Paolini, *Navigating Modernity: Postcolonialism, Identity, and International Relations* (Boulder, Colo.: Lynne Rienner, 1999); L. H. M. Ling, *Postcolonial International Relations: Conquest and Desire between Asia and the West* (Basingstoke: Palgrave, 2002); and Gita Chowdhry and Sheila Nair, eds., *Power, Postcolonialism and International Relations: Reading Race, Gender and Class* (London: Routledge, 2002).

18. Smith, "The Self-Images of a Discipline"; Krishna, chapter 4 in this volume.

19. For example, Chowdhry and Nair, *Power, Postcolonialism and International Relations*; Ling, *Postcolonial International Relations*; and Philip Darby, "Pursuing the Political: A Postcolonial Rethinking of Relations International," *Millennium: Journal of International Studies* 33, no. 1 (2004): 1–32.

20. For an elaboration of this argument regarding the misappropriation of Fanon by certain strands of postcolonial theory, see the chapters by Neil Lazarus, E. San Juan Jr., and Nigel Gibson in Anthony Alessandrini, ed., *Frantz Fanon: Critical Perspectives* (New York: Routledge, 1999).

21. Michel-Rolph Trouillot, *Silencing the Past: Power and the Production of History* (Boston: Beacon Press, 1995), 107; see also Said, "Secular Interpretation," 38–39.

22. Said, *Culture and Imperialism*, 16.

23. Issa G. Shivji, "The Life and Times of Babu: The Age of Liberation and Revolution," *Review of African Political Economy* 95 (2003), 111, citing Frank Furedi, *The New Ideology of Imperialism: Renewing the Moral Imperative* (London: Pluto Press, 1994), 99.

24. See, for example, Richard Wyn Jones, ed., *Critical Theory and World Politics* (Boulder, Colo.: Lynne Rienner, 2001); Mark Neufeld, *The Restructuring of International Relations Theory* (Cambridge: Cambridge University Press, 1995); Andrew Linklater, *The Transformation of Political Community: Ethical Foundations of the Post-Westphalian Era* (Cambridge: Polity Press, 1998); and Kimberly Hutchings, *International Political Theory: Rethinking Ethics in a Global Era* (London: Sage, 1999).

25. Frantz Fanon, *The Wretched of the Earth* (Harmondsworth: Penguin, 1967), 169.

26. The documentary film *Rousseau in Africa: Democracy in the Making* is an Open University film, broadcast in Britain on BBC2 on 20 October 2005. It is described as follows: "Filmed in Cape Town, South Africa, this programme looks at the changes to the country since Nelson Mandela was elected and how the vote has changed the way people feel about themselves as citizens. The film shows why the previous apartheid system would have been regarded as illegitimate by Jean-Jacques Rousseau, the eighteenth-century philosopher, who argued that people who form themselves into a civil society undergo a 'remarkable change.'" <http://www.roland-collection.com/rolandcollection/section/38/1507.htm> (accessed October 15, 2005).

Part I

Eurocentric Origins and Limits

Chapter One

International Relations as the Imperial Illusion; or, the Need to Decolonize IR

Julian Saurin

If imperialism, expressed primarily as colonialism, was the foundation of world order in the nineteenth century and before, so international or interstate relations became the foundation of world order in the twentieth century. It is against this standard and orthodox characterization of world history that uncertainty regarding the reformation of world order in the twenty-first century is contrasted in the vast commentary, academic and popular, on the shape and form of a new world order. The most common yet unfailingly enigmatic or convoluted response from across the political spectrum is to suggest that "globalization" has come to form the basis of world order in this new century. In such a historiography of world ordering and, hence, world history, it is axiomatic not only that the nation-state is a historical relic superseded or at least radically transformed by globalized powers but also that, a fortiori, colonialism and imperialism are descriptions of a long-past, even ancient, world order.[1] Thus, we might begin by asking why, given the anachronisms of colonialism and imperialism, in a globalized world should we be preoccupied with the need to decolonize International Relations (IR)? Isn't the decolonizing of IR a distracting and marginal matter?

Two initial responses can serve to orient the proceeding argument. First, the basic story of the general historical transition from imperial to international world order and from international to globalized world order is highly questionable. Even if one were broadly to accept such an account, this historiography is insensitive to the continuities of earlier orders and not appreciative of the long shadow of history on current developments. Second, in any case, the substantive and concrete transformation of the world over two centuries has not entailed a corresponding transformation in the concepts, theories, methods, and language through which those concrete transformations are accounted. In these respects, then, one is faced with two fundamental problems that need investigation. First, to what extent is the world today organized in a noncolonial or nonimperial manner? Second, to what extent can the world today be accounted for in a conceptual lexicon and theoretical register shorn of its imperial and colonial derivation? In essence, I want to argue that world order continues to be determined largely by imperialism, including neocolonial political forms, and that the assumptions, concepts, and language of inquiry in IR remain infused with imperial and colonial reasoning. Thus, the necessity to decolonize IR is as urgent as ever.

COLONIAL ORDER, INTERNATIONAL ORDER, GLOBAL ORDER: IMPERIAL ORDER

There are many who insist that the discipline or scholarly inquiry that came to be known as IR came into the world in 1919, the year in which the revolutionary doctrine of "national self-determination" was enunciated ostensibly to usher in a new world of sovereign national equality but actually ensuring that the year concluded with a peace to end all peace.[2] However, the opening contention here is that far from the post–World War I settlements reflecting a radically new political reality, thereby perhaps warranting a new and peculiar disciplinary inquiry prompting the creation of new university departments, IR was from the moment of its disciplinary conception, together in substance and spirit, imperial and national in character. Its inheritance, to continue the biological metaphor, was of course already to be found in those progenitors, colonialism and nationalism.

Nationalism in Europe and Wilson's ill-thought-out principle of national self-determination, which was reluctantly and rarely honored by colonial powers, were the firstborn institutions of imperialism.[3] Whether one sees World War I as a necessary consequence of interimperialist rivalry or the fatal logic of Great Power secret treaties and alliances or the consequence of the realization of long-repressed national dreams, two historical developments are beyond doubt. First, European colonial rule did not diminish but continued to expand, not reaching its zenith until 1947 (and after yet another war to end all wars). Second, at the same time, nationalism and the principle of national self-determination became the core precept around which world order seemed to be organizing as evidenced by the establishment of the League of Nations and its successor, the United Nations. On the surface at least, "nation" replaced "empire" as the elemental component of world order. It thus appeared as if inter-national relations, often of national rivalry, had displaced dynastic struggles between empires or imperial conquest as the motor of world ordering. Of course, the fundamental organization of the world through imperialism, of world ordering through accumulation by dispossession,[4] remained formally unrecognized and indeed comprehensively ignored by established authorities, including by the now-official guardians of workers' interests, communist states, and the Third International, or Comintern.[5]

These opening historical observations are necessary in order to begin to specify what kind of knowledge or science of the world we are referring to and, in turn, to begin to explain why such knowledge of the world could have a colonial or imperial character that would thereafter need "decolonizing." Necessarily, the predicate to the call for a decolonizing of IR must be that IR is already colonized or that IR is colonial. To put the conclusion of this chapter at the beginning, the problem of decolonizing IR will not be resolved by ever-greater sensitivity to the multiple histories that are demanded by the postcolonial turn in historical and cultural studies—though one can never be too intrigued by the varieties of experience and representation. Instead, it requires a reengagement with method, philosophy of science, and history on the one hand and a political economy of knowledge on the other. The assertion of Western supremacism and its corresponding discounting or silencing of "the rest" is not primarily an intellectual or, for that matter, an epistemological trick, conspiracy, or malign intent but rather a matter of structured production. In this sense, to decolonize IR requires the active production of a different international social order. Imagination and new imaginaries and the promulgation of theoretical alternatives is simply not a sufficient methodological, still less political, response. Furthermore, from the outset, one has to clarify precisely what is at stake in the call for decolonizing of IR. It is one task to decolonize IR for reasons of normative and "political" objection to colonialism and imperialism, but it is quite another task to decolonize IR prompted by an ambition to clarify and better explain the production of particular world orders and world organization. To be sure, these two tasks can be interrelated, but they are not equivalent, and therefore I conclude that no amount of epistemological and historiographical sympathy for the subaltern and oppressed—whether hybridized or essential—can substitute for a critical political economy of power. The underlying curiosity of this inquiry regards whether there are forms of social power that are, perhaps, peculiar and particular to imperialism and world order. This inquiry therefore concludes by arguing that decolonizing IR is necessary not primarily because colonialism or imperialism is a politically or morally offensive organization of the world, though it is indeed that, but because a colonized IR mystifies, obscures, misidentifies, misrecognizes, and mistakes the basis and manner of the production of world order.

So the first task is to show in what principal ways IR as a body of knowledge and international relations as a social practice or set of social relations remain colonial, colonized, or imperial in character. With this in mind, a historical examination of the continuities of international order is called for together with an examination of the continuities in the methods, concepts, tropes, and representations of world order in IR.

The second task is to begin to examine in what ways IR may be decolonized and, most important, to at least begin to indicate what difference to social inquiry and knowledge about the world such a decolonization might produce. A decade ago, Pieterse and Parekh argued, "The decolonisation of the western imagination means reviewing Western horizons in the light of the collusion with empire and colonialism, and with the ongoing asymmetries of global power . . . [but] [t]his is not merely a matter of disentangling the effects of power . . . but of understanding the interweaving of progress and power, and to reflect on the role of power in history."[6] Their call for reimagination thus begins by dismissing any possibility of a crude and ready distinction between the colonizer on the one hand and the colonized on the other. In turn, they quote favorably the purpose expressed by Mehrez that "decolonisation comes to be understood as an act of exorcism for both the colonizer and colonised. For both parties it must be a process of liberation from dependency in the case of the colonised; and from imperialist, racist perceptions, representations, and institutions . . . in the case of the coloniser."[7] But again, it would be mistaken to conclude that the necessary double exorcism could be conducted on two discrete and essential bodies, as if they were informed by two separate formative histories. We can take this common purpose into the field of IR as long as it remains clear that decolonization is not secured through a simple reversion of rule to the colonized or achieved through some corrective occidentalism or some spirited appeal to the universal but subaltern Other. Thus, decolonizing IR (or anything else for that matter) cannot be reduced to the task of undoing history or "reverse engineering" the mechanisms of imperial world ordering.[8]

THREE ELEMENTS OF A DECOLONIZING METHOD

The dominant representations of world order in IR reflect, I shall argue, what James Blaut has called "the coloniser's model of the world" and what Sophie Bessis has identified as an expression of "western supremacism."[9] However, the production of colonizers' models of the world or such expressions of supremacism have long and varied manufacturing histories with enormously complex divisions of labor. Thus, the presentation of the colonized land and indigenous people in Defoe's *Robinson Crusoe* is significantly different from that in Conrad's *Heart of Darkness*; the encounter and treatment of the Maya and Aztec recorded in Bernal Diaz's *Conquest of New Spain* not only tells of a quite different world to the European engagement with Arab and Ottoman rule in Gertrude Bell's *The Desert and the Sown* but are differentially absorbed both into the colonial imaginations and into modes of imperial rule.[10] Similarly, though Ngũgĩ wa Thiong'o's preoccupation with the struggle between imperial and indigenous language addresses the question also posed by C. L. R. James regarding ownership of the means of cultural production, the specific differences between the history of British colonialism in East Africa on the one hand and the Caribbean and United States on the other are crucial.[11] It is necessary to underline these obvious matters because, though there is no substitute for a close examination of the particular genealogies of colonial and imperial praxis and while refusing the tendency in IR to flatten out the often steep contours characteristic of highly differentiated imperial histories, one can nevertheless begin to outline how IR has inherited a colonizer's model of the world or arrogated to itself a supremacist disposition.

Critical realists often begin their inquiries with a variation on the single question addressing the conditions of possibility. That is, the inquirer is asking what conditions and mechanisms must be (1) present and (2) operative for such and such an effect, including phenomena, to be possible. While I don't pretend to be able to properly or fully address these questions in this chapter, it is in this spirit that I proceed. However, rather than draw heavily from the probably more unfamiliar critical realist engagement,[12] perhaps it is better to set course from a more familiar Marxist critique. There are two truisms from *The German Ideology* and from "The Eighteenth Brumaire of Louis Bonaparte" that, though prompted by peculiarities of national and imperial experiences in Europe, both reflect Marx's method and, through that method, can provoke the critique of colonial thinking that informs this chapter by raising the notion of "the illusion of the epoch." As already implied, we might properly ask not only why we should decolonize IR but also, most significant, *how* we decolonize IR. In short, method (and theory) are at least as significant—perhaps more so—to the decolonization of IR than is normative or political intent.

First, then, is the assertion that "the class which has the means of material production at its disposal, has control at the same time over the means of mental production, so that thereby, generally speaking, the ideas of those who lack the means of mental production are subject to it."[13] This leads Marx to conclude that the ideas of the ruling class "are the ruling ideas of the epoch." If we move now into the field of colonial IR, by definition, the dominant or ruling ideas of what constitutes world order and how world order is constituted (i.e., the dominant notion of "the international") are the ideas of those who control the means of international mental production. Knowledge of the world, in this sense, is produced and organized colonially.

Second, Marx famously argues that "men make history, but not of their own free will; not under circumstances they themselves have chosen but under the given and inherited circumstances with which they are directly confronted."[14] Not only is history made (allowing for agency) and not given, but also their inheritance is given (acknowledging preconditions), entailing that the very telling and meaning of history is simultaneously rewritten and bequeathed as an imperial or colonial history. The historiography of IR is, therefore, to be understood both as much a product of mental production as any other ideological form and as much a consequence of inherited circumstances as any other material with which we are confronted. Marx's historical method signaled here requires neither a determinist view of history, a rigid structuralism, nor a totalizing metanarrative before which the infinite pluralities of historical experience and sense must fall into line.[15]

Following these two opening claims, a vital distinction needs to be made regarding the examination of world order. Broadly speaking, there are two traditions of thinking about colonialism. The first and dominant tradition argues that colonialism is a transhistorical phenomenon differentiated only by the particular forms of external rule and administration, degree of colonial settlement, or nature of subjugation to alien rule. For this tradition, it makes sense to, for example, conduct a comparative history of empires that likens and contrasts the Roman Empire with the Habsburg Empire or the American Empire, and in which it is the superficial likeness of the colonial form that invites comparison. For this tradition, the period of decolonization from about 1947 represents the clear historical demise of colonialism and ushers in a period of national freedom.[16] After all, it is claimed, by the end of the twentieth century there were no colonies (as understood in international law), leaving only a remnant of self-administering "overseas" territories. The preeminent historical subject for this tradition is the nation, presented as a historically frustrated but ever-immanent possibility that finally was able to either negotiate or violently liberate itself from imperial subordination into a nation-state. The distinguishing language of this tradition is in its use of a vocabulary of "national freedom," "sovereignty," "independence," and "self-determination," all of which are realized through decolonization. In turn, therefore, it makes sense in this tradition to speak of a postcolonial period; that is, the "colonial" is something of the past, and therefore any call today to decolonize IR is either otiose or fatally postlapsarian.[17]

The second minority tradition—primarily Marxist and specifically Leninist in origin—maintains that classical colonialism was but a phase, albeit a crucial one, in the historical development of capitalist imperialism. In this view, the impetus and logic of imperial expansion comes from and must be primarily explained in reference to the exigencies of capitalism. Thus, insofar as capitalism is not a transhistorical phenomenon, it follows that any explanation of the forms of imperialism and world order, including colonial empires, must be rooted in an analysis of the historical peculiarities and particularities of the development of world capitalism. In this view, comparing the feudal Carolingian Empire with the capitalist empire of twentieth-century imperial Japan is a fool's errand.

In responding to the call to decolonize IR, which of these two paths is taken is the decisive question, and the reason for taking the second path can be argued by invoking a third argument from Marx, namely, what he refers to as "the illusion of the epoch," which draws together the production of ruling ideas with the notion of inherited circumstances into the telling of history. Before elaborating the notion of the illusion of the epoch in IR, suffice to say for the moment that we need to see imperialism as the fundamental problem for the study of international relations and that colonialism and empires are either (1) periodic and peculiar expressions of imperialism or (2) otherwise derivative of imperialism. Regardless, because colonialism and imperialism are neither equivalent nor synonymous, we should at least be aware that limiting our ambition to that of decolonizing IR may do little to diminish IR's imperialist character.

It is not unimportant, then, to ask whether the call to decolonize IR is a call to postcoloniality or a call to anticolonialism (or anti-imperialism). To continue from the premises of the first tradition may, at best, result in a postcolonial IR, still redolent with the illusory forms of international order. To be provoked by the sensibilities of the second tradition provides the conditions of possibility for both an anticolonialism and an anti-imperialism. The dominant traditions of IR, including international theory, serve to reflect international order and organization rather than explaining the reasons for the emergence of that order and the defeat of alternative immanent orders. Redescribing a social order, including an international order, does not in and of itself constitute an explanation of that order. For example, retelling the story of the international through the perspective of another or as experienced by a historical agent who had hitherto been silenced, while necessary to a more adequate explanation of social change, remains insufficient. This clearly raises a delicate historiographical and scientific problem regarding, to use Wolf's phrase, "the people without history."[18] While in scholarly terms the recovery, reintroduction, or reappearance of people without history back into history may be relatively uncontroversial (though the supremacist historiographical attitude described by Bessis, Blaut, Guha, Wolf, and others demonstrates a strength and pervasiveness of view that suggests a continuing and bitter fight) it is, we well know— from the origins of subaltern studies to Freirean pedagogy and from theologies

of liberation to Rastafari dub poetry—deeply political. But I'm jumping ahead
of myself, for Rastafari dub poetry does not constitute the historical narrative
behind the illusion of the epoch, whereas nationalism, racism, supremacism,
and state-centrism are central to that illusion. Specifically, Marx writes that
"the exponents of this conception of history have consequently only been able
to see in history the political actions of princes and States, religious and all
sorts of theoretical struggles, and in particular in each historical epoch have had
to share the illusion of that epoch."[19] Marx has the correct emphasis here: the
illusion is expressed and contested at a theoretical level, as an abstraction, as a
"sovereign consciousness" and not as a substantive historical process. After all,
following Edward Said, the illusion is both produced and maintained because
"if the Orient [or the colonized, subaltern, or otherwise dispossessed] could
represent itself it would; since it cannot, the representation [by the colonizer]
does the job, for the West."[20] The imperialist arrogates to himself both the
production of world order and the description and explanation of that selfsame
world order. The illusion is that world history has no dispossessed.

What of this epochal illusion? How does it manifest itself? International
theory typically presumes the fragmentation of the social and natural world
into the constituent domains of politics, economics, society, culture, religion,
and so on, for each of which there has developed a dedicated and specialist
discipline of scientific doctrine. International theory has as its object of inquiry
the international political order and the organizations or polities that make up
that international order. As we know, IR is preoccupied with one particular
kind of political organization or polity, namely, the state. In turn, the transformation and status of the state preys over international theory, although I would
contend that international theory has typically been negligent of historical differentiation and discounting of the historical specificities of individual states
and societies. It is not surprising, therefore, to find that international theory
typically oscillates between oppositional dyadic abstractions: thus communi-
tarianism versus cosmopolitanism, inside against outside, domestic or foreign,
cooperation or conflict, order or justice, anarchy versus stability, and so on.
The battle of abstractions or the generation of illusions continues as long as
the wretched of the earth are kept out.

The consequence of the illusion of the epoch lies in mistaking the products of
international ordering for international ordering itself. It is imperialism, I argue,
that produces international polities and organizations and that in turn pitches
the social world into dyadic oppositions. The illusions are the explanandum, but
the explanans is imperialism. The illusion of the epoch is, therefore, to persist
with the mistake that the explanation of international order and organization
of the world remains to be found in the examination of the nation-state and
inter-national organizations. Changing the descriptive vocabulary of world

order from colonial to international, from imperial to national, neither reflected a fundamental shift in world ordering principles nor signaled an improvement in the adequacy of scientific explanation. Again, Marx's criticism of the critics is apt: "They forget, however, that to these phrases they themselves are only opposing other phrases, and that they are in no way combating the real existing world when they are merely combating the phrases of this world."[21] The success and longevity of this illusory ambition is to be measured by the constant return by scholars to the examination of the abstracted state or the juridical ideal subject of positivist international law and a corresponding discounting of the history of subalterns or of those in the "waiting room of history."

Central to orthodox IR is the assumption that to leave the waiting room of history and gain historical recognition can be achieved only through the assumption of national identity and state form. The European historical trajectory shows the way to all that may follow. Since the nationalist principle underpins the discipline of IR, once-subjugated polities and peoples were able to follow analogous nationalist incitements, especially with the fall of formal empires, to that of risorgimento leader Massimo d'Azeglio when he declared, 'Fatta l'Italia, bisogna fare gli italiani"—with Italy made, the Italians must now be made.[22] It seem to me that the nationalist principle that informs imperialist visions of progress is the necessary corollary to the widely held historiographical excuses that take the form of "they couldn't stand in the way of progress," "they were destined to die out," "they were too weak a civilization," "their savagery deserves no pity," or simply "exterminate all the brutes." As a discipline, IR served first and foremost to nationalize social scientific investigation. As suggested by Louis and Robinson, the ending of colonial rule can have at least two reasons.[23] The first is that colonialism was ejected and substituted by novel and distinctive forms of rule, but the second is that colonialism, being just one form of imperialism, metamorphosed in such a way as to retain the fundamental powers of imperialism while shedding the outward forms of colonialism. Where orthodox IR adopts the first assumption and in so doing enshrines the nationalist principle, the critique outlined here seeks to demonstrate the strength of the second claim. Thus, in this vein, we can also speak of IR's account of the shift from a colonial world order to an international world order but beneath which the essential attributes and disposition of imperialism continue to shape and inform world order. In this light, the central problem for the study of international relations is not so much colonialism and the need for decolonizing IR but that the emergence of the international itself is the story identical with that of imperialism. Nationalism—and the international—is imperialism's alter ego and not its successor.

Provoked by Ranajit Guha's insightful description, imperialism was always "a joint operation of war and words," and the argument presented here is that the imperial character of international relations is demonstrated most frequently through the use of organized violence, the dispossessing of both the means of production of life and the means of producing one's own life account of that dispossession. It is in this combination of telling one's own story of one's own life that the subordinated histories of the colonized confront, often violently, the imperially authorized history of world order.

IDENTIFYING THE COLONIAL IN INTERNATIONAL RELATIONS

One can identify a number of distinguishing characteristics of colonialist knowledge that are pervasive in orthodox IR. Crucially, this knowledge continues to be produced in and through an imperial (or colonial or neocolonial) economy. How and in what ways do the conventions of IR appropriate and represent the colonial or imperial world? Answering these questions will provide at least an initial characterization of colonial knowledge in IR.

There is to begin with a number of simple empirical tests for assessing the veracity of the contention that informs this chapter, namely, the claim that IR theory is an expression of Western supremacism and therein perpetuates the epochal illusion. This test could be undertaken through a number of iterations, each slightly varied. Thus, we could ask how many works in international theory take as their historical referent or object of inquiry any non-Western states. Next we could ask how many and what proportion of works in IR are published in Western journals and publishing houses. We could also examine how many theoretical traditions or perspectives are Western in origin or derivation. Further, we could ask how many authors from non-Western countries have published in IR journals. In asking these historical questions, which can, in principle, be resolved empirically (and later statistically), we would be well on the way to outlining a profound and chronically structured distribution of scientific power. To be sure, the problem of isolating and defining what was meant by the "West" or what counts as "an object of inquiry" or a "Western theoretical perspective" might remain problematic but certainly not something that those well versed in methodological positivism couldn't settle through careful technical specification. It is at this point, if you will, that a sociology of knowledge production would reveal that it is not a North–South split or any other geographical or spatial distinction that is the primary determinant of the current structure of IR knowledge but rather one determined by the ownership of the means of production. There is an intimate relationship between the development of capitalism on a global scale, the development of imperialism (including colonialism), and the theoretical expression of Western supremacism. Through no accident, the structure of the knowledge economy of the world maps rather neatly onto the structure of imperial dispossession and appropriation.[24]

Whatever the paucity of references to or uses of the history of the colonized (subaltern and otherwise dispossessed), IR scholarship is able to present the colonized as much through omission and unspoken assumption as by direct reference. There are four principal (and no doubt complementary) paths one can take in exposing the nature and effects of these omissions and assumptions. First, there is the general critique of Eurocentrism in which the now global dominance, indeed intellectual hegemony, of the European "enlightenment" social scientific traditions has effected the silencing or permanent subordination of subaltern knowledge, including historical knowledge. Here, "subaltern" and "colonized" are synonymous. Second, there is the profoundly important critique of "orientalism" in which the Western imagination tells us little or nothing about "the rest" but everything about the West. Here, "nothing" and "the rest" are synonymous. Third, there is the recording, tracing, and critique of the profound political economic inequalities that were generated by colonial (or imperial) international order and that have resulted in the perennial extermination of the colonized. Here, "colonial order" and "inequality" are synonymous. Finally, one could demonstrate the contradiction, partiality, differentiation, and inconsistency of ostensibly universalist doctrines, most obviously of human rights and human equality, in the constitution of the colonial (or imperial) order. Here, "partiality" and "universality" are synonymous.

The removal or discounting of the subordinated from their own history is secured often through the simplest of techniques, such as in the repetition of simple phrases. Thus, in his critical assessment of Said's work, Bruce Robbins takes Disraeli's imperial dictum that "the East is a career" and comments that his phrase

> is briefly and brilliantly offensive. Activating the convention by which an empty, immobile point on the compass is held capable of condensing millions of undescribed personal destinies, the sentence equates these missing millions with a single individual's rising curve of professional accomplishment. The individual who is to enjoy the career is elided, as if in pretense of equal exchange for the elision of the colossal human diversity that is to be its raw material; in the space of symmetrical impersonality thus cleared, the static East can be spurred into movement, metamorphosed into the kinesis of a (Western) "pursuit."[25]

So, in a phrase, is captured the essence of imperial administration and the attitude to subject peoples. And it is the task of overturning a deep and long-established attitude that any call for decolonizing IR must face. This attitude in fact tells the story of Western supremacy—its historical and historiographical evolution—by presupposing Western supremacism. Guha identifies the problem clearly when he counterposes Hegel's characterization of world history with what is historically entailed in the production of that world history. Thus, quoting Hegel,

> world history moves on a higher plane than that to which morality properly belongs. . . . The deeds of great men who are individuals of world history . . . appear justified not only in their inner significance . . . but also in a secular sense.[26]

In this way, the historical function and purpose of the imperial nation or state is presented as already peculiar and elevated and not prone to the limiting conditions and considerations that characterize the subordinate. What does this abstraction mean concretely? Imperialism is author of history, author of law, author of historical subject, author of indictment, author of judgment. For example, "By inventing a universal humanity and endowing this juridical abstraction with inalienable rights, it absolved Europe of crimes both past and future," Bessis opines before asking whether "Enlightenment thought, like storm-bearing clouds, already carries future horrors within it, formulating the limits of universality in such a way as to make Europe its sole guardian?"[27] Correspondingly, Guha argues that

> from the point of view of those left out of World-history this advice amounts to condoning precisely such "world-historical deeds"—the rape of continents, the destruction of cultures, the poisoning of the environment—as helped "the great men who [were] the individuals of world history" to build empires and trap their subject populations in what in the pseudo-historical language of imperialism could describe as Prehistory.[28]

Imperial rule makes itself known as imperial rule through the power of universalizing its own story and self-validating its own story. The twin of this is to deprive the subordinated of the capacity to tell their own story and to determine an alternative legitimation and self-validation.

Key to the reproduction of this trope is the disciplining effect of the historiography of Western progress and world development, best expressed in the phrase "the colonizer's model of the world" or summarily expressed as: in the beginning there was Europe, then the Enlightenment . . . and only then 'the world.' Even "critical" theories of imperialism (i.e., the broadly Marxist tradition) have inadvertently focused their attention and developed their explanations of IR through a concentration on the histories of Europe and North America. Eurocentrism, in this respect, is not simply a function of theory but also an attitude to the world. It is startling how international theory is motivated by either (1) stories of origination in which claim to originality and hence authenticity are crucial for legitimacy or (2) social or temporal proximity to the foundational metaphors of the IR canon. Thus, closeness or similarity to (e.g., Eastern Europe, Turkey, or South Africa) or even derivation from (Canada, Australia, or even the United States) confers legitimacy. But also the foundational metaphors and analogues of IR are essentially European, be they from Thucydides, Machiavelli, Hobbes, Locke, Kant, or Lenin. Rather than the critical metaphors and analogues of IR being reshaped in the light of an imperial world ordering, world-historical experience is reshaped to correspond with the already established imperial conceptual lexicon. The imperialist historiography that I have argued informs the conventions of IR is one in which world histories, in all their diversities and particularities, are dispossessed from their historical subjects, appropriated, and recast in the service of a colonial or neocolonial project. A few words are in order to indicate the manner in which the science, law, language, economy, and violence of imperialism are reflective of a common pattern of dispossession.

From this overarching imperial presentation of world history, perhaps the single most effective yet most often unreflective technique in the attitude of colonial IR has been to regard subordinated histories, including that of nationalist histories, as imitations or duplications of the path already forged in Western history. Indeed, we have seen recently, in the new imperial wars of the United States and the United Kingdom, that deviation from the approved forms of historical development prompts the deployment of imperial criticism. When the development of world order does not correspond with imperial prescription, violence itself is redefined. Thus, Mamdani laments the manner by which "political violence in modern society that does not fit the story of progress tends to get discussed in theological terms."[29] This capacity for asserting authorship, for claiming exclusive authority over accounts of world history, is a vital element in the supremacist armory. Not only are lines of historical descent defined, but qualification or legitimacy remains the preserve of imperialism. It is these unreflected imperial tropes that IR has inherited and reproduced. As indicated earlier, IR is predicated on the nationalist principle, and the nationalist principle is the most consistently articulated myth of origination. Those who can be shown not to originate (i.e., aliens) cannot be part of the nation; if so, where or what is their historical place? The central illusion of IR is thereby reinforced from the inside and from the outside. Without myths of origination, there is no IR.

Allied to this notion of authorized duplication is imperialism's refusal to interpret or translate. That is, the attitude of Western supremacism is secured because the immense diversity of historical subjects and historical experience is rendered meaningful only through an imperial vocabulary. Eric Cheyfitz, in a fascinating work, *The Poetics of Imperialism*, argues that "this process of translation, initiated by Columbus and perpetuated by the European voyagers who follow him, prepares the way for and is ever involved in the dispossession by which the Native American land was translated (the term used in English common law to refer to transfers of real estate) into the European identity of property."[30] And this meant title deed, written in English, comprehensible only in the history of English law. (Jill Lepore's *The Name of War* illustrates the matter in a similar fashion.)[31] Imperialism is the imposition of meaning and the refusal to negotiate. It is a one-way translation from the subordinated to the superordinate, from the subaltern to the expropriator.

Imperialism, as indicated earlier, seeks to secure its order through monopolizing the means of mental production, and it is in this manner that there is a reproduction of colonialist knowledge in IR. More than that, what unites the various expressions of imperialism are the refusal of the imperial to interpret, to engage in dialogue. Instead, imperialism is a permanent if varying attempt to dispossess, to eliminate self-provision and self-definition, and to render unto itself on its own terms all that once pertained to others. In this sense, imperialism and imperialist historiography (including IR, I have been arguing) have been, in Guha's words, "a joint operation of wars and words."[32]

The irony is, perhaps, that theories of imperialism, including ostensibly critical theories of imperialism, have adopted and adapted to exactly these characteristics of imperialism. Whatever the intellectual provenance of these traditions, they exclusively derive from Europe (or to a lesser extent North America). Thus, ironically, the principal accounts of imperialism recognized by IR speak of and from the imperial heart and not from the colonial experience.[33] In the classical traditions, however much they are "updated," the imperium has history—indeed is history; the colony is without history, is tabula rasa. Any pretensions we might have of a radical anti-imperial critique should leave us with no doubt that we have an enormous amount of work to do. Axiomatic to the dominant traditions of postcolonial studies, as we have seen, has been the effort to hear the voice of the voiceless. But, as Appiah has sharply observed,

> postcoloniality is the condition of what we might ungenerously call a comprador intelligentsia: a relatively small, Western-style, Western trained group of writers and thinkers, who mediate the trade in cultural commodities of world capitalism at the periphery. In the West they are known for the Africa they offer; their compatriots know them both through the West they present to Africa and through an Africa they have invented for the world, for each other, and for Africa.[34]

This may be an ungenerous criticism, but it is an easy and proper one to make because, once again, the postcolonial theorists' chosen ground for battle has been that of the claim to authenticity, truth, and origin. Put another way, however much postcolonial theorists reject the essentialisms of authenticity, as long as their chosen political contestation is to represent the people without history, the argument will be lost. To use an old-fashioned and now rarely heard phrase, there is an "unfavorable correlation of forces" between an imperial knowledge economy and a postcolonial knowledge economy.[35]

What I am suggesting is that the postcolonial yapping and nibbling at the heels of imperialism is a forlorn endeavor. Instead, I am proposing that a decolonization of IR needs to be recast as an anti-imperialism and that the first task is to explain imperialism's production and reproduction and not to be preoccupied by one particular historical form of imperialism, namely, that of colonialism. While important, the preceding discussion does not condense down just to the question, "Who tells the stories?" Even though it is axiomatic to imperialism that the history of imperialism has been told as an apologia; even though the colonized have been largely silenced or are heard, only to be immediately discounted; despite acknowledging that what is allowed to be heard, those who are authorized to be heard, are the hybrids (i.e., those able to speak the language of imperialism); and even if today we concur, corrupting Sartre's observation that "the poor don't realize that their function in life is to exercise our generosity," that the colonized don't realize that their function in life is to exercise our (i.e., the West's) humanitarianism, yet it remains the case that the central historiographical battle is a political battle over ownership of the means of production of memory and the definition of progress.

CONCLUSION

The argument hitherto has been that the demand to decolonize IR can begin to be answered by exposing the character and composition of the central "illusion of the epoch." That illusion is one that presents world order of the second half of the twentieth century as a fully realized international order, confirming of national freedoms, first enunciated and confirmed in Europe. However, resolving the problems of historical subordination, whether material or ideational, is not exclusively (perhaps not even primarily) an intellectual or mental task but instead a substantive political task: thesis eleven. A forceful supporting testament to this claim comes from the unlikely source of Samuel Huntington when he writes that "the West won the world not by the superiority of its ideas or values or religion (to which few members of other civilizations were converted) but rather by its superiority in applying organized violence. Westerners often forget this fact; non-Westerners never do."[36] By not forgetting this, one can acknowledge that even with the effort to decolonize IR by bringing the forgotten subaltern and multiple histories back in, by more fully elaborating and exposing the delusions of orientalism, by demanding an equal or fair political-economic order, and by insisting on a fulfillment of universal rights and duties, one still is not equipped to fulfill thesis eleven. Although the previously mentioned strategies allow for recognition of the past and while they may also permit partial corrections for historical injury, they do not explain historical transformation or provoke emancipation. In this sense, these investigative strategies are postcolonial; they are not anticolonial. This is especially important given the siren enticements made by postcolonial studies, which, I argue, do not offer a means of decolonizing IR as much as providing vibrant color to the colonial picture, of acknowledging the myriad varieties of oppression and exploitation, of recognizing the multiplicity of identities and of stating—what has always struck me as blindingly obvious but has taken a whole academic industry to obfuscate—that identities are hybrid, variegated, fluid, and historical and not essential, fixed, and natural. This is, after all, precisely what Marx meant by the historical and the social.[37]

It is not unimportant, then, to ask whether the call to decolonize IR is a call to postcoloniality or a call to anticolonialism (or anti-imperialism). Guha identifies both the difficulty and the significance of such a call as this to decolonize IR when he writes that "a call to expropriate the expropriators, . . . is radical precisely in the sense of going to the root of the matter and asking what may be involved in a historiography that is clearly an act of expropriation."[38] Similarly, we might properly ask not only why we should decolonize but, most significant, *how* we decolonize IR. Method (and theory) is at least as significant—perhaps more so—to the decolonization of IR than is the normative intent or political intuition. Still more, I have suggested, we should also be cautious that decolonization does not constitute the yet more thorough capture of societies and histories to the projects of imperialism. I have argued that only if decolonizing IR is driven by an anti-imperialism and not satisfied by a pale postcolonialism can we speak of hope. Decolonizing IR therefore requires not just the willingness—which was always there—of the subordinated to write world history but also, crucially, the means of production of that world history to be recovered by the dispossessed, by agreement, or by force.

NOTES

1. Symbolic of the changing foundation of world order, one can take the Congress of Vienna (1815), guided by dynastic and sanguinary legitimation of rule; the General Act of the Berlin Conference (1885) dividing the African world wholly regardless of consideration of the colonized with order based on "spheres of influence"; the

post–World War I Paris "peace" treaties, especially that establishing the League of Nations at Versailles (1919), predicated on "open, just, and honorable relations between nations" or more readily translated as great power paternalism and imperial perfidy; and the Charter of the United Nations (1945), founded on nominal state equality and substantive inequality. Whatever the differences, all were variations on imperial order.

2. Archibald Wavell's judgment on the Paris peace conferences was "after 'the war to end war' they seem to have been pretty successful in Paris at making a 'Peace to end Peace'" (cited in the epigram and title of David Fromkin, *A Peace to End All Peace: The Fall of the Ottoman Empire and the Creation of the Modern Middle East* [London: Deutsch, 1989]).

3. Macmillan notes that American legations in Europe, when asking for elaboration from President Wilson as to what "self-determination" actually meant, were met with silence from the president and his office—a catchy slogan but a fatally ambiguous "principle" (Margaret Macmillan, *Paris, 1919* [New York: Random House, 2003], 11).

4. See David Harvey, *The New Imperialism* (Oxford: Oxford University Press, 2003).

5. Both the Second International (Socialist and Social Democratic parties) and the Third International (Comintern, Moscow-aligned communist parties) were effectively nationalist in orientation and colonialist in sympathy. Parties that were members of either the Second and the Third International, which came to form parties of government across the world, continued to pursue domestic and foreign policies of colonial, militarist, and profoundly racist kinds. This is an important point: socialism was neither guarantee nor insurance against either colonialism or imperialism.

6. Jan Nederveen Pieterse and Bhikhu Parekh, "Shifting Imaginaries: Decolonisation, Internal Decolonisation, Post-Coloniality," in *The Decolonization of Imagination: Culture, Knowledge and Power*, ed. Jan Nederveen Pieterse and Bhikhu Parekh (London: Zed Books, 1995), 3.

7. Quoted in Pieterse and Parekh, "Shifting Imaginaries," 4.

8. There is, of course, a vast literature on the relationship between colonizer and colonized. Indispensable primary references include Albert Memmi, The *Colonizer and the Colonized* (London: Souvenir Press, 1965); Frantz Fanon, *Black Skin, White Masks* (London: Pluto Press, 1986); and Frantz Fanon, *The Wretched of the Earth* (Harmondsworth: Penguin, 1967). Other excellent secondary commentaries include Ania Loomba, *Colonialism-Postcolonialism* (London: Routledge, 1998); Patrick Williams and Laura Chrisman, eds., *Colonial Discourse and Post-Colonial Theory* (London: Harvester Wheatsheaf, 1993); Arif Dirlik, *The Post Colonial Aura: Third World Criticism in the Age of Global Capitalism* (Boulder, Colo.: Westview Press, 1997); and, of course, the work of Edward W. Said, *Orientalism* (London: Vintage, 1978), and the subaltern studies movement, key writings of which are collected in the eight-volume series edited by Ranajit Guha, *Subaltern Studies* (New Delhi: Oxford University Press, 1982).

9. James M. Blaut, *The Colonizer's Model of the World: Geographical Diffusionism and Eurocentric History* (London: Guilford Press, 1993); Sophie Bessis, *Western Supremacy: The Triumph of an Idea?* (London: Zed Books, 2003).

10. Daniel Defoe, *The Life and Adventures of Robinson Crusoe* (Harmondsworth: Penguin, 1965); Joseph Conrad, *Heart of Darkness* 1925, reprint, (Harmondsworth: Penguin, 1995); Bernal Diaz, *The Conquest of New Spain* (Harmondsworth: Penguin, 1963); Gertrude Bell, *The Desert and the Sown* (London: Heinemann, 1907).

11. Ngũgĩ wa Thiong'o, *Decolonising the Mind: The Politics of Language in African Literature* (London: James Currey and Heinemann, 1986); C. L. R. James, *American Civilisation* (1950; reprint, Oxford: Blackwell, 1993), and *At the Rendezvous of Victory* (London: Allison and Busby, 1984).

12. For helpful introductions to critical realism, see Andrew Collier, *Critical Realism: An Introduction to the Philosophy of Roy Bhaskar* (London: Verso, 1994), and Margaret Archer, Roy Bhaskar, Andrew Collier, Tony Lawson, and Alan Norrie, eds., *Critical Realism: Essential Readings* (London: Routledge, 1998).

13. Karl Marx and Friedrich Engels, *The German Ideology* (London: Lawrence and Wishart, 1968), 64.

14. Karl Marx, "The Eighteenth Brumaire of Louis Bonaparte," in *Surveys from Exile: Political Writings*, vol. 2 (1869; reprint, Harmondsworth: Penguin, 1992), 147.

15. I have no sympathy for orthodox Marxism, which claims that the problem of bourgeois history is largely one of mistaking the key historical subjects or of misidentifying key historical "laws of movement." Marxism has to address the open-ended and multiple histories and give account of why some and not other renditions of history become dominant.

16. This historiographical interpretation relies on a rather casual forgetting or discounting of the 1824–1825 period, which marks the end of Spanish colonial rule in most of the Americas.

17. Whether from the garden or the colony, whether seen as an expression of human freedom or historical predestination, the form of exit is inconsequential compared to the sheer fact of the fall from the old and the unavoidable necessity of the new.

18. Eric R. Wolf, *Europe and the People without History* (Berkeley: University of California Press, 1997).

19. Marx and Engels, *The German Ideology*, 60.

20. Said, *Orientalism*, 21.

21. Marx and Engels, *The German Ideology*, 41.

22. Quoted in Eric R. Wolf, *Pathways of Power: Building an Anthropology of the Modern World* (Berkeley: University of California Press, 2001), 65.

23. William Roger Louis and Ronald Robinson, "The Imperialism of Decolonisation," in *The Decolonisation Reader*, ed. James Le Seuer (London: Routledge, 2001), 49.

24. This major problem is discussed briefly with reference to Africa in the final section of the concluding chapter of this volume.

25. Bruce Robbins, "The East Is a Career: Edward Said and the Logics of Professionalism," in *Edward Said: A Critical Reader*, ed. Michael Sprinker (Oxford: Blackwell, 1992), 48.

26. Ranajit Guha, *History at the Limit of World-History* (New York: Columbia University Press, 2002), 4, citing Georg W. F. Hegel, *Lectures on the Philosophy of World History: Introduction* (Cambridge: Cambridge University Press, 1975), 141.

27. Bessis, *Western Supremacy*, 22–23.

28. Guha, *History at the Limit of World-History*, 4.

29. Mahmood Mamdani, *Good Muslim, Bad Muslim: America, the Cold War, and the Roots of Terror* (New York: Pantheon Books, 2004), 4.

30. Eric Cheyfitz, *The Poetics of Imperialism: Translation and Colonization from The Tempest to Tarzan* (Philadelphia: University of Pennsylvania Press, 1991), 126. Instances of this process of imperial "translation" are examined by Krishna (chapter 4 in this volume) with regard to language and alphabet and by Gathii (chapter 6 in this volume) with regard to property.

31. Jill Lepore, *The Name of War: King Philip's War and the Origins of American Identity* (New York: Knopf, 1998).

32. Ranajit Guha, quoted in Arundhati Roy, *An Ordinary Person's Guide to Empire* (Cambridge, Mass.: South End Press, 2004), 8.

33. On the few occasions that IR does remember imperialism, the standard sources are invariably Lenin, Hobson, and perhaps Luxemburg. There are, of course, major accounts of imperialism by the colonized, but these are generally ignored altogether.

34. Kwame Anthony Appiah, "Is the Post- in Postmodernism the Post- in Postcolonial?," in *Contemporary Postcolonial Theory: A Reader*, ed. Padmini Mongia (London: Arnold, 1996), 62–63, quoted in Loomba, *Colonialism-Postcolonialism*, 246.

35. I write this in a month of renewed bloody brutality in Iraq, Colombia, Chechnya, Sudan, and elsewhere. At this time, a leading IR journal finds the most compelling and pressing subject for its conference, which is titled "Between Fear and Wonder: International Politics, Representation and 'the Sublime,' " at which the following will preoccupy its worldly IR scholars: "The sublime, as an aspect of aesthetics that signifies engagement with the inexplicable and incalculable, captures many modes of interpretation. Taming the sublime through art and poetry for example, challenges the foundation and reach of our communicative knowledge. Therefore, sublime experiences, events and moments can shatter the consensus of constitutive meaning through which we give order to our lives. How epistemology responds to and incorporates the sublime, from aesthetic conception to representation, is consequently a deeply political question. Who, with what words and what authority, expresses or interprets 'the sublime' in our world?" Oh, what a lovely war. (*Millennium: Journal of International Studies*, Annual Conference, 2005, <http://www.lse.ac.uk/Depts/intrel/millenn/Conf2005_Sublime/Conference_2005.htm> [accessed September 15, 2005].)

36. Samuel P. Huntington, *The Clash of Civilizations and the Remaking of World Order* (New York: Simon and Schuster, 1997), 51. It is, though, impossible to agree with Huntington's assessment of conversion. How would we account for the transformation of indigenous Latin American and African civilizations and people without reference in substantial part to conversion? Huntington, of course, has a partial, dismissive, and arrogant definitional response: historically, African societies don't count as civilizations! Africa is omitted in his list of civilizations on pages 45 to 46, though by page 47 Africa "possibly" could have a distinct civilization. In a seminal book of about 350 pages, "African (possibly)" is as confident as Huntington will get.

37. It bears repeating, particularly in the light of the postcolonial preoccupations, that Marx was a philosopher, not an economist. A great deal of his most important

work was in what we would now call cultural studies, history, or social theory. To the extent that he was an "economist," his was, crucially, a critique of political economy. No one who has read *The Holy Family, The Jewish Question, The German Ideology, The Poverty of Philosophy, The Economic and Philosophic Manuscripts*, most of his journalism, or, for that matter, *Capital* or the *Grundrisse* could seriously conclude that Marx was either (1) primarily an economist or (2) concerned only with the "empirical" world of goods and services.

38. Guha, *History at the Limit of World-History*, 2.

Chapter Two

International Relations Theory and the Hegemony of Western Conceptions of Modernity

Sandra Halperin

Theories about the structures, processes, and events that define and recur within the international realm are based to a large extent on the history of the European states system and its role in world affairs since the sixteenth century. Critiques of these theories have focused primarily on their Eurocentricity as well as on fundamental silences and distortions in the historical accounts on which they depend. However, critical theorists have yet to draw attention to two of the most problematic aspects of these accounts.

The first of these relates to our understanding of the "European experience." While critical perspectives have done much to elucidate European representations of non-European "others," they have left wholly unexamined Europe's representation of *itself*. Consequently, they tend to reproduce Europe's profoundly erroneous, highly ideological representation of its own history.[1] They frequently assume, wrongly, that knowledges and practices universalized by Europeans were grounded in European history when, in many cases, these neither originated in Europe nor were even part of the European experience. Because European history remains fundamental to our understanding of the contemporary world, "decolonizing" International Relations (IR) theory requires that we not only "bring in the rest of the world" but also "bring in" a more accurate account of how Europe itself developed. Until we do, critical perspectives will ultimately serve only to reinforce rather than undermine the historical underpinning of mainstream IR theory.

43

Second, critical theories generally accept the basic unit of analysis of mainstream IR theory. Although they maintain a critical stance toward nationalist historiography and binary schemas, they tend, nonetheless, to focus on whole nations or regions.[2] In common with mainstream IR theory, they assume that development has been a process of nationally organized economic growth and that *globally* organized economic growth is something that is only now beginning to emerge. However, nationally organized economic growth has rarely been the case; it has only recently characterized a few countries and for only a few decades. Discussions of transnationalism and of global capitalist classes usually assume that these phenomena are new when, in fact, they have underpinned world economic processes continuously since at least the end of the eighteenth century. By focusing on whole nations and their interactions with each other, critical perspectives reproduce many of the silences and distortions that characterize mainstream IR theory.

Critical theories leave intact much of the historical as well as the ontological basis of mainstream IR theory. Consequently, their critique remains partial and limited in its impact. The aim of this chapter is to bring into view an alternative history and ontology. It first highlights a number of myths that distort our understanding of the broad historical period on which much of contemporary IR theory is based. It then endeavors to show how structures and processes obscured by these myths produce elements of an alternative ontology. The first section discusses several myths concerning modernity and the "rise of Europe," which are factually wrong and analytically unproductive. They obfuscate the cultural, social, and intellectual advances that were achieved previous to and that made possible the "rise of Europe" as well as the nature and basic structures of European expansion. The second section focuses on myths concerning industrialization and democracy in Europe in the nineteenth century. It endeavors to show that capitalist development, both within and outside Europe, has everywhere and from the start involved not whole nations or societies but only sectors or geographical areas within states.

All the chapters in this volume are engaged in rethinking the history and ontology of mainstream theory. Some illuminate materials from which alternative narratives or histories can draw; others demonstrate how contrapuntal analysis can deepen and expand our understanding of both history and the contemporary world. Above all, what is needed is to confront the hegemonic perspective with an unassimilable difference, one that cannot be rendered compatible or incorporated but that, if accepted, makes it impossible to retain the dominant account.

Focusing on transnational/cross-regional structures and developments before, during, and after the "rise of Europe" dissolves the binarisms characteristic of existing approaches (core/periphery, colonizer/colonized, West/rest, modern/ traditional) and brings into focus the synchronic and interdependent development of dynamic focal points of growth throughout the world shaped, both within and outside Europe, by translocal interaction and connection as well as by local struggles and social relations. Emphasizing the development and interaction of classes, groups, and social networks rather than of states and regions analytically shifts the axis of view from the vertical (states, regions) to the horizontal (classes, networks). By bringing different processes and relationships into view, this "horizontal" perspective enables different questions to be asked and different accounts to be told. It is this that may ultimately enable us to develop a more adequate understanding of world-historical developments.

THE RISE OF EUROPE: FOUNDATIONAL MYTHS

According to conventional Western historiography, Europe's rise began as a result of more or less natural processes of expansion impelled by dynamic developments within Europe itself—the spectacular growth of agricultural productivity and trade and of European towns and cities. With the same spirit of discovery and exploration that had given rise to this dynamism, Europeans succeeded in navigating the great seas and oceans. These explorations led to the European "discovery" of a primitive and backward "new" world, hitherto untouched by civilization. Meanwhile, back at home, European dynamism was generating world-historical "revolutions" in science and technology, agricultural and commercial practices, intellectual life, and social and political institutions. These revolutions, together with the discovery of a primitive new world, imbued Europeans with a sense of mission: to use European technological and institutional advances to lift out of darkness both the backward and impoverished new world to the West as well as the stagnant and dissolute "old" world to the East that had proved incapable of regenerating itself.

This section focuses on factors in the "rise of Europe" that are obfuscated by this story. Europe's rise began with the brutal and bloody expansion of a European military aristocracy in Europe itself. Eventually, changes in the conduct of warfare and, later, advances in military technology enabled this military expansion to extend beyond Europe. With the precious metals gained through conquest of the "new" world, Europeans invested heavily in developing the military capability necessary to conquer areas of the world that were in significant ways more advanced than itself. In fact, it was cultural, social, and intellectual advances achieved in the non-European world that had made Europe's military expansion possible and that provided the basis for and, to varying degrees, the content of its revolutions.

The Nature of European Expansion

The rise of Europe was accompanied by the most destructive military expansion in human history. It began with the outward movement of a western European military aristocracy that, in the eleventh, twelfth, and thirteenth centuries, established conquest states and colonial societies throughout Europe. Two features of this expansion should be noted. The first is its brutality. The expansion of this "conquest aristocracy" changed the rules of warfare "towards a new cruelty, brutality and bloodthirstyness" that, along with the conquerors' appetite for domination, was noted by both European and Muslim observers.[3] Second, wherever conquest led to the establishment of colonies, it became mythologized "as a founding moment and a defining breach in time."[4] As Robert Bartlett explains, those who settled in the newly conquered and colonized parts of Europe were concerned to invalidate preconquest legal and other claims to possessions and privileges. The notion of a sharp break between preconquest barbarism and postconquest progress and development helped provide a basis for a new definition of property rights in the conquered areas.[5] Thus, in an early version of the "civilizing mission of the newcomer," settlers characterized the presettler history of the newly colonized regions as dark, primitive, underdeveloped, impoverished, and barbarous and characterized their own activities as progressive and transformative.

In the eleventh century, conquering western European elites advanced to Greece, Andalusia, Ulster, and Prussia and established colonial bridgeheads and bastions outside Europe. Europe set about conquering a dominant Asian economy by means of predatory acquisitions, armed ships, and a predatory worldview. By the latter half of the eleventh century, a dense network of Italian trading, piracy, and settlement was developed by "aggressive merchants-cum-pirates-cum-crusaders" trading in the large ports (Constantinople and Alexandria), plundering (al-Mahdiyyah in North Africa), or trying to establish crusading principalities (Antioch and Lattakieh).[6]

By mid-thirteenth century, Europe and the Orient were becoming more evenly balanced, though Asia was still more developed technologically and institutionally.[7] At the end of the fifteenth century, Europe was at a common level of development with Asia and was progressing at a common rate. After the fifteenth century, the growth of Asia and the Middle East began to slow relative to Europe. By the end of the sixteenth century—and using the precious metals of the New World to invest in military organization, supplies, and shipping—Europe had achieved a worldwide military lead based on naval superiority. This was facilitated by the demise of the once-powerful Chinese navy and consolidated with the failure of Ottoman naval construction to keep pace with developments that took place in Europe in the seventeenth and eighteenth centuries.

The world system that at that time stretched from western and southern Europe through the Middle East to China was, according to Janet Abu-Lughod, a relatively peaceful one, governed by unwritten laws and rules of reciprocity. But by the sixteenth century, Portuguese men-of-war were violating the rules of the game by burning or boarding ships and confiscating cargo of indigenous and unarmed merchant fleets of the area.[8]

A predatory European worldview was evident from the first conquests made outside Europe. The capture of Jerusalem in Palestine came four years after the proclamation of an ideology of crusade by Pope Urban II at Clermont, France, in 1095. A narrative of Christian-Muslim holy war, developed to accompany the European crusade against Ummayyad Spain, was used to misrepresent intra-Christian battles in Spain (such as the slaughter of Charlemagne's rear guard by Basques)[9] and to define a division between East and West that either had not existed or had not been recognized in medieval times.[10]

Like the conquest of Europe itself, conquests outside Europe were mythologized as defining a breach in time in the conquered realm between a dark and barbarous age and one of progress, reason, and enlightenment. The notion of a breach between Europe and the rest of the world was related not to Europe's technological, cultural, or intellectual progress but to its concern with consolidating European domination over other parts of the world. Europeans did not extend their modernity or seek to modernize their colonies or subjects. Neither European colonizers nor their sponsored intermediaries supported the development of institutions that would empower or enrich the masses lest they become a threat to imperialist interests.

The European Discoveries

In Western historiography, the term "discovery" is commonly used to describe the process by which, from the fifteenth century on, Europe and more especially western Europe set about discovering "the rest of the world." The dominant image is of the European explorer "discovering barbaric peoples in strange and remote places." But there is another story that begins earlier in which the European explorer "is himself an exotic barbarian discovered and observed by enquirers from the lands of Islam."[11]

Muslims viewed the lands to the north and west of the Ottoman Empire "in much the same way as Europeans were to view the Americas from the sixteenth to the eighteenth century": as "rich and barbarous lands to which it was their sacred mission to bring religion and civilisation, order and peace—while reaping the customary rewards of the pioneer and frontiersman."[12] Muslims saw the Islamic community as "the sole repository of truth and enlightenment, surrounded on all sides by an outer darkness of barbarism and unbelief."[13]

Islamic Andalusia was a multiethnic, multilingual, and religiously pluralistic state that fostered a culture of tolerance.[14] When Europeans reconquered Spain in the thirteenth century, the threat to Muslims was not cultural, religious, ideological, or philosophical but political and military.[15] The thirteenth-century western European assault on Córdoba and the Mongol assault on Baghdad were probably experienced as barbarian invasions of a similar kind.

The rise of the West occurred within a complex and prosperous world system linked by trade and intercultural exchange. As Europe's military expansion advanced through the eleventh, twelfth, and thirteenth centuries, among the many discoveries Europeans doubtless made were the cities of Constantinople, Kaifeng, Baghdad, and Córdoba. These, at the time, were the largest cities in the world and major centers both of commerce and culture. Some of the notable achievements that they would have found there were paved streets, street lamps, sewage systems, freshwater systems provided by aqueducts, and businesses and stores that stayed open twenty-four hours a day. They must have discovered that China, which until the fifteenth century remained the world leader in technology, industry, and commerce, had developed coal and steel industries, an armaments industry, and market-regulated commerce. China had also developed mariners' compasses and constructed massive sailing vessels with pivoting sails and watertight compartments. When Europeans discovered the new world, it was as a result of the achievements of generations of non-European seafarers, geographers, astronomers, and cartographers who had laid the foundation for the modern period of geographic exploration. In fact, Europe's discovery of America owed much to the Muslim doctrine of the sphericity of the earth, a theory to which scholars had long subscribed at the Islamic center of scientific studies at the University of Toledo and one accepted by Christopher Columbus.

A network of trade linked Europe with the Muslim world and with India and China. Europe imported a wide range of important Muslim, Indian, and Chinese commodities, including silks and other textiles, spices and aromatics, timber, metals, and ceramics. However, it was not until European colonization of the Americas and the establishment of commercial outposts in the east that Europe, for the first time, had a range of goods for export to the east. By the late eighteenth century, a range of European exports had been developed and had brought about a change in the balance of trade in favor of Europe.

Before the European age of "discovery," there existed not only a prosperous and far-flung trading network but an active and important network of intercultural exchange as well. Muslim scholars internationalized learning, translating Greek, Indian, and Persian works on medicine, astronomy, mathematics, and philosophy; studying science and alchemy, history, theology, geography and cosmology, and botany; and setting up universities, libraries, translation bureaus, observatories, and medical schools. Never before had intercultural exchanges "linked as many political societies and encompassed as many different fields of thought."[16] From the eighth through the tenth century, the Islamic caliphate in Baghdad undertook a "massive and systematic" translation into Arabic "of the universe of Greek learning." For about 200 years, the translation of ancient Greek scientific and philosophical texts was the focus of extraordinary expenditures of time, effort, and money. This was not "a mechanical or curatorial effort to 'preserve' the Greeks for posterity" but rather an effort to understand and adapt the Hellenistic intellectual universe and reintegrate it "back into a living culture."[17]

The European Revolutions

According to conventional accounts of modern European history, in the seventeenth century Europe experienced scientific, military, intellectual, commercial, agricultural, political, industrial, and technological advances that together laid the foundations of modernity and the modern world. A sixteenth- and seventeenth-century "secular revolution," followed by a political revolution (in England) and the beginning of scientific, commercial, price, and military revolutions, are thought to have set in motion trends of thought and change that helped launch the eighteenth-century intellectual revolution known as "the Enlightenment." It is generally assumed that the European Enlightenment was a, if not *the*, major turning point in the advance of modernity, laying the foundations for the eighteenth-century American and French revolutions, which in turn coincided with the beginning of the industrial revolution.

The European Enlightenment was characterized at the time by the thinkers most associated with it, as well as by others, as representing a radical and absolute break with the past.[18] Conventional accounts of modern European history continue to promote this view. However, the radical rupture that the story of the European revolutions suggests is more fiction than fact. What these "revolutions" represented was the extension into northwestern Europe of scientific, intellectual, technological, industrial, and military developments originating in other areas and cultures. Their adoption by Europeans produced modest changes that, in fact, amounted largely to modifications of old practices and beliefs. The ideas of the European Enlightenment, generally considered to have provided the context for the development of the modern world, were influenced greatly by the cultures of China and the Middle East during the medieval period and by Stoic ideas that had been influential for some 2,000 years. The ideas that Enlightenment thinkers and historians called European did not come from a Hellenic culture that "originated" from and then "returned to" Europe, as is often asserted: they were rejuvenated and developed by Islamic civilization from the Hellenic heritage that it shared with Christian Europe.

In sum, the term "European revolutions" was used to describe processes of change that were not really European, sudden or explosive, or really discontinuous with the past. The notion that the European Enlightenment and other revolutions represented a profound break in human history was a continuation of the theme of breach and disjuncture that had developed through centuries of European expansion and conquest. The view of European cultural and intellectual superiority, by further defining relations between Europe and the rest of the world in terms of advanced and primitive societies, provided additional ideological support for European conquest and domination. One of the most important contributions of the Enlightenment to this project was the development of a new historiography centered on the notion of progress. Cyclical conceptions that had characterized notions of social and historical change for much of history began to give way, and linear conceptions of historical change came to dominate social thought. By the eighteenth century, European philosophers, theologians, scientists, and historians had converged on the view of European history as a chronicle of progress in the advance of reason and freedom.

MYTHS OF THE INDUSTRIAL REVOLUTION AND MODERN EUROPEAN DEVELOPMENT

It is generally assumed that the separation of Europe from the non-European world began with advances achieved during what has been called "the long sixteenth century"; that, by the end of the eighteenth century, as a result of technological, scientific, and intellectual revolutions, Europe had achieved a level of development that made possible world-historic industrial and democratic revolutions; and that these European revolutions set in motion processes of industrialization and democratization that opened up a sharp division between what would come to be characterized as the "advanced industrial world" and the "third world." This section argues that none of these events marked the decisive period of European advance and that, in fact, European economic and political history diverged decisively from that of the rest of the world only after 1945.

Scholars have argued for over a century that the period we call the industrial revolution was not the radical break with the past that the term suggests, and recent research confirms this.[19] However, with the publication in 1884 of Arnold Toynbee's *Lectures on the "Industrial Revolution,"* the expression was adopted by the purveyors of European triumphalism and, despite objections, incorporated into historical terminology.

It is certainly true that Europe experienced enormous growth during its "long sixteenth century."[20] But the assumption that, as a consequence, western Europe had become rich compared to other parts of the world by the start of the industrial revolution[21] is erroneous. In the seventeenth century, European growth was halted and, in some areas, reversed. Thus, on the eve of the industrial revolution, the level of gross national product per capita in Europe was, in fact, about even with that of the non-European world.[22]

During the classic industrial revolution, Britain actually experienced only gradual industrialization.[23] However, Europeans in the late nineteenth century, impressed by the technological advances of the time, accepted the idea that Europe's level of economic well-being and its rate of progress were incomparably superior to anything that had gone before.[24] Such beliefs became deeply embedded in the historical consciousness of that and subsequent generations. They did so, most likely, because they helped shape the identity of Europe in relation to areas of the world being exploited by European governments and peoples and were used, in fact, as a rationale for that exploitation. Despite the general acceptance of these beliefs, however, the incomparable advance of Europe was more myth than reality.

The level of income in Britain by the middle of the nineteenth century and in Germany or France in 1870 was comparable with that of classical Greece. Colin Clark calculates that the real earnings of a typical British factory worker in 1850 and those of an Italian worker in 1928 were approximately equivalent to those of a free artisan in Rome in the first century A.D.[25] Europe's rate of growth, though faster than it had been, was not spectacular in the nineteenth century; compared to European rates after World War II (4.5 percent), its annual growth (0.9 to 1.0 percent) was slow.[26] Nor was Europe's growth spectacular relative to the rest of the globe.[27] The growth of some tropical countries matched that of European and North American performance until the outbreak of war in 1914.[28] Between 1870 and 1913, per capita national income in Britain and France and in much of central and southeastern Europe was growing slower than in Colombia, Brazil, and Mexico.[29]

Most accounts of modern European history focus on dynamic (but actually limited and scattered) focal points of growth found throughout Europe in the nineteenth century. They tend to emphasize processes of urbanization, industrialization, liberalization, urban working-class movements, and democratization and to ignore or downplay the persistence of rural, preindustrial, feudal, and autocratic structures of power and authority. European societies were, in fact, characterized by all the features associated with contemporary "third world" dependent development: weak middle classes and alliances between the state, traditional landowning elites, and new industrial classes; enclave economies oriented to foreign markets; sharp inequalities and increasing poverty; and unstable and partial democracy. On the eve of World War I, all these features were as characteristic of Europe as they are of the so-called developing world today, while Europe as a whole had achieved a level of economic well-being about equal with that of Latin America.[30] Europe was still "pre-eminently pre-industrial," as Arno Mayer has argued.[31] In all of Europe except England, agriculture was still the single largest and weightiest economic sector. Even after World War I, France still drew its wealth principally from agriculture, and approximately half the population was engaged in agricultural pursuits.[32] Central Europe had not yet begun its industrial takeoff; eastern and southern Europe had neither developed industrially nor moved significantly into agricultural exports; in fact, on the eve of World War I, these areas of Europe were exporting less primary products than Latin America.[33] In 1914, most of Europe was still rural,[34] and most of rural Europe had not changed substantially since the Middle Ages.

Europe's Nonrevolutionary Industrialization

According to conventional accounts, industrial development in Britain was "promoted and led by an independent capitalist middle class which fought against the old aristocracy as well as against the restrictive power of the state."[35] These accounts assume that "bourgeois revolutions" occurred in Britain and France when middle-class elements (the Independents in the English Revolution and the Montagnards in the French Revolution) fought and won a struggle for state power against merchant and financial monopolists that had originated in the feudal land aristocracy (the Royalists and Monarchists of the English and French revolutions). Barrington Moore argued that, as a result, Britain had a "fully capitalist bourgeoisie" in the nineteenth century that, with "minimum help from the state, was able to convert a large part of the globe into [its] trading area."[36]

This is largely a fiction. It was the aristocracy that led and won the revolt against absolutism both in Britain and elsewhere in Europe, and, though concessions were granted to wealthy nonaristocratic industrialists after the 1848 revolutions, the aristocracy remained the dominant faction of the bourgeoisie throughout the nineteenth and early twentieth centuries. In consequence, it was traditional elites that led capitalist development in Europe and formed the basis of its "capitalist class."[37]

Many have argued that this elite had become bourgeoisified by the eighteenth or nineteenth century. However, throughout the nineteenth century, the most effective elites were traditional and aristocratic, landowning and rent receiving, and oligarchic. This elite dominated the state apparatus and used it to channel industrial expansion into noncompetitive, ascriptive, monopolistic forms that ensured the continuity of rural, preindustrial, feudal, and autocratic structures of power and authority. Thus, claims that the establishment of nation-states in Europe represented the emergence of rationalized, "autonomous" state institutions that operated to advance "state" or "national" interests and the influential body of writing concerning the "new" liberal age are misleading. The end of absolutism and the creation of the bourgeois state and bourgeois law brought about not the separation of economic (class) power from political (state) power but rather a structure of power that fused both for extraction of surplus, locally and abroad, by extraeconomic compulsion.

With the so-called industrial revolution, traditional elites in Europe used the wealth and privileges that they had acquired in the past to ensure that processes of industrialization would not adversely affect their interests.

Throughout the nineteenth and early twentieth centuries, various forms of economic protection and monopoly, as well as restrictions on labor organization and political participation, enabled Europe's small elite of landowners and wealthy industrialists to monopolize land as well as the entire field of industry and trade. This produced a "dual" pattern of development that, in all aspects, resembles the dual economies described by theories of contemporary "third world" development.[38]

Dual economy models were developed to explain the economies of colonial countries and, in particular, their most characteristic feature: the existence of an island of western economic institutions and organizations surrounded by traditional communities and institutions and an underdeveloped economy. Many developing countries today are characterized by a sharp division between a dynamic foreign-oriented, "corporate" sector and the larger traditional economy and society. There is no investment beyond this sector: profits are either reinvested there or exported. Improvements in technology do not diffuse outward to agriculture or to cottage industry. What income distribution takes place is confined to the corporate sector and does not occur between it and the noncorporate sector. Thus, the economy as a whole is characterized by a lack of internal structural integration and dependency on outside capital, labor, and markets. Most perspectives on development, whether liberal or Marxist, assume that this kind of dualism is unique to the contemporary developing world and that, in the industrializing countries of the West, there were "leading sectors" (such as cotton textiles in the British takeoff from 1783 to 1803 and railroads in France from 1830 to 1860) that were essentially indigenous and closely interwoven with the other sectors of the economy.

But European countries were also characterized by a lack of internal structural integration and dependency on outside capital, labor, and/or markets. Great Britain, France, Italy, Germany, Spain, Portugal, the Austro-Hungarian Empire, Russia, Belgium, and much of the Balkans all had dynamic, foreign-oriented economic sectors that failed to transform the rest of their economies and societies. Some European countries experienced widespread growth, though less widespread and much later than is usually supposed; but in most, modern industrial sectors oriented to and dependent on international markets formed enclaves within nonindustrial, mainly agricultural and backward hinterlands linked not to other sectors of the domestic economy but to similar industrial enclaves in other countries. Production was largely for external markets, trade was external, and capital was invested abroad. Concerned to consolidate and maintain their control of labor while at the same time mobilizing it for the expansion of production, elites sought to increase profits through a dualistic system of internal restriction and external expansion.

Europe's economic expansion was based on the use of production methods that deskilled labor and kept it fragmented and impoverished. Profits increased not through increasing the productivity of labor in wage goods industries but by applying large quantities of unskilled or semiskilled labor to production, as is typical of primary export production in the contemporary "third world." In Britain, whole families (women and children) were put to work to earn, together, the same wage that once had been paid to a single "head of household." By making it necessary for the whole family to contribute to its reproduction rather than a single "head of household," the employer got more workers for no additional cost. Profits increased also by increasing the duration or the normal intensity of labor by making workers work longer, faster, and with fewer, shorter breaks. Cheap food was imported from abroad to further decrease the cost of labor. Workers were forced to consume poorer-quality food either by dismantling regulations prohibiting the adulteration of basic foodstuffs or, as in Ireland, by making them dependent on the potato crop for sustenance. Because the workforce was, by these means, rendered too poor to function as a factor of consumption, the dynamic sectors of European economies were dependent on the development of exogenous demand and consumption. The export of British goods and capital played a leading role in creating an international circuit of investment and exchange for this purpose.

Europe's dualistic economic system expanded production and increased profits for a transnational landowning and industrial elite while at the same time limiting the geographic and sectoral spread of industrialization, mass mobilization for industrial production, and the rise of new classes at home. A generally low level of industrialization and the production of high-cost goods for export avoided the need for both redistribution of the national income—the need to provide workers with the purchasing power to consume the goods that they produced—and a significant factory proletariat. This ensured that the benefits of expanding production would be retained solely by the property-owning classes.

The property-owning classes of European states were part of a single trans-regional elite whose broadly similar characteristics, interests, capabilities, and policies were constituted and reproduced through relations of interaction and connection, which had for centuries created similarities and interdependencies among states. As the various economies of Europe began to expand in the nineteenth century, their advanced sectors became tied more closely to those within other European economies than to the more backward sectors within their own. Economic development in Europe took place within and was crucially shaped by an increasingly interdependent industrial system.

Democratization

It is frequently claimed that, in contrast to the political evolution of societies in the contemporary "third world," "in the early part of the twentieth century" most western European societies "were either political democracies, or well on the way toward becoming so."[39] The French Revolution is thought to have introduced "the first experience of democracy"[40] and, thus, to have begun a "democratic revolution" that, following the Revolution, spread equality and liberty into increasingly wider domains. However, the actual impact of the Revolution in terms of inaugurating change was far more limited. Because restrictions in sites of production and throughout economies were reproduced by maintaining them throughout the polity, political participation in Europe remained highly restricted until the era of the world wars.

Before 1945, what has uncritically been accepted as "democracy" in Europe was a severely limited form of representative government that was everywhere constructed on the basis of a highly restrictive, means-tested suffrage that excluded the majority of the population from participation in the political process. Like democracy in the ancient world, it was really an "egalitarian oligarchy" in which "a ruling class of citizens shared the rights and spoils of political control."[41] The great majority of adults were excluded from participation: men below the age of twenty-five or thirty-five and women. Given that the life expectancy in Europe before World War I was between forty-one (as in Austria and Spain) and fifty-five years of age, this meant that those who had the vote were men in the last third of their life (see table 2.1). If the same system prevailed in the West today, the vote would be restricted to men over fifty-four years of age.

Table 2.1. Life Expectancy and Voting Age in Europe in 1910

	Life Expectancy	Voting Age
Belgium	47	25
Germany	47	25
Denmark	55	35
Norway	55	25

Source: Adapted from Robert J. Goldstein, Political Repression in Nineteenth Century Europe (London: Croom Helm, 1982), 241.

Universal adult suffrage would have enfranchised 40 to 50 percent of each country's population. In 1910, only some 14 to 22 percent of the population was enfranchised in Sweden, Switzerland, Great Britain, Belgium, Denmark, the Netherlands, and Germany (see table 2.2).

In some places, the suffrage included members of the poorer classes. However, three-class and other weighted and plural voting systems, as well as open balloting and restrictions on and biases against working-class organizations and parties, made it futile for poor people to vote. Thus, the previously listed figures do not reflect the actual number of people who were permitted to vote under the systems existing at the time.

Although the tendency to equate the existence of parliaments with democracy is no longer a feature of studies of contemporary developing countries, it continues to be accepted in studies of European political development. The development of parliamentary institutions in nineteenth-century Europe did not affect the character of popular representation in Europe. Before World War I, parliaments in Europe functioned rather more like royal courts than the parliaments and other legislative bodies that exist today in the West. On

Table 2.2. Percentage of European Population Who Were Enfranchised in 1910

Finland	45%	Austria	21%
Norway	33%	Sweden	19%
France	29%	UK	18%
Spain	24%	Denmark	17%
Bulgaria	23%	Portugal	12%
Greece	23%	Romania	16%
Serbia	23%	Russia	15%
Germany	22%	Netherlands	14%
Belgium	22%	Italy	8%
Switzerland	22%	Hungary	6%

Source: Adapted from Robert J. Goldstein, Political Repression in Nineteenth Century Europe (London: Croom Helm, 1982), 241.

the eve of World War I, hereditary transmission of sociopolitical status was still widespread. The British House of Lords, a purely hereditary body monopolized by the great landowning families, had absolute veto power over legislation proposed by the House of Commons until 1911.

It was not until the middle of the twentieth century that stable, full liberal democracy was established in western European societies. Until then, Europe, in common with parts of the contemporary "third world," experienced partial democratization and reversals of democratic rule. On the eve of World War I, Norway was the only country in Europe with universal and equal suffrage. Everywhere else, democracy was partial and unstable. Constitutions and democratic civil liberties were continually thwarted by extralegal patronage systems and by corruption. Great Britain had still not enfranchised the whole male working class, and its electoral system was corrupted further by plural voting. Only after World War II did universal, equal, direct, and secret suffrage become the norm throughout western Europe.

In sum, political institutions in nineteenth-century Europe were established by elites for the purpose of preserving and extending their social and economic power and, as a result, were continually compromised and undermined by efforts to preserve privilege and to forestall the acquisition of power by subordinate groups and classes. Political participation was severely limited. Where liberal electoral politics were introduced, governments had difficulty in maintaining them for sustained periods of time. Parliaments were dissolved, and election results were disregarded. To preserve privilege and to forestall the rise of socialism, constitutions and democratic civil liberties were continually thwarted by conservative restorations and reaction and by extralegal patronage systems, corruption, and violence. Thus, despite the massive population movements within and outside Europe and the appearance of great flux and change over the entire surface of European life, traditional bases of social and political power remained intact.

CONCLUSION

Of all the areas of study that have developed within the social sciences, the field of IR has relied, perhaps more than any other, on history. But, as this chapter has argued, the historical accounts on which much of mainstream IR theory depends are shaped by a profound mythology about modern European history, one that wrongly places Europe at the root and center of modernity and the modern world and transforms Europe's brutal expansion and political-military hegemony into a story of enlightenment and progress. The notion of European modernity was produced as part of a hegemonic project. Our continued acceptance of it and use of it as a basis of theory building contributes to the continuation of that project.

Recently, new Islamic groups have challenged the economic, political, and military dominance of the West and, taking up earlier currents of Islamic thought,[42] the hegemony of Western conceptions of modernity and progress. These challenges have prompted a wide range of theoretical and epistemological discussions in the social sciences and humanities. However, such discussions have hardly been acknowledged in the field of IR. As a discipline, IR continues to be largely a record of recent Western political experiences and one that, in addition, presents a highly idealized account of them. It remains stubbornly Eurocentric both in its unwillingness to accept non-Western political thought and in its refusal to analyze politics from a non-Western perspective.[43]

It is interesting, in this regard, to contrast the view of history that has characterized much of Western scholarship with the view that characterized the scholarship produced in the Islamic empires of the past. In the great Islamic centers of learning, scholars embraced a view of history as transcending the history of a particular culture or period. This was the impetus behind their massive undertaking to revive the knowledge of the past between the eighth and fifteenth centuries. In contrast, Western thinkers and historians, from the European Enlightenment to the present, have promoted the view that Europe's rise defined a radical disjuncture and breach with all that occurred previously. Middle Eastern scholars had recognized the immense significance for their own time of Chinese, Indian, and, above all, Hellenistic culture[44] and respected the material and intellectual achievements of other cultures. In contrast, Western scholars have defined everything outside the West and before its rise as inferior and without value, characterizing as *Western* achievements that in fact owed much to advances achieved by the non-Western world.

Unless IR scholars are willing to critically explore the assumptions that have shaped Western self-understanding, they will continue to contribute to the Western hegemonic project as it enters a new global age by reproducing, in research and writing on globalization, the biases and exclusions of conventional IR theory. The development of methodological approaches and analytical concepts adequate to the task of grasping the nature and direction of current trends of change requires a perspective that places "the West" in a larger global system and its rise within the context of a world history that was critically shaped by Islam. The challenge is to study global developments in ways that analyze all regions of the world both in a world-historical and comparative perspective and within a broader arena of human experience.

The historical critique sketched out in previous sections points to aspects of a different ontological basis for understanding world history and world affairs. Most accounts of the development of capitalism begin with the "rise of Europe." The story they tell is that following the European Dark Ages (or, certainly, by the eve of Europe's "industrial revolution"), the "lights went on" in Europe, in a surrounding world of darkness. Then, as a result of European exploration, settlement, colonization, and conquest, lights of varied brightness and color gradually appeared in non-European areas of the world over the course of the next two centuries.

However, this story is no longer convincing. As Janet Abu-Lughod and others have shown, the rise of Europe took place within an already existing system, stretching from western and southern Europe through the Middle East to China and characterized by a prosperous and far-flung network of trade and intercultural exchange. European military expansion into this system did not displace or destroy it: when the "lights went on in Europe," they remained on elsewhere in the world. The actual pattern of economic expansion throughout the world resembled (to borrow an image from James Blaut) "a string of electric lights" strung across Asia, the Middle East, Africa, Latin America, and Europe.[45] These lights illuminated small islands of urbanized industrial society and export sectors in Asia, Latin America, Europe, and elsewhere, each surrounded by traditional communities and institutions and underdeveloped, weakly integrated local economies. This pattern developed around the world as elites and ruling groups, seeking to expand production while at the same time avoiding the social leveling required for the production of articles for mass local consumption, produced largely for external markets. As a result, both within and outside Europe, domestic markets remained weak and poorly integrated, and economic expansion proceeded through a translocal/cross-regional exchange of capital and commodities among governments, ruling groups, and elites.

From the start, capitalist development has been essentially transnational in nature and global in scope, involving not whole societies but rather the advanced sectors of dualistic economies not only in Latin America, Asia, and elsewhere but in Europe as well. Europe *itself* was the model for the dualism and other features associated with what theorists have described as third world "dependent development"; Europe was also the initial focus of European racism, exploitation, and imperial domination. Thus, when European powers encouraged the development of dualism and dependence and practiced racism, exploitation, and imperial domination overseas, they were replicating abroad the same social structures and processes that they had created at home. Moreover, European colonialism and imperialism was a collaborative project that crucially depended for its success on governments, ruling groups, and elites around the world. Colonialism did not disadvantage whole societies. It further enriched or helped create privileged classes.

An account of history that recognizes, among other things, colonialism and exploitation in the West; the role of local elites in "third world" development and their connection with Western elites; and the highly uneven, partial, and limited nature of Europe's own history of industrialization reveals the inadequacy of assuming whole nations or regions as the basis for social inquiry. The real history of Europe, as opposed to the widely accepted myths, prompts us to shift analysis to transnational/cross-regional networks and structures—to a horizontal set of connections, relations, and processes. From this perspective, much of what mainstream IR theory obscures may become more visible: the anatomy of social power throughout the world; its relationship to different developmental outcomes; how it has evolved over time locally, transnationally, and cross regionally; and the factors and conditions that, historically, have proved necessary for its reproduction and transformation.

NOTES

1. Subaltern studies and the postcolonial critique, in contrast to nationalist and Marxist challenges to colonialism and its legacies, is concerned to break free from Eurocentric discourses and accounts (Gyan Prakash, "Subaltern Studies as Postcolonial Criticism," *American Historical Review* 99, no. 5 [1994]: 1475). Their critique of the West focuses not just on "the colonial record of exploitation and profiteering" but also on "the disciplinary knowledge and procedures it authorized—above all, the discipline of history" (1483). According to Prakash, in subaltern studies, "Europe" refers to an *imaginary* (though powerful) entity. Dipesh Chakrabarty's call for the "provincialization of Europe" is animated by this recognition ("Postcoloniality and the Artifice of History: Who Speaks for 'Indian' Pasts?" *Representations* 37 [winter 1992]: 1–26, and *Provincializing Europe: Postcolonial Thought and Historical Difference* [Princeton, N.J.: Princeton University Press, 2000]). But the key concern is generally with the ways in which "Europe works as a silent referent in historical knowledge" (Chakrabarty, "Postcoloniality," 1) and *not* with the fact that what operates as a "silent referent" is a fictitious view of Europe's development and history. For instance, when critics assail the tendency of subaltern studies to write of non-Western histories in terms of failed transitions (e.g., to bourgeois democracy and industrialization), they are concerned that this replicates Europe's universalizing project rather than that it replicates a mythology about European development (see the discussions in Prakash, "Subaltern Studies"; Chakrabarty, "Postcoloniality"; and Frederick Cooper, "Conflict and Connection: Rethinking African History," *American Historical Review* 99, no. 5 [1994]: 1516–45).

2. As Jorge Klor de Alva has argued with respect to critical studies of Latin America, it is the nation that is generally treated as the object of independence, decolonization, and postcolonialism. However, independence and decolonization does not always take place for classes and ethnic groups within newly independent nation-states (J. Jorge Klor de Alva, "The Postcolonization of the [Latin] American Experience: A Reconsideration of 'Colonialism,' 'Postcolonialism,' and 'Mestizaje,'" in *After Colonialism:*

Imperial Histories and Postcolonial Displacements, ed. Gyan Prakash [Princeton N.J.: Princeton University Press, 1995], 241–77). Aijaz Ahmad has also assailed the tendency for critical studies to define the "third world" by a "unitary experience of national oppression" (*In Theory: Classes, Nations, Literatures* [London: Verso, 1992], 99–100, 102–30).

3. Robert Bartlett, *The Making of Europe: Conquest, Colonization and Cultural Change, 950–1350* (Princeton, N.J.: Princeton University Press, 1993), 86, 88.

4. Bartlett, *The Making of Europe*, 92.

5. Bartlett, *The Making of Europe*, 94–96.

6. Bartlett, *The Making of Europe*, 183.

7. Janet L. Abu-Lughod, *Before European Hegemony: The World System A.D. 1250–1350* (New York: Oxford University Press, 1989), 5.

8. Abu-Lughod, *Before European Hegemony*.

9. Maria Rosa Menocal, *Ornament of the World: How Muslims, Jews, and Christians Created a Culture of Tolerance in Medieval Spain* (Boston: Little, Brown, 2002), 71. The Christian monarch of the combined kingdoms of Castile and Leon, Ferdinand I, had Muslim allies against the Christians from Normandy and Aquitaine whom he considered enemy intruders (Menocal, *Ornament of the World*, 135).

10. Adda B. Bozeman, *Politics and Culture in International History: From the Ancient Near East to the Opening of the Modern Age*, 2nd ed. (New Brunswick, N.J.: Transaction, 1994), 417.

11. Bernard Lewis, *The Muslim Discovery of Europe* (New York: Norton, 1982), 11.

12. Lewis, *The Muslim Discovery*, 29.

13. Lewis, *The Muslim Discovery*, 39.

14. Menocal, *Ornament of the World*.

15. Lewis, *The Muslim Discovery*, 152.

16. Bozeman, *Politics and Culture*, 425.

17. Menocal, *Ornament of the World*, 205–6.

18. The thinkers associated with the Enlightenment include d'Holbach (1723–1789) and the Encyclopedists in France, David Hume (1711–1776) in Scotland, and Kant (1724–1804) in Germany.

19. Douglass C. North, *Structure and Change in Economic History* (New York: Norton, 1981), 162; Michael Fores, "The Myth of a British Industrial Revolution," *History* 66, no. 217 (June 1981), 181–98; and Rondo Cameron, "The Industrial Revolution: A Misnomer," in *Wirtschaftskrafte und Wirtschaftwege: Festschrift für Hermann Kellenbenz*, vol. 5, ed. Jurgen Schneider (Stuttgart: Komission bei Klett-Cotta, 1981), and "A New View of European Industrialization," *Economic History Review* 38, no. 1 (February 1985): 1–23.

20. Fernand Braudel, *The Mediterranean and the Mediterranean World in the Age of Philip II* (New York: Collins, 1972); Immanuel Wallerstein, *The Modern World System I* (New York: Academic Press, 1974).

21. See, for example, David Landes, *The Unbound Prometheus* (Cambridge: Cambridge University Press, 1969).

22. Paul Bairoch, "The Main Trends in National Income Disparities since the Industrial Revolution," in *Disparities in Economic Development since the Industrial Revolution*, ed. Paul Bairoch and Maurice Lévy-Leboyer (London: Macmillan, 1981); *Economics and World History: Myths and Paradoxes* (London: Harvester, 1993), 105–6; Angus Maddison, "A Comparison of Levels of GDP Per Capita in Developed and Developing Countries, 1700–1980," *Journal of Economic History* 43 (1983): 27–41; "Measuring European Growth: The Core and the Periphery," in *Growth and Stagnation in the Mediterranean World in the 19th and 20th Centuries*, ed. Erik Aerts and Nuno Valério (Leuven: University of Leuven Press, 1989), 82–118; *The World Economy in the Twentieth Century* (Paris: Development Center of the Organization for Economic Cooperation and Development, 1989).

23. Nicholas F. R. Crafts, "British Economic Growth, 1700–1813: A Review of the Evidence," *Economic History Review* 36 (1983), 177–99.

24. Colin Clark, *The Conditions of Economic Progress*, 3rd ed. (London: Macmillan, 1957), 652.

25. Clark, *The Conditions of Economic Progress*, 652, 654.

26. The figure for the nineteenth century comes from Paul Bairoch, "Europe's Gross National Product 1800–1975," *Journal of European Economic History* 5, no. 2 (1976): 309. The latter figure is for the period 1950–1970 and comes from Bairoch, *Economics and World History*, 142.

27. See Sandra Halperin, *In the Mirror of the Third World: Capitalist Development in Modern Europe* (Ithaca, N.Y.: Cornell University Press, 1997), Statistical Appendix, tables 10 and 11.

28. W. Arthur Lewis, *Growth and Fluctuation, 1870–1913* (London: George Allen & Unwin, 1978), 223–34.

29. Lewis, *Growth and Fluctuation,* 216; Celso Furtado, *The Economic Growth of Brazil* (Berkeley: University of California Press, 1965), 162–65.

30. See Halperin, *In the Mirror*, Statistical Appendix, tables 1 and 2.

31. Arno J. Mayer *The Persistence of the Old Regime: Europe to the Great War* (New York: Pantheon Books, 1981), 187, 301.

32. Frederick A. Ogg, *Economic Development of Modern Europe* (New York: Macmillan, 1930), 185.

33. Lewis, *Growth and Fluctuation*, 166.

34. See Halperin, *In the Mirror*, Statistical Appendix, table 4.

35. Daniel Chirot, *Social Change in the Twentieth Century* (New York: Harcourt Brace Jovanovich, 1977), 223.

36. Barrington Moore Jr., *Social Origins of Dictatorship and Democracy* (Boston: Beacon Press, 1966), 32.

37. The position remains true, however, for the United States, New Zealand, Canada, Australia, and perhaps South Africa as well.

38. And erroneously restricted in their application to that world. The argument is more fully developed in Halperin, *In the Mirror*.

39. Chirot, *Social Change*, 222.

40. Françoise Furet, *Penser la Révolution Française* (Paris: Gallimard, 1978), 109.

41. Robert MacIver, *The Modern State* (London: Oxford University Press, 1932), 352.

42. For instance, Al-Afghani, who emphasized the Islamic roots of modernity and the difference between modernity and westernization. He considered modernization to be an Islamic project and westernization to be a project of cultural alienation and dependency.

43. World systems and dependency theories, which seemed to provide a way forward out of these limitations, tend to reproduce them by treating conditions in non-Western areas as stemming from the manner in which they had been incorporated into a system born in the West and dominated by a core of Western capitalist countries.

44. Bozeman, *Politics and Culture,* 417.

45. James M. Blaut, *The Colonizer's Model of the World: Geographical Diffusionism and Eurocentric History* (London: Guilford Press, 1993), 171.

Chapter Three

Liberalism, Islam, and International Relations

Mustapha Kamal Pasha

Each universal ideological notion is always hegemonized by some particular content which colours its very universality and accounts for its efficiency.

—Slavoj Žižek[1]

The last two decades of the twentieth century saw an invigorating process of contestation, critique, and construction of alternatives within the field of International Relations (IR). With the arrival of a so-called cultural turn[2] and the promise of new encounters less encumbered by supremacy and prejudice, the softening of hard orientalism with awareness and apprehension of difference,[3] and growing critical awareness of the question of identity in IR,[4] the world of IR had seemed astonishingly reflexive and heterodox. No singular worldview fully ordered things or was the order of things.

Yet in times of crisis, assumed danger, or emergency, these autonomous spaces in IR can swiftly shrink and recognizable patterns of convergence or complicity with power return. In the post-9/11 climate of political closure, the tenuous character of alternative voices becomes self-evident. Without much resistance, securitization has resumed hegemonic status, with political realism redefining the tenor of IR with renewed vigor. Neorealist orthodoxy, only recently facing challenge from a wide variety of locales within the IR community, has made a spectacular comeback, showing an erstwhile imperviousness to questions of identity and difference as well as the compulsions of political economy. The promise of diversity and openness offering prospects for a more ecumenical discipline has been apparently short lived. Buttressed by an ethos of xenophobia seeking legitimation in a reputed "clash of civilizations,"[5] a reversal seems to be already materializing.

The apparent resecuritization of IR and growing closure to multivocality and difference in the wake of dramatic recent events underscore the enormous difficulty of sealing off discursive from nondiscursive worlds. The pervasive militarization of public space[6] and normalization of the state of exception[7] parallel an all-encompassing *mentality of securitization*. This mentality is expressed more tangibly in the hardening of borders and political closure in the centers of global power[8] with a simultaneous attrition in sovereign claims for independence or autonomy in the peripheral zones of the global political economy. A dual framework of dispensation is crystallizing with the subsumption of sovereignty by empire. The Third World lies porous and vulnerable in the face of declining multilateralism within a fractured post-Westphalian order minimally authenticated in international law and organization. By contrast, the centers of global power (mainly in the West) are increasingly sealed off from threatening populations from the South, mostly the Islamic world.[9] Securitization is also manifested in a pervasive fear psychosis from alleged enemies of civilization:[10] the binaries of the civilized and the barbarian or the saved and the damned condition the Western social milieu.

To be certain, though, the extant politics of closure suggests deeper hegemonic tendencies now easily provoked by power. While no one-to-one correspondence exists between the world of IR and the world it seeks to interpret, the fusion of the two worlds suggests deeper tendencies *within* theory to respond to events in particular ways. These hegemonic tendencies emanate from particular negotiations with otherness, both cultural and intellectual. It is these deeper historical tendencies within IR that form the central concern of this chapter, as their recognition is central to the possibility of decolonizing IR.

The resistance of Western IR to alternative forms of knowledge is not a question of malice, conspiracy, or ignorance or a sudden reaction to unprecedented events. Rather, the current response to recent developments exposes the limits of the canon drawn principally from durable cultural imaginaries and patterns. The dependence of IR on these imaginaries and patterns directs inquiry away from presentism or primitive functionalism to an appreciation of historical and ideological strands. In the first instance, Western IR congeals the burden of historical encounters with otherness. Despite appeals to universalism, the hegemonic proclivity to deny alternatives legitimacy and a simultaneous quest to either annihilate opposition or to assimilate otherness conditions the historical past of the discipline. In the second instance, as Sandra Halperin's account in this volume reveals, the mystification of a particular story as *the* story remains the durable plank of Western IR. In this ideological construction,

Westphalia parades as the foundational moment of IR, as a preamble to the canon. In either historical or ideological terms, Western IR shows an elective affinity to the career of modernity in a culturally embedded form. The official account of IR (as with the history of modernity) appears largely as a biography of Western triumph, of encounters premised on a consolidation of Western power, not weakness.

Within this framework, this chapter sees *IR as an instantiation of Western liberal-modernity*, a set of mutually overlapping mappings, performances, and engagements with the social and political world. IR personifies the career of spatially determinate social forces in relation to perceived and actual Otherness. IR carries the baggage of historical encounters, including established patterns of discrimination and classification, definite ways of addressing the mundane and the metaphysical, discernible rules for separating inside from the outside, discrete symbolic economies of representation, discrete trajectories of what is regarded as the proper character of social or political life, and in typical cases an implicit self-awareness among social agents that their framework or model of organizing the social world is the natural order of things—legitimate, superior, and paradigmatic. Given the hegemonic status of Western (notably American) IR,[11] other practices appear deviant, inferior, and illegitimate.

This chapter proposes Western IR as a particular realization of the liberal-modernist imaginary with four durable attributes giving it a distinctive character: the Westphalian legacy, including a preference for secularism; a modernist confidence in progress, initially secured within the framework of the modern-state but also obtainable within secure spaces of a pacific international community; the ontological primacy of the individual above society; and the innate superiority of capitalist exchange as the principle of allocating resources and preferences and structuring social interaction and cohesion. In terms of basic philosophical orientation, these attributes help structure a unified field of engagement with the world, emerging from actual historical experience and the presumed ascent of the West.[12] The salience of cultural encounters is paramount to a fuller recognition of the cultural limits of Western IR, particularly in the crystallization of the principal elements. Through interaction with other worlds, notably the Islamic civilization, the self-image of Western IR has evolved and consolidated. It is not against the idea of a state of nature that a particular (liberal) notion of social organization has emerged but through competition with the social order conditioned or provisioned by Islam. The putative deficiencies of the latter provide the backdrop to an evolving self-confidence and hubris.

The centrality of Western liberal-modernity to IR can be measured by a mere glance at the career of popularly recognized competitor fields. Comparative politics or area studies, for instance, tend principally to record the scope of variance from archetypal attributes of Western experience. Hence, whether the Westphalian imaginary has fully captured the hearts and minds of ex-colonials remains a persistent theme in extant analyses.[13] The recent normative discourse on "failed states"[14] is yet another reminder of the hegemony of "Westphalian common sense" in IR.[15] Similarly, secularism and its presence marks the boundaries of "civilization" based on reason against others that allow irrational forces to occupy salience in societal interaction.[16] On this view, modernist belief in material progress within the secure confines of a sovereign nation-state distinguishes the West from societies that subordinate the drive toward acquisition to a nonmaterial ideal or entertain an alternative conception of the "good life." The primacy of the unencumbered individual is yet another crucial feature of Western civilization. Societies privileging community, group, or family appear necessarily deficient against the normative supremacy of the autonomous self. Closely linked to this facet, of course, is the hegemony of capitalist exchange, both as an ideal-typical modality of social connectivity as well as for organizing society itself. Emerging out of the particular historical experience of the rise of capitalism, the modern state, and bureaucratic rationalization, these attributes provide the West an ideal-typical benchmark and norm to evaluate non-Western performance in all social fields. The rigidity of commitment to these elements undergirding IR can also help account for the enormous difficulty of according legitimacy to alternative modes of thinking and behavior. Typically, alternative cultural priorities and life patterns appear either too deviant or simply reflective of a primitive stage of development.

To the extent that mainstream IR remains intrinsically *Western* in its articulation, its claim of universality must be placed in relation to its cultural limits. If this intuition has any merit, then the task of decolonizing IR begins with an appreciation of those limits. Provincializing the West then becomes a necessary step toward a counterhegemonic discourse.[17] Recognition of the cultural underpinnings of the canon, nevertheless, is only a first step toward a calibrated process of deconstruction and reconstruction. This task is made more difficult by the hegemonic status of Western culture globally but specifically the embrace of modern rationality and its institutional manifestations. What spaces are available to visualize and materialize alternatives in the context of hegemony? Those alternatives may themselves contain significant traces of hegemonic thinking and practices. The process of recovering new perspectives more attuned to the social and life world of the silent majority is compounded by the globalization of liberal modernity. Few spaces remain "outside" the imperium of capitalism or the modern state. The syntax of social existence is deeply conditioned by the logic of exchange and rationalities of modern power. To propose otherwise, as in orientalist constructions of Otherness, is to deny the burden of colonial impact or unequal power relations in the postcolonial setting but also the universality of the modern.

The quest for alternatives, though decidedly complex, must nonetheless proceed from an accounting of tensions, paradoxes, and contradictions within hegemonic thinking to release new spaces of enunciation and counterhegemony. There is no firm assurance that self-correcting mechanisms of cooptation within IR will not contaminate any alternative that might emerge.[18] This elementary caution can guard against exaggerated hope of a discursive turn or, more optimistically, revolutions of a Kuhnian kind.[19] In the final analysis—and this is the crucial insight of Julian Saurin's argument in chapter 1—alternatives are tied to social forces and their capacity to generate new and durable political options. Theory is a necessary and indispensable complement to meaningful transformation, but an appreciation of the historicity of IR is central to any decolonizing exercise. It minimally allows the option of challenging the natural authenticity of certain forms of knowledge and their claim to universalism. Similarly, historicity can lend temporality to otherwise timeless understandings of human nature, social organization, and connectivity. To that end, a mapping of some key paradoxes within the canon, made more explicit in the recent response to dramatic events, can be a helpful beginning.

SECURITIZATION, LIBERALISM, AND ISLAM

This chapter develops a mapping of central paradoxes that define the essentially liberal canon of IR by exploring three dimensions of the inherent impulse toward securitization: first, the historical burden of Western encounters with Islam; second, the necessary limits of liberal tolerance; and third, the quest for cultural hegemony through secularization.

The securitization impulse arises most immediately from the popular image of a threatening political Islam. The relative ease with which old symbols have been successfully deployed to evoke predictable responses directs inquiry toward the historical sources of IR. The first claim to be explored is therefore the intimate relationship between the *securitization* of contemporary thinking and historically conditioned knowledge structures drawn from encounters between the West and Islam,[20] which have produced the fiction of deeply felt incommensurable differences between the two worlds.[21]

Second, securitization is not the antithesis of liberalism but, in fact, its underside. The emergence of a "siege" mentality in the wake of terrorist attacks, which appears to depart from the natural terrain of liberalism, is not as radical as it seems or unprecedented. There are other historical parallels when the barricades have gone up and xenophobia is promoted to a normal state of mind, especially in addressing encounters with particular ethnic or religious minorities. The reaction to Islam is specific, however, as argued in the first section. It draws on deep historical currents implicating an intimate enemy, admired, reviled, pitied, and feared under different historical circumstances. In the zone of politics, the reaction to Islam brings to the surface enduring fault lines within liberalism, always perched uneasily between the contradictory promise of freedom and sovereign demands. In times of emergency, hospitality gives way to self-preservation. It is argued that this represents not a departure from but a necessary continuation of liberalism.

Third, a crucial plank linking securitization and liberalism is the aspiration of creating homogenized cultural space, which remains the fundamental aim of hegemony. Difference—especially incommensurate difference—may offer productive uses to create domestic hegemony, but it can potentially undermine a more international (or global) quest. The enemy outside can help solidify the "nation" or "civilization" (the extant expression) but nags a global enterprise except in conceptions of a bifurcated world forever torn apart. There are no obvious resolutions to the dilemma. In part, though, the global drive toward secularization becomes explicable in this context. Secularization seeks to transform the world in the image of the West. This claim redirects focus on secularization, to be seen as a "softer" variant of securitization.

Paradoxically, the drive toward secularization may heighten the necessity for securitization as threatened cultural and religious communities may choose to resist. On the other hand, securitization may diminish the appeals of liberalism (and secularism), principally showing the beastly side of (Western) civilization. In either case, the failure or inability to recognize difference *on its own terms* reveals the constrictions of liberalism as a framework of tolerance. In the case of Islam, these constrictions become fairly recognizable as both secularization and securitization confront Islam's cultural and political expression, Islam as an alternate design to organize the social world or to tame liberal-modernity. Although largely unsuccessful, as the conclusion to this chapter argues, so-called resurgent Islam can be best grasped as both a container of modern politics and an oppositional force. Misrecognition of "political" Islam as an atavistic throwback or as a reactive social phenomenon merely recycles orientalism or strengthens the liberal conceit of expansiveness and mutual tolerance. The dual uses of Islam, as negation and as tolerance, underscore the ambivalences inherent to liberalism. In the first instance, Islam represents all that liberalism ostensibly negates, Islam's assumed closure, irrationality, belligerence, and bigotry. In the second instance, liberalism opens its doors to difference, tolerating the otherness of Islam, extending reason to the cultural worlds of Islam.

Islam as the Radical Other

The orientalist apprehension of Islam is central to the self-construction of IR and Western identity through marking a boundary between civilization and pathology. This section explores the relationships between the Western perception of Islam as radical Other and the various reactions that take the form of securitization, in an apparent abandonment of liberal norms.

The intensity of reaction to the events of 9/11 is self-evident given the brazen nature of the terrorist attacks in the heart of the imperium. However, the pervasive securitization that has followed, especially the targeting or profiling of Muslim populations to secure Western civilization, betrays deeper motivations and motives. The reappearance of the "Islamic peril" bears historical resonance, Islam being the unwelcome familiarity, a fact scarcely concealed in nominal appeals to mutuality and cultural interdependence. To the extent that the cultural boundaries of the West have been drawn from a sharp religious separation between Christendom and the world of Islam,[22] the current mood congeals religious proclivities despite presumed Western secularization.

The hegemonic image of a monolithic, homogeneous Islam draws from a *longue durée* of encounter between Christendom and the worlds of Islam. Although there is considerable fluidity in the actual encounter, the hegemonic image is one of divergence, of incommensurable difference. What defines the contours of this image is a uniform Islam devoid of contradictions in its vast, heterodox worlds. With orientalist efficiency, the signature of Islam is one of an undifferentiated, unchanging radical Other.[23] The notion of a singular, radical Other renders Islam as an outpost of modernity. Discrete cultural boundaries sharply mark off the modern from the traditional. The latter can be read as "deficient, if modernizing, other."

A key implication is the equation of (Islamic) politics as pathology. The idea of Islam as boundary marker, of both the West and modernity, spatializes difference, but to guarantee that boundaries are not relaxed, temporality offers the most economical resource.[24] Outside progress, the world of Islam remains a medieval oddity, unyielding to centuries of Western contact and the latter's positive impact. Its quest for modernization is mired in futility, colonized by politics that appears as a social pathology of a religious world unwilling to secularize. It is the absence of secularism that accounts for Islamic extremism, gender oppression, irrational politics, and economic stagnation or misery. With secularism, moderation would prevail. Freedom from the stranglehold of religion would relax gender relations in the direction of greater equality. Politics, in turn, would reflect reasoned dialogue and deliberation, not passionate attachments colored by religiosity. Similarly, impediments to a self-expanding market economy dictated by religious taboos would be lifted. In sum, secularization holds the only promise for a better life.

Compounded by the return of binary tropes and the injection of a totalizing religious idiom of enunciation in popular consciousness, the otherness of Islam now appears absolute. Hospitality yields to apprehension, difference fully materialized in strangeness. Secularization or the evacuation of Islam from its public settings now works as an essential precondition for full membership into civilized society. Securitization guarantees that failures of secularization are not unattended.

In the economy of representation, extremist Islamic currents take on the appearance of an archetypical pathology of atavistic rage,[25] a generalizable feature of Muslim society. This sentiment is strengthened by deeper anxieties of peril for Western civilization both inside its confines in the shape of the suspicious Muslim immigrant who defies assimilation and outside in the form of evil.[26] At the core of securitization is the question of (Western) identity, how to secure it in the face of barbarism. Securitization is characterized by a reinscription of danger,[27] the ontology of inside/outside,[28] and an irreconcilable friend/enemy distinction.[29] Other values emanating from morality, cosmopolitanism, or international obligation[30] must be subordinated to a primal necessity of survival and self-preservation. The reprivileging of the state, recently downgraded to the whims of globalization and the promises of a rising global civil society, becomes explicable on this account. Once again, the state fortifies its hold on the mind, pushing to the sidelines other social actors. The radical otherness of Islam necessitates civilizational framing, or, as Krishna argues in chapter 4 in this volume, "strategies of containment"; but only the state can erect boundaries and keep the intimate enemy at bay. The notion of "homeland security" captures this paradox.[31]

Popular imaginaries rarely escape the effects of hegemony. As Gramsci noted, common sense betrays its imprint.[32] Ideas and attitudes pervade the entire social body, acquiring self-reproducing veracity. The possibility that a latent (hostile) orientation toward Islam has served as the recessive side of the liberal West, the manifestation of specific attitudes, becomes less opaque. The consolidation of a "natural attitude"[33] toward Islam, in the aftermath of the events of 9/11 in the United States and the more recent London bombings of 7/7, demonstrates therefore not only the effects of securitization but also, in a deeper sense, the determinate boundaries of cultural cartographies. Unsurprisingly, both state and civil society in Western polities reveal predictable responses to an assumed Islamic threat, often competing for more zealous expression.

Theory and event have different but not completely autonomous temporal registers. Both are permeated by specific modalities of thought. Cultural zones bearing the imprint of Islam (as in the medieval past), therefore, have been redesignated as zones of danger, representing a menacing geopolitical presence, requiring barricades and surveillance. Civilizational lines that have been neither fixed nor so rigid are once again fortified to split humanity into conflictual zones despite the pronounced coming of a "flat" world.[34] The rise of Islamophobia (like erstwhile anti-Semitism) becomes intelligible in this context, ensuring that the enemy *inside* is recognizably even more treacherous than the undifferentiated Other, outside. Polite racism has easily succumbed to blatant expression of prejudice and hatred with the figure of the "Muslim" providing complete nourishment to a pervasive climate of paranoia as recent hate crimes in Western polities with renewed ferocity show.[35] Neither tolerance (a concession to permissive, if insurmountable, difference) nor recognition (appreciation of its legitimate cultural existence and agency) is now the preferred option of social contact and interaction between "liberal" majorities and "illiberal" Muslims.

Securitization as Liberalism's Backstop

We have seen how Western fear of Islam as the radical Other generates responses of securitization that apparently entail abandoning the more normal commitment to liberal norms. It is argued in this section, however, that securitization has always been an inherent and necessary component of liberal modernity, a contradiction that reveals liberalism's own orientalist foundation. The seeming proclivity of mainstream IR to readily succumb to cultural hubris in the face of new dangers suggests the presence of determinate limits that are neither easily apparent nor functionally reducible to presentist currents. These limits are deeply embedded in liberal thought, in its differentiated practice in distinct spatial and temporal zones. Against these limits, universality assumes an ideological character. Liberal modernity and its project of rationalization of the globe cannot proceed without ideological rationale. Securitization may provide psychic certainty, but it is unable to generate modernization, help produce wealth and freedom, or emancipate humanity from barbarism and misery. The assumed deficiencies of non-Western areas and Islamic cultural zones (ICZs) in particular can be removed only under a liberal dispensation, but imminent danger presents serious impediments. Hence, the present constellation is imbued with contradictory tendencies within liberalism.

To the extent that the foremost political duty of the state, which is now reprivileged, is to secure the "inside," there is no contradiction between universalism and its particular instantiations. Liberty can never be absolute in the presence of sovereign demands; it must accede to the Leviathan, as Hobbes or Schmitt would suggest. The uneven spread of civil liberties within the imperium (or the modern state) is a constant reminder of the fateful paradox inherent to the Enlightenment. Without eliminating real or potential threats to sovereign power, the "good life" is a phantom quest. Securitization rests on this liberal paradox. Some values are more sacrosanct than others. The ability to distinguish friend from enemy lies at the base of sovereign power. Freedom, on this view, is contingent and conditional. The plethora of negative, *not* positive, freedoms within a liberal social order is not coincidental. Limits on sovereign authority are inherently provisional and in a state of emergency, nonexistent. Securitization is thus built into the fabric of the liberal order and fully captured in the principle of sovereignty. The persistent unease noticeable among liberal circles concerning the alleged erosion of civil liberties in the "defense of the realm" is therefore misplaced. Liberals tend to ignore the inherently tenuous footing of the liberal project, at once accommodating of difference but repelling its advances. The current undeclared global state of emergency presents in stark proportions the liberal paradox. Exceptional circumstances require exceptional procedures.

Tensions within liberalism, however, run deeper. In the first place, the chief aim of the Leviathan to desecuritize the polity (and its international instantiation) assumes demarcations between the market and state and the evacuation of security from civil society.[36] However, this fictitious separation between the realms of economics and politics is readily exposed, particularly in international space. In a neomercantilist world, the assumed disjointing evaporates. In an ideal liberal world of market hegemony, the separation appears opaque, concealed by hegemony and its instantiation. Yet it *is* hegemony that guarantees market conquest. Invariably, the founding moment of hegemony is violence in its naked and less pronounced forms, but to sustain hegemony, coercion remains a pivotal factor.[37] In the second place, hegemony cannot be established in neutral space. The lines dividing the "inside" from the "outside" often breached cannot be fully transcended.

The post–Cold War constellation, it is widely conceded, was going to be an uncertain moment in world affairs despite the assumed triumph of Western liberalism and its model of structuring social and political life.[38] In hegemonic policy circles, political Islam, the principal idiom of stateless barbarity and successor to totalitarian communist savagery, simply extended the scope of uncertainty following the demise of the Second World. Yet the particular ways in which IR thought and practice have responded to the events of 9/11 and 7/7 go beyond ideology to culture. More stable orientalist dispositions seem to be implicated. Familiar answers to a global peril have been discernible, but deeper historical forces may be involved. The crucial element giving established modes of response particular definition is the deployment of recessive anti-Islamic sentiment.

Against the liberal paradox between sovereignty and liberty, the response to recent events, notably the terror attacks of 9/11 and 7/7, become explicable. The refrain that "everything has changed" disguises fault lines within Western liberalism. Although the utterance commands us to faithfully acquiesce to a self-evident truth given its elegant rhetorical economy, it fails to show why particular choices have emerged. The despatialization of violence in a world stoically committed to a post-Westphalian imaginary ends up producing a strictly statist reaction. It was argued earlier in this chapter that the invocation of religiously charged vocabulary, with references to evil, arises from cultural wellsprings that can help mobilize passion and policy against an unconventional (stateless) enemy. In the last analysis, however, it is the deployment of sovereign power against known and hidden adversaries that offers ultimate security.

The fault lines within liberalism exposed in the current conjuncture of global emergency have always been more visible beyond the West: the non-Western world is usually exempt from the application of liberal principles. The exception is the rule in that context. Historical practice has shown that tensions within liberalism—between universal freedom and its partial instantiation, claims of sovereignty and demands of liberty, secular public space and private religiosity, or thin and thick cosmopolitanisms—afflict the liberal mission, if not altogether eroding grounds of legitimation. The new rules now being assembled to structure the self-acknowledged impossible task of assimilating of Muslim minorities are extracted from past colonial practice. Today in the West, as in the former colonies, liberalism suppresses its universalistic claims of liberty in favor of security, order, discipline, and punishment. On balance, though, these developments in hegemonic centers only faintly mirror the military terror unleashed in the ICZs. Liberal pretensions secured at home are easily abandoned to fight evil abroad. In those hapless areas, the fury of Western power acknowledges few limits.

Colonial practice provides ample testimony to uneven and unequal application of liberal principles in the realm of economics, law, or politics as well as the realization of the Westphalian promise. The unevenness and contradictory application of liberal principles in colonial contexts raises deeper questions concerning their origins and intent. In many instances, liberal governmentality is a progeny of colonial practice, brought from the colony to the metropolis and not the other way around. The colony, on the other hand, rarely experienced the brighter face of liberalism.[39] There seems to be implicit recognition that liberal principles apply only to (Western) liberal societies; the colony is perpetually in a state of emergency, though at different levels of threat.

It is now a truism in postorientalist accounts that the reduction of Islam to an ideology of closure and violence emanates from orientalist underpinnings of liberalism. Orientalism, however, has historicist and nonhistoricist forms.[40] The latter, a clumsier articulation of strategies of dealing with Otherness, as in the case of racism, assigns fixity to the Other. A subtler, perhaps more effective form is the historicist variant that views otherness temporally. For the most part, Western orientalist constructions of Islam have oscillated between the nonhistoricist and historicist versions, often mixing the two. Despite its avowed commitment to univeralism, liberalism rests on orientalist constructions of geopolitical and cultural space: the fluidity and changeability of the West measured against a rigid "East" resistant to both reason and material progress. Political economy essentializes this Kiplingesque divide, qualified by a story of progress through time. Without Western contact and input, goes the argument, the non-West is condemned to varying degrees of barbarity. Relations between the West and Islam are an essential part of that story.

Despite celebrations of past Islamic achievement, an evolutionary, teleological liberalism has rigidly assigned ICZs a lower position on the totem pole of social development with the story of stagnation readily on offer. Once a great civilization, the script goes, the Islamic civilization was unable to generate orientations with elective affinity to things patently modern.[41] Endogenous factors ultimately account for Islamic stagnation in this script, with the role of exogenous forces (notably imperialism) aiding, not undermining, modernization in the ICZ. Eventually, though, these regions will "catch up" and modernize. Time can bring the worlds together, yet, paradoxically, it helps establish distance between civilizations in the first place. The kinship between orientalism and liberalism is palpable in this account, the former providing the diagnosis, the latter the remedy.

Orientalism, though, also serves another important purpose. Tied to hegemony, it serves as a backstop to liberalism. Given the unbridgeable gulf between claims of liberty and sovereignty that have plagued liberal thought, in times of crises the progressive inclinations within liberalism can be repressed in favor of a stage theory of development. Conversely, the "outside" world can be allotted the status of an outcast beyond the pale of civilization. Both tendencies can be found in the practice of Western liberalism in relation to Islam.

Creating Homogeneous Cultural Space

Thus, the tightening of boundaries and the coercive construction of security and order have always been inherent to rather than the antithesis of liberalism, above all in the colonies and in the historical encounter with Islam. Securitization has discernible limits, however. Conceived centrally as a response to exceptional circumstances, its temporal horizon is constricted. A state of emergency is not consistent with the drive for capitalist accumulation.[42] If the "good life" hinges on wealth creation in a monetized exchange-driven economy, the coercive features of liberal-modernity can only be transient. Hence, securitization cannot be assigned permanence. Rather, self-seeking and internalization of its logic alone can ensure the fulfillment of the liberal dream. There is the additional problem of dealing with Islamic heterogeneity. A binary separation between "us" and "them," in itself arbitrary and capricious, leaves out zones of entanglement between Islam and the West. Neither annihilation nor assimilation can deliver civilizational security. The compulsions of global capitalism accentuate the problem. The ICZs are an integral part of the capitalist world, obeying its dictates but also servicing its key sectors. Although peripheral, the ICZs are not marginal to processes of world accumulation—hence the tension between securitization and the demands of capitalist reproduction on a world scale. This tension accounts for alternative modalities of securing the "volatile" ICZs. The temporal limits of securitization require a more enduring solution: a hegemonic quest to create a homogeneous cultural world through secularization. Needless to say, these modalities—securitization or secularization—are not strategic or policy options but corollaries of a particular field of vision.

The more similar the rest of the world, the more secure it is. An implicit assumption guiding Western orientations toward Islam is the belief that a secular world is a freer and more peaceful world. This belief is first and foremost a legacy of savage European experience, as highlighted by Sandra Halperin (chapter 2 in this volume), an experience of brutality and war wrought by religion. Universalizing the secularization thesis, the post-Westphalian order has aptly sought freedom from religion in realizing the principle of sovereignty. Second, this view solidly rests on the assumption that religion has been expelled from public life in the Western world, replaced by reason. The presence of religion in non-Western regions, notably the ICZs, undermines the process of establishing a social order sheltered by rational principles. The essentialization of ICZs as regions possessed by religious sensibility to the exclusion of any compulsions of political economy, material considerations, or nonreligious ideals directly flows from an orientalist mapping.

The liberal belief in equating progress with secularization, however, rests on amnesia and erasure. Liberalism tends to disown its own theological underpinnings.[43] The conceptual apparatus of liberalism contains significant theological elements, including subjective morality, salvation, and the work ethic. It is inconceivable to separate "modern" notions of subjective morality and religiously sanctioned conduct. The idea of salvation, in turn, has been crucial to establishing a determinate linkage between particular behaviors and conduct and the teleological promise of reward, both worldly and otherworldly. Without necessarily embracing Weberian rationality in its fullness, the notion that the underlying principles of work ethic are not simply drawn from lay experience also suggests the proximity of religion to quotidian practice. Finally, a capitalist economy is inconceivable without trust in exchange. Again, the idea of trust draws heavily from both religious thought and practice. Similarly, secularism rests on a sharp demarcation between public and private spheres. Yet, in practice, the formal place of religion becomes the private zone, while its real effects can be disbursed throughout the social body to the point of opaqueness. Once religion is seemingly exiled from public space, it serves as a basis to make political judgment of cultural zones outside. Presence of religion in the public sphere, therefore, signals a problem, a marker of premodernity or incomplete instantiation of modernity. Forgotten in this hegemonic discourse is the place of religion within Western liberalism, its ties to notions of subjective morality and ethics. Moreover, silent in this discourse is the transformation of religion into ideology qua modernity.

Secularization can guarantee the creation of a homogenized cultural space but also advance the aims of security. The presumed threat to civilization comes from political communities and their inhabitants who are unable to separate worldly from religious affairs. The epithet "fundamentalism" is often used to designate phenomena reflecting fusion between the two. On this account, secularization and progress become indistinguishable. Missing in this conversation is the contradictory nature of Western secularism and its paradoxical relation to religion but also the propensity of generalizing the transition from Christendom to Westphalia beyond Europe (and later North America). Absent in this discourse also is the historical context of the formation of modern non-Western states, particularly in the ICZs. Invariably, the latter process has been consummated under colonial or semicolonial arrangements, conditioning the content, character, and form of sovereignty and negotiations between religious and lay authority. These silences permit transparent yet distorted answers to complex historical processes. The quest to create a homogeneous cultural space qua secularization disguises the implicit religious underpinnings of the project. To the extent that secularism is a particular resolution to the problem of sovereignty (the transition from heaven to earth) in actually existing (Western) cultural zones, it cannot avoid transmission of specific values and orientations. These values and orientations are inescapably trapped in a logic promoting cultural particularism. Secularization, on this view, is an enunciation and realization of Western strategies of addressing the emergence of new subjectivities released by capitalist modernity and the rationalization of politics.

CONCLUSION

The urgent task of decolonizing IR knowledge requires, as a first step, recognition of its own cultural form and limits, a step that will undermine IR's pretension to universal validity. This chapter has argued that the limits of IR are intrinsic to its historical constitution, rooted in practice under the shadow of Western power and hegemony. Theory sprouts not from nowhere but from determinate if spatially dispersed societal currents.[44] Neither power nor hegemony is simply an empty signifier; it is impregnated with actual historical material. On this reading, post- 9/11 IR offers a useful site to reexamine contradictory impulses: professions of universality abruptly challenged by particularlistic norms and practice, commitments to inclusion subdued by exclusionary performance, or "enclavization"[45] into civilizational fortresses erected to ward off the infidel or the barbarian despite assertions of the "end of history"[46] and the arrival of a global civil society. On the face of it, these tropes underscore the inextricable nexus between theory and history but in a more durable sense suggest the presence of unresolved tensions within IR and its philosophical homeland, liberalism. Although Western liberalism (on a hegemonic reading of history) has triumphed as the first secular global religion, dampening prospects of alternative visions of organizing international social life, the fault lines persist and may even have widened.

To the extent that the liberal-modernist imaginary is globalized, it poses serious impediments to pacific relations between political communities less enamored by exiling religion from public life and Western polities that have evolved a particular resolution to the public-private question. Crusading secular attempts to eliminate certain forms of religious commitment embody a fundamentalist logic of closure to difference. The assumption that there is an absence of internal friction and fracture within the ICZs, to evolve new pathways between spirituality and material life or religion and politics, serves the liberal mission well. Appreciation of discord and dialogue would greatly diminish the certainty that missionary zeal requires to secure the Holy Land.

The failure to recognize fractures also misrepresents the scope of modernity's presence within the segmented world of the ICZs. To be sure, the grammar of internal dialogue and contestation within ICZs remains intrinsically modern, recognizable in contestations over the nature of political community, the structure of the economy, ends of government, technological and economic progress, and IR. Recognition of this facet, as well as appreciation of the form and content of liberal modernity in the social worlds of Islam, defies the obverse orientalist conception of the self-constitution of ICZs. Historicity appears at three levels. First, liberal modernity enters the ICZs with established images of otherness, as a civilizing force against stagnant or stagnating barbarism.

Although the colonial project is punctured or punctuated by many empathetic orientalist protagonists, the framing context is decidedly of a missionary kind. Salvation or modernization appears as its principal goal. Second, liberal modernity is conditioned by Western military and economic power against weaker adversaries who are unable to successfully resist. It has been argued here that securitization has always been inherent to liberalism, especially in its historical encounters beyond the West. The texture of liberal modernity as well as resistance captures the one-sided effects of power. In important ways, power reinforces and rationalizes the missionary spirit. On the other hand, the colonial project provides power with its raison d'être. Given nobility of aims, the exercise of power appears just and legitimate. Echoes of the past seem to persist in the colonial present.[47] Finally, liberal modernity in the ICZs retains the mixed effects of the colonial project, institutionalized principally in the character of the postcolonial state. The latter plagiarizes the myth of progress via modernization but also the self-conception of colonial paternalism. Hence, the dominant classes in the ICZs—and the state that ensures their economic and political fortune—face Muslim masses as subjects, not as citizens. The structuration of differentiated citizenship remains one of the principal legacies of the colonial project and its postcolonial instantiation as modernization. This larger context is further sustained by the consolidation of a rentier sensibility in the arena of global political economy.

Voices of resurgent Islam[48] appear in two principal forms, first as a plea for inclusion into global cultural space and second as a protest against rejection. In the former instance, there is an aspiration to participate in globality with sensitivity to its particularism. In the second case, resurgence appears as a reminder to a fateful resistance to difference. Clearly, there is considerable variance in resurgent Islam, but in its diverse expression there is a common quest for participation in modernity. To the degree that political Islam seeks a resolution to the problem of sovereignty, it embraces the logic of modernity, institutionalized either as political economy or as the nation-state. Although the idiom of enunciation betrays signs of pre- or antimodern temperament, the desire to bridge heaven and earth remains an intrinsically modern quest. Political Islam is ensconced in national, not transnational, space, notwithstanding its popular representation as a global and globalized phenomenon.[49] Islamicists seek to capture or transform the *modern* nation-state against moral or ethical claims drawn from presumably an alternative (religious) source. On the other hand, the dismissive repudiation of Islamicists by secular nationalists as "traditionalists" or enemies of modernization strengthens their belief in the totalizing closure of the modern world to an alternative (Islamic) mapping of the social world. Rejectionist Islam, therefore, records a protest against modernity.

We have seen that IR has consistently portrayed Islam, the radical Other, as a pathological form beyond the pale of modernity. Political Islam is inherently modern, however, in three significant ways. First, it aims to resolve the question of authority within the framework of sovereign power. Compulsory references to the Scriptures provide a framework for accountability, but there is no escaping the secular import of the state and its institutional accoutrements. The centrality of the modern state to the establishment of a just social order defies the image of a self-sustaining community of believers successfully negotiating a City of God. Second, modern rationalities of governance and governmentality, of technical reason and bureaucratization, invade the political horizon of political Islam. On this view, the fiction of a premodern "band of brothers" quickly evaporates. Finally, political Islam is a particular resolution to the question of a new form of subjectivity informed by the emergence of the modern economy, family, and civil society. The compulsions of exchange, privacy, and intimacy secured in a bourgeois mode, and individual pursuits enabled by nonfamilial social ties speak to the modernity of the social world of political Islam.

We have also seen how IR's orientalist apprehension of Islam as homogeneous and static issues in an essentialized and tautological understanding of violence, as inherent to Islam's pathological and traditional otherness. However, it is the *fractured character of liberal modernity* in the ICZs that partially explains trends toward nihilism and violence. Nihilism is an implicit recognition of the implausibility of realizing the promise of either the City of God or the City of Man, an appeal to the most affected sectors within the hegemonic world of capitalism and modern rationality. Hence, nihilism and its realization as terror underscore either the death of politics, the inability to forge a future drawn from alternative wellsprings, or the near absence of potential to create parallel political projects. Few spaces remain outside modernity and its Western global expression. Yet the West appears inhospitable to difference. The political closure nourished by difference actively transforms dissent into rejection.

In sum, alternatives, both realized and potential, are deeply conditioned by the liberal-modernist imaginary and its institutionalized presence in ICZs. These limits suggest cross contamination. A key aspect of decolonizing IR is to uncover its historical origins that bear an unbridled stamp of Western cultural practice. The conceptual apparatus underpinning IR, therefore, needs to be relativized against its universal claims. A second necessary element of intellectual decolonization is the recognition that alternatives to IR also have real limits given both cross contamination and the historicity of engagement with the orthodoxy. Appreciation of fractures with the mainstream narrative of IR and identification of contradictions, silences, and repressions merely are first steps toward building viable alternatives. The deployment of IR theory as international practice, in all its contradictory and heterodox manifestation, presents an additional avenue toward seeking alternatives. Neither uniform nor self-evident, the foundations of IR must be uncovered to release it from its own fetters.

NOTES

1. Slavoj Žižek, "Multiculturalism, or, the Cultural Logic of Multinational Capitalism," *New Left Review* 225 (September–October 1997): 28.

2. Yosef Lapid and Friedrich Kratochwil, eds., *The Return of Culture and Identity in IR Theory* (Boulder, Colo.: Lynne Rienner, 1997).

3. Naeem Inayatullah and David L. Blaney, *International Relations and the Problem of Difference* (London: Routledge, 2004).

4. Cameron G. Thies, "Progress, History and Identity in International Relations Theory: The Case of the Idealist-Realist Debate," *European Journal of International Relations* 8, no. 2 (June 2002): 147–85.

5. Samuel P. Huntington, *The Clash of Civilizations and the Remaking of World Order* (New York: Simon and Schuster, 1997).

6. Derek Gregory, *The Colonial Present: Afghanistan, Palestine, Iraq* (Malden, Mass.: Blackwell, 2004).

7. Giorgio Agamben, "On Security and Terror," *Frankfurter Allgemeine Zeitung*, trans. Soenke Zehle, September 20, 2001, <http://www.egs.edu/faculty/giorgioagamben.html> (accessed 22 August 2005).

8. Carl Levy, "The European Union after 9/11: The Demise of a Liberal Democratic Asylum Regime," *Government and Opposition* 40, no. 1 (2005): 26–59. See also Edna Keebel, "Immigration, Civil Liberties and National/Homeland Security," *International Journal* 60, no. 2 (2005): 359–72; Jef Huysmans, "Minding Expectations: The Politics of Insecurity and Liberal Democracy," *Contemporary Political Theory* 3, no. 3 (2004): 321–41; and Mark B. Slater, "Passports, Mobility and Security: How Smart Can the Border Be?" *International Studies Perspectives* 5, no. 1 (2004): 71–91. For a sophisticated theoretical background on this issue, see Didier Bigo, "Security and Immigration: Toward a Critique of the Governmentality of Unease," *Alternatives* 27 (2002): 63–92.

9. Sally Howell and Andrew Shryock, "Cracking Down on Diaspora: Arab Detroit and America's 'War on Terror,'" *Anthropological Quarterly* 76, no. 3 (2003): 443–62.

10. Eli Zaretsky, "Trauma and Dereification: September 11 and the Problem of Ontological Security," *Constellations: An International Journal of Critical and Democratic Theory* 9, no. 1 (2002): 98–105.

11. Steve Smith, "The United States and the Discipline of International Relations: 'Hegemonic Country, Hegemonic Discipline,'" in *International Relations and the New Inequality*, ed. Mustapha Kamal Pasha and Craig N. Murphy (Malden, Mass.: Blackwell, 2002).

12. William H. McNeill, *The Rise of the West: A History of the Human Community* (New York: New American Library, 1963).

13. Robert H. Jackson, *Quasi-States: Sovereignty, International Relations and the Third World* (Cambridge: Cambridge University Press, 1990).

14. For a very insightful critique of the "failed states" discourse, see Pinar Bilgin and Adam David Morton, "From 'Rogue' to 'Failed' States? The Fallacy of Short-Termism," *Politics* 24, no. 3 (2004): 169–80.

15. Siba N. Grovogui, "Regimes of Sovereignty: International Morality and the African Condition," *European Journal of International Relations* 8, no. 3 (September 2002): 315–38.

16. Elizabeth Shakman Hurd, "The Political Authority of Secularism in International Relations," *European Journal of International Relations* 10, no. 2 (June 2004): 235–62.

17. Dipesh Chakrabarty, *Provincializing Europe: Postcolonial Thought and Historical Difference* (Princeton, N.J.: Princeton University Press, 2000).

18. As recent reworkings of constructivism in IR theory bear out, neorealism has efficiently incorporated the language of constructivism without yielding to the latter's logic. See especially Alexander Wendt, *Social Theory of International Politics* (Cambridge: Cambridge University Press, 1999). For an overview of the so-called constructivist turn, see Jeffrey Checkel, "The Constructivist Turn in International Relations Theory," *World Politics* 50, no. 1 (January 1998): 324–48.

19. Thomas S. Kuhn, *The Structure of Scientific Revolutions*, 2nd ed. (Chicago: University of Chicago Press, 1970).

20. Norman Daniel, *Islam and the West: The Making of an Image* (Edinburgh: The University Press, 1966).

21. Bernard Lewis, "The Return of Islam," *Commentary*, January 1976, 39–49. By the same author, see also *What Went Wrong? Western Impact and Middle East Response* (New York: Oxford University Press, 2002).

22. Aziz Al-Azmeh, *Islams and Modernities* (London: Verso, 1993).

23. As Al-Azmeh puts it, "The evil which was Islam became a want, a deficiency in the natural order of things which was this order itself seen, from the Enlightenment onwards, as the culmination of universal history. Islam once evil vying with good, thus became an anachronism, a primitive stage in an emergent historicist notion of things" (Al-Azmeh, *Islams and Modernities*, 16).

24. Johannes Fabian, *Time and the Other: How Anthropology Makes Its Object* (New York: Columbia University Press, 1983).

25. Bernard Lewis, "The Roots of Muslim Rage," *Atlantic Monthly* 266, no. 3 (1990): 47–60.

26. Tony Blair, "Speech on the London Bombings Delivered at the Labour Party National Conference," BBC, 9 July 2005, <http://news.bbc.co.uk/1/hi/uk/4689363.stm> (accessed 5 August 2005).

27. David Campbell, *Writing Security: United States Foreign Policy and the Politics of Identity* (Minneapolis: University of Minnesota Press, 1998).

28. R. B. J. Walker, *Inside/Outside: International Relations as Political Theory* (Cambridge: Cambridge University Press, 1993).

29. Carl Schmitt, *On the Concept of the Political*, trans. George Schwab (Chicago: University of Chicago Press, 1996).

30. Immanuel Kant, "Perpetual Peace," in *Immanuel Kant, Perpetual Peace and Other Essays*, trans. Ted Humphrey (Cambridge: Hackett Publishing Company, 1983), 107–43. See also Michael Doyle, "Kant, Liberal Legacies, and Foreign Affairs," *Philosophy and Public Affairs* 12, nos. 2 and 3 (summer and fall 1983): 205–35, 323–53.

31. The American terminology of "homeland security" has crossed the Atlantic to Europe. In June 2006, Brussels hosted the second *Homeland Security Europe* conference, drawing together "the people and agencies who detect, protect and respond to threats." See "Homeland Security 2006: The Second Annual European Homeland Defence Conference," <http://www.wbresearch.com/homelandsecurityeurope/index.html> (accessed 13 October 2005).

32. Antonio Gramsci, *Selections from the Prison Notebooks*, ed. Quintin Hoare and Geoffrey N. Smith (New York: International Publishers, 1971).

33. Seyla Benhabib, "Unholy Wars," *Constellations: An International Journal of Critical and Democratic Theory* 9, no. 1 (2002): 34–45.

34. Thomas L. Friedman, *The World Is Flat: A Brief History of the Twenty-First Century* (New York: Farrar, Straus and Giroux, 2005).

35. Alan Cowell, "Faith-Hate on Rise in UK," *New York Times*, 3 August 2005, <http://www.iht.com/articles/2005/08/03/news/London.php> (accessed 10 August 2005). See also "Hate Crimes against U.K. Muslims Soar," *CBC News* 3 August 2005, <http://www.cbc.ca/story/world/national/2005/08/03racism050803.html?print> (accessed 9 September 2005).

36. Barry Buzan and Ole Wæver, *Liberalism and Security: The Contradictions of the Liberal Leviathan* (Copenhagen: Copenhagen Peace Research Institute, Working Paper, April 1998), <http://www.cianet.org/wps/bub02> (accessed 22 August 2005).

37. Mustapha Kamal Pasha, "Islam, 'Soft' Orientalism and Hegemony: A Gramscian Rereading," *Critical Review of International Social and Political Philosophy* 8, no. 4 (2005): 543–58.

38. John J. Mearsheimer, "Back to the Future: Instability in Europe after the Cold War," *International Security* 15, no. 1 (1990): 5–56.

39. Recall Frantz Fanon's depiction of the colonial context: "In the colonial countries . . . the policeman and the soldier, by their immediate presence and their frequent and direct action maintain contact with the native and advise him by means of rifle butts and napalm not to budge. It is obvious here that the agents of government speak the language of pure force. The intermediary does not lighten the oppression, nor seek to hide the domination; he shows them and puts them into practice with the clear conscience of an upholder of the peace; yet he is the bringer of violence into the home and into the minds of the native" (*The Wretched of the Earth* [Harmondsworth: Penguin, 1967], 29).

40. For a paradigmatic discussion of orientalism, see Edward W. Said, *Orientalism* (London: Vintage, 1978), and *Culture and Imperialism* (London: Vintage, 1994). A good overview is offered in Mona Abaza and Georg Stauth, "Occidental Reason, Orientalism, Islamic Fundamentalism: A Critique," in *Globalization, Knowledge and*

Society, ed. Martin Albrow and Elizabeth King (London: Sage, 1990). For provocative discussions of orientalism, see Armando Salvatore, "Beyond Orientalism? Max Weber and the Displacement of 'Essentialism' in the Study of Islam," *Arabica Revue d'Etudes Arabes* 43 (1996): 412–33, and Fred Halliday, "'Orientalism' and Its Critics," *British Journal of Middle Eastern Studies* 20 (1993): 145–63.

41. Lewis, *What Went Wrong?*

42. For a different view, see Susan Roberts, Anna Secor, and Matthew Sparke, "Neoliberal Geopolitics," *Antipode: A Radical Journal of Geography* 35, no. 5 (2003): 886–97.

43. "In much nineteenth-century evolutionary thought, religion was considered to be an early human condition from which modern law, science, and politics emerged and became detached" (Talal Asad, *Genealogies of Religion: Discipline and Reasons of Power in Christianity and Islam* [Baltimore: The John Hopkins University Press, 1993], 27).

44. Robert W. Cox, "Gramsci, Hegemony and International Relations: An Essay in Method," *Millennium: Journal of International Studies* 12, no. 2 (1983): 162–75.

45. Michael J. Shapiro, "Samuel Huntington's Moral Geography," *Theory and Event* 4 (1999), <http://muse.jhu.edu/journals/theory_and_event/> (accessed 15 September 2005).

46. Francis Fukuyama, *The End of History and the Last Man* (New York: Free Press, 1992).

47. Gregory, *The Colonial Present.*

48. John L. Esposito, ed. *Voices of Resurgent Islam* (New York: Oxford University Press, 1983).

49. Nazih Ayubi, *Political Islam: Religion and Politics in the Arab World* (London: Routledge, 1991).

Part II

The Colonial and Racial Constitution of the International

Chapter Four

Race, Amnesia, and the Education of International Relations

Sankaran Krishna

Aren't all cultures and civilizations just screens which men have used to divide themselves, to put between that part of themselves which they are afraid of and that part of themselves they want to preserve?

—Richard Wright

This chapter argues that the discipline of International Relations (IR) was and is predicated on a systematic politics of forgetting, a willful amnesia, on the question of race. Historically, the emergence of a modern, territorially sovereign state system in Europe was coterminous with and indissociable from the genocide of the indigenous peoples of the "new" world, the enslavement of the natives of the African continent, and the colonization of the societies of Asia. The discipline of IR maintains its ideological coherence via crucial strategies of containment that normalize the coeval emergence of modern sovereignty and dispossession on a global scale. One such strategy, "abstraction," is the focus of my critique in this chapter.

IR discourse's valorization, indeed fetishization, of abstraction is premised on a desire to escape history, to efface the violence, genocide, and theft that marked the encounter between "the rest" and the West in the post-Columbian era. Abstraction, usually presented as the desire of the discipline to engage in theory building rather than in descriptive or historical analysis, is a screen that simultaneously rationalizes and elides the details of these encounters. By encouraging students to display their virtuosity in abstraction, the discipline brackets questions of theft of land, violence, and slavery—the three processes that have historically underlain the unequal global order we now find ourselves in. Overattention to these details is disciplined by professional practices that work as taboo: this approach is deemed too historical or descriptive, that student is not adequately theoretical and consequently lacks intellectual rigor, so and so might be better off specializing in comparative politics or history or anthropology, such and such a question does not have any direct policy relevance, and so on.

The first section illustrates an exemplary act of abstraction that is central to the self-construction of the discipline of IR—the depiction of nineteenth-century Europe as a pacific zone (the Hundred Years' Peace) orchestrated by diplomatic virtuosity. A brief reading of this same century from the vantage of outside the imperium illustrates the possibilities of contrapuntal readings of IR discourse. Here, I further elaborate what I mean by "strategies of containment" and how they have worked to constitute IR discourse as a "political unconscious." This section is critical to understanding the very nature of contemporary IR discourse, its characteristic anxieties and obsessions, and the reasons why it is a quintessentially "white" discipline constructed around an amnesia on the question of race. In the second section, I examine three distinct encounters between the rest and the West. In each case, abstraction works as a strategy of containment to discipline what is considered legitimately within the purview of "proper" IR discourse and what ought to be left on the cutting room floor. The fetish for abstraction thus has to be understood as deeply political and depoliticizing. I conclude this chapter by considering the implications of such a contrapuntal analysis for the "education of international relations," that is, how it might and should impact on our pedagogy as practitioners of something called "IR discourse."[1]

Two central conceptual themes recur in this chapter: abstraction and contrapuntality. Abstraction is an inescapable analytical device that makes knowledge practices possible in the first place; without strategies of abstraction, the infinity of reality would overwhelm us. Yet abstraction is never innocent of power—the precise strategies and methods of abstraction in each instance decide what aspects of a limitless reality are brought into sharp focus and what is left literally out of the picture. In related ways, both Michel Foucault and Martin Heidegger sensitize us to this fact. Heidegger consistently foregrounds the fact that every effort at knowledge is ineffably accompanied by a simultaneous and unavoidable concealment of the plenitude of being from which that which is sought to be understood is "disclosed." The process of knowledge production is from the very outset regarded as the flip side of a process of concealment and unknowing. Whether one is for or against abstraction is therefore an irrelevant question—it is an unavoidable moment in the constitution of knowledge. Rather, one ought to be ever vigilant about what it is that abstraction simultaneously conceals as it reveals and to give up the illusion that our devices of abstraction can ever give us a final and omniscient purchase on reality.[2] Similarly, Foucault's injunctions on the imbricated character of power and knowledge remind us that the precise nature of our abstractions hinges on the productive ends toward which they are deployed—that "reality" is always already an impositional interpretation.[3] Both writers enjoin us to be aware of the inevitability of abstraction but also its intimate and uninnocent relationship to power.

In his magisterial *Culture and Imperialism*, Edward Said offers at least three closely interrelated definitions of "contrapuntal" analysis. First, "by looking at different experiences contrapuntally, as making up a set of . . . intertwined and overlapping histories, [one can] . . . try to formulate an alternative both to a politics of blame and to the even more destructive politics of confrontation and hostility." Elaborating, Said suggests that "we must be able to think through and interpret together experiences that are discrepant, each with its particular agenda and pace of development, its own internal formations, its internal coherence and system of external relationships, all of them co-existing and interacting with others." Further, one needs "a simultaneous awareness both of the metropolitan history that is narrated and of those other histories against which (and together with which) the dominating discourse acts."[4]

One can scarcely conceive of a discipline more hostile to contrapuntality than mainstream IR discourse. Resting on the nonnegotiable and immense edifice of a fragmenting device called "sovereignty," the discipline emerges from and is oriented to the reproduction of an alienated way of being. To understand why and how IR discourse produces an amnesia on the question of race through the device of abstraction, one has to contrapuntally restage the encounters between the West and the rest, encounters that produced the originary alienation that inaugurated the modern (post-Columbian) world and necessitated the discipline of IR to suture it. The essence of what it means to be the "West" or "India" or "Africa" or "American" was produced coevally and dialectically during these modern times. Contrapuntality serves as the device through which to historicize the fundamental epistemic categories (sovereignty, nation, property, and state) of an IR discourse that privileges the priority and eternal character of its conceptual categories through its devices of abstraction.[5]

ABSTRACTION AS A STRATEGY OF CONTAINMENT IN IR DISCOURSE

When still a newcomer to the discipline of IR, I found the dominant characterization of the nineteenth-century "world" as "the Hundred Years' Peace" maintained by the Concert of Europe somewhat baffling. To describe the period from 1815 to 1914 as "peaceful" in any sense of that term seemed astounding to anyone familiar with the history of empire. Consider the following incomplete list of wars, insurrections, mutinies, conquests, and territorial expansions engaged in by the British for just part of the nineteenth century:[6]

1839–1842: Opium Wars in China
1840s: Wars against South African Kaffirs and New Zealand Maoris and the
    conquest of Punjab
1854–1856: Crimean War
1854: Conquest of Lower Burma
1856–1860: Second China War
1857: Attack on Persia
1857–1858: Suppression of Indian Revolt/Mutiny
1856: Governor Eyre case in Jamaica
1866: Abyssinian expedition
1870: Repulse of Fenian expansion in Canada
1871: Maori resistance destroyed
1874: Decisive campaign against the Ashanti in West Africa
1882: Conquest of Egypt

This list does not include the periods 1815–1839 or 1882–1914 or any of the similar activities engaged in by the other European powers of France, Germany, Spain, Portugal, Italy, and Belgium. In thinking of what it is that allows these numerous and violent encounters between different peoples to fall out of the history of international relations, it becomes obvious that a certain principle of abstraction is at work here, centering on the concept of "sovereignty." Wars are defined exclusively as the acts of sovereign powers on each other in a tradition that goes back a long way in IR discourse, whereas the impressive list here constitutes merely encounters between various forms of quasi states, native principalities, warlords, tribes, territories, and puppet regimes on the one hand and a sovereign state on the other. Such encounters can hence be excised from the genealogy of international relations. Thus, the Revolt of 1857 that swept across northern India, that resulted in tens of thousands of deaths, and that at one point looked likely to bring a forcible end to the British Raj there does not count: it is not between two settled sovereign bounded entities that mutually recognize each other as authentic states. Rather, it is seen as a hiccup in the pacification of Empire, a mere "Mutiny" as it came to be called, a "domestic" issue by its very definition incapable of altering the Hundred Years' Peace.

The operation of this abstraction of sovereignty to deny the bloody history of the nineteenth century is no aberration. The same sovereign definition of "war" informs David Singer's voluminous data-gathering enterprise on conflict, it underlies the effort by Bueno de Mesquita to assess the rational utility calculations of war initiators, and it allowed Rudy Rummell to claim that "democracies" rarely, if ever, initiate wars with each other or produce genocides and for still others to claim (against all the evidence of the incredibly sanguinary twentieth century) that the Cold War brought stability and peace to the world order.[7] By deftly defining inter*national* as the encounter between sovereign states, much of a violent world history is instantly sanitized. Bernard Nietschmann found that of the 120 wars that were ongoing in 1987, only four were between sovereign states. The vast majority of insurgencies and civil wars were unnoticed because "the media and academia are anchored in the state. Their tendency is to consider struggles against the state to be illegitimate or invisible. . . . They are hidden from view because the fighting is against peoples and countries that are often not even on the map."[8] Among other things, what this sovereigntist abstraction accomplishes is simple: the loss of lives during encounters between states and nonsovereign entities is of no consequence. It needs to be mentioned that the overwhelming number of these casualties were either brown or black while sovereignty remained lily white.

IR discourse's valorization and fetishization of "theory" becomes more comprehensible as a "strategy of containment," in Frederic Jameson's term. For Jameson, a strategy of containment allows the wielders of a body of interpretive work to "project the illusion that their readings are somehow complete and self-sufficient." With a sharper political edge, he further defines a strategy of containment as a process that "allows what can be thought to seem internally coherent in its own terms, while repressing the unthinkable . . . which lies beyond its boundaries."[9] Clearer still, a strategy of containment is

> a means at once of denying those intolerable contradictions that lie hidden beneath the social surface, as intolerable as that Necessity that gives rise to relations of domination in human society, and of constructing on the very ground cleared by such denial a substitute truth that renders existence at least partly bearable.[10]

In Jameson's "strategy of containment," one can discern clear echoes of Heidegger's idea of knowledge as the simultaneous act of disclosure/concealment. Founded on discourses that justified, abstracted, and rationalized the genocide of the populations of the new world, the enslavement of Africans, and colonization of the Asians, the discipline of IR is one giant strategy of containment, "a substitute truth that renders existence at least partly bearable." It is also, then, a quintessentially white discipline. It is not that race disappears from IR; it is rather that race serves as the crucial epistemic silence around which the discipline is written and coheres. That which is made to appear in IR discourse is that which conceals the silent presence of race. "Postcolonial

IR" is thus an oxymoron—a contradiction in terms. To decolonize IR is to deschool oneself from the discipline in its current dominant manifestations: to remember international relations, one needs to forget IR.

The disciplining moves within the pedagogy of IR—the taboo against overly historical and descriptive narratives; the fetish for quantitative analyses that compress centuries of contested historical narratives into eviscerated numbers; the reduction of socially sentient human beings into rational utility maximizers; the preference for problem-solving theory (in the guise of policy relevance) rather than for critical or genealogical theory; the putative anarchy of the system of nation-states that discredits possibilities of imagining nonnational ways of being; the hypermasculine tetchiness and insecurity on questions of gender, androgyny, and queer identity; and, most significant, the elision of themes such as the theft of land, racism, slavery, and colonialism—these can be collectively understood as a series of extraordinarily effective moves that preserve the ideology of IR discourse.

Jameson makes a point of some significance for IR discourse when he notes that "strategies of containment are not only modes of exclusion; they can also take the form of repression in some stricter Hegelian sense of the persistence of the older repressed content beneath the later formalized surface."[11] I argue peremptorily that the obsessive anxiety displayed by IR discourse on issues such as terrorism, third world immigration, the spread of infectious diseases such as AIDS or the Ebola virus, illegal drugs, refugees, or Islamic fundamentalism—as Mustapha Pasha has elaborated in chapter 3 in this volume—is the return of the repressed. The ideology of IR discourse, with its gothic apparitions, premised as they are on an originary alienation and estrangement between a "civilized" West and a dangerous, incomprehensible, and barbaric "rest," is unable to repress the entailments of that alienation through its multiple strategies of containment—they resurface as IR gothic, perhaps the dominant literary genre in the discipline. They return to haunt the habitus of a discipline destined never to be at peace with itself because its origins and reproduction owe to a process of abstraction that represses the violent preconditions of its very locus of enunciation.[12]

The very foundations of IR discourse should be interpreted as an attempt at overcoming an originary alienation that clefts humanity with the "discovery" of the new world by Columbus in 1492 and the slavery that accelerates thereafter. The encounter with the "other" constituted both the self of Europe from this point in time and space and the steady estrangement of the world thereafter into an enclosed zone that reserved for itself the attributes of civilization, culture, religiosity, science, rationality, private property, and humanity and attributed to the other the precise opposites—barbarity, a lack of history, superstition, lack of private property, and inferiority. It is perhaps unsurprising that this originary alienation, an alienation that goes to the very heart of the modern condition, is sought to be energetically overcome by the creation and sustenance of a discipline that exemplifies the alienation and through its devices of abstraction seeks both expiation and transcendence. To understand international relations, then, seek out that which IR discourse represses, hides, elides, conceals, and prematurely closes off as avenues for inquiry. As Toni Morrison has it on the impact of this originary alienation on the content of modernity,

> Modern life begins with slavery. . . . Slavery broke the world in half, it broke it in every way. It broke Europe. It made them into something else, it made them slave masters, it made them crazy. You can't do that for hundreds of years and it not take a toll. They had to dehumanize, not just the slaves but themselves. They had to reconstruct everything in order to make that system appear true. It made everything in world war two possible. It made world war one necessary. Racism is the word we use to encompass all this.[13]

PRIMAL ENCOUNTERS: CONTRAPUNTAL READINGS ACROSS THREE CONTINENTS

In this section, I demonstrate how some of the critical conceptual building blocks of IR discourse—sovereignty, property, nationness, and international law, to mention some—were all emergent in the encounter between the West and the third world. Rather than being timeless qualities embodied in Europe prior to contact, concepts such as property and sovereignty acquired their particular valences as a consequence of the need to both differentiate and privilege Europe in contrast to its other. Further, to put it rather bluntly, they enable the theft of lands and the annihilation of the other. Since each of the encounters examined across the continents of Africa, Latin America, and Asia is a vast terrain of relationships over time, I have chosen to focus on slivers that highlight the power of abstraction in empowering the colonizer in its relations with the colonized.

Grotius in Africa

For IR discourse, Hugo Grotius is a founder of international law and a conservative supporter of absolutism in the aftermath of the Thirty Years' War. He is regarded as having authored some of the most influential tracts in the evolution of the discipline of international law—on the freedom of the seas, separation of church and state, the right to acquisition of found properties, and on just war. The balance and moderation of his works have consequently attached his name to a paradigm that attempts the melioration of Machiavellian realpolitik with Kantian cooperation.[14]

The image of Grotius in the disciplinary lore is that of a universalist and abstract thinker: he is appropriated purely intellectually, as an impartial logician and rule maker for an emergent order of nation-states in Europe, whose pathbreaking work rightly serves as the foundation for the evolution of international law over the centuries thereafter. The world that allows for such an inscription of Grotius is one that begins and ends with Europe and its interstate rivalries. Let us turn to how a contrapuntal approach to world politics produces a rather differently inflected Grotius. The difference highlights the need to rewrite the conceptual building blocks of IR discourse—sovereignty, territoriality, security, and the nation-state—and its major figures, including Grotius, in terms of their conjoined origins in the colonial encounter and of the ways in which Europe's dealings with non-Europeans critically informed and influenced the content of such terms and scholarship. Siba Grovogui points out in impressive detail that most of Grotius's work served first to empower the Dutch in their arguments and battles with the Spanish and the Portuguese over the rights to trade with the colonies, in both Asia and Africa as well as with the new world, and second to coalesce an incipient Europe against the "other," variously defined as the Islamic Middle East, the despotic Asians, the propertyless Indians of the new world, and the slaves of Africa.[15] He shows that Grotius's influential *Mare Liberum*, the renowned tract on the freedom of the seas, was occasioned by the Dutch East India Company's desire to hang on to a Portuguese galleon captured by them in the Straits of Malacca. (Grotius was hired by the Dutch East India Company to write this tract.) This occurred in the context of the Dutch rebelling against Spanish hegemony and seeking to enlarge their share of colonial trade during the decline of the Spanish and Portuguese empires. Similarly, the incipient secularization of Grotius's arguments against the pope's, whose various edicts and bulls had favored Spain and Portugal, has to be contextualized against a rising Dutch economy that was predictably antimercantilist. As Grovogui notes, Grotius's

> defense of the relative autonomy of Asians was not a manifestation of his concern
> for their right to sovereignty. Rather, it was a springboard from which to reject
> the papal arbitration that had granted exclusive rights over portions of the globe
> to Spain and Portugal. Grotius' central concern was the immediate effects of the
> 1493 papal bulls on the emerging power of the Netherlands. Indeed, Spanish and
> Portuguese privileges stood in the way of the development of Dutch commerce
> and navigation.[16]

The key step in the canonization of the work of Grotius within the field of IR, the step that anoints him as a founder of modern international law, is an act of abstraction, that is, shearing the theoretical principles of his various works away from the historical contexts within which they emerged, the purposes they were meant to serve, the interests they were furthering, the specific peoples they were simultaneously dispossessing and empowering, and the acts of epistemic and physical violence that they set in motion. Abstraction, in this sense, is to denude a historical process of its sociality and to instead reify it into disembodied principles of change and evolution. Grovogui notes in a trenchant summary that

> the modern law of nations has been proposed by a select group of nations, not as the ethical basis of a universal order, but as a means to hegemony. As a result, international law has been composed of morally deficient and unrelated, albeit complementary, principles and norms. The legal provisions that have applied to non-Europeans have been culturally specific, enabling Europe to undermine the other's subjectivity and sovereignty in the international order ... most [Western theorists] have omitted the importance of non-European alterity to the structures and hierarchies of international law. From the mid-sixteenth century onward, the relationship between European powers and non-Europeans was constructed upon the twin principles of either denying or suppressing the subjectivity of the latter. These principles manifested themselves in two related developments: the diminution of the juridical capacity of the other, a necessary condition for Western hegemony; and the institution of extraterritoriality, that is, the application of Western laws outside of Europe ... although the West has proclaimed the universality of the principles of international law (e.g.; liberty, free trade, and property rights), Western praxis has excluded the other from equal participation in the international order. This praxis has also generated jurisprudence, that is legal doctrines and juridical idioms. The formulation of these doctrines and the determination of these idioms have mirrored historical sensitivities and the ethos of their times. Modern western jurisprudence has endorsed or condoned, but in either case perpetuated, the violent exclusion of the other.[17]

Western abstraction in the discourse of international law worked not merely to fragment the other, deny it its subjectivity and specificity, and justify the appropriation of its lands. The same process of abstraction also worked to consolidate Europe and to produce the "West" as a category:

> During the early phase of Dutch hegemony, Grotius built on the right of booty, unilateral appropriation, self-defense, and retribution to develop specific rules that protected Dutch interests and encouraged Christians to engage in mutually beneficial relationships. In his writings, he demonstrated his inclination for inter-European accommodation and dialogue, which would benefit the Netherlands as an emerging power...he advised that in their relations with one another, Christians were obliged to keep their promises, to restore unjust gains, and to make reparations for wrongful acts.[18]

While it is true that the idea of Europe would remain a checkered one for centuries to come and would be punctuated by the worst wars of humankind, both direct and proxy, the residual notions that would eventually consolidate this space as the ultimate repository of civilization—the metric of justice and the arbiter of international fairness—are already evident in the contrapuntal process that Grovogui charts here.

Antiquating Europe in New Spain

I approach the issue of sovereignty somewhat elliptically in this chapter. While conventional definitions emphasize the realm under the writ of a king or an executive or state, I argue that modern sovereignty is more powerfully underlain by a bounded self-spatialization that names itself as a destiny, a genius, a culture, a civilization, or a homeland—a contiguous and identifiably discrete and separate entity. Imputing a certain coherence to a space through its culture or language, ethnicity, religion, or history is a critical step in the production of sovereignty. The importance of language in this regard is critical—as noted by, among others, Benedict Anderson's seminal work.[19] It is crucial to remember, as Eugen Weber suggests, that modern European languages such as French became "national" only very recently and through a process that was anything but one of pacific gradualness.[20] In the early encounter between Spain and the new world, the "standardization" of Castilian into a modal Spanish is a critical step for the production of a sovereign realm that would eventually become the contemporary nation-state of Spain. By rereading the standardization of Castilian and by charting its rise to a hegemonic language over other competing dialects, one is charting the presencing of sovereignty. In 1492, Castilian was one of a number of competing dialects—its emergence as the lingua franca of a nation is something that owes immensely to the accident of its being the tongue of the conquistadores.

In his seminal work on this issue, Walter Mignolo shows how Castilian came to define itself, acquire a grammar, reestablish its interrupted linkages with Latin, and then, in the century following contact, become the template on which the Mesoamerican languages and their grammar were scripted.[21] One of the consequences over the longer run of this primal need for communication alongside conquest is the consolidation of a national imaginary—or the production of modern, sovereign space. The subtitle of Mignolo's first chapter indicates the coeval production of Spanish sovereignty and its colonial fragments: "The Linguistic Unification of Spain and the Linguistic Diversity of the Indies." Language becomes the vehicle for the gradual consolidation of a national imaginary in Spain (in other words, the production of Spanish sovereignty) while it simultaneously fragments the social and linguistic landscape of the new world as their picto-ideographic languages are fit into the Procrustean grammar of Castilian.

Mignolo contrasts the alphabetized fixity of Castilian with the picto-ideographical fluidity of the Mesoamerican languages. While both scripts are undoubtedly abstractions, Mignolo is sensitive to the comportments that this difference often entails. Among other things, the alphabetized fixity of Castilian renders Spanish Christianity a religion of the book and encourages a Spanish attitude that presents the Mesoamericans with a depressing choice— either assimilate into us via conversion or assert your religious recalcitrance and face the consequences of accepting your subhuman status, namely, annihilation. Mignolo's work reveals how the fixity of Castilian makes it a facile vehicle for the expropriation of the lands of the Indians: an abstract, alphabetized language is more conducive to the writing up of land deeds, the proclamation of new ownership, and the calculation of debt. The language of the conquistador enables the expropriation and consolidation of the "property" of the Indians (a process discussed by both Anghie in chapter 5 and Gathii in chapter 6 in this volume), especially as one considers simultaneous changes occurring in the world of mapmaking at this time. A prominent grammarian of this time in Spain, Nebrija, revealed an appreciation for this. Mignolo ventriloquates Nebrija: "A language whose destiny is to unify a native territory and to subjugate a conquered people could not . . . be left open to the variations of speech."[22]

The acquisition of an abstract and alphabetized language, in contrast to picto-ideographic languages, becomes a principle of hierarchy. For grammarians such as Nebrija and Aldrete, that the Amerindians lacked the alphabet sufficed to equate them with naked savages, who also lacked science, literature, and civility. Alphabetized languages, by their greater fixity of meaning in comparison with oral cultures, it was argued, preserved meaning and enabled continuity and incremental growth of knowledge over generations. (As a counterfactual exercise, one can easily construct a series of invaluable civilizational values and comportments that might be better preserved by oral cultures in comparison to written ones—for example, respect for elders as they are seen as the repository of culture and knowledge rather than decaying bodies and minds. More than anything else, the reasoning of the colonizers is an instance of affirming the consequent, that history belongs to the victors. Thus, central to the reclaiming of colonized history has been a struggle over the legitimacy of oral sources as of equal worth in the production of historical knowledge—see Ayers, chapter 7 in this volume).

The culmination of this hierarchy in the universalization of Europe as metric is indicated in a famous episode wherein Franciscan missionaries arrived in 1524 in the wake of the conquest of Mexico by Cortes. They learned the indigenous languages and created their grammar. The latter, of course, is not an innocent process. The encounter between an alphabetized and an ideographic language at different levels of power and control necessarily remade the latter on the template of the former. As Mignolo notes, understanding in this encounter was exclusively on Castilian terms:

> A glance at the Amerindian language grammars written by Castilian friars in Mexico during the sixteenth and seventeenth centuries shows that the majority of them began with a discussion of the letters of the alphabet and by identifying those letters Amerindian languages did not have. None of them showed any concern with the script of the classic civilizations in the central plateau. . . . The new preoccupations expressed by the grammarians suggest that the letter had been promoted to an ontological dimension with a clear priority over voice as well as any other writing system. The classical tradition was inverted, and the letter no longer had the ancillary dimension attributed to it by Aristotle but had become the voice itself, while nonalphabetic writing systems were suppressed.[23]

The consolidation of Europe as norm and normal quickly follows, as the Franciscans make an astounding pronouncement on the Mexican language: they aver that it lacks seven letters. The only basis on which the newly encountered language can be described in terms of such a lack is by the simultaneous elevation of the "old" language to a universal yardstick. And the degree to which we have internalized the yardstick is revealed by the fact that the observation of lack was astounding then but is banal and factual now.

This excursus through language demonstrates that the consolidation of a Spanish national imaginary and the fragmentation of the political authority structures of the new world were coeval, simultaneous processes. A genealogy of sovereignty that is confined to a Europe with its drawbridges up is necessarily an incomplete genealogy—one that is complicit with the attendant universalization of Europe.

The Queen's English in India

A number of recent works reexamining British colonialism in India and elsewhere have suggested that it might be more accurate and certainly fruitful to regard imperialism as a social formation that importantly transformed both colonizer and colonized rather than a resistanceless and one-sided imposition of an already constituted "superior" culture on a supine recipient.[24] One of the most consequential arenas of encounter between the British and the Indians during the centuries of colonialism was obviously that of land and land revenue extraction. All histories of empire, whether they see it as an absentminded and intentionless acquisition on the part of Britain or whether they impute it to the inexorable logic of insatiable capital, are agreed that the critical turning point was the East India Company's acquisition of the right to collect the land revenue of a diwani in Bengal in the mid-eighteenth century. Thereafter, the entire edifice of the Raj was built literally on the back of the Indian peasant, as it was the land revenue eked out from under him that constituted its mainstay. While the literature on the ideology, methods, amounts, and effects of British land policy in India is vast, I focus on one small sliver of this contested literature to highlight a few central points salient to this chapter. Specifically, I show how the device of abstraction empowered the British as they sought to comprehend a bewildering array of highly localized practices relating to the land. Abstraction allowed them to claim that they "understood" India because such an understanding was part of an overall emerging scientific ethos. This valorization of abstraction (knowledge relatively unencumbered by the need for empirical validation via ethnographic observation) was intimately connected with the reigning belief that what distinguished the orderly mind of the British was precisely this genius for abstraction in contrast to the undisciplined and emotional Indian who tended to get lost in the details and therefore miss the forest for the trees. The classic instance of this is, of course, James Mill's six-volume history of India, written without ever having set foot in that country and, in addition, claiming that very fact constituted the best proof of the veracity of his scientific observations and dispassionate analysis.[25]

Abstraction, in this instance, allows for an assimilative and intra-European understanding of the Indian situation—the British see India exclusively through lenses ground in the history of England. Ironically (or perhaps not so ironically or unexpectedly), it is the eloquent exponents of nineteenth-century liberalism in England—James and John Stuart Mill, Bentham, and Macaulay—who were the most forceful exponents of empire, while it is the conservative Edmund Burke who is sensitive to the excesses that such a liberal will to knowledge embodies. Burke is humbled by the prospect that the "other" is perhaps ineffably unknowable and is deeply skeptical of strategies of abstraction that ultimately "know" only by reducing the other to the "same."

At the outset, to those of us accustomed to the thoroughly self-contained histories of Western political thought, it will come as a surprise to realize how much time, energy, and space British thinkers accorded to the relationship with India. From Adam Smith and Hume through Ricardo, the Millses (father and son), Macaulay, Marx, and Bentham and all the way down to Keynes, the encounter in the subcontinent formed a staple in their writings, to the point where Eric Stokes, in his landmark work *English Utilitarians and India*, notes that "it is remarkable how many of the movements of English life tested their strength upon the Indian question."[26]

In 1793, after nearly four decades of trying to fathom the intricacies of landownership (or the lack thereof) in Bengal, the viceroy Cornwallis enacted the infamous Permanent Settlement. The Permanent Settlement fixed in perpetuity the amount of land revenue to be paid by the zamindars to the British colonial government in Calcutta. This, it was anticipated, would give the zamindars an incentive to improve their lands and cultivation practices (as all surplus over and above the fixed assessment would now be theirs to keep), constitute them as the bulwark of a Company regime still very unsure of its ability (or willingness) to hold on to its distant empire, limit opportunities for the outright plunder and pillage of the Bengal countryside by the English servants of the East India Company that had been ongoing from the late 1750s to 1793, eliminate the uncertainty involved in assessing land revenue subject to annual fluctuations in crop yields, and, in conformity with the Whig sentiment of governance, remove the Company Raj from its presence in the intricacies of rural India to a more becoming and distant presence in Calcutta.

Whether the Permanent Settlement met its many objectives is an essentially contested question. That it sought to re-create a faithful native simulacrum of the landed classes that underwrote the legendary stability of the British political and social order is not in doubt. At the very moment of its enactment, in the decades that followed, and in the two centuries of scholarship on the issue since then, the effects of the Permanent Settlement—both good and bad— are intensely debated and contested. The Settlement, while it was welcomed by the Anglo-Indian community of the Bengal presidency, was vehemently opposed by the administrations of the Madras and Bombay presidencies as well as in the newly acquired territories in the northwest, notably the Punjab.[27] It is held, especially by generations of Indian historians, variously to have accelerated the decline of the Bengal agrarian economy, promoted rack-renting and absentee landlordism, irretrievably destroyed the customary and mutually obligatory relations that wove the (largely Hindu) zamindars and his (largely Muslim) tenants, made the avaricious moneylender a greater presence than ever before, caused the terrible famines that began to depopulate the countryside with a depressing regularity, and so on. On the other hand, it may be (in a backhanded way) credited with providing the early nationalists of Bengal with the material and ideational basis from which to articulate their demands for self-government and, in the longer run, independence.

I focus here on the first half of the nineteenth century—a time when the Company's charter was up for renewal and occasioned much debate within the British parliament and among the attendant public in London and Calcutta on a number of issues, including the proper role of English governance in its distant outpost in Bengal. The Permanent Settlement of 1793 and the highly "interventionist" policies in areas such as law, religion, social reform, and education entered into by the British colonial regime in the period from about the 1810s to the late 1850s marked a momentary and vehemently contested triumph of a liberal sentiment on empire in Britain. The purpose of empire, it was argued by the liberals, was to bring the light of science, reason, English language, literature, and culture and, with it, progress to the benighted Indian. Unraveling the overlapping (and sometimes violently antagonistic) constituencies of liberals, utilitarians, evangelicals, free-traders, Anglicans, and others as British policy for its Indian colony was being debated would take us too far afield. But the opposition between the liberals and the conservative Edmund Burke on the appropriate British comportment toward its Indian colony offers a fascinating window into the role of abstraction in this encounter.

For Mill and the rest of the liberals in England at this time, the specifics of India are literally irrelevant because the content of what was India had already been unlocked within an overpowering narrative of science, reason, evolution, and the modern script of history. Armed with this rationalist vision of their own time and locus of enunciation, when they turned their gaze to India, all they could see was the empirical confirmation of their thesis regarding British reason and Oriental irrationality. Or, as Mehta has it,

> The historian in James Mill, the legislator in Bentham, the educator in Macaulay, and the apostle of progress and individuality in J. S. Mill, all . . . fail in the challenge posed by the unfamiliar; because when faced with it they do no more than "repeat," presume on, and assert (this where power becomes relevant) the familiar structures of the generalities that inform the reasonable, the useful, the knowledgeable, and the progressive. These generalities constitute the ground of a cosmopolitanism because in a single glance and without having experienced any of it, they make it possible to compare and classify the world. But the glance is braided with the urge to dominate the world, because the language of those comparisons is not neutral and cannot avoid notions of superiority and inferiority, backward and progressive, and higher and lower.[28]

The content of India is overdetermined in the liberal gaze—its details narrated a priori by an epistemic frame that, for all its inductivist and empiricist claims anchored in experimental science, proved incapable of seeing anything that it was not already programmed to encounter. It is this same rationalist vision that serves as the basis on which to deny the Indian his coevalness with the British and simultaneously justify colonialism as a civilizing mission to uplift the infantile and backward Indian (but never to the point where he might be ready for self-government).

Thus, the author of *On Liberty* proceeds to justify, through his three limiting conditions, why its prescriptions stop short of the subcontinent: his second condition reserves liberty for mature and advanced societies, not for "backward" ones such as India, which will have to do with the benign despotism of an Akbar, if it should be so fortunate. This liberal inability to ever "really be surprised by the stranger, for he or she is always recognized as . . . familiar, though deformed"[29] offers an interesting contrast with Burke, who takes issue with the entire enterprise of colonialism at this time. And, interestingly enough, in making his case, Burke trains his eye precisely on the fetish for abstraction that governs liberal reason. With Hume and Smith, Burke recognizes the possibility that the very valorization of freedom could become a principle by which classes and nations come to be hierarchized. He is aware that the revolutionary championing the cause of freedom could use that very idea as his vehicle for domination over others not so similarly inclined—a move clearly revealed by the liberals, particularly J. S. Mill, in the previous sections. Such a critique of the domineering possibilities inherent in an ideology of freedom had made Burke's reputation as the classic conservative thinker in his opposition to the excesses of the French Revolution. But, as Mehta demonstrates, more so than even that celebrated instance, Burke himself regarded his labors in attempting to curtail the excesses of British imperialism in India to be the archetypal, if also unsuccessful, transmutation of his thought into practice. In contrast to the abstract appropriation of India by liberal thought, Burke privileges what might be called more spatially bounded structures of feeling or sentiment that form a people into a nation. In making that move, Burke anticipates the Levinasian respect for the ineffable alterity of the other—he entertains the possibility that reality may not be complicit in our efforts to comprehend it, that it is not obliged to turn to us a legible face (as Foucault has it somewhere)—that India might in fact be unknowable to the imperial gaze.

In constructing his counterarguments to the liberal desire to know the other in the image of the same, Burke's

> thought is pitched at a level that takes seriously the sentiments, feelings, and attachments through which peoples are, and aspire to be, "at home." This posture of thought acknowledges that the integrity of experience is tied to its locality and finitude. . . . By doing so it is congruent with the psychological aspects of experience, which always derive their meaning, their passionate and pained intensity, from within the bounded, even if porous, spheres of familial, national, or other narratives. For Burke, in contrast with both the Mills, the significance of experience and the forms of life which they are a part of is not provisional on their incorporation in a rationalist teleology. Reason, freedom, and individuality, as nineteenth century liberals understood them, are not, for Burke, the arbiters of the significance of these forms of life; when they are assumed to be such arbiters, he is aware that it was usually by relying on an implicit alliance with political and other forms of power.[30]

Burke is fully cognizant of the role that abstraction plays in the power of the liberal doctrine to marry its (proto-)Darwinist hierarchies to the interests of empire. His "well-known suspicion of abstract forms of reasoning" stem from his reservations that "by diminishing the significance of 'circumstances' they glide over the very things that give texture and meaning to human experiences."[31]

Lest it be thought that Burke (or Mehta or myself) subscribes to some naive theory of knowledge that uncritically valorizes lived experience or fails to recognize that abstraction is an inevitable and inescapable part of any effort at comprehension, it is not abstraction per se that Burke opposes. It is the hubris that accompanies this will to knowledge that he wishes to alert us to.[32]

CONCLUSION

These three encounters together amount to an effort at unsettling the hierarchies that inform IR discourse. In its mainstream variants, the fetish for theory and abstraction in IR discourse encourages us to see the world as populated by nation-states that have somehow traveled sui generis through time and without their histories having intertwined and overlapped. From such a construction, IR discourse can then array these spaces in terms of their proximity to an ideal—the sovereign, developed, and secure nation-state—or their distance from it—the sorry, lackey quasi states destined for perpetual anarchy within and without. The contrapuntal readings offered here disturb the effort of mainstream discourse to sustain the originary alienation that inaugurated the modern disposition of nation-states.

I conclude by pointing to some of the implications of contrapuntal analysis for the education of international relations—for our pedagogic practices as teachers in this discipline. First, we need to ask ourselves, What are the political entailments of the specific forms of abstraction that we valorize? What is the will to knowledge that our aesthetic privileging of ahistorical theorizing embodies? What is the relationship between our practices of abstraction and the disappearance of questions of race from the field of international relations? Second, we need to be sensitive to the routine, everyday policing of the study of international relations by the very strategies we use to demarcate our field from others, such as history, comparative politics, anthropology, literature, and cultural studies. Why is it that, at the end of these disciplining moves, we find ourselves inhabiting a discipline that has excised questions of inequality, genocide, and the theft of lands and cultures and that has, in their stead, centered on issues such as combating terrorism, securing sovereignty, and winning the games that nations play? Third, in what ways are our own pedagogical practices complicit with the narration of international relations as the quintessential "prose of counterinsurgency"—on the side of the state and against the imagination of nonnational ways of being? Fourth, what is the relationship between the political unconscious of our discipline—the repressed stories of racism, genocide, violence, and theft—and the obsessions of our craft—terrorism, illegal immigration, insecurity, and secrecy? I have said enough to indicate that a relentlessly contrapuntal approach to the multiple histories that have produced the present dispensation is at least a beginning. If we are to work and see around the dazzling blindness of white IR and its abstractions, accepting and reiterating the conjoined histories that constitute us and our craft will tell us what to do tomorrow.

NOTES

I would like to thank Randy Persaud, Jorge Fernandes, Mustapha Kamal Pasha, Mike Shapiro, Itty Abraham, Naeem Inayatullah, Jonathan Goldberg-Hiller, Konrad Ng, Rob Walker, and Siba Grovogui for their comments and friendship over the years. Special thanks as well to Branwen Gruffydd Jones for her support and for organizing the wonderful conference in Aberdeen in April 2005. The epigraph is from Richard Wright, *The Outsider* (New York: Harper and Row, 1965), 135.

1. I deliberately use *IR discourse* rather than *IR theory*, *IR literature*, or just *IR* in order to inflect theory, discipline, or any social narrative with considerations of power. Walter Mignolo explicates his choice of *colonial discourse* over *colonial literature* in his work on the Renaissance: "*Discourse* used in this sense has an enormous advantage over the notion of literature when the corpus at stake is colonial. While *colonial literature* has been construed as an aesthetic system dependent on the Renaissance concepts of poetry, *colonial discourse* places colonial discursive production in a context of conflictive interactions, of appropriations and resistances, of power and domination" (*The Darker Side of the Renaissance: Literacy, Territoriality, and Colonization* [Ann Arbor: University of Michigan Press, 1995], 7).

2. See Rudiger Safranski, *Martin Heidegger: Between Good and Evil*, trans. Ewald Osers (Cambridge, Mass.: Harvard University Press, 1998), and Michael Dillon, *Politics of Security: Towards a Political Philosophy of Continental Thought* (New York: Routledge, 1996).

3. See Michel Foucault, "Truth and Power" and "Two Lectures" in his *Power/Knowledge: Selected Interviews and Other Writings 1972–1977*, ed. Colin Gordon (New York: Pantheon, 1980), 109–33 and 78–108.

4. Edward W. Said, *Culture and Imperialism* (London: Vintage, 1994), 19, 36, 59.

5. For more on the enablements of such a conjoined reading of modern history and its refusal to either drop anchor in nativism or forego the invaluable legacy of "European" ideas such as freedom and democracy, see Dipesh Chakrabarty, *Provincializing Europe: Postcolonial Thought and Historical Difference* (Princeton, N.J.: Princeton University Press, 2000).

6. See V. G. Kiernan, *Poets, Politics and the People*, ed. Harvey J. Kaye (London: Verso, 1989), 134.

7. See J. David Singer, ed., *The Correlates of War*, vols. 1 and 2 (New York: Free Press, 1979); Bruce Bueno de Mesquita, *The War Trap* (New Haven, Conn.: Yale University Press, 1981); and Rudolph J. Rummel, *Power Kills: Democracy as a Method of Non-Violence* (New Brunswick, N.J.: Transaction, 1997).

8. Bernard Nietschmann, "The Third World War," *Cultural Survival Quarterly* 11, no. 3 (1987): 1, 7, quoted in Michael Shapiro, *Violent Cartographies: Mapping Cultures of War* (Minneapolis: University of Minnesota Press, 1997), 176–77.

9. Frederic Jameson, *The Political Unconscious: Narrative as a Socially Symbolic Act* (Ithaca, N.Y.: Cornell University Press, 1981), 10, 53.

10. This is from one of Jameson's best interlocutors, William Dowling, in his *Jameson, Althusser, Marx: An Introduction to the Political Unconscious* (Ithaca, N.Y.: Cornell University Press, 1984), 54.

11. Jameson, *The Political Unconscious*, 213.

12. Dowling elucidates how abstraction works in the context of economics: "Classical and neoclassical economics function as strategies of containment . . . not simply through their premature closure (closing off inquiry before it can lead to ultimate questions about history and society) or even through their repression of history (repressing the sense in which the market economy described in their texts could not exist without exploitation and oppression), but through the *way* they accomplish this closure and repression, treating the workings of an emergent capitalism as eternal and objective economic laws" Dowling, (*Jameson, Althusser, Marx*, 79). Rick Ashley inaugurated this line of argument within IR by his analysis of the way "economism" works within and as the discipline in "Three Modes of Economism," *International Studies Quarterly* 27, no. 4 (1983): 463–96, and "The Poverty of Neo-realism," *International Organization* 38, no. 2 (1984): 225–86.

13. From Paul Gilroy's interview with Toni Morrison, published as "Living Memory: Meeting Toni Morrison" in Paul Gilroy, *Small Acts* (London: Serpent's Tail, 1993). Quote reproduced from Gilroy, *Black Atlantic* (Cambridge, Mass.: Harvard University Press, 1993), 221.

14. James Der Derian, *On Diplomacy: A Genealogy of Western Estrangement* (Oxford: Basil Blackwell, 1987), 16.

15. Siba N. Grovogui, *Sovereigns, Quasi Sovereigns and Africans: Race and Self-Determination in International Law* (Minneapolis: University of Minnesota Press, 1996).

16. Grovogui, *Sovereigns*, 58. In his text *War and Peace*, Grotius had already argued that slavery was legally acceptable.

17. Grovogui, *Sovereigns*, 43–44, 63.

18. Grovogui, *Sovereigns*, 61.

19. Benedict Anderson, *Imagined Communities: Reflections on the Origin and Spread of Nationalism* (London: Verso, 1991).

20. Eugen Weber, *Peasants into Frenchmen: The Modernization of Rural France 1870–1914* (Stanford, Calif.: Stanford University Press, 1976).

21. Mignolo, *The Darker Side of the Renaissance*.

22. Mignolo, *The Darker Side of the Renaissance*, 42.

23. Mignolo, *The Darker Side of the Renaissance*, 46.

24. Mrinalini Sinha, *Colonial Masculinity: The "Manly" Englishman and the "Effeminate Bengali" in the Late Nineteenth Century* (Manchester: Manchester University Press, 1995); Anne McClintock, *Imperial Leather: Race, Sexuality and Gender in the Colonial Contest* (London: Routledge, 1995); Chakrabarty, *Provincializing Europe*;

Ashis Nandy, *The Intimate Enemy: Loss and Recovery of Self under Colonialism* (Delhi: Oxford University Press, 1983); Said, *Culture and Imperialism*; Gauri Viswanathan, *Masks of Conquest: Literary Study and British Rule in India* (New York: Columbia University Press, 1989).

25. "In Mill's History the specific, but, more relevantly, the strange and the unfamiliar, are at the epistemological mercy of a rationality that is vouched for in advance of 'viewing' and certainly experiencing the strange and the unfamiliar. The project of the empire is inscribed in the judgments of that way of 'doing' history, which relentlessly attempts to align or educate the regnant forms of the unfamiliar with its own expectations. Liberal imperialism is impossible without this epistemological commitment—which by the nineteenth century supports both progressivism and paternalism—that is, the main theoretical justifications—of the empire" (Uday Singh Mehta, *Liberalism and Empire: A Study in Nineteenth-Century British Liberal Thought* [Chicago: University of Chicago Press, 1999], 18).

26. Eric Stokes, *English Utilitarians in India* (Oxford: Clarendon Press, 1959), quoted in Mehta, *Liberalism and Empire*, xii. Mehta's is a worthy successor to Stokes's classic work and is an exemplar in political theory of what I have, following Said, called a contrapuntal approach to understanding international relations.

27. For a superb explication of the differing ethos of governance that animated these presidencies in comparison with Cornwallis's Bengal, see Stokes, *English Utilitarians in India*. The other classic occasioned by the debate on the Permanent Settlement is, of course, Ranajit Guha's *A Rule of Property for Bengal: An Essay on the Idea of Permanent Settlement* (1963; reprint, Durham, N.C.: Duke University Press, 1996).

28. Mehta, *Liberalism and Empire*, 20.

29. Mehta, *Liberalism and Empire*, 33.

30. Mehta, *Liberalism and Empire*, 21.

31. Mehta, *Liberalism and Empire*, 41.

32. It is important as well to register the limits to Burke's critique of empire. His attitude to empire was a difference of degree, not of kind, from that of the liberals. A flaming anti-imperialist he was not by any means. His overwhelming concern at all times is not the fate of the Indian but rather of what the rapacious colonialists would do to democracy to England on their physical or ideational return to the homeland.

Chapter Five

Decolonizing the Concept of "Good Governance"

Antony Anghie

RACE, INTERNATIONAL RELATIONS, AND INTERNATIONAL LAW

What does it mean to "decolonize" a discipline? "Good governance" is a term that acquired considerable prominence in the field of international law in the 1990s. Although the term lacks any specific legal meaning, it became a way of organizing, interpreting, and deploying a number of international law doctrines, particularly those relating to international human rights law. It is by attempting to provide what might be broadly termed a "postcolonial" analysis[1] of the emergence and use of this concept and by contesting conventional accounts of its development and utility that this chapter seeks to illuminate aspects of the project of decolonizing a discipline. My analysis focuses on international legal materials. But my general sense is that many commonalities exist between International Relations scholars and international law scholars who are attempting this difficult and important task.[2]

Both International Relations and international law use the concept of sovereignty as a founding principle for their respective disciplines, as Krishna has already highlighted in chapter 4 in this volume. But equally important, both International Relations and international law characterize and analyze imperialism, which is surely a central phenomenon in each discipline, as somehow incidental to the discipline proper and explicable in terms and categories that derive from European experience and history. This is one of the ways in which both disciplines can be regarded as "Eurocentric."[3] This elision of the importance of imperialism for both disciplines seems especially problematic because it results in a systematic blindness, a failure to understand the continuing and decisive presence of imperialism in the contemporary international system. One of the consequences of current U.S. policy and the war in Iraq in particular is that it has made imperialism a central and inescapable aspect of contemporary analysis. This sudden recognition of the presence of imperialism—numerous recently published books aspire to deal with the issue—carries with it certain dangers. Most immediately, imperialism is understood to be something akin to "classical" nineteenth-century British and French imperialism. As a consequence, the more subtle and enduring forms of imperialism remain concealed from view and analysis. Even more importantly obscured is the need to develop an alternative conceptual vocabulary, one that can be used to reveal imperialism and its effects in all their multifarious forms. The sort of explicit imperialism that is now being enacted is discussed principally in the conventional vocabularies that this volume of writings seeks to displace.

The manner in which the concept of "race" has been treated in both International Relations and international law might illustrate some of these concerns. Both International Relations and international law scholars have asserted how race, which was such an integral aspect of imperialism, plays very little role, as an analytic category, in the explanation of international affairs.[4] It is important to understand, then, the mechanisms by which the significance of race to the disciplines of international law and International Relations have been suppressed. One of the most notable aspects of the complex relationship between race and international law is the extent to which the character of that relationship has apparently changed over the past one hundred years. At the beginning of the twentieth century, international law explicitly furthered racism, whereas now, at the beginning of the new millennium, international law appears forcefully committed to the eradication of racism.

The historical centrality of race for the discipline of international law is clearly revealed by a study of nineteenth-century jurists. These jurists were preoccupied with the question of the limits of international law, with the issue of whether international law was capable of encompassing, governing, and accommodating peoples belonging to very different societies. Race is perhaps the most powerful and obvious marker of difference, the apparently stable and self-evident foundation on which further and more elaborate ideas of difference—focusing on culture, "civilization," and backwardness—may be constructed. Race, transmuted into the more comprehensive notion of "civilization," is central to the very definition of international law. Thus, even in

1928, international law was defined as "the name for the body of customary and conventional rules which are considered legally binding by civilised States in their intercourse with each other."[5]

Race served the very important function of determining the issue of membership within the family of nations. It usually signified not merely difference but inferiority—the characteristics of which were comprehensively elaborated on by the writers of that time when they detailed the nature of African or Asiatic societies. The characterization of non-European societies as backward and inferior played a large role in justifying both the conquest of these peoples and the civilizing missions undertaken by European powers—quite often acting in the name of the "international community"—to remedy backwardness and barbarity. Race, at the most basic level, signified a difference that had to be overcome by the assimilative powers of international law, if international law was to become truly universal. In this way, the concept of race is inextricably connected with one of the defining characteristics of international law: its universality.

An examination of the brief histories offered at the beginning of some of the major textbooks of international law provides insight into how the relationship between international law and race, established so powerfully in the nineteenth century, has shifted in the intervening years. Whereas international law was then exclusively European, it is now most prominent for its open and cosmopolitan nature, including within its ranks all sovereign states regardless of their cultures and social structures. Indeed, instead of promoting conquest and domination, international law and institutions, beginning with the League of Nations and continuing more prominently with the United Nations, have sought to promote decolonization, the acquisition of sovereign statehood by entities that had previously been denied this status by international law. In this way, international law dissociated itself from the colonial past.[6]

The rejection by international law of the racism that it had previously propagated and, indeed, that established the very foundation of the discipline was further articulated, particularly in the field of human rights. It is not easy to identify any area of international law where racial distinctions are still maintained. Rather, a study of international instruments suggests that racism now is a phenomenon that exists principally within states. Indeed, the norm against racism appears to be one of the most established and uncontroversial of the many internationally recognized human rights; it is noteworthy, for example, that the International Convention on the Elimination of All Forms of Racial Discrimination[7] was adopted by the United Nations in 1965, preceding by almost a year the International Covenant on Civil and Political Rights.[8]

A singular transformation was thus effected: whereas the concept of race—and its cognates, the concepts of the uncivilized non-European—had been explicitly constitutive for the discipline of international law, it was now characterized as an aberration, as external to the discipline. Indeed, the discipline became forcefully committed to eradicating racism, which was now understood as existing at the local, national level but not in the international realm.

It is against this background that a growing number of scholars have explored the enduring significance of race in terms of its role in shaping the character of international relations and international law. One of the principal concerns that unites these scholars is their attempt, in various fields from international economic law to immigration law,[9] to uncover "the ongoing dynamics of racialized power, and its embeddedness in practices and values which have been shorn of any explicit, formal manifestations of racism."[10] The "war on terror" relies on a set of techniques that certainly derive from earlier racist practices in order to invoke the "fundamentalists" and "terrorists," the great threats that are so essential to the conduct of that war.

In this chapter, I explore how the study of history contributes to the project of identifying the "ongoing dynamics of racialized power." The study of history offers one means of understanding why people of color continue to be, on the whole, the most disadvantaged and marginalized. The study of history is in many respects a practical exercise, a means of facilitating and furthering the reconstructive project that a number of scholars, whether they belong to the movement of critical race theory, Lat-Crit theory, or Third World Approaches to International Law, have in common. What is required is a *critical* engagement with existing histories of international law, the histories that suggest that racism is a problem that has now been successfully overcome. This raises a series of questions: what are the concerns of conventional histories,[11] what place is occupied by people of color within these histories, how are non-Western people characterized in these histories, and what function do they serve within these histories in explaining the progress and development of international law? Further, how do these conventional histories, which focus on Europe as the center, create the conceptual categories that govern the discipline itself? In studying this connection, we might better understand how specific, European history assumes the guise of the international. Against these conventional histories, what may be required is the telling of alternative histories—histories of resistance to colonial power, histories from the vantage point of the peoples who were subjected to international law and that avoid the tendencies of conventional histories to assimilate the specific, unique histories of non-European peoples within their broader concepts and controlling structures.

The work of postcolonial scholars has played a major role in examining how conventional histories have addressed the phenomenon of colonialism.[12] These scholars have attempted to show the tragedies and violence inherent in the colonial encounter and how the very methodology of conventional history suggests progress and improvement. This task remains daunting, however, for the reasons outlined by Dipesh Chakrabarty, who argues that

> insofar as the academic discourse of history—that is, "history" as a discourse produced at the institutional site of the university—is concerned, "Europe" remains the sovereign, theoretical subject of all histories, including the ones we call "Indian," "Chinese," "Kenyan" and so on. There is a peculiar way in which all these other histories tend to become variations on a master narrative that could be called "the history of Europe."[13]

The suggestion is that the discipline of history is so powerfully structured by concepts that derive from European thought and experience that, in attempting to present an alternative and distinctive history of non-European societies, the employment of the very categories of historical inquiry has the effect of affirming that Europe remains the "sovereign subject" of all histories.

While recognizing some of the problems inherent in the study of history, this chapter sketches a critical and historically based analysis of a specific initiative that was enthusiastically embraced by the international community, the project of "good governance." In adopting a historical approach to this issue, I seek to address a series of questions: What are the underlying structures of conventional history which in a complex way affirm and explain the initiatives undertaken? How does our understanding of the project of good governance differ if we examine these histories from a different perspective? From a perspective that suggests that the histories of the relationship between Europe and the non-European world involve a complex set of interactions that cannot be studied simply as the extension of a European set of ideas into the non-European world? My broad interest lies in attempting, first, to excavate the connections of the good governance initiative with earlier, colonial enterprises and, second, to illustrate how the use of the concept may serve to further what are, in essence, colonial relations. Through the study of history, then, it may be possible to examine the colonial past and attempt to identify the underlying dynamic of racialized power and the role it plays in reproducing colonialism rather than to associate colonialism with a specific vocabulary and set of practices in a particular period. It then may be possible to examine how this dynamic is reproduced and reenacted in a language that lacks any "formal manifestations of race" and that, furthermore, is animated—as colonialism always has been—by the irreproachable ambition to better human well-being.

GOVERNANCE IN CONTEMPORARY SETTING

"Good governance," like "development" before it, is a capacious term that has a number of meanings.[14] Like "development," furthermore, "good governance" has a very powerful and apparently universal appeal: all peoples and societies would surely seek good governance—in much the same way that all peoples and societies were seen as desiring development. While good governance may be seen, then, as an "essentially contested term" that could justify a whole series of different and perhaps inconsistent projects and initiatives, there is a powerful strand in the whole system of ideas related to governance that, when scrutinized closely, suggest that "good governance" has a particular significance for developing countries, for these are the countries that lack governance. The concept of good governance, particularly because of its reliance on universal international human rights norms, may appear to be a neutral concept that is potentially applicable to all states. Whatever the political crises and corruption that afflict advanced industrial states, however, these are rarely if ever discussed in terms of internationally articulated norms of "good governance." In practice, then, good governance is a concept that has developed in relation to and that is principally applied to third world states. Good governance provides the moral and intellectual foundation for the development of a set of doctrines, policies, and principles, formulated and implemented by various international actors to manage, specifically, the third world state and third world peoples. Attempts by Western states to promote "good governance" in the non-European world are simply one example of a much broader set of initiatives—relating to the promotion of democracy, the promotion of free markets, the promotion of the rule of law—which have a basic structure in common. In all cases, the basic task is that of reproducing in the non-European world a set of principles and institutions, which are seen as having been perfected in the European world and which the non-European world must adopt if it is to make progress and achieve stability.[15]

The idea that the major problems confronting third world peoples may be attributed to the absence of "good governance" is now both powerful and commonplace.[16] Consequently, important international actors—international human rights groups and international financial institutions (IFIs) such as the World Bank and International Monetary Fund (IMF)—have, within their own spheres of competence, sought to promote "good governance." In very broad terms, "good governance" involves the creation of a government that is, among other things, democratic, open, accountable, and transparent and that respects and fosters human rights. Thus, good governance is linked, in international human rights law, with ideas relating to democratic governance and legitimate governance.[17] Further, human rights lawyers focus on the ways in which human rights norms regarding political participation and free speech may be used to achieve the overarching goal of good governance.[18] Development institutions, most prominently the World Bank, have focused on the importance of good governance for the purposes of achieving development and have, accordingly, formulated policies that would foster such governance. The World Bank claims to be engaged in a common task with human rights institutions in promoting its particular version of good governance.[19] The Bank and the IMF are in a powerful position to implement their concepts of good governance because the vast majority of third world countries depend on the IFIs for financial assistance. Consequently, the IFIs can make their financial assistance conditional on borrowers reforming their governmental structures and political institutions. The sweeping and intrusive character of IFI conditionalities are suggested, for instance, by the IMF requirement that Asian countries seeking its assistance following the financial crisis of 1997 had to meet "50 to 80 detailed conditions covering everything from the deregulation of garlic monopolies to taxes on cattle feed and environmental laws" in return for assistance.[20]

The World Bank powerfully suggests that its good governance agenda complements and furthers that of human rights scholars and activists who emphasize the importance of democratic governance.[21] The Bank, as a development agency, is prohibited from interfering in the political affairs of a state.[22] Recently, however, the Bank has sought to shape and reform the political and economic institutions of member countries, arguing that such reform is essential for successful economic development. The Bank asserts that "at least as important as the policies and the resources for development are the efficiency and transparency of the institutions that carry out the policies."[23] The Bank is now involved in a whole range of issues, including legal reform, and claims that its initiatives complement and promote human rights:

> The World Bank helps its client countries build better governance. This assistance in improving the efficiency and integrity of public sector institutions—from banking regulation to government auditing functions to the court system—has a singularly important, although indirect, impact on creating the structural environment in which citizens can pursue and continue to strengthen all areas of human rights.[24]

The IFIs' concern for "good governance" must be in seen in the context of their principal preoccupation, the furtherance of neoliberal economic policies through structural adjustment programs involving privatization, trade liberalization, and currency devaluation. The IFIs play a major role in furthering a particular form of globalization based on neoliberal economic policy. The IMF exerts considerable pressure on developing countries to remove all restrictions on capital flows, enhancing the mobility of capital at the cost of making developing countries far more vulnerable to volatility and economic instability.[25] Further, the IFIs use their considerable financial power to compel countries to open their financial sectors to foreign investors. Thus, Korea was required to open its financial and automobile sectors to foreign investors and Thailand its banking sectors in return for loans.[26]

Broadly, then, good governance, dubiously claiming affinities with international human rights law, is a means of promoting a number of controversial economic policies that essentially seek to expand the market and that often disadvantage the inhabitants of third world countries who are continuously postulated to be the beneficiaries of this process.[27] The Bank and the IMF vigorously promote globalization despite intensifying inequalities both within and between states.[28]

My argument is that the project of governance, heralded as a new advance in the development of international law, has a very old lineage. Since the beginnings of the modern discipline in the sixteenth century, international law has devised a number of doctrines and technologies directed at shaping and reforming the government of the non-European state. Most typically, this project of reform involves two elements that are often characterized as inseparable: the furtherance of commerce and the advancement of civilization. In short, international law has sought to create non-European governments that would facilitate European commercial expansion into the colonies and, in so doing, civilize and develop the backward natives. Trade and civilization have been the principal justifications for the colonial project through the centuries. My argument is that the contemporary project of governance, particularly as it is promoted by the powerful IFIs, replicates in significant ways the civilizing mission that has given colonialism its impetus and that continues to be an important aspect of contemporary relations between the "developed" and the "developing" worlds.

Good Governance and Human Rights

Good governance exerts an extraordinarily powerful influence on the thinking of the international community for a number of reasons—because it is connected with human rights, the universal language in this "age of rights,"[29] and because it suggests that the problems of the third world lie within the third world itself. Beginning with these propositions, it follows that the problem of addressing international justice can be achieved largely through the project of good governance. For many scholars, however, the project of good governance, however it is justified as liberating the oppressed peoples of the third world from local dictators, raises serious concerns. As Wickramasinghe has put it,

> In this new approach the aim is nothing less than to change the world-system by reforming the fundamental institutions of the recipient state.[30]

Because of its affinity with human rights, the governance agenda appears to be a modern project originating in international human rights law. Under classic nineteenth-century international law, respect for the sovereignty of a country prevented international law from scrutinizing or legally assessing the character of government of a state. How the government of a state was conducted, particularly in terms of the relationship between government and its citizens, was a matter entirely outside the proper scope of international law. As Gregory Fox argues,

> States in the nineteenth century, caught increasingly in the throes of aggressive nationalism, saw their domestic political institutions as essential components of a unique national culture. In order to protect these institutions from external pressures, the dominant states of Europe shaped an international law that carved out an exclusive sphere of domestic jurisdiction. A fortress-like conception of state sovereignty endowed governments with "a monopoly over fundamental political decisions, as well as over legislative, executive and judicial power."[31]

Seen in this way, doctrines of "good governance" or "the right to political participation," which intervene in what has been regarded as within the domestic jurisdiction of a state, represent a fundamental departure from classic international law.

GOVERNANCE AND COLONIALISM

The Concept of Government in Sixteenth-Century Law

If we examine the concept of good governance from the perspective of the experiences of non-European states, however, an entirely different genealogy emerges of the relationship between government and international law. First, it is clear that international lawyers have been concerned about the proper function of government in non-European societies since at least the modern beginnings of the discipline in the sixteenth century. Francisco de Vitoria was a Spanish priest whose work, *De Indis*,[32] is regarded as one of the earliest and most important works of the modern discipline of international law. Vitoria's work "On the Indians Lately Discovered" focused on the numerous legal issues generated by Columbus's unprecedented voyage and discoveries and, in particular, on the question of the legal basis of Spanish rule over the Indians of America.

Governance, the manner in which the Indian rulers governed their people, is a matter that features prominently in Vitoria's deliberations. While Vitoria asserted that the Indians were human beings who were bound by universal natural law, the jus gentium, he is equally emphatic in claiming that they were not of the same stature as the Spanish themselves. The Indians were children who required the guidance and protection of the Spanish. Vitoria makes this assessment, focusing quite explicitly on governance to demonstrate the inferiority and inadequacy of the Indians:

> Although the aborigines in question are . . . not wholly unintelligent, yet they are little short of that condition, and so are unfit to found or administer a lawful State up to the standard required by human and civil claims. Accordingly they have no proper laws nor magistrates, and are not even capable of controlling their family affairs.[33]

While the Indians may have established their own forms of governance, these are found wanting once measured against the universal "standard required by human and civil claims." As such, the Spanish, in the interests of the Indians themselves, "might undertake the administration of their [the Indians] country, providing them with prefects and governors for their towns and may even give them new lords."[34] The Indians are now characterized as infants or wild beasts, and for Vitoria it follows that "their governance should in the same way be entrusted to people of intelligence."[35] Vitoria stressed that Spanish rule over the Indians was to take place in the interests of the Indians and that the Spanish could not profit from it.[36]

It is the test of government, deployed in completely different ways, that is crucial to Vitoria's overall argument: on the one hand, the existence of some form of government suggests that the Indians possess reason, and it is because of this that they are bound by universal natural law; on the other, Indian government is inferior, and its failure to comply with universal standards suggests the need to develop an entirely new set of technologies for the purposes of remedying this deficiency. Unsurprisingly, the "universal" standard is revealed, on further scrutiny, to be an idealized European standard. Once characterized as aberrant, however, Indian society becomes a legitimate subject for reform by the agency of natural law, the Spanish. In the case of the Indians, then, government was a construction of the Spanish acting in the name of enforcing international norms. It is this same natural law, furthermore, that justifies the Spanish intervening on behalf of the Indians to rescue them from their tyrannical rulers.[37]

For Vitoria, however, governance is not merely about reforming the primitive or rescuing the innocent. Accompanying these arguments, which rely heavily on images of backwardness and barbarity, are an equally if not more compelling set of ideas that focus on property, trade, and commerce. Several of Vitoria's most important arguments are based on the notion of property, which, among other things, is closely connected in Vitoria's thought with legal personality and sovereignty. Thus, the crucial consequence of being recognized as a legal person, as possessing reason, is the acquisition of the right to own property.[38] With regard, more broadly, to commerce, Vitoria argues that the right to travel in Indian lands and the right to trade are fundamental principles of natural law to which the Indians must adhere.[39] Vitoria appeared to make such rights apply completely equitably, asserting that "it is certain that the aborigines can no more keep off the Spaniards from trade than Christians can keep off other Christians."[40] Any Indian action that amounts to hindering such trade and commerce is treated as a violation of the jus gentium, which could amount to the ultimate sanction of war.[41] Governance, as Vitoria suggests earlier, includes the creation of a system of administration that protects and upholds these sacrosanct rights.[42] Apart from this, any Indian opposition to the violent Spanish incursions into their territories was treated as an act of war that would justify retaliation, the commencement of a just war by the Spanish, which in turn legitimized the complete dispossession of Indian lands. It is through the waging of such a just war that, Vitoria concludes, the Spanish legally acquired sovereignty over the Indians. In the final analysis, the failure of non-European government to comply with European concepts of governance and to enable the furtherance of European interests would lead to annexation.

Government in Nineteenth-Century International Law

Vitoria's interest in how international law might promote proper government in non-European states and the proper role of such government persisted in international relations over the centuries, particularly the nineteenth century, when colonial expansion was at its height. Many of the maneuvers evident in Vitoria's work, authored within a naturalist jurisprudence, are reenacted by means of the very different lexicon of nineteenth-century positivist international law. Natural law prescribed, broadly, that all states and entities were subject to an overarching system of law that emanated from reason and that transcended state will. As such, in the Vitorian universe, the Spanish, no less than the Indians, were subject to the overarching law of jus gentium. Under the positivist philosophy that emerged by the end of the nineteenth century, when colonialism approached its apogee and European states competed among themselves to amass the largest empires, international law was created by the will and actions of states or, more particularly, civilized states. The state was no longer subject to a higher, transcendent authority. It was in this phase that, with respect to Western states, the positivist emphasis on the primacy of sovereignty established that the manner in which a sovereign behaved within its own territory was entirely outside the scope of international scrutiny.

The experience of the non-European world was completely different. As the discussion of Vitoria suggests, the governance of non-European states would be subjected to a special scrutiny that resulted in interventions that were endorsed by international law once those states had been rendered inferior or aberrant by the concepts and categories that prevailed at the time. In the late nineteenth century, this maneuver was effected by the distinction in positivist jurisprudence between civilized and noncivilized states, which relied principally on racial categories. The non-European states were excluded from the realm of international law, which now made a distinction between civilized states, which were sovereign and possessed full personality, and noncivilized states, which were not properly members of the "family of nations" and hence lacked complete legal personality. Under positivist jurisprudence, sovereign states were the authors of international law. This meant that the nonsovereign, non-European states existed within the system largely as objects; as these states were not fully sovereign, they were legally disempowered from opposing the actions taken by European states that embodied international law.[43] In effect, European states could play an enormously important role, in a manner sanctioned by international law, in shaping the character of non-European states, even in those circumstances where those states were not simply absorbed into colonial empires. Thus, international law developed, once again, a series of doctrines that focused on governance—and its lack—in non-European states.

The concept of government played a crucial role in this jurisprudence; for the jurists of the nineteenth century, government was the crucial test of whether a state was indeed civilized.[44] Even those states such as China that were recognized as possessing an ancient civilization did not necessarily meet the test of government, which essentially required states to create conditions in which Europeans could feel both familiar and secure. States were civilized only when Europeans encountered within them a government "under the protection of which the former [the Europeans] may carry on the complex life to which they have been accustomed in their homes."[45] No pretense was made that both European and non-European states were governed by an overarching and universal set of norms; rather, it was explicitly asserted that non-European polities had to transform themselves, radically, into the image of Europe if they were to be recognized.[46]

One of the central tests used to assess the status of native governance was its capacity to tolerate, protect, and facilitate European trade. Native government was legally required, in essence, to be the instrument that enabled Europeans to engage in the commerce that was such an imperative of the European presence there; nor was any attempt made to separate commerce from governance, as it was understood that the whole purpose of governance was to facilitate the inexhaustible expansion of European commerce:

> The inflow of the white race cannot be stopped where there is land to cultivate, ore to be mined, commerce to be developed, sport to enjoy, curiosity to be satisfied.[47]

The intimate and inextricable links between commerce and governance were such that European trading companies controlled and governed territories. Native peoples, being uncivilized, lacked sovereignty; but the East India Company, Dutch East Indies Company, Imperial East Africa Company, and British South Africa Company—corporations that sought to make profits from the exploitation of native peoples and their territories—could be vested with important sovereign rights, including the right to acquire territory. The East India Company was basically an extension of the British Crown, for whom "the company is as much an organ as the department of its government ostensibly entrusted with the conduct of its foreign affairs."[48] As Krishna discusses in chapter 4 in this volume, the East India Company pioneered the British presence in India; it entered into treaties with local rulers and took possession of and administered Indian states such as Bengal, Bihar, and Orissa.[49] Here, commerce and governance are not merely complementary but identical: a company exercises the rights of government. Proper government was essential to the protection and propagation of commerce, and where native governments were incapable of creating and maintaining the conditions that supported the inevitable European annexation of their own territories, Westlake argued, "government should be furnished."[50] Wars of colonial conquest followed, and conquest and annexation were recognized as legitimate bases for title. But where this was not possible, a number of other techniques were devised to enable European powers to exercise a massively intrusive control over the ways in which non-European states governed. Even where non-European states nominally retained their autonomy, the manner in which they were governed was determined more by external pressures exerted by European powers than by local needs and will; indeed, this is exactly the situation in Iraq today, as James Gathii demonstrates in chapter 6.

Governance and Humanitarianism

In time, rather than focus explicitly on commercial acquisition, the European powers formulated a more nuanced and morally acceptable basis for colonialism. The essential purpose of the Berlin Conference was to divide up the

African continent among competing European powers in such a way as to prevent the escalation of inter-European rivalries. Thus, the conference was centrally preoccupied by commercial considerations. Nevertheless, the participants were careful to assert that promotion of such commerce served a far greater purpose than the mere maximization of European profits. Bismarck remarked that the imperial government was guided by the conviction that all the governments invited share the wish to bring the natives of Africa within the pale of civilization by opening up the interior of that continent to commerce.[51]

Importantly, slavery was abolished, and the Berlin Treaty included provisions relating to native welfare. Nevertheless, there was no inconsistency between these apparent changes in policy and the furthering of commerce. As Lord Lugard noted in condemning the institution of slavery, "It is economically bad, for the freeman does more work than the slave, who, moreover, is indifferent to the productivity of the soil and careless of posterity."[52] The Berlin Conference developed a new rationale for colonialism, comprising the twin themes of commerce and civilization, the policy of the "dual mandate" magesterially and comprehensively elaborated by Lord Lugard, its foremost exponent.

The expansion of European commerce was no longer simply a mechanism for the economic exploitation and subordination of non-European peoples but also a means of effecting the entry of the backward peoples into the world of civilization. As Bismarck's comments suggest, these humanitarian goals were to be furthered by the expansion of commerce. Lord Lugard makes clear the reasons underlying the scramble for Africa:

> The vital importance of the control of the tropics for their economic value had, however, already begun to be realised by the nations of Europe, and France, Germany, and Italy, laying aside their ambitions in Europe, emerged as claimants for large "colonies" in Africa.[53]

Even while driven by commerce, the humanitarian aspect of the rhetoric of governance developed an extraordinarily complex and resilient character such that, in the new framework of the dual mandate, all manner of economic policies could now be justified and refined as advancing humanitarian causes. It is precisely through this affiliation between economic and humanitarian concerns that various policies that would have appeared nakedly exploitative could now be presented as appropriate and even desirable. Essential aspects of the dual mandate policy, pithily summarized by Joseph Chamberlain, were cited by Lugard in an epigraph to his book: "We develop new territory as Trustees of Civilisation for the Commerce of the World."[54] Importantly, Chamberlain presents colonial policy as deriving its authority from the international community and directed toward benefiting that entire community. The resources of non-European peoples were characterized as belonging to the international community, with Britain acting on behalf of that community through their exploitation. The immutable "right to trade" was cited by European powers to legally justify their entry into non-European societies, as indicated by the British in China, the French in Europe, and the Spanish in the Americas. Non-European sovereigns were required, by force if necessary, to comply with this right. Once European powers acquired control and sovereignty over these same African and Asian territories, however, the right ceased to exist, and intra-European rivalries developed precisely because England would deny access to French traders in European colonies, for example.

Whatever the rhetoric, commerce was the controlling preoccupation of colonial governance. This resulted in the disintegration of native institutions and ways of life and, with this, the social formations that had offered people protection and meaning; this phenomenon was noted and commented on by experts on colonial policy even prior to the process of decolonization.[55] In addition, the government of the colony operated in accordance with the needs of the metropolis. The economy of the colony was integrated into the overall structure of the economy of the metropolis. Furthermore, the institutions, government, and "rule of law" established in the colonies were directed, essentially, at furthering this commerce.[56]

My overall argument, then, is that the non-European world is different, that the governance of these societies has been intimately shaped by international actors, imperial European states, whose actions have been sanctioned and enabled by international law. Over the centuries, international law developed a sophisticated series of technologies, doctrines, and disciplines that borrowed in important ways from the broader justifications of colonialism to address the problem of the governance of non-European peoples. It is hardly surprising, then, that this was a subject of considerable scholarship and that authors such as M. F. Lindley compiled, described, and analyzed these techniques in a book revealingly titled *The Acquisition and Government of Backward Territories in International Law* in 1926.[57] At a time when government within European states was entirely immune to regulation by international law, government in non-European states was a matter that international law could dictate. It must be noted that the purpose of this exercise was often to grant the indigenous peoples some measure of protection. But the fundamental purposes animating governance remained the same. As classically formulated by Joseph Chamberlain, the governance of native peoples consisted of the dual mandate: civilization and commerce. A study of much earlier works, such as those of Vitoria and Westlake, suggest that this has been a consistent theme—trade and civilization—a theme that finds its contemporary expression in a variety of forms in this era of globalization, which ostensibly provides freedom and the market. Another version of this same theme has been articulated by the former president of the World Bank, James Wolfensohn, who speaks of "human rights and property."

The World Bank's current governance agenda may be historically understood as an essential continuation of these same themes. The mandate system of the League of Nations represents the first instance of an international institution undertaking the responsibility of protecting the well-being of native peoples. The work of the World Bank may be understood, in many respects, as continuing the practices of the mandate system, which represented the first occasion on which an international institution, not limited in any way by the sovereignty of a state, could play a direct and unimpeded role in shaping the government, political institutions, and economy of a state. The World Bank exercises a similar degree of power over third world countries, which are required to comply with the Bank's strictures in order to receive assistance. In pointing to these continuities, I do not wish to suggest that nothing has changed since the time of Vitoria. The ongoing struggles by the people who have had to confront these imperial structures led to decolonization. Third world peoples have at least achieved formal sovereignty, and the challenge remains of devising new strategies to combat these new forms of a very old and enduring set of imperial practices.

CONCLUSION

Given this brief historical survey of the different manifestations of a concept that has acquired great significance in contemporary international relations, what can we observe regarding the broader issue that initiated this inquiry: the question of the relationship between history, colonialism, and international law?

First, it is evident that the civilizing mission is a fundamental aspect of international law; it continues in a number of different ways despite radical changes in jurisprudence—the changes from naturalism in the time of Vitoria to positivism in the time of Westlake to pragmatism in the League of Nations era. What is remarkable is that despite these changes, which in conventional histories of international law mark important disruptions in the discipline, the basic structure of the civilizing mission is reproduced: government in non-European states is wanting, the essential characteristics of good government is government that furthers trade and civilization where trade is understood to mean the trade conducted by westerners seeking to advance their commercial interests in the non-European territory, and appropriate and detailed standards must be developed to ensure that good government is achieved.

Second, virtually all these initiatives—of "good governance," "democracy," the "rule of law," or indeed the earlier initiatives of "sovereignty"—represent a basic movement from West to East. They involve the transference of a set of institutions and practices that have ostensibly been perfected in the European world and that must now be adopted in the non-European world if it is to make any progress. As this discussion on governance suggests, however, the liberatory potential of such initiatives must be viewed with skepticism given that they are inevitably mired in a complex and ongoing set of power relations between the European and non-European worlds. At the very least, these initiatives suggest, often with an insidious and patronizing benevolence, that peoples in the non-European worlds are lacking in their own ideas as to how their societies should be structured and what values they should prescribe and adopt.

Third, we may note that a focus on the specific histories of non-European states and the ways in which international law has attempted to establish their status and place them within the overall system of international law reveals that many of the doctrines and practices now regarded as recent developments of a new and progressive international law have a very old lineage. The non-European world has, on the whole, been rendered nonsovereign by international law over the course of the past three centuries.[58] It is precisely in the non-European world that international law can extend and expand its reach and develop and refine a series of technologies directed toward creating good government. The domestic sphere, which is entirely immune to international law in the case of European states, is entirely vulnerable to international law in the case of the non-European states. It is in the non-European world that these technologies and doctrines have been developed over the past five centuries, and it is in the third world that the technologies are once again being deployed—for basically the same purpose.

Fourth, the vocabulary of race is no longer required in its explicit form largely because international law has developed an extraordinarily rich and complex vocabulary to represent non-European peoples in terms that appear natural and uncontroversial. The most notable example is the representation of non-European peoples as "undeveloped." This terminology is supported by a comprehensive set of theories involving an interrelated set of concepts that complement each other: development as something requiring the free market, civil society, and good governance, all of which are lacking in the non-European world. International law and the initiatives it creates are not in themselves seen as racist or discriminatory. Rather, international law and institutions are responding to the realities of third world poverty, violence, and lack. It can hardly be doubted that third world peoples suffer enormous hardships and difficulties. But what must be questioned in the narratives that support international initiatives such as "good governance" is the worldview that suggests, for example, that the causes of poverty are entirely indigenous, that poverty may be alleviated by the redeeming and neutral mechanism of the market, and that political failure is due entirely to indigenous corruption. It is through the historical study of the complex relationship between race and international law, then, that it may be possible to identify how these initiatives simply serve to replicate colonial structures.

NOTES

Many thanks to Branwen Gruffydd Jones and all participants at the workshop "Decolonising International Relations" held at the University of Aberdeen for a very stimulating event and for helpful suggestions. This chapter is based in part on my earlier work, "Civilization and Commerce: The Concept of Governance in Historical Perspective," *Villanova Law Review* 45, no. 5 (2000): 887–911.

1. For earlier attempts to apply the methods of postcolonialism to international law, see, for example, Philip Darby, ed., *At the Edge of International Relations: Postcolonialism, Gender and Dependency* (London: Pinter, 1997).

2. The two disciplines have always been interconnected in complex ways. See, for example, Anne-Marie Slaughter, "International Law and International Relations Theory: A Dual Agenda," *American Journal of International Law* 87, no. 2 (1993): 205–39, and Christian Reus-Smit, ed., *The Politics of International Law* (Cambridge: Cambridge University Press, 2004). For connections between the two disciplines relating to the issue of colonialism, see, most prominently, Siba N'Zatioula Grovogui, *Sovereigns, Quasi Sovereigns, and Africans: Race and Self-Determination in International Law* (Minneapolis: University of Minnesota Press, 1996); see also Edward Keene, *Beyond the Anarchical Society: Grotius, Colonialism and Order in World Politics* (Cambridge: Cambridge University Press, 2002).

3. James Thuo Gathii, "International Law and Eurocentricity," *European Journal of International Law* 9, no. 1 (1998): 184–211.

4. See Gita Chowdhry and Sheila Nair, eds., *Power, Postcolonialism and International Relations: Reading Race, Gender and Class* (London: Routledge, 2002), 17 ff.

5. Lassa Oppenheim, *International Law: A Treatise Vol. 1: Peace*, 4th ed., ed. Arnold McNair (London: Longmans, 1928), 3–4.

6. For an account of the importance of race for international relations and the anxieties that shaped the emerging antiracism that began in the interwar period and continued into the UN period, see Frank Furedi, *The Silent War: Imperialism and the Changing Perceptions of Race* (London: Pluto Press, 1998).

7. International Convention on the Elimination of All Forms of Racial Discrimination, 660 U.N.T.S. 195, adopted by the UN General Assembly on December 21, 1965 (G.A.Res. 2106, 20 GAOR, Supp. 14, U.N.Doc. A/6014 at 47); opened for signature on March 7, 1966; entered into force on March 7, 1966.

8. *International Covenant on Civil and Political Rights*, Annex to G.A.Res. 2200, 21 GAOR, Supp. 16, U.N.Doc. A/6316 at 52 (1966).

9. See "Symposium. Critical Race Theory and International Law: Convergence and Divergence," *Villanova Law Review* 45, no. 5 (2000): 827–1220, and "Colloquium. International Law, Human Rights, and LatCrit Theory," *University of Miami Inter-American Law Review* 28 (1997): 177–302.

10. Kimberlé Crenshaw, Neil Gotanda, Garry Peller, and Kendall Thomas, eds., *Critical Race Theory: The Key Writings That Formed the Movement* (New York: New Press, 1995), xxix.

11. For example, Arthur Nussbaum, *A Concise History of the Law of Nations* (New York: Macmillan, 1954).

12. See, in particular, the work of the subaltern studies collective, for example, Ranajit Guha, ed., *A Subaltern Studies Reader 1986–1995* (Minneapolis: University of Minnesota Press, 1997).

13. Dipesh Chakrabarty, "Postcoloniality and the Artifice of History: Who Speaks for 'Indian' Pasts?" in *A Subaltern Studies Reader 1986–1995*, ed. Ranajit Guha (Minneapolis: University of Minnesota Press, 1997), 263. However, note here the important argument regarding "Europe's own history" set out by Halperin in chapter 2 in this volume.

14. For different treatments of "governance," see, for example, Richard A. Falk, *On Humane Governance: Toward a New Global Politics* (University Park: Pennsylvania State University Press, 1995), and Commission on Global Governance, *Our Global Neighborhood: The Report of the Commission on Global Governance* (New York: Oxford University Press, 1995). For attempts by third world scholars to provide an understanding of governance that would be more useful for third world peoples, see Edward Kofi Quashigah and Obiora Chinedu Okafor, eds., *Legitimate Governance in Africa: International and Domestic Legal Perspectives* (The Hague: Kluwer Law International, 1999).

15. For a telling examination of this phenomenon in relation to "democracy promotion," see William P. Alford, "Exporting the Pursuit of Happiness," *Harvard Law Review* 113, no. 7 (2000): 1677–715 . The argument that all societies must adopt the model established by Western societies has been most famously made by Francis Fukuyama in his *The End of History and the Last Man* (London: Penguin, 1992).

16. I have chosen to use the term "third world" here for reasons in part discussed in B. S. Chimni, "Third World Approaches to International Law: A Manifesto," in *The Third World and International Order: Law, Politics and Globalization*, ed. Antony Anghie, B. S. Chimni, Karin Mickelson, and Obiora Okafor (Leiden: Martin Nijhoff, 2003).

17. See, for example, Linda C. Reif, "Building Democratic Institutions: The Role of National Human Rights Institutions in Good Governance and Human Rights Protection," *Harvard Human Rights Journal* 13 (2000): 1–69, and Thomas M. Franck, "The Emerging Right to Democratic Governance," *American Journal of International Law* 86, no. 1 (1992): 46–91.

18. Henry J. Steiner, "Political Participation as a Human Right," *Harvard Human Rights Yearbook* 1 (spring 1988): 77–134; Gregory H. Fox, "The Right to Political

Participation in International Law," *Yale Journal of International Law* 17 (1992): 539–607; Christina M. Cerna, "Universal Democracy: An International Legal Right or the Pipe Dream of the West?," *New York University Journal of International Law and Politics* 27 (winter 1995): 289–329.

19. World Bank, *Development and Human Rights: The Role of the World Bank* (Washington, D.C.: International Bank for Reconstruction and Development/World Bank, 1998), <http://www.worldbank.org/html/extdr/rights/> (accessed 2 September 2005).

20. Devesh Kapur, "The IMF: A Cure or a Curse?" *Foreign Policy* 111 (summer 1998): 114–29. For detailed studies of IFI policies and conditionalities in Africa, see James Thuo Gathii, "The Limits of the New International Rule of Law on Good Governance," in Quashigah and Okafor, *Legitimate Governance*, and John-Jean B. Barya, "The New Political Conditionalities of Aid: An Independent View from Africa," *IDS Bulletin* 24, no. 1 (1993): 16–23.

21. See Ibrahim F. I. Shihata, "Democracy and Development," *International and Comparative Law Quarterly* 46 (1997): 635–43.

22. The Bank's involvement in governance issues raises complex questions as to how this may be justified in terms of the Bank's Articles of Agreement, which assert that "the Bank shall not interfere in the political affairs of any member" (World Bank, Articles of Agreement, Art. IV.10).

23. World Bank, *Development and Human Rights*, 11.

24. World Bank, *Development and Human Rights*, 11.

25. Robert Wade, "The Coming Fight over Capital Flows," *Foreign Policy* 113 (winter 1998): 41–54.

26. Martin Feldstein, "Refocusing the IMF," *Foreign Affairs* 77, no. 2 (1998): 20–33; Kapur, "The IMF," 118.

27. See James Thuo Gathii, "Good Governance as a Counter-Insurgency Agenda to Oppositional and Transformative Social Projects in International Law," *Buffalo Human Rights Law Review* 5 (1999): 107–74.

28. See the annual *Human Development Reports* of the UN Development Program, in particular those of 2005 (chapter 2) and 1992; Nancy Birdsall, "Life Is Unfair: Inequality in the World," *Foreign Policy* 111 (summer 1998): 76–93.

29. See Antony Anghie, "Universality and the Concept of Governance in International Law," in Quashigah and Okafor, *Legitimate Governance*.

30. Nira Wickramasinghe, "From Human Rights to Good Governance: The Aid Regime in the 1990s," in *The New World Order: Sovereignty, Human Rights and the Self-Determination of Peoples*, ed. Mortimer Sellers (Oxford: Berg, 1996).

31. Fox, "The Right to Political Participation in International Law," 545.

32. Franciscus de Victoria, *De Indis Et Ivre Belli Relectione* (1557; reprint, Washington, D.C.: Carnegie Institute of Washington, 1917). I have adopted the spelling of "Vitoria," which is most commonly used.

33. Vitoria, *De Indis*, 161 para. 407.

34. Vitoria recognizes that the Indians "have polities which are orderly arranged and they have definite marriage and magistrates, overlords, laws and workshops" (*De Indis*, 127, para. 333).

35. Vitoria, *De Indis*, 161, para. 408.

36. This idea became the basis of the League of Nations mandate system and its successor, the UN trusteeship system. Vitoria is mentioned in virtually all books dealing with these subjects. Interestingly, Vitoria himself did not regard this argument of guardianship as his most powerful legal vindication of Spanish conquest, stating more tentatively, "There is another title which can indeed not be asserted, but brought up for discussion, and some think it lawful" (*De Indis*, 160, para. 18).

37. Vitoria, *De Indis*, 159, para. 403.

38. This is reflected in Vitoria's extensively argued position that since the Indians possess reason, they were "true owners alike in public and private law before the advent of the Spaniards among them" (*De Indis*, 115, para. 303).

39. Vitoria asserts that "the Spaniards have a right to travel to the lands of the Indians and to sojourn there, so long as they do no harm, and they can not be prevented by the Indians" (*De Indis*, 150 para. 383) and that "it was permissible from the beginning of the world (when everything was in common) for any one to set forth and travel wheresoever he would" (*De Indis*, 151 para. 386).

40. Vitoria, *De Indis*, 153 para. 389.

41. Vitoria states that "to keep certain people out of the city or province as being enemies or to expel them when already there, are acts of war" (*De Indis*, 151 para. 382).

42. Vitoria does impose some limits on the rights to trade, suggesting that it was Spain alone that discovered the New World and hence that Spain alone could trade with it (*De Indis*, 157 para. 398).

43. The non-European states could not, of course, be ignored, particularly since interactions had taken place between European and non-European states. European states had to observe various legal doctrines in their dealings with non-European states; however, these doctrines were directed more toward preventing intra-European rivalries than out of a concern to protect the rights of non-Europeans.

44. John Westlake begins one section of his book with the heading "Government Is the Test of Civilization" in *Chapters on the Principles of International Law* (Cambridge: Cambridge University Press, 1894), 141.

45. Westlake, *Chapters on the Principles of International Law*, 141.

46. Japan succeeded in clearing this formidable threshold, principally as a consequence of defeating a major European power, Russia, in the battle of Tsushima in 1905.

47. Westlake, *Chapters on the Principles of International Law*, 142.

48. Westlake, *Chapters on the Principles of International Law*, 191.

49. Westlake, *Chapters on the Principles of International Law*, 195.

50. Westlake, *Chapters on the Principles of International Law*, 142.

51. Cited in Mark F. Lindley, *The Acquisition and Government of Backward Territory in International Law: Being a Treatise on the Law and Practice Relating to Colonial Expansion* (London: Longmans, Green and Co., 1926; reprint, New York: Negro Universities Press, 1969), 332.

52. Lord Frederick J. D. Lugard, *The Dual Mandate in British Tropical Africa* (London: Frank Cass, 1965), 64. A very complex relationship exists between these humanitarian practices and economic consequences: I do not mean to suggest that the abolition of slavery was a subtle conspiracy that was intended to always further

economic exploitation under a new and apparently benevolent guise; rather, my argument is that the abolition of slavery in itself did not prevent—indeed, it sometimes furthered—the type of trade and commerce that the European powers sought to promote. It is significant that one of the central actors of this period—Lugard is regarded as the preeminent colonial administrator of his time—recognized the possible economic benefits resulting from the promotion of these humanitarian policies.

53. Lugard, *The Dual Mandate in British Tropical Africa*, 10.

54. Lugard, epigraph in *The Dual Mandate in British Tropical Africa*.

55. For example, John S. Furnivall, *Progress and Welfare in Southeast Asia: A Comparison of Colonial Policy and Practice* (New York: Institute of Pacific Relations, 1941).

56. "The main object of colonial policy during the Liberal experiment was the promotion of commerce. This required direct administration on Western principles, allowing free play within the law to economic forces" (Furnivall, *Progress and Welfare in Southeast Asia*, 21).

57. See also Charles G. Fenwick, *Wardship in International Law* (Washington, D.C.: U.S. Government Printing Office, 1919), and Alpheus H. Snow, *The Question of Aborigines in the Law and Practice of Nations* (New York: G. P. Putnam's Sons, 1921).

58. Indeed, it seems to me that the more developed the concept of sovereignty becomes in the West, since the beginning of the seventeenth century, the more wanting and excluded becomes the sovereignty of non-European peoples.

Chapter Six

Dispossession through International Law: Iraq in Historical and Comparative Context

James Thuo Gathii

The confiscation of private property during wartime is prohibited under customary international law. However, the U.S.-led invasion of Iraq in 2003 has been accompanied by confiscation of private property. The purpose of this chapter is to demonstrate that the contraventions of international law wrought by the confiscation of private property in the war and occupation of Iraq are not exceptional but part of a long history of the uneven application of international law in situations of colonial and imperial conquest and the routine disregard and subordination of non-European peoples to the interests of European powers. A primary reason accounting for the uneven and inconsistent application of rules prohibiting the confiscation of private property on conquest has been to facilitate the political expediencies and hegemony of conquering states over weaker and vulnerable states. For example, U.S. courts have held that treaties embodying this rule that private property rights shall be inextinguishable on conquest are subject to the overriding constraint of their compatibility with national policy during times of war.[1] In the United States, such views have been fortified by judicial attitudes reluctant to use international law to restrain the executive branch, especially with regard to wartime decisions.[2]

I argue that this attitude has greatly facilitated the dispossession of the private property rights of citizens of weaker and often non-European states. By contrast, the private property rights of citizens of powerful Western states have traditionally received an especially high level of protection. I also examine the fundamental restructuring of the Iraqi economy following the U.S.-led conquest in 2003 and its incompatibility with rules of international law. A major theme of the chapter is to reveal the historical continuity of the dispossession of non-European countries by Western countries. The radical transformation of the Iraqi economy into a free market in the twenty-first century has conferred enormous benefits to Western multinational corporations at the expense of Iraqi citizens in much the same way that European acquisition of the territory of indigenous communities in the Americas, Africa, and elsewhere benefited white settler interests at the expense of indigenous communities in the nineteenth century and before.

THE EFFECT OF CONQUEST ON PRIVATE PROPERTY UNDER CLASSICAL CUSTOMARY INTERNATIONAL LAW

Customary international law and the laws of war embody specific rules prohibiting the confiscation or destruction of private property on conquest and occupation. The primary prohibition against destruction of enemy property by belligerents is embodied in article 23(g) of the 1907 Hague Convention Respecting the Laws and Customs of War on Land, which *especially* forbids the destruction or seizure of an "enemy's property, unless such destruction or seizure be imperatively demanded by the necessities of war."[3] This strict rule was adopted by the U.S. Supreme Court in 1833 in *United States v Percheman*, where the Court observed that it is "very unusual, even in cases of conquest, for the conqueror to do more than displace the sovereign and assume dominion over the country."[4] The Court further noted,

> The modern usage of nations, which has become law, would be violated; that sense of justice and of right which is acknowledged and felt by the whole civilized world would be outraged, if private property should be generally confiscated and private rights annulled. . . . If this be the modern rule even in cases of conquest, who can discount its application to the case of an amicable cession of territory?[5]

This rule was also affirmed in leading cases such as *Ware v Hylton*[6] as well as by political leaders like Alexander Hamilton who supported the prohibition against confiscation, stating in part that "no powers at my command can express the abhorrence I feel at the idea of violating the property of individuals, which, in an authorized intercourse, in time of peace, has been confided of our Government and laws, on account of controversies between nation and nation."[7]

Various reasons have been advanced to justify these rules. The laws of war are predicated on a distinction between civilian and military aspects that arose in the practice of states that have professional militaries.[8] Accordingly, the laws of war seek to reduce war's adverse consequences on noncombatants, particularly civilians, the sick, and the wounded of the belligerent and neutral states. The rules of international law governing the conduct of warfare are based on a presumed set of clear distinctions: between states and individuals, between a relatively stronger occupying state in relation to a weaker state, between the government and the people, between public and private property, and between civilians and combatants. Under classical customary international law, war was conceived as something that occurs between states rather than between individuals.[9] Where an individual of enemy nationality and her property are domiciled abroad, her property is not regarded as having an enemy character and, if seized, cannot be confiscated. Where citizens of an enemy state are domiciled within the territory of the opposing belligerent state, she and her property may assume an enemy character. In particular, where the resources of such a citizen were applied toward aiding the enemy, she and her property automatically acquire an enemy character and become subject to confiscation.[10]

Since at least the eighteenth century, it has been regarded as unjust and impolitic that debts and contracts between individuals who had confidence in each other and entered into obligations should have that trust and confidence destroyed as a result of national differences or in the event of war.[11] Further, some authorities hold that it is prudent to suspend rather than to abrogate loan payments owed by subjects of an enemy to the subjects of the opposing belligerent until the conclusion of the war and the return to peacetime.[12] Although as a general matter the doctrine of nonintercourse prohibits commerce between belligerent states, the strictness of this doctrine was held by the end of the nineteenth century to have been attenuated by the "rapid advances in civilization," "progressive public opinion," and the "influence of Christianity" such that it was possible to differentiate between military as opposed to civil affairs and between the conduct of war and of commerce.[13] Thus, in the United States, as well as in the United Kingdom, trading with the enemy requires special licenses.[14]

Considerations of humanity are another justification given for the rule against extinction of property rights on conquest. One of the most eloquent exponents of this view was John Basset Moore, who argued for

> the protection of property not militarily used or in immediate likelihood of being so used against destruction, not, as writers sometimes seem to fancy, because of humane regard for insensate things, but because of the belief that, in the interest of humanity, war-stricken peoples should not be reduced to a condition of barbarism or savagery, but should, on the contrary, be enabled to resume the normal processes of peaceful life as soon as possible.[15]

According to Moore, the basis of this rule lay in "a moral revolt, a new creed," a "loftier conception of the destiny of and rights of man and of a more humane spirit" according to which the confiscation of property was necessary to "assure the world's commerce a legitimate and definite freedom."[16]

HEGEMONIC EROSION OF A CUSTOMARY INTERNATIONAL LAW CANON DURING THE TWENTIETH CENTURY

The classical customary international rule forbidding the extinction of contracts and private property rights on conquest has been undermined by uneven and inconsistent application. One of the reasons advanced for this inconsistency is that the rule is ancient and therefore does not reflect the practice of states in all cases.[17] The Hague Regulations were negotiated at the end of the nineteenth century at a time when it was in the interest of the United States to comply with rules of international law.[18] Some have argued that the subsequent growth of the political and economic power of the United States justifies a less significant role for international law in governing the U.S. role in international affairs.[19] One commentator has concluded that international law serves as a tool for U.S. power as opposed to a restraint of U.S. power in the world today.[20] Thus today, almost a hundred years after the Hague Regulations came into force, the United States asserts its global military and political dominance unilaterally in a manner unthinkable a century ago.[21] This global dominance, according to adherents of this view, has resulted in reducing the constraints of international law on the United States.[22]

Twenty-first century warfare, as conducted by powerful countries such as the United States, is vastly different from nineteenth-century warfare. It has been argued that high-tech warfare is more precise, with a decrease in the death of civilians and destruction of their private property. However, the trebled lethality of high-tech warfare has in fact multiplied rather than reduced the impact of war on civilian populations and property for various reasons.[23] First, powerful states with such weaponry have made sophisticated legal arguments to justify narrowing distinctions between soldiers and civilians that legitimize civilian casualties and destruction to civilian property as collateral damage.[24] Countries such as the United States have adopted doctrines justifying the use of overwhelming military force, including using unchallenged heavy precision-guided aerial bombs and missiles to support few but well-equipped battalions in enemy territory.[25] Second, the traditional humanitarian constraints on the use of military force have been mobilized to lend credibility to new visions of military necessity and military action.[26] As Upendra Baxi and others have argued, the post–Cold War doctrine of militarized humanitarianism has had adverse human rights and economic consequences for nondominant cultures and peoples.[27]

In the nineteenth century, the classical rule restricting the vitiation of contracts and private property on conquest was founded on the view that war occurred between states. While there are instances in the history of international relations where armed force was exercised against nonstate actors, such as the threat of piracy,[28] the War on Terrorism declared after September 11, 2001, by the United States and later endorsed by the United Nations has contributed to the continued erosion of the view that war occurs between states.[29] The War on Terrorism has come to be defined almost exclusively as against nonstate actors. The Bush administration's *National Security Strategy* of 2002 states,

> The enemy is not a single political regime or person or religion or ideology. . . . The struggle against global terrorism is [therefore] different from any other war in our history. It will be fought on many fronts against a particularly elusive enemy over an extended period of time.[30]

In addition to preemptive strikes against suspected terrorists, the United States has adopted an aggressive effort to "disrupt and destroy" terrorist organizations and their operations around the world by various means, including disabling terrorist groups' material support and finances. These efforts have been given imprimatur by the United Nations[31] although the preemptive use of force is clearly prohibited under international law.[32] The Counter Terrorism Committee, established by the United Nations to monitor global antiterrorism activities, has legitimated broad powers to block and confiscate private property belonging to groups (including religious organizations and charities that have been shown to have little or nothing in common with terrorists) and individuals suspected of terrorism without any due process and in clear violation of UN human rights mandates.[33] By refusing to act within the confines of international law and with due process in the blocking and confiscation of private property, both the United States and the Counter Terrorism Committee depart from prior practice, under which peace treaties between belligerent states exempted property belonging to religious bodies and charitable organizations from confiscation and liquidation.[34]

Thus, the changing nature and circumstances of war during the twentieth century undermined the rules prohibiting the confiscation of private property on conquest in a number of ways. However, there is a much longer history of uneven application of this rule, to which I now turn. This differential application of the rule against extinction of private property rights and contracts on conquest is, I argue, a systemic expression of the hegemonic power of conquering states that goes back decades and centuries in the history of international law.

THE UNEVEN APPLICATION OF INTERNATIONAL LAW AGAINST NON-EUROPEANS

In this section, I reveal a distinct hegemonic impulse to override the private property rights of non-Europeans on conquest in the history of international law. To set the stage, I first discuss a 1905 House of Lords decision that explicitly found that the rule against extinction was preempted by the prerogatives of the Crown. I then discuss an earlier decision of the Supreme Court where Native American ownership of land in early American history was treated as mere possession on conquest and in the various peace treaties between the United States and Spain, while similar possession of land by white colonial settlers was held to constitute unimpeachable private property rights.

In the case *West Rand Central Gold Mining Co. v The King* in 1905, the question before the House of Lords was whether, after annexation, a conquering state becomes liable to discharge the financial obligations of the conquered state due to individuals or corporations.[35] The relevant facts of the case were that the Republic of South Africa had seized over 2,617 ounces of gold from the West Rand Central Gold Mining Company for "safekeeping." Following the Anglo-Boer War, Britain conquered the Republic of South Africa and thereby came into possession of the seized gold. West Rand Central Gold Mining Company brought suit seeking recovery of the gold on the premise that conquest or change of sovereignty by cession ought not affect preexisting contractual rights. The company relied on *United States v Percheman*, arguing that the whole of the civilized world would be outraged if private property should be generally confiscated and private rights annulled by the British conquest.

Unpersuaded, the House of Lords held that "where the King of England conquers a country it is a different consideration, [from peaceable cession], for there the conqueror by saving the lives of the people conquered *gains a right and property in such people, in consequence of which he may impose upon them what law he pleases.*"[36] In effect, the court declined to extend protection to the private property rights of a South African corporation by drawing a distinction between the circumstances under which such protection applies and those in which it does not.

In light of the court's observation that the Crown was freed of any constraints in deciding what law to apply to a conquered people, it is plausible to argue that the decision was made to match the demands of colonial expediency rather than because the doctrine required such an outcome on any principled basis except those consistent with the designs of the expanding British Empire. This case reveals the malleable and contradictory applications of this customary international law rule's saving benediction of private property and contracts on conquest. Sometimes it was held to apply, but in cases like this, the King's prerogatives over a conquered state overrode the applicability of the rule.

Unlike in *West Rand Central Gold Mining Co.*, the rule against extinction of private property rights was successfully applied in the earlier case of *Strother v Lucas* in 1838 to facilitate the survival of land grants made by the Spanish Crown to white settlers.[37] In addition, use and occupation of territory by Spanish and other white settlers that had not been recognized by the Spanish Crown as constituting private property rights enjoyed the saving benediction of the rule against extinction of private property rights after Spain ceded its territories to the United States.[38] In this case, conquest transformed the use and occupation of land into private property rights on Spanish cession of territory to the United States. However, this transformation did not work in favor of a Native American who occupied and used the land in the same way as the Spanish and other white settlers.

Native American use and occupation of land was held not to enjoy the same status as similar use and occupation of land by Spanish and other white settlers. This attitude of early American courts toward Native American land rights as falling below private property rights is further evidenced by cases like *Johnson v M'Intosh*, in which the Supreme Court held that conquest impaired Native American rights to land.[39] The rationale for nonrecognition of Native American rights to land espoused by Justice Marshall was that the "tribes of Indians inhabiting this country were fierce savages, whose occupation was war, and whose subsistence was drawn chiefly from the forest [and that] to leave them in possession of their country, was to *leave the country a wilderness*."[40] Conquest and cession thus applied differently as between Native Americans on the one hand and Spanish and white settlers on the other. While Spanish and white settlers had their use and occupation of land treated as equivalent to land grants or titles that survived conquest or cession of territory, similar use and occupation of land by Native Americans was not recognized as private property capable of surviving conquest or cession.

Even more strikingly, in *Strother*, the Supreme Court recognized "local laws," "usages," and "customs" as evidenced by "informal writings," "parole agreements," and "possession alone, for long time" and even common/collective as well as private ownership of property in land all on behalf of the Spanish and white settlers but not for the Native Americans. The Court's lengthy exposition of how title was acquired informally through the "laws, customs and usages of Spain in relation to the grants to the grants, transfers and tenure of village property"[41] eerily parallels non-European settlement patterns, including those of the Native Americans.[42] These processes were informal insofar as they differed from formal grants conferred by written authority of the Crown or the Crown's representatives. Parole evidence to prove occupation and cultivation consistent with local laws, customs, and usages was permissible for the white settlers but not for the Native Americans who similarly occupied and cultivated their land in accordance with their customs, usages, and practices. Notwithstanding Native American occupation of land that was analogous to settler practice, the Court found that lands not so occupied or cultivated by the settlers in Louisiana were parts of the King's dominions. The Court reinforced this difference by noting that local authorities should treat Native Americans with "mildness, gentleness and moderation, with verbal, and not judicial, proceeding."[43] Thus, evidence of use, occupation, and cultivation by Europeans that was presented in *Strother* was given the status of a private property right and granted the saving benediction of the customary international law rule that preserves property rights on conquest or cession. Yet similar evidence could not yield a similar outcome for Native Americans.

This was not dissimilar in British colonial Africa. In 1926, the Privy Council held in the *Tijani* case that

> the title of the native community generally takes the form of a usufructuary right, a mere qualification of a burden on the radical or final title of whoever is sovereign.... Such a usufructuary right ... may be extinguished by the action of a paramount power which assumes possession or the entire control of the land.[44]

The Privy Council, like the Supreme Court in *Johnson v M'Intosh*, held that since the Crown had radical title to territory, its acquisition of lands held under the rights, laws, and customs of natives could not "legally interfere" or invalidate an exercise of the Crown's sovereign powers.[45]

Neither Native American nor African land use and occupation constituted property rights under the Western system. British courts shared the view with American courts that international law and treaties between conquering colonial powers did not recognize non-European occupation and use of land as establishing rights over territory and that, if such rights existed, they were extinguished by the superior title of the conquering sovereign. In both *West Rand Central Gold Mining Co.* and *Strother*, it is clear that with regard to both the private property interests of a corporation and the occupation, use, and property of a non-European community over land, the Crown's authority on conquest or cession more often than not overrides the customary international law rule's saving benediction of these property interests from extinction. This absolute power to acquire title to territory and to abrogate preexisting rights is an extreme authority associated with colonial acquisition of territory. It is based on the racist premise that non-European land was *terra nullius*, or open land, belonging to no one. Under this premise, use and occupation of territory by non-Europeans was insufficient to establish title over the territory. That only a Western state was capable of owning territory was the accepted view in nineteenth-century international law, which in turn served to justify the abrogation of the rights of non-European peoples to their land.

The uneven and inconsistent application of customary international law norms forbidding the confiscation of private property resulted in the conquest and dispossession of non-European peoples. This was integral to the establishment, protection, and expansion of a particular world order in which distinctions between European and non-European peoples determined the nonrecognition of the private property rights of non-European peoples and that forms the precursor to today's imperial world order, which is legitimized largely in humanitarian terms.

PRIVATIZING IRAQ

I have demonstrated thus far that the classical international law rule forbidding extinction of private property rights has been applied unevenly and inconsistently in the history of international law. In this section, I show that the conquest of Iraq is exhibiting a parallel process of privileging and protecting foreign economic interests while underprotecting the property rights of Iraqis under the U.S.-led war and occupation of Iraq.

While generally conquest does not vitiate preexisting private property and contract rights, under military occupation these rights enjoy a much lower threshold of protection under international law.[46] Although the occupying power is required to respect private property, interferences with it are permissible where they accord with the following rules. Existing rules of "assessment and incidence" enable the occupant to collect taxes and tolls, the proceeds of which must be used to defray the costs of administering the territory. No general punitive pecuniary penalties can be imposed on the population on account of acts involving specific individuals not imputing the general population. All contributions must be made under written order and are effective only when they are "as far as possible in accordance with rules of assessment and incidence of the taxes in force." Requisitions, where so demanded from individuals for the needs of the army of occupation, shall, as far as is possible, be paid in cash. Only assets belonging to the state may be taken into possession. Where the assets and resources of individuals are seized, they must be returned and "compensation fixed when peace is made." The property of municipalities, religious institutions, charities, educational institutions, and the arts and sciences are to be treated as private property whose seizure, destruction, or willful damage is forbidden.[47]

Under the Hague Regulations, an occupying power is an administrator or usufructuary. Article 55 reiterates the obligation of an occupying state to safeguard the capital of public properties and "to administer them in accordance with the rules of usufruct."[48] An occupant does not own public property in occupied territory and cannot, therefore, "sell or otherwise transfer ownership of the property to third parties."[49] Consequently, the occupier is authorized only to "take possession" of movable assets including cash, funds, realizable securities, depots of arms, and so on, but only where necessary for use in military operations. Seizure of private property for use in military operations "must be restored and compensation fixed when peace is made."[50] It follows that article 53 of the Hague Regulations does not authorize taking possession of objects that cannot be used for military purposes.[51]

The right of an occupying power to administer occupied territory under article 43 must be justified by its duty to restore and ensure public order, and it must respect the laws of the occupied territory unless "absolutely prevented." As such, large-scale social and economic transformations of a conquered territory, unless justified by considerations of public safety, are outside the purview of article 43. In some contexts, massive societal transformations by an occupant fall within the *debellatio* doctrine, which presumes the complete dissolution of the occupied state. Proceeding from analogous reasoning, the allied powers of the post–World War II period justified their occupation of the Axis states on the basis of "New Order in Europe."[52] Such expansive powers on the part of conquest and occupier states suggest an agenda of imposing their social, economic, and political systems and values on less powerful conquered and occupied states.

The U.S.-led conquest and occupation of Iraq has failed to observe the previously mentioned rules of international law both with regard to the destruction of property belonging to individual Iraqi citizens and with regard to the transformation of Iraqi society and economy undertaken under the authority of the occupying power. The Anglo-American invasion of Iraq was premised primarily on finding weapons of mass destruction to preempt their use in future terrorist attacks. Ad hoc reasons justifying going to war with Iraq without Security Council authorization ranged from enforcement of Security Council resolutions going back a decade to ending mass murder and torture. Since the late 1990s, it has been a policy of the United States to assist in regime change by replacing Saddam Hussein.[53] Lurking behind these justifications and the inability of the United States and the United Kingdom to build a coalition authorized by the Security Council was the question of Iraqi oil. Arguably, then, dispossession was at the heart of the war.

During the war, thousands of Iraqis had their private property, including agricultural land, destroyed; thousands more deserted their property in the wake of war.[54] Some of the buildings were occupied by the advancing forces to secure supply lines and to restore law and order. The looting of the period immediately following the fall of the Saddam regime in early 2003 resulted in further loss of private and public property and significant cultural artifacts.[55] The insecurity resulting from the looting and the insurgency against the occupation has developed into a low-intensity violence that continues to disproportionately affect Iraqis both in terms of human loss and suffering and in terms of further destruction of their private property. Further casualties and loss of property have resulted from U.S. cluster munitions, "accidental" bombings, and other related military activities that evidence the "inescapable brutality of modern warfare."[56] These include claims relating to property damage arising from the movement of occupying-power tanks and military vehicles, including injury or death to Iraqi livestock, bicycles, and so on.[57] In Iraq as elsewhere, women are affected differently and, arguably, more adversely by conquest and war than men.[58]

Having toppled Saddam's regime, the question arose whether the U.S.-led coalition would follow the laws governing occupants of a territory on conquest or turn the country over to the United Nations to oversee the transition toward a new government. The coalition opted to be governed by the law of occupation. However, without a role for the United Nations, there was no institutional context that would hold the coalition accountable under the law of occupation. In addition, the coalition needed the legitimacy it had failed to get by going to war without Security Council authorization. By the vaguely worded Resolution 1483 of May 2003, the Security Council gave the coalition authority the imprimatur of legitimacy to administer Iraq.[59] Though the preamble called on the occupying powers to comply with the Fourth Geneva Convention and the Hague Regulations of 1907, it did not expressly decide that the scope of the power of the occupying Coalitional Provisional Authority (CPA) would be determined by either of these sets of international obligations. Nor did the Security Council establish an accountability mechanism.

The U.S.-led occupation of Iraq was governed not only by the Hague Regulations but also by rules of international humanitarian law that form part of customary international law. The U.S. State Department has referred to the Hague Regulations of 1907 regulating private property as codifying existing international law.[60] American federal courts have also recognized the application of the Hague Regulations. The U.S. Uniform Code of Military Justice also recognizes these rules, and there is persuasive authority that multilateral conventions apply to belligerent occupation.[61]

Nevertheless, the vagueness of Resolution 1483 and lack of an accountability mechanism enabled the occupying states to justify expansive powers under the ostensible cover of maintaining international peace and security.[62] During the occupation period, the U.S.-led coalition exploited the formal ambiguity of the governing law to initiate far-reaching economic and other reforms in Iraq. Such an outcome would have been far less likely or possible if Iraq had been administered by a UN-led transitional authority with a clearly planned mandate meeting the needs of Iraq and Iraqis, as some commentators at the time argued should be the case.[63]

The U.S.-appointed civilian governor of Iraq after the 2003 conquest, Paul Bremmer, single-handedly issued a series of wide-ranging orders authorizing, among other things, foreign investors to own up to 100 percent interests in Iraqi companies (without profit repatriation conditions) in virtually all sectors of the economy[64] while leaving the oil industry in the hands of a professional management team who would be independent from political control,[65] the appointment of a former Shell Oil Company chief executive officer to be chair of an advisory committee to oversee the rehabilitation of Iraq's oil industry,[66] a flat tax,[67] a U.S.–Middle East free trade area,[68] the privatization of the police force,[69] formation of a stock market with electronic trading, and the establishment of modern income tax, banking, and commercial law systems under the direction of U.S. contractors.[70]

The CPA was dissolved after the appointment of the interim Iraqi government in June 2004 by UN Special Envoy Lakhdar Brahimi under authority of a UN Security Council resolution.[71] The transitional administrative law of Iraq carried forward all the CPA's economic reforms.[72] Indeed, the task of this interim government was not to develop a new policy framework for Iraq but rather to draft a new constitution. In January 2005, a transitional National Assembly was elected, and in May 2005, an Iraqi transitional government assumed authority.[73] Its Council of Ministers has confirmed its intention to continue the market reforms of the CPA.

The basis of the CPA's economic reforms as carried forward by the current transitional government is embodied in the plan "Moving the Iraqi Economy from Recovery to Sustainable Growth," drafted in part by U.S. Treasury Department officials. This plan is widely regarded as a blueprint for reorganizing the Iraqi economy according to free market principles.[74] Two primary premises of the privatization program underpinning this strategy are that Western-based firms are capable of making Iraq assets and resources more productive and that private ownership at a time when there is no stable government in the country is preferable to public ownership of assets.[75] It is furthermore held that a future Iraqi government organized on the model of free market democracy would be unlikely to become as dictatorial and inclined to developing weapons of mass destruction as Saddam Hussein's regime.

These expansive powers to transform Iraq into a free market economy were justified as falling within the scope of the CPA's mandate of promoting "the welfare of the Iraqi people through the effective administration of the territory" and "economic reconstruction and the conditions for sustainable development."[76] The Security Council resolution is at best a controversial source of such expansive authority.[77] It is scarcely debatable that the powers the CPA exercised in signing privatization contracts lack legitimacy among a broad range of Iraqis and may be subject to reversal by a postoccupation, postelection Iraqi regime exercising its internationally recognized sovereignty over its natural and other resources.[78] Justifying a broad mandate on the premise that it is consistent with the welfare of the Iraqi people is clearly reminiscent of the "sacred trust of civilization" under which European countries justified their mission of colonial rule and administration.[79]

These expansive powers to radically transform the Iraqi economy and society are also questionable under article 43 of the Hague Regulations. As Nisuke Ando has argued, such major transformations without the consent of the occupied people are inconsistent with the temporary nature of occupation governance and the principle of self-determination under international law.[80] An occupier engaged in regulating and transforming social and economic values and institutions, beyond restoring and ensuring order as envisaged under article 43, is invariably an interested party and cannot claim to be in the position of a neutral trustee.[81] The fact that the authority for making these reforms now rests with a supposedly sovereign Iraqi transitional government does not remove the stain of their origin in the crucible of occupation.

COMPARING AND CONTRASTING DE-FASCISTIZATION, DE-BAATHIFICATION, DE-NAZIFICATION, AND THE LIQUIDATION OF JAPANESE ZAIBATSU

The uneven and irregular application of law regarding property rights of non-Europeans under occupation is clearly revealed by considering the case of Iraq alongside other major instances of occupation and reconstruction: Germany, Italy and Japan.

The de-Fascistization program of the Allied forces in Italy involved the impounding of the private property and assets of Fascist organizations and their affiliates that had been disbanded. The illicitly acquired property of individual members and sympathizers of these organizations was confiscated, and they were ejected from government jobs; they were, however, allowed to maintain their pension rights. Moreover, since a majority of government jobs were held by members of the Fascist Party, the Allied powers did not eject all of them to allow the continuity of Italian civil administration. After the occupation, Italian courts that were invited to test the validity of occupation measures found them consistent with the Hague Regulations.[82] In Germany, the Allied occupation was justified as necessary to ensure the elimination of Nazism and militarism, engage in disarmament, recover reparations, control industry and all aspects of the economy, reform education, and ensure the democratic reconstruction of Germany through political decentralization.[83] The U.S. occupation of Japan was motivated by similar objectives of demilitarization and democratization through measures aimed at purging militarists and ultranationalists as well as liquidating big business combines (Zaibatsu) and the private property of individuals involved in these businesses.[84]

The similarity of the foregoing occupation measures in Italy, Germany, and Japan on the one hand and in Iraq on the other is that they all sought to fundamentally change the very foundations and values of the political, economic, and social institutions in these countries as they existed before occupation. However, in Japan, unlike in Italy and Germany, the U.S. occupation measures—such as the transfer to the Japanese government of the private property of individual members of the liquidated Zaibatsu combines, the restriction of economic transactions on the part of some of these individuals, denials of pensions, and expropriation of their farmland—were arguably inconsistent with the Hague Regulations.[85]

The de-Baathification of Iraq was one of the most important objectives of the U.S.-led occupation and was continued by the interim and transitional Iraqi government. The proposed constitution binds future permanent Iraqi governments to continue this process of de-Baathification.[86] It has involved the dissolution of not just the Baath Party but a whole continuum of entities affiliated with Saddam Hussein, including defense, security, information, and intelligence organs of government and the entire structure of the Iraqi military, including paramilitary units. All the property and assets of the Baath Party are under order to be seized and transferred to the CPA "for the benefit of the people of Iraq." Individuals in possession or control of Baath Party property are required to turn it in to the Coalition. An Iraqi Property Claims Commission is authorized to return seized private property. The Iraqi De-Baathification Council (now renamed Committee) is charged with the location of Baathist officials and the assets of the party and its officials with a view to eliminating the party and its potential to intimidate the population.

The de-Baathification of Iraqi institutions, such as the judiciary, proceeds apace with their Americanization.[87] As Tony Blair stated in his address to Congress,

> Ours are not Western values, they are the universal values of the human spirit.... Anywhere, anytime ordinary people are given the chance to choose, the choice is the same: freedom not tyranny; democracy, not dictatorship; the rule of law, not the rule of the secret police. The spread of freedom is the best security for the free.... And just as the terrorist seeks to divide humanity in hate, so we have to unify it around an idea. And that idea is liberty. We must find strength to fight for this idea and the compassion to make it universal.[88]

For Blair, a particular set of neoliberal values are universal, and so it follows that the de-Baathification and reconstruction of Iraq is no less neutral than those universal values. Yet, while repressive regimes that violate people's rights must be held accountable, military action that legitimizes wholesale reorganization of a militarily weaker society also necessarily involves the imposition of the will of the conquering state(s).[89] Otherwise well-intended processes such as de-Baathification have threatened or resulted in the loss of employment and income for thousands of Iraqi professionals in the health and education sectors for simply being ordinary members of the Baath Party.[90] The dissolution of the Iraqi army added to the unemployment and disillusionment of thousands of Iraqis. Such outcomes, which have had a negative and cascading effect on the families and dependents of those who have lost their incomes, originate in the unilateral and undemocratic nature of the unaccountable authority of the CPA.

Hence, like in Japan, the process of re-creating the occupied country has adversely affected the private property rights of these non-Western nationals to a far greater degree than similarly situated individuals in the Western states of Italy and Germany. It is argued here that, in light of the unevenness and inconsistency of applying norms of international law demonstrated earlier in this chapter, such an outcome is neither coincidental nor random.

CONCLUSION

Throughout this chapter, I have shown that rules of international law governing what happens on conquest favor the interests of powerful Western states at the expense of conquered states, especially where the conquered states are non-Western. I have also shown that the rules of occupation with regard to private property protect peoples of non-Western states less than they protect the property of Western owners similarly situated and affected by conquest and occupation.

This vulnerability is enhanced with regard to states such as Iraq and Afghanistan, in part because the image of a terrorist as a bearded Muslim in a turban has become ensconced in Occidental culture, above all in the United States. This enduring orientalist image of the Islamic "radical Other" existed long before September 11, 2001, as Pasha argues in chapter 3 in this volume. This popular image has been effectively mobilized to lend credence to loosening both the civil liberties protections and the private property rights for Arabs and Persians of the Muslim faith.

The peculiar nature of the international law applied toward non-European peoples is a reflection of a unique form of Western, American, or European power rather than a direct translation of international law as such. The importance of the rule of law in international relations, especially with regard to relations between powerful hegemonic states on the one hand and weaker vulnerable states on the other, cannot be overstated. Indeed, the official discourse of American exceptionalism and unilateralism is not new in the context of relations between conquering and conquered states, as we have seen throughout this chapter, nor is the sanctification of the economic interests of American and Western investors in the so-called developing countries. These discourses and practices must be exposed, as I hope I have done here, and resisted, challenged, and protested. Otherwise, such discourses will prevail and consolidate, being evoked and reenacted in successive waves, awaiting moments like the unfortunate terrorist attacks of September 11, 2001, for reinforcement and reiteration. By resisting, challenging, and protesting hegemonic goals of powerful countries, institutions, and corporations, we also serve to delegitimize the American and European self-images of privilege and rule over non-European peoples.

This chapter has revealed systematic differences in the historical application of both the rule against extinction of private property and contract rights and the status of private property rights under occupation as between Europeans and non-Europeans. These findings may be mistakenly traced to a theory of cultural politics that suggests that non-Europeans do not recognize private property rights, private property being an inherent and unique feature of European or Western society. Such a view is mistaken to the extent to which it does not recognize that the disregard of non-Western property rights of whatever form, private or otherwise, is born out of the crucible of the encounter between a self-righteous Western cultural project and non-Western civilizations often designated as backward, barbaric, poor, smelly, and lazy.

Further, the massive privatization of publicly owned Iraqi assets initiated by the U.S.-led occupation CPA and carried forward by the Iraqi interim and transitional governments is questionable under norms of international law recognizing the Iraqis' sovereignty over their resources. Placing the massive resources of the Iraqis in the hands of foreign firms without giving Iraqis an opportunity to participate in their ownership and management raises questions about the legitimacy of the process. The sustainability of decisions taken by the occupying government is doubtful under any future Iraqi government that is truly independent.

Part of the challenge confronting the Iraqi people at the moment is a larger question of seeking the best arrangements at the national level that would simultaneously recognize the human rights of all individuals regardless of their background while at the same time respecting their diverse cultures and religions, particularly those of minorities and women. The current constitutional proposal of radically decentralizing power may not, however, achieve this objective. At the international level, the challenge is not different. It must be recognized that projects of imperial conquest facilitated by orientalist images of Arabs and Persians as terrorists do not serve the goals of global security but actually work against global security. The human rights of all non-Western people vulnerable to conquest must be upheld. By upholding these rights, the peoples of the vulnerable states of the world would not have to live in the fear that powerful countries will run over them and appropriate or confiscate their private property while privatizing their public assets. In Iraq, this is happening at a time when Iraqis can least afford to lose their public and private assets to the powerful and organized business interests swarming over their country as if it were fallen prey. The deposition of dictators like Saddam Hussein should make a great nation and people not *less* but *more* able to control their destiny.

NOTES

1. See *Clark v Allen*, 331 US 503, 513–14 (1947), and *Techt v Hughes*, 128 NE 185 (NY 1920), *cert. denied*, 254 US 643 (1920).

2. See *Guzman v Tippy*, 130 F3d 64, 66 (2d Cir 1997), holding that executive decisions prevail over international law, and *Hamdi v. Rumsfeld*, 316 F3d 450, 463–64 (4th Cir 2003), explaining that courts are bound to defer to executive branch decisions during wartime since the executive branch, rather than the courts, is best equipped to make such decisions.

3. See Hague Convention (IV) Respecting the Laws and Customs of War on Land and its annex Regulation concerning the Laws and Customs of War on Land, October 18, 1907, art. 23, 36 Stat. 2277, T.S. 539; referred to hereinafter as Hague Regulations.

4. *United States v Percheman*, 32 US (7 Pet.) 51, 86.

5. *United States v Percheman*, 86–87.

6. *Ware v Hylton*, 3 US (3 Dall.) 199 (1796).

7. Otto C. Sommerich, "A Brief against Confiscation," *Law and Contemporary Problems* 11 (1845): 156.

8. Coleman Phillipson, *The Effect of War on Contracts and on Trading Associations in Territories of the Belligerent* (London: Stevens & Haynes, 1909), 29.

9. According to Edmund H. Schwnek, "Legislative Power of the Military Occupant under Article 43, Hague Regulations," *Yale Law Journal* 54 (1945): 393, 403, the Hague Convention was developed at a time when war was "waged against sovereign and armies and not against subjects and civilians."

10. Phillipson, *The Effect of War*, 34–35.

11. See *Treaty of Amity, Commerce, and Navigation*, November 19, 1794, US-GB, 8 Stat. 116 (1794), <http://www.yale.edu/lawweb/avalon/diplomacy/brit/jay.htm> (accessed 28 March 2004), at art. 10.

12. Phillipson, *The Effect of War*, 45.

13. Phillipson, *The Effect of War*, 49.

14. For the United Kingdom, see F. A. Mann, "Enemy Property and the Paris Peace Treaties," *Law Quarterly Review* 64 (1948): 492, 499. For the United States, see *Trading with the Enemy Act*, Public Law 65-91, 65th Cong., 1st sess., 6 October 1917, chapters 105, 106, which forbids trade with enemies during times of war.

15. John Bassett Moore, *International Law and Some Current Illusions and Other Essays* (London: Macmillan, 1924), 5.

16. Moore, *International Law*, 13–14.

17. See Davis P. Goodman, "The Need for Fundamental Change in the Law of Belligerent Occupation," *Stanford Law Review* 37 (1985): 1573–608; and David J. Scheffer, "Beyond Occupation Law," *American Journal of International Law* 97, no. 4 (2003): 842–60.

18. Stewart Jay, "The Status of the Law of Nations in Early American Law," *Vanderbilt Law Review* 42 (1989): 845.

19. Jules Lobel, "The Limits of Constitutional Power: Conflicts between Foreign Policy and International Law," *Virginia Law Review* 71 (1985): 1104.

20. See Nico Krisch, "Weak as Constraint, Strong as Tool: The Place of International Law in US Foreign Policy," in *Unilateralism and US Foreign Policy: International Perspectives*, ed. David M. Malone and Yuen Foong Khong (Boulder, Colo.: Lynne Rienner, 2003).

21. "The United States possesses unprecedented—and unequalled—strength and influence in the world" (U.S. Government, *The National Security Strategy of the United States of America* [Washington, D.C.: The White House, 2002], <http://www.whitehouse.gov/nsc/nss.pdf> ([accessed 13 October 2005], 1). The strategy makes it the responsibility of the United States to make the world safe and better. It declares the doctrine of preemption:

Defending the United States, the American people, and our interests at home and abroad by identifying and destroying the threat before it reaches our borders . . . [and] if necessary, to exercise our right of self-defense by acting preemptively against such terrorists, to prevent them from doing harm against our people and our country. (6)

22. See Curtis A. Bradley, "The Charming Betsy Canon and Separation of Powers: Rethinking the Interpretive Role of International Law," *Georgetown Law Journal* 86 (1998): 479–537.

23. See Thomas W. Smith, "The New Law of War: Legitimizing Hi-Tech and Infrastructural Violence," *International Studies Quarterly* 46, no. 3 (2002): 355–74.

24. See Roger Normand and Chris af Jochnick, "The Legitimation of Violence: A Critical Analysis of the Gulf War," *Harvard International Law Journal* 35 (1994): 387–416.

25. For a description of the Powell doctrine, see Stan Crock, Paul Magnusson, Lee Walczak, and Frederik Balfour, "The Doctrine of Digital War," *Business Week* April 7, 2003, <http://www.businessweek.com/magazine/content/03_14/b3827601.htm> (accessed 13 October 2005).

26. Smith, "The New Law of War," 367–70.

27. Upendra Baxi, "'The War on Terror' and the 'War of Terror': Nomadic Multitudes, Aggressive Incumbents, and the 'New' International Law," *Osgoode Hall Law Journal* 43, no. 1/2 (2005): 7–43.

28. See Edward Channing, *The Jeffersonian System, 1801–1811* (New York: Cooper Square, 1968).

29. See Security Council Resolution 1483, UNSCOR, 4761st meeting, UN Doc. S/RES/1483 (2003) [hereinafter SC Res. 1483]. By this resolution, the Security Council appears to have effectively legitimated the Iraq War that it had previously declined to authorize.

30. U.S. Government, *National Security Strategy*, 5.

31. See Security Council Resolution 1373, UNSCOR, 4385th meeting, UN Doc. S/RES/1373 (2001).

32. James Thuo Gathii, "Assessing Claims of a New Doctrine of Pre-Emptive War under the Doctrine of Sources," *Osgoode Hall Law Journal* 43, no. 1/2 (2005): 67–103.

33. José E. Alvarez, "Hegemonic International Law Revisited," *American Journal of International Law* 97 (2003): 873–88.

34. Mann, "Enemy Property and the Paris Peace Treaties," 503.

35. *W. Rand Cent. Gold Mining Co. Ltd. v The King*, 2 KB 391, 391 (1905).

36. *W. Rand Cent.*, at 410–11 (emphasis added).

37. *Strother v Lucas*, 37 US 410 (1838).

38. See *Strother*, 438.

39. *Johnson v M'Intosh*, 21 US 543, 574 (1823).

40. *Johnson*, 543, 590 (emphasis added).

41. *Strother*, 300–301, 304–5, 306–14, 432, 435, 449, 458.

42. See Carlos Scott López, "Reformulating Native Title in Mabo's Wake: Aboriginal Sovereignty and Reconciliation in Post-Centenary Australia," *Tulsa Journal of Comparative and International Law* 11 (2003): 21–110.

43. *Strother*, 439–40.

44. *Sobhuza II v Miller*, App. Cas. 518, 525 (1926).

45. *Sobhuza*, 528.

46. See Hague Regulations, art. 42.

47. Hague Regulations, arts. 46, 48, 49, 50, 51, 52, 53, 54, 56.

48. Hague Regulations, supra note 5, at art. 55.

49. Eyal Benvenisti and Eyal Zamir, "Private Claims to Property Rights in the Future Israeli-Palestinian Settlement," *American Journal of International Law* 89 (1995): 295–340.

50. Hague Regulations, art. 53.

51. Ernst H. Feilchenfeld, *The International Economic Law of Belligerent Occupation* (Washington, D.C.: Carnegie Endowment for International Peace, 1942), 52.

52. See Benvenisti and Zamir, "Private Claims," 57–58, 64–65, 92–96.

53. See section 7 of the Iraqi Liberation Act of 1998, <http://www.fcnl.org/issues/int/sup/iraq_liberation.htm> (accessed 14 October 2005).

54. Brian MacQuarrie, "For Iraqis, a Struggle to Recoup Loss," *Boston Globe*, August 6, 2003, A1; Agence France-Press, "US Forces Demolish Iraq Homes," March 3, 2003, <http://www.news.com.au/common/story_page/0,4057,7942137%5E1702,00.html> (accessed 4 March 2004), reporting that the U.S. military was destroying Iraqi homes as punishment for the insurgency during the occupation period; United Nations, "Humanitarian Appeal for Iraq: Revised Inter-Agency Appeal 1 April–31 December," 2003, <http://www.reliefweb.int/appeals/2003/files/irq03flash2.pdf> (accessed 29 March 2004).

55. See John Daniszewski and Geoffrey Mohan, "Looters Bring Baghdad New Havoc," *Los Angeles Times*, April 11, 2003, A1. Article 56 of the Hague Regulations provides that the property of municipalities and institutions dedicated to education, the arts, and sciences shall be treated as private property and forbids the seizure, destruction, and willful damage of the foregoing properties, historic monuments, works of art, and science. Article 47 prohibits pillage. The pilfering by looters, including U.S. soldiers, of Iraq's rich cultural artifacts in its Baghdad museums clearly violated the foregoing provisions of the Hague Regulations (Hague Regulations, arts. 56, 47). See SC Res. 1483 addressing this problem.

56. Nehal Bhuta, "A Global State of Exception? The United States and World Order," *Constellations: An International Journal of Critical and Democratic Theory* 10, no. 3 (2003): 371–91.

57. See Vanessa Blum, "After the War, a Time to Pay: How JAG Lawyers Settle Foreign Claims over Non-Combat Damage," *Legal Times*, April 21, 2003, 1.

58. Judith G. Gardam and Michelle J. Jarvis, *Women, Armed Conflict and International Law* (The Hague: Kluwer Law International, 2001), 19–51.

59. See SC Res. 1483, calling on the "Authority, consistent with the Charter of the United Nations and *other relevant international law*, to promote the welfare of the Iraqi people through the effective administration of the territory" (emphasis added).

60. U.S. State Department Memorandum of Law on Israel's Right to Develop New Oil Fields in Sinai and the Gulf of Suez, October 1, 1976, *International Legal Materials* 16, no. 733 (1977): 750–53.

61. See Theodor Meron, "Applicability of Multilateral Conventions to Occupied Territories," *American Journal of International Law* 72, no. 3 (1978): 542–57.

62. Alvarez, "Hegemonic International Law Revisited," 882–83.

63. Scheffer, "Beyond Occupation Law," 859.

64. Coalitional Provisional Authority Order No. 39: Foreign Investment, Sept. 19, 2003. <http://www.cpa-iraq.org/regulations/> (accessed 20 February 2004).

65. Chip Cummins, "State-Run Oil Company Is Being Weighed for Iraq," *Wall Street Journal*, January 7, 2004, A1.

66. See Neela Banerjee, "A Retired Shell Executive Seen as Likely Head of Production," *New York Times*, April 2, 2003, B12.

67. Coalitional Provisional Authority Order No. 37: Tax Strategy for 2003, September 19, 2003, <http://www.cpa-iraq.org/regulations/> (accessed 20 February 2004).

68. Jess Bravin and Chip Cummins, "US Offers Concessions to U.N. in Bid to Lift Sanctions on Iraq," *Wall Street Journal*, May 9, 2003, A1.

69. Andrew Higgins, "Contract Cops: As It Wields Power Abroad, US Outsources Law and Order Work," *Wall Street Journal*, February 2, 2004, A1.

70. Neil King Jr., "Bush Officials Draft Broad Plan for Free-Market Economy in Iraq," *Wall Street Journal*, May 1, 2003, A1; Bob Sherwood, "Legal Reconstruction: Investors Want Reassurance over Iraq's Framework of Commercial Law," *Financial Times*, November 3, 2003, 14.

71. Security Council Resolution 1546, UNSCOR, 4987th meeting, UN Doc. S/RES/1546 (2004).

72. The orders and decisions of the CPA were carried forward under article 26(c) of the Transitional Administrative Law of Iraq (2004).

73. The transnational National Assembly was charged with the responsibility of drafting a new Iraqi constitution, which it completed and approved on August 28, 2005. The Constitution was presented for approval in a referendum on October 15, 2005. Article 25 of the Constitution essentially ratifies the economic reforms of the CPA by providing that "The state shall guarantee the reforming of the Iraqi economy according to modern economic bases, in a way that ensures complete investment of its resources, diversifying its sources and encouraging and developing the private sector." Article 26 on its part provides that "The country shall guarantee the encouragement of investments in the different sectors." Finally Article 110 of the Constitution provides that "The federal government and the governments of the producing regions and provinces together will draw up the necessary strategic policies to develop oil and gas wealth...relying on the most modern techniques of market principles and encouraging investment."

74. King, "Bush Officials Draft Broad Plan."

75. For similar views, see Allan Gerson, "Peace Building: The Private Sector's Role," *American Journal of International Law* 95, no. 1 (2001): 102–19.

76. SC Res. 1483, paras. 4, 8(e).

77. In March 2003, the top legal adviser to U.K. Prime Minister Tony Blair wrote a subsequently leaked memo warning that "the imposition of major structural economic reforms might violate international law, unless the Security Council specifically authorized it" (Dephne Eviatar, "Free-Market Iraq? Not So Fast," *New York Times*, January 10, 2004, 9). See Brett H. McGurk, "Revisiting the Law of Nation-Building: Iraq in Transition," *Virginia Journal of International Law* 45 (2005): 451–64, who argues that the CPA did everything the international law of occupation appeared to prohibit.

78. General Assembly Resolution 1803, UNGAOR, 17th sess., 1194th plenary meeting Supp. No. 17, 15. UN Doc. A/5217, (1962). Article 1 provides, "The right of peoples and nations to permanent sovereignty over their natural wealth and resources must be exercised in the interest of their national development and of the well-being of the people of the State concerned." Article 7 thereof provides, "Violation of the rights of peoples and nations to sovereignty over their natural wealth and resources is contrary to the spirit and principles of the Charter of the United Nations and hinders the development of international cooperation and the maintenance of peace." The Preamble of SC Res. 1483, in addition, provides for "the right of the Iraqi people freely to determine their own political future and control their own natural resources." Note that Resolution 1511, adopted on October 16, 2003, underscored "that the sovereignty of Iraq resides in the State of Iraq" and reaffirmed "the right of the Iraqi people freely to determine their own political future and control their natural resources" (Security Council Resolution 1511, UNSCOR, 4844th meeting, UN Doc. S/Res/1511[2003], at second preambular paragraph).

79. See James Thuo Gathii, "Geographical Hegelianism in Territorial Disputes Involving Non-European Land Relations: An Analysis of the Case concerning Kasikili/Sedudu Island (Botswana/Namibia)," *Leiden Journal of International Law* 15, no. 3 (2002): 614–15.

80. Nisuke Ando, *Surrender, Occupation, and Private Property in International Law: An Evaluation of US Practice in Japan* (Oxford: Clarendon Press, 1991), 125.

81. Benvenisti and Zamir, "Private Claims," 210.

82. Ando, *Surrender*, 53, 69–71.

83. Ando, *Surrender*, 59, 73.

84. Ando, *Surrender*, 105.

85. Ando, *Surrender*, 106, 112–14.

86. This discussion draws on Coalition Provisional Authority Orders and Memoranda, <http://www.cpa-iraq.org/regulations/> (accessed 29 March 2004).

87. Jim Edwards, "Rebuilding Iraq's Judicial System from the Ground Up," *New Jersey Law Journal*, October 27, 2003, <http://www.law.com/jsp/article.jsp?id=1066605424932> (accessed 15 August 2005), reports that a judicial assessment team sent to Iraq by the Justice Department recommended detailed judicial reforms in Iraq along the lines of the U.S. legal system, including extension of Miranda-style rights, attorney compensation, case management, and so on.

88. Prime Minister Tony Blair, Address to a Joint Meeting of Congress (July 17, 2003), *Congressional Record* H7059 (2003), 149.

89. Maxine Marcus, "Humanitarian Intervention without Borders: Belligerent Occupation or Colonization," *Houston Journal of International Law* 25 (2003): 102, 133–34.

90. Jonathan Steele, "US Decree Strips Thousands of Their Jobs," *The Guardian*, August 30, 2003, 16.

Part III

Toward Decolonized Knowledge of the World and the International

Chapter Seven

Beyond the Imperial Narrative: African Political Historiography Revisited

Alison J. Ayers

The inadequacy of historiography . . . is nothing other than a measure of the dominance exercised by a mode of colonialist knowledge.

——Ranajit Guha[1]

Fundamental to the project of Western imperial domination has been the appropriation of the past. Imperial historiography, epitomized by the ideology of "World-history," has done violence to indigenous history/histories, supplanting them with narratives that are typically modern and Western.[2] This chapter contributes to the intrinsically radical endeavor of recovering the past—or, as Guha argues, the expropriation of the expropriators. Through examination of subordinate history/ies, it seeks to critique the imperial historiography of Africa and contribute to the recovery of African historicality.

Arguably more so than any other "peoples without history," Africa has been excluded from History. Hegel's infamous characterization denied Africa inclusion within so-called "world-historical" peoples: "Africa proper, as far as History goes back, has remained . . . shut up," being nothing more than the "land of childhood, which, lying beyond the day of history, is enveloped in the dark mantle of Night." Hegel takes his leave of Africa: "not to mention it again [for] it is no historical part of the World; it has no movement or development to exhibit." What we properly understand by Africa, he argued, "is the Unhistorical, Undeveloped Spirit, still involved in the conditions of mere nature . . . only on the threshold of the World's History."[3] Not belonging within History, Africa could be cast from the concert of humanity, erased from "civilization."

Underpinning Hegel's philosophy of history is an illicit claim to universality. He proclaims to give us the World: "The subject of this course of Lectures is the Philosophical History of the World . . . by this must be understood Universal History."[4] This universal history ends absolutely in Europe—not only in the sense of the culmination of the historical trajectory but also as the zenith of human achievement. Europe proclaims itself to be both author and embodiment of the "universal," although its universal is so peculiar, its global is so local.[5]

While Hegel provides the foundations of this far-reaching philosophy of history, its moral and ideological antecedents can be traced from Renaissance Europe and the conquest of the "New World." As we have seen in earlier chapters, the violence and pillage that characterized European expansionism was accompanied by a comprehensive project of discrimination whereby

> Renaissance Europe learned to identify itself by the otherness of a multitude of races, religions, languages, and cultures. Names and categories were invented to enable the knowledge systems of the Old World to cope with the exigencies of the New. One such invention that was to find a place for itself fairly soon in the expanding lexicon of alterities is the concept of "people without history."[6]

The late fifteenth and sixteenth centuries witnessed therefore the birth of the mythical West through the forging of a new and totalizing ideology that placed its putative legitimacy on a new foundation and gave meaning both to expulsion and appropriation.[7] This ideology spawned a racial and racialized ontology of "whites" and "nonwhites," full persons and subpersons, that has provided the ideological architecture underpinning an entire history of European atrocity against "nonwhites"—through the Enlightenment's hostility to non-European "races" exemplified by Hume and Kant to the imperialism of our time.[8]

Current manifestations of racism may be less vulgar than that of Hegel's ignorant calumny, but they are no less insidious. The architectonic of exclusion manifest in the ideology of "world-history" continues to frame the relationship between Euro-America and Africa. As Olufemi Taiwo argues, the outlines, if not the exact content of Hegel's philosophy of History, have continued to structure the understanding of Africa in the consciousness and institutions of Hegel's descendants.[9]

Principal among these is the exclusionary and Eurocentric bias within Hegel's philosophical schema. Europe's historical experience is privileged as the expression of the Universal, and only the concepts of European social philosophy are assumed to contain within them the possibility of universalization: "This assumption implies that only by expanding and enriching these concepts can one encapsulate non-European processes as the particulars of a universal history whose theoretical subject is, and will always remain, Europe."[10] The concepts of European social philosophy assume therefore the status of touchstone or pedigree.

According to this ideological frame, the conjoining of "African democracy" invariably provokes calls to justify the attachment of the epithet "African" to the substantive "democracy." But as Taiwo has noted, such debates become mired in arguments about pedigree that cannot be won since pedigree arguments always serve an imperial purpose. The person clamoring to be convinced that such notions merit inclusion in the sanctified spaces that carry the name "democracy" (or some other equivalent)

> already presupposes that *his* characterization is unproblematic, is not particular, is universal, and therefore, supplies the metric by which all others must be measured. Even when it is unintended, especially when it is unintended, this sort of demand smacks of the bastard Universality that we have already encountered in Hegel at the beginning of his enterprise.[11]

That in the twenty-first century peoples libeled by Hegel are challenged by his progeny to show—*only on terms acceptable to them*—that Africa is part of humanity and its history is testament "to the intellectual arrogance and insufferable imperialism that have seized the ground of determining the contours of human being."[12] Refuting such delusions and vilifications only confers a gratuitous respectability to the suggestion that Africa and its people are required to justify admittance in the concert of humanity. The purpose of this chapter, however, is to engage with scholars serious about questions of democracy who, while unapprised of the history (or histories) of political community and democratic traditions in Africa, do not a priori assume their absence.

DEMOCRATIZATION AND THE GHOST OF HEGEL

The vituperations of imperial historiography reverberate far beyond the confines of the academy. Just as Hegel's writings on philosophy informed contemporary imperial practice, Africa's peculiar and continued absence from History asserts itself in the current imperial project of "democratization."[13] African notions and forms of political community and democracy have been rendered invisible and therefore negated. As Dickson Eyoh has detailed, the dominant discourse of democratization in Africa has been marked by sparse regard for "the African debate."[14] The dominant social agents of the democratization project have presumed a nonhistory of democracy within Africa, or what the pseudohistorical language of imperialism would characterize as Prehistory.[15]

According to this imperial narrative, it is widely presumed that African societies and cultures are nondemocratic. In distinct echoes of the "civilizing mission," Western neoliberal democratic values, norms, and institutions are to be inculcated through the activities of the social agents of the "democratization" project. Deputy Managing Director Alassane Ouattara of the International Monetary Fund proclaims, for example, that "most African countries are only at the start of the arduous process of developing a tradition of democracy, and establishing the institutions that safeguard it." With time, he argues, democratic institutions "will become an accepted part of the social fabric in Africa, but we are still at the stage of building them up. We must protect and nurture them."[16]

Inherent within the democratization project is the false universalism encountered in Hegel. The orthodox notion of democracy assumes universality. Thus, the government of Sweden asserts, "The rule of law, freedom of expression, political pluralism and multi-party systems are *universally valid.*" Similarly, Canadian government policy proclaims that the "fundamental principles of human rights, democracy and good governance are *universal,*" and the Development Advisory Committee of the Organization for Economic Cooperation and Development states that there are "certain *universal* standards that cannot be compromised."[17] But such claims to universality are highly problematic. The orthodox notion of democracy constitutes a Western neoliberal procedural notion of democracy that is culturally and historically specific.[18] In constructing the universal, the project illicitly elevates its peculiarity into a universality.

The "cold hands of Hegel"[19] are palpable in this exclusionary, Eurocentric bias. European historical experience is privileged, while the historical specificity and legitimacy of the African condition is rendered invisible. Moreover, as Halperin's account has demonstrated, it is a partial and highly mythologized version of Europe's history that is held up as the universal standard. The dominant social agents of the democratization project have sought to turn the historical and cultural dynamics of modern Europe, sanitized of its own flaws, into the basis of a general and prescriptive theory whereby democracy is understood as a "turnkey institutional import." Thus, African reality has meaning only insofar as it is seen to reflect a particular stage in the development of an earlier history—that of modern Europe.[20]

The principal consequence of such a methodological approach is to abstract phenomena from context and process. The result, as Mahmood Mamdani asserts, is a history by analogy rather than history as process.[21] In seeking to understand Africa through analogies, mainstream Africanists have been unable to analyze or explain the concrete historical condition of neocolonial Africa.

As Mamdani's pathbreaking analysis in *Citizen and Subject* illuminates, the failure to contend with the historical specificity of the African experience—including the nature and impact of the colonial encounter—has beleaguered attempts to realize a more substantive and meaningful democratization in the neocolonial period.

The purpose of this chapter is not to rehearse these complex and contested debates, which tend to polarize around modernist and communitarian tendencies. Rather, it seeks to counter the imperial historiography of Africa through examination of African political history and systems in the nineteenth century—in the period immediately preceding the "European Scramble"—based on empirical evidence drawn primarily from Ghana and Uganda. The chapter does not claim that these political systems were necessarily democratic, nor does it suggest that political entities of the nineteenth century were "pristine" human societies.[22] It does contend, however, that there is an African history (or histories) of political community and democracy autonomous of the orthodox Western neoliberal notion that dominates the so-called democratization project. Inquiry and understanding of African political history and systems necessitate a methodological commitment to concrete historiographical research, in contrast to the commonplace imperial practice whereby judgment is conferred on the basis of inadequate or nonexistent evidence or *prior to* an assessment of the evidence.[23]

Much analysis of African political systems is based on records derived from social memory, such as customs, rituals, religious beliefs, proverbs, myths, and oral narratives. As Jan Vansina has argued, "Imperfect as they are, no one can imagine any longer a history of Africa reconstructed without any recourse to oral traditions.... Much of what they have to say no other voice can tell."[24] But also at stake in the retrieval of social memory is the *legitimacy* of oral genres. The absence of a written history constitutes a key aspect of discrimination within imperialist historiography. Inherent to Renaissance thought was the notion "that people *without writing* were people without history and that people without history were inferior beings."[25] Through such feints, imperial historiography has privileged the written word and constructed the spurious and debilitating dichotomy of first- versus second-order narratives and history versus myth.

Several hundred years later, Hegel's reformulation introduced the state as a further defining characteristic. History, according to Hegel, is a rational process. Its ultimate subject is Spirit (*Geist*), and the essence to which it tends is Freedom.[26] To undertake this movement, Spirit becomes embodied in the state: the rational state is therefore Spirit objectified. As such, the Renaissance principle "No writing, no history" was transformed to read "No state, no history." Writing remained a necessary condition, but it was not sufficient: since writing to be historical needed the state to write about, it became incorporated in the latter. Such revision

> followed inexorably from the logic of historical developments in the West. The formative energies and expansionist drives of its new nations would henceforth be invested in the state as the locomotive of that most modern and dynamic of inventions called World-history.[27]

AFRICAN POLITICAL SYSTEMS AND DEMOCRACY IN THE NINETEENTH CENTURY

This chapter seeks to retrieve indigenous African history/ies displaced by the modern and Western narratives of imperial historiography. Three broad modes of political community in nineteenth-century Africa are identified: segmentary political systems, centralized polities formed through internal differentiation, and conquest polities. The notion of modes of production highlights strategic political-economic relationships that underlie, orient, and constrain interaction in nineteenth and early twentieth-century Africa. These modes are not "types into which human societies may be sorted nor stages in cultural evolution" but "constructs with which to envisage certain strategic relationships that shape the terms under which human lives are conducted."[28]

Segmentary Political Systems

Segmentary political systems have been variously referred to as "stateless," "acephalous," or "nonstate" orders.[29] Such terminology denotes this mode of political community in terms of what it is *not*, that is, the residual other to the analytical value accorded the "state" or the "head." As Ifi Amadiume has argued, "The ethnocentrism of European scholars has directly influenced the classification and definition of these societies, seeing them as 'lacking something,' such as rulers, states, order, a head."[30] However, these societies may possess and exhibit an *anti*centralization moral philosophy and consciousness, and as such, the terminology "segmentary political systems" is more appropriate.

Segementary systems were highly decentralized and arguably democratic forms of organization.[31] Social differentiation was minimal. Systems and practices geared toward the preservation of order and harmony were prevalent, although formal judicial and political institutions were minimal. Such political systems, it is claimed, demonstrate that so-called anarchy can lead to solidarity—social order does not always and necessarily depend on the existence of states or statesmen—in contradistinction to Hobbes and subsequent political philosophers of the liberal tradition.[32]

Although segmentary societies are commonly portrayed as bound by kinship, notions of kinship were highly contested, and considerable variation existed in terms of the extent and intensity of kinship relations and the ways in which obligations and claims were established. In those situations in which resources were widely and openly available, kinship tended to operate at the familial-domestic level, creating relations among persons—partnerships among shareholders in social labor—through marriage and filiation. Conversely, where access to resources was restricted and available only to claimants with a "kinship license," extended kinship on the jural-political level subsumed and organized kinship on the familial-domestic level.[33]

The form and extent of internal oppositions and, as such, the democratic status of segmentary kin-ordered societies remain highly contested issues. Disputes have focused particularly on gender relations, the nature of the relationship between elders and other members of the society, oppositions between original settlers and newcomers and those between lineages. There is a degree of consensus, however, that although societies organized under the rule of elders, "they contained re-distributive mechanisms that thwarted tendencies to reproduce inequalities in a cumulative fashion."[34] The prominence of leaders was checked by kinspeople and their allies, and kin ordering set upper limits to internal differentiation. This is not to argue that inequalities did not persist under conditions of closed resources but rather to recognize that kin-ordered units possessed mechanisms to contain and resolve tensions and conflicts. When cumulative conflict exceeded the capacity of kin-based mechanisms, groups would break up and fission. Significantly, the tendencies toward inequalities in function were greatly enhanced when kin-ordered groups entered into relationships with tributary or capitalist societies.[35]

In Uganda, segmentary societies include agricultural and pastoral communities in northern Uganda, such as the Karamajong, Iteso, Kuman, Langi, Kakwa, and Lubara. Iteso society is examined in detail as one of the largest and most documented of segmentary societies in Uganda. Iteso sociopolitical organization was constituted on a kinship basis, although age-set groupings were more prevalent in areas of primary settlement. In Ghana, segmentary societies include the Kokomba, the Lowiili, the LoDagaba, and the Tallensi—all located in the north of Ghana and constituted on a segmentary, kinship basis. This chapter examines the case of the Tallensi, the most studied and documented of segmentary societies in Ghana. Throughout the nineteenth century, production in both Iteso and Tallensi society was characterized by a kin-ordered mode of production, constituted in terms of "extended" kinship—kinship on the jural-political level.

The Iteso of Northern Uganda

The present-day Iteso are the descendants of a fusion of multiple ethnicities and historical migrations. The notion of a consciously identified and clearly bounded ethnic ("tribal") identity may not have become fully developed until colonial rule, when imperial administrators were preoccupied with "tribe" and intent on drawing district boundaries on a perceived ethnic basis.[36]

Examination of the sociopolitical system of the Iteso reveals a highly decentralized, largely egalitarian society in which social groups enjoyed significant autonomy concurrent with social unity forged through elaborate interrelationships based on kinship, marriage, age, and locality. The pursuit of justice and the maintenance of law, order, and harmony were highly important tenets, harmony being achieved through the overriding principle of consensus. Iteso society was governed by elders, and the nature of their relationship with other members of society is contested. But, although elders were vested with influence and widely respected, they possessed limited power—power being held and exercised by the people. Elders could not compel any member of their kinship group to accept their collective decisions. Individuals and groups were at liberty to migrate to other areas if they did not concur.

Iteso sociopolitical organization was based primarily on kinship associations, although age-set groupings were prevalent in areas of primary settlement. The basic unit of kinship was the household (*ekale*), several of which constituted a homestead (*ekek*); a number of these constituted the *ateker*. The members of these groups were bound by a common origin and observed a common taboo system, *etale*. The *ateker* constituted the principal unit of agropastoral production. Land tenure was communal, and claims to land were complex and rule bound.[37] Notions of leadership and authority were highly decentralized and nonhierarchical. Three fundamental and interrelated institutions of leadership ensured a system of checks and balances within Iteso society: the military leader, *Aruon*; the foreteller, *Emuron*; and the spokesperson and arbiter, *Ekeraban*. There was also an *Apolon ka etale*, the most senior woman in the *ateker*, responsible for the decisions that governed the taboos of the *ateker*. Fragmentation of *atekerin* was commonplace because of factors such as shortage of land in a locality or opposition between generational groups. In such cases, members could migrate elsewhere, establishing areas of primary settlement. By the nineteenth century, the social system consisted of a highly segmented network of lineage groupings (*atekerin*) that, unlike recognized clan systems, were not united under a common ancestor or totem.[38]

The *atekerin* were united (or at least in permanent cooperation) through the system of age sets. Whereas an *ateker* was composed exclusively of people of common descent, an age set comprised a cross section of people from various descent groups. Members of an age set were bound by the observance of the regulations of their ritual group (*etem* or *ewoe*). The age sets united a large number of people from different *atekerin*, contributing to the unity of the Iteso during the nineteenth century.[39]

In addition to cooperation within lineages and age sets, territorial units of cooperation existed, the *eitela* (equivalent to a parish) being the principal sociopolitical units. Within an *eitela*, integration was ensured through *ateker* and *etem* linkages, further strengthened by ties of intermarriage. There was no *eitela* head but rather government by elders.[40] Within the *eitela*, there were established legal procedures for settling disputes. Law and order was maintained on a communal basis, based on the *eisuil*, council of elders. This long-standing convention constituted a communal method of settling disputes between two or more *atekerin* within a given *eitela* or between adjacent *itela*.[41] Iteso society was therefore rule based: "the search for justice and good understanding within an *ateker* and among *atekerin*, was a very important political aspect of pre-colonial Iteso society."[42] Although the practice of reconciling disputes varied, certain principles were widespread as means to maintaining social order: first, that harmony was achieved through consensus; second, the recognition of leadership that possessed influence but little power; and, finally, the seniority of age over youth.[43]

The seniority of age over youth is evident in that one had to become an elder—*Apolon*—in order to assume the claims and privileges of an adult male. Various authors have suggested that "running parallel to the egalitarian nature of the system between homesteads and clans was an almost tyrannous respect demanded by the elders from youth."[44] However, the authority of the elders was *not* absolute: leaders of a particular *ateker* could not compel the individual members of that *ateker* to accept and conform to their decisions. If members of the *atekerin* considered the decisions of the elders unacceptable, they could move away, and it was not permissible that such migrant groups be coerced into returning or conforming.[45] Furthermore, juniors or nonelders possessed certain "claims" in the case of familial disputes.

Throughout Teso, the norm appears to have been that the *Aruok* and *Iker-abak* of individual *atekerin* were the recognized leaders within each *eitela*. No political hierarchy existed within the *eitela* inasmuch as the leaders of the various *atekerin* were considered equals, although one could be recognized as the overall leader of the *eitela*, on the understanding that he was "first among equals." The norms of Iteso political philosophy and practice dictated that the overall *Aruon* or *Emuron* could not enforce policies or decisions. Nor could leaders of a particular *ateker* compel the individual members of that *ateker* to accept and conform to their decisions. Decisions within precolonial Iteso society were the result of collective decision making, the various leaders being expected to implement the collective decision. These leaders were spokespersons, arbiters, and mediators, people of influence but little power. Power came exclusively from consensus among the people.[46]

The onus on consensus and collective decision making reflected Iteso notions of egalitarianism and leadership. As Grace Akello has elaborated, the Iteso were "highly egalitarian, democratic people" who upheld "the value of consultation and two-way communication." Elders were required to "nurture the spirit of cooperation and unity amongst the people" and could be criticized, for example, through the commonplace occurrence of singing songs condemning aberrant behavior. For example, the notion that all people are equal is expressed in the following Iteso song:[47]

Oooni Iteso ibangaaka!	We Iteso are foolish!
Ooo eyala, ooni Iteso	No joke, we Iteso
Ibangaaka	are foolish
Ooo, tooto!	We are foolish indeed!
Imoromoroi ijo eong	Why do you despise me
Eong da kolo	When even I
Ekoni kwape ajo	was born like you.
Auuruni eong totoka	When my mother gave birth to me
Auuruni eong totoo oo!	Born like you indeed!

Nor could leadership be utilized as a means to accumulate individual wealth. Instances where influence and standing were used to increase wealth were severely condemned.[48] A person could enjoy relative wealth, for example, in cattle, but this could not bring recognition as a leader: "Wealth employed to feast the people, wealth as an instrument of generous hospitality, brought respect and prestige, but not necessarily leadership."[49] Nor, as Okalany argues, could the judicial system be manipulated to favor the wealthy over the poor. If a wealthy *ateker* refused to negotiate with a poorer one it had offended, the former would find itself opposed not only by the aggrieved but also by third and fourth clans that played the role of mediators and arbitrators in the dispute.[50]

The Tallensi of Northern Ghana

The Tallensi in the nineteenth century constituted a segmentary, egalitarian society. Social stratification was minimal, and power and influence were highly devolved. The Tallensi have no clearly demarcated boundaries with their neighbors, the Gorisi, Namnam, and Kusasi. "Rather their borders merge with those of their neighbours in such a way that in the transitional zones one finds communities linked with both." Kwaku Nukunya explains that

> up to about 1910 there was no one with authority over the whole of Taleland. Demarcation of clear-cut boundaries would presuppose the existence of such an authority. Rather, the largest political authority was the clan or lineage head. Beyond him there was no one to unite even two clans.[51]

It is not surprising, therefore, to learn that the Tallensi never amassed as such for war with their neighbors—although individual clans and their allies did conflict periodically with neighboring groups.

Conflicts did occur between different Tallensi clans, particularly between Namoo and Tali clans. The latter are said to be the original occupants of the land, while the former are the descendants of migrants from the Mamprusi area to the south.[52] Relations between newcomers and original settlers constituted a potential form of internal opposition within kin-ordered societies, not least as the Tallensi were formed from a fusion of original inhabitants and newcomers headed by chiefs tributing slaves to the Asante[53]—suggesting considerable potential for internal opposition, at least in the initial constitution of a Tallensi social formation. However, relations between Namoo and Tali clans in each locality are mediated through various institutions, detailed below.

Tallensi lineage is segmentary. Within the institution of kinship, segmentation allows for considerable fluidity in relations between groups.[54] The smallest unit is the household, several of which comprise the compound; a group of compounds constitutes the inner lineage, a number of which form the maximal lineage. Two or more maximal lineages constitute a clan.[55] There are leaders at every level of the segmentary process up to the lineage head, the *kpeem*. Power and influence are therefore highly devolved, and representation of all members of the society is thus ensured.

The Tallensi subscribe to the notion of a high god or supreme being, *Nayi-wum*, said to be the creator of the world and everything in it and the source of all powers therein. The small gods, or divinities, responsible for immediate concerns of the world, are controlled by and derive their powers from the *Nayi-wum*. The Earth is also an object of worship, the Earth priest (the *tendaana*) being an important functionary within Tallensi society. It is the reverence for the ancestors, however, that is most apparent. The belief among the Tallensi is that death is not absolute. When death occurs, it is that of the physical body, while the soul joins the spirit world, from where the deceased oversee the affairs of the earthly world. As such, ancestral rites constitute an important means of social control.

The Tallensi, in common with many other segmentary societies, are characterized by an absence of formal law enforcement organs. Such societies are rule based, nevertheless, in that they possess mechanisms for settling disputes and maintaining social order. Within the lineage or clan, fear of the ancestors and the pressure of the elders tended to induce virtuous behavior and respect for political authority. The complementary roles of *na'am* and *tendaana* during great festivals also ensure order and harmony through the balance of forces. Both are expected to perform vital rites required for the prosperity of the community. *Na'am* is the *kpeem* of the principal Namoo clan in a locality and the medium through which the mystical forces of Tale religion are mobilized to ensure the well-being and fecundity of humans, animals, and crops. The *tendaaana* is the *kpeem* of the principal Tali clan in a locality and regarded as the custodian of the Earth cult, ensuring the beneficence of the Earth. Both are required for the prosperity of the community, obliging the two to remain on good terms.

Beyond the clan or lineage, there are no formal authorities to mediate disputes, but there are various institutions that mitigate and resolve conflicts and ensure social order. Although descent groups are politically autonomous in the sense that allegiance is not owed to anyone outside the descent group, cooperation and reciprocal relations exist between clans. For example, cooperation in funerals and rituals among neighboring clans does take place. The ties of kinship and affinity that exist between certain maximal lineages of adjacent clans also ensure that clans that are so linked do not engage in conflict with each other. Even those not so linked may have common allies who help arrange settlements. Matrilineal ties also reduce tensions and resolve conflicts. In the case of an offense being committed, compensation must be equal to the loss incurred. Thus, if someone kills a person from another clan, the offender's party is expected to replace the victim with a person of the same standing from his clan or have himself or a fellow clansman killed.

The Tallensi practice a patrilineal system of kinship; that is, an individual belongs to his or her father's descent group, the agnatic group. This comprises persons descended through the male line from a common ancestor. Succession and the inheritance of property are transmitted through the male line. The perceived gender inequities inherent in a patrilineal kinship system have led many to contest the democratic status of such societies. Classical anthropologist Meyer Fortes, for example, claimed that jural and ritual authority were vested in the father, and, as such, the Tallensi conception of the person was "an adult male who has reached old age and lineage" and would become worshipped as an ancestor. Women, therefore, could never attain full personhood as they remained in a status of jural and ritual minority.[56] This claim and his subsequent focus on the male (as father and son) led Fortes to conclude that Tallensi domestic relations constituted a typically patrilineal joint family.

However, as Ifi Amadiume has shown, Fortes constructed a masculinized system for the Tallensi rather than appreciating that a dual-gendered system formed the basis of social organization. Amadiume's insightful account of gender relations in Tallensi society shows there were other gender systems, such as the matricentric production unit, the system of the females, and the *soog* relationship of maternal kin. These provide an alternative, matriarchal kinship-based moral ideology and system in discourse with and opposition to the patriarchal system. Fortes's European masculinized and patriarchal paradigm suppressed the system of matriarchy and thus misrepresented the dialectic of gender and the system of checks and balances of Tallensi society.[57]

Centralized Polities Formed through Internal Differentiation

The transition from a segmentary to a more centralized mode of sociopolitical organization has often been conceptualized as one from a kinship-based to a territorially based authority. However, the conflict between kinship and administrative modes of organization existed at varying degrees of intensity, and the outcome varied. The overwhelming tendency throughout Africa was that kin-based groups were able to defend their custodianship of land and prevent it becoming private property and that centralized administrative authority remained circumscribed by that of clans and lineages.[58]

Tribute was nevertheless extracted by *political* or *military* means, even where primary producers retained access to the means of production, notably land. The mobilization of social labor in this mode is a function of the locus of political power. Competition for power between groups or estates of nonproducers leads to variable patterns of power distribution within a tributary mode of production.[59] Common to such modes was a cultural component that underlined the status of the surplus takers and the social distance separating them from others, together with claims to supernatural origins and validation.

In the Great Lakes region of eastern Africa, by the nineteenth century, centralized modes of organization characterized the kingdoms of Bunyoro, Toro, Buganda, Busoga, Nkore, Buha, Buhaya, Buzinza, Rwanda, and Burundi. Although only Bwamba, Bukonzo, and part of Kigezi were classified as segmentary societies, segmentary lineages persisted as a form of political organization at the local level even in the centralized kingdoms. The emergence of centralized polities and the conflict between kinship and territorial modes of political community differed considerably between kingdoms. In Bunyoro-Kitara, Nkore, Buhaya, Burundi, and Rwanda, centralizing tendencies emerged from the encounter between the original, decentralized, agricultural communities and immigrant northern pastoral communities. In the cases of Buganda, Busoga, and all other Bantu kingdoms from Congo through Zambia and

Zimbabwe to South Africa, centralizing tendencies emerged from within existing social formations.[60]

In the nineteenth century, as Archie Mafeje argues, the interlacustrine kingdoms were constituted, at least partially, according to a tributary mode of production: surplus product was extracted by noneconomic means, the organization of production was based on use rather than exchange value, and dominance was achieved largely through ideology, including the role of local religions and beliefs. Here the cases of Buganda and Bunyoro are explored. Each kingdom emerged from a widely differing historical trajectory, but in both polities, centralizing tendencies were considerable by the late nineteenth century.[61]

The Kingdom of Buganda

Buganda was an agricultural society with no pastoral tradition, and, as such, land was a prime asset. Initially, the king of Buganda, *Kabaka*, was first among equal heads of patrilineages or clan heads, *bataka*. However, by the middle of the nineteenth century, in a largely unprecedented move, the king had usurped clan heads and declared himself *Saabataka* (head of all clan heads). He then dispensed with the *bataka* as custodians of clan or lineage lands and arrogated the right to distribute land solely unto himself. As the Kiganda proverb states, the *Kabaka* "had eaten up the country."

The *Kabaka*'s domination was facilitated, in part, through enhanced interregional trade that was concentrated under the direct control of the king, thus increasingly bypassing the prerogatives of the Baganda lineages.[62] His position was consolidated by ideological claims to divine validation, including kingship rituals and ceremonies such as the new-moon ceremonies, the jawbone oracles, and Balubale cults, all of which referred to the superhuman attributes of the kings.[63] Having assumed control of all land in Buganda, the king administered it by appointing his own territorial chiefs, *bakungu*. Chieftainship was accorded on a clan basis according to personal merit. The king emerged supreme, therefore, but with an administrative hierarchy composed of personnel from both humble and noble origins: the line of chiefs recruited from ordinary citizens (administratively appointed commoner chiefs) predominated over hereditary (traditional) chiefs. Moreover, challenging the widespread Baganda custom of patrilineal descent, the centralizing king/s decreed that monarchs be affiliated to the maternal lineage in order to prevent any single clan from becoming too powerful and prevent the development of entrenched dynasties.[64]

Although by the nineteenth century Buganda had gone furthest in abrogating the principle of kinship as a basis for political organization, it was not the case that a similar degree of historical transformation had occurred in its organization of the labor process and the realization of property relations. Buganda maintained communal land rights, with a shift to private property in land occurring only with the advent of British colonial rule. In addition, beyond the fulfillment of certain public services and the payment of tributes, peasants or tenants were not obligated to work for individual patrons, maintaining the right of removal, *kusenguka*.[65]

The Kingdom of Bunyoro

The formation of Bunyoro, the earliest of the interlacustrine kingdoms, has been widely attributed to the in-migration of pastoralists from northern areas of Uganda. While this created an admixture of ethnic groups, the creation of the polity of Bunyoro was not attributable to a particular ethnic group, nor did ethnic groups persist throughout its history. Rather, the ascendancy of dynasties such as the Bachwezi and Babito, like the rise of an official bureaucracy, should be seen more as nascent "class" phenomena than as ethnic relations.[66] Political organization in nineteenth-century Bunyoro was largely bureaucratic. Apart from a hereditary Babito dynasty, the bureaucracy consisted of appointed chiefs who differed in rank. The king, *Mukama*, appointed administrative chiefs, but chieftainship was not restricted to any estate or category of persons. The senior chiefs held official estates in fief directly from the *Omukama*, but the tendency was toward heritable wealth in land, pending approbation from the king. All chiefs were entitled to tribute from tenants and collected taxes on cattle, dairy, and agricultural products. They also recruited labor for public works. There was no direct exploitation of tenants as labor, however. The extraction of economic value took a political form. In Bunyoro, the tendency was toward the consolidation of a landed aristocracy with heritable wealth who continued to curtail the centralizing ambitions of the king.

In the cases of both Buganda and Bunyoro, centralization had proceeded apace during the course of the nineteenth century. However, even in highly centralized polities, lineages persisted as a form of political organization at the local level. In Buganda, which had gone farthest in abrogating the principle of kinship, open conflict between the *Kabaka* and the clan leaders led to a state of disequilibrium for nearly fifty years. In other interlacustrine kingdoms, centralizing monarchs accommodated clan and lineage groups by allowing them effective occupation of the land while subordinating them to the demands of a territorial bureaucracy.[67] The organized power of lineages and clans continued to function therefore as a popular check on both the kings and the appointed administration. Tension between the different modes of sociopolitical organization led to differentiation between kin-based, hereditary traditional chiefs and state-appointed administrative chiefs. Moreover, both forms were in turn checked by clan- and lineage-based village councils that in many or most places retained the right of access to land and regulated all other natural resources, the movement of livestock, protection of crops, markets, long-distance trade, and personal obligations and claims.

Nineteenth-Century Conquest Polities

The previously mentioned institutions were the "traditional" institutions of nineteenth-century Africa through which village-based communities regulated social and economic affairs, but they were not its only institutions.[68] This was a period of intense historical change rather than the stable reproduction of customary relations and saw the emergence of nineteenth-century conquest polities and the associated rise of the administrative variant of chiefship. However, restraint on authority within nineteenth-century political systems was derived from distinct but related tendencies: one from peers, the other from the people. The nature and form of these constraints is evident from empirical examples of nineteenth-century conquest polities. Even within the Zulu, Xhosa, and Swazi polities of south-central Africa, considered some of the more centralized and despotic forms of political authority in nineteenth-century Africa, power was not absolute. At the other end of the spectrum of nineteenth-century conquest polities were the loose confederations established among the Akan peoples of West Africa, particularly the Asante and the Fante, which exhibited a highly elaborate system of governance.[69]

The Asante Confederacy

The Asante kingdom emerged as a distinct political entity toward the end of the seventeenth century, when, according to Asante history, the *Sika Dwa*, or Golden Stool, descended from the Akan high god Onyame, uniting the previously autonomous Asante clans under the *Asantehene* (King). The Golden Stool contains the soul or spirit, *sumsum*, of the Asante.

Associated with the Golden Stool was a unifying rule-based political system that defined the structure of the government, the division of labor, and the main elements of early Asante political culture.[70] The Asante polity is constituted according to the *Abusua*, or lineage system. Four or five *Abusua* make up a clan. All administrative units are constituted according to the *Abusua* system, whose essential feature, Obeng argues, "is its truly democratic character, namely, that every member of the community is represented."[71] The *Abusua* is matrilineal, every child belonging to its mother's *Abusua*. Each child also belongs to another social grouping, the *Nton*, which is patrilineal and through which the child inherits his or her father's spirit or deity. A child is believed to be the embodiment of two groups, the mother's blood or *mogya* (*Abusua*) and the father's spirit or *kra* (*Nton*).[72] All Asante Stools are *Abusua* Stools, only members of a particular *Abusua* being eligible for election to a particular Stool. The heads of the various lineages in a village constituted the *Mpaninfoo* (elders) in peacetime and the *Asafohene* (captains) in times of war. In addition to the Family Stools, a stool was also created for the headwoman of each lineage group in the village. The young men in a village, the *Asafo*, who formed the bulk of the Asante army, also had their own head, the *Nkwankwahene*. At a meeting of the village elders, every young man had a right to be present and to speak.[73]

The Kumasi polity functioned in a dual capacity: it was an ordinary member of the Confederacy (one of the six polities that comprised the original union), but it was also the locus of political power in the Confederacy. The *Asantehene* was the head of Kumasi district, the center connecting all the lineage heads, and the most venerate person in Asante because of his position as the occupant of the Golden Stool. However, the *Asantehene* was "not an autocrat . . . the stages through which his election to the Golden Stool passes ensure the rights of the people and safeguard the democratic principles of the monarchy."[74] He worked within the confines of checks and balances. Among the six divisional chiefs, the *Asantehene* was considered the "first among equals," and he could be destooled by his own people. The Queen Mother, *Asantewaa*, was regarded as the (symbolic) mother of the *Asantehene* and the ruler of women, safeguarding women's interests and concerns within the Asante polity. The Queen Mother was one of the principal advisers to the *Asantehene*, particularly, for example, during periods of crisis, war, and chieftaincy disputes.[75] Nor was it unheard of for the Queen Mother to go to war. Nana Yaa Asantewaa, for example, led the Asante army against the British in 1900.[76]

Integral to this loosely bound confederacy was the practice of decentralization. Over time, the authority of the chief had come to be so "limited and severely defined" that "a whole series of injunctions . . . were publicly recited before him on his enstoolment." The most important of these was "never to act without the advice and full concurrence of his counsellors, who were in turn subject to similar restraints."[77] Tell him, the assembled people would admonish a newly enstooled person, "that we do not wish for greediness, we do not wish that his ears should be hard of hearing, we do not wish that he should act on his own initiative"; rather, he should consult with representatives of the people.[78] Policy was discussed at various levels, in the old Oman or national councils and in the Omansin (subdivision), before a final decision could be taken constitutionally. At such gatherings, the *Ohene* (chief) and his attending counselors "were never anything more . . . than vehicles of communication." Should a chief make "the least attempt to act on his initiative," it was considered "a legitimate cause for destoolment." The community of freemen (and it

Dua-koro gye mframa a ɛbu—One tree cannot stand the might of a great storm (one person's palm cannot cover the sky, or one person cannot fight a dozen; i.e., one person cannot rule alone).

Praeɛ wɔ hɔ yi, woyi baako a ɛbu; woka bɔ mu a ɛmmu—The twig of a broom can easily be broken, but when they are fastened together, they will be strong and cannot be broken (there is strength in unity).

Ɔhene tufoantie na odi ntakraboa a ɔnni tire—A chief or leader who does not heed good advice eats a headless bird (a chief or leader who tramples over good counseling by his elders many a time falls into trouble).

Deɛ ɔretwa sa no nnim sɛ n'akyi akyea—He who fashions a footpath does not know that behind him the path is crooked (a leader may not know of his mistakes save the led or onlookers draw his attention to them).

Wobu ɔkɔtɔ kwasea a Onyame hwɛ wo to—God looks at you when you cheat the crab (if you cheat a poor or miserable person, God watches your actions and may punish you for it).

Ɔhɔhoɔ biara ɔnyɛ aboa wokɔ ne kurom a, wobɛhunu ne suban—No stranger is a beast, you will know him better if you visit his hometown (have respect for strangers).

Wosuro asɛntenten a, wonte mpaninsɛm—If you detest listening to the talk from our elders, you may not be well informed of past events and history (learn to listen patiently because what you learn may be useful).

Wosum borɔdeɛ dua a, sum kwadu bi—When you support the plantain plant with a tree, it is also advisable for you to do likewise to the banana plant (do not put all your trust in one thing or venture; you may live to regret it when it fails you. For example, in the Akan extended family system, it is a widely held belief that one should look after one's children but not lose sight of extending one's hand to one's nephews and nieces as well).

Ɛnyɛ adehyeɛ nyinaa na wɔfata kyiniiɛ ase—It is not all the royals that are eligible to be enthroned or come directly under the umbrella (before a royal is enthroned, they must have satisfied the queen, kingmakers and majority of the subjects' demands or aspirations, such as being intelligent, respectful, hardworking, tactful, brave, upright, generous, and so on).

Figure 7.1. Proverbs of the Akan

should be noted that others were unfree) among the Akan constituted a genuine "public opinion."[79]

Present-day Asante chiefs continue to stress the importance of consensus building and collective decision making: "When the council sits, the sub-chiefs all participate in the discussions, in order that public opinion and different interests are represented. . . . The chiefs' council consists of the heads of all the lineages in an area, they sit on Stools themselves by virtue of their lineage, they are not chiefs by appointment of the king. The lineage chiefs are appointed

through lineage electoral colleges. . . . The council members often pre-date the
Ohene." Reciprocity between the ruler and ruled and the system of checks
and balances on a chief are also considered significant: "if a council member
is not performing well, the chief cannot dismiss the member arbitrarily. The
respective elders are called to the council meeting and the decision taken by the
council, it is not a 'one-man show,' our traditional constitution does not allow
that." Similar procedures exist for the destoolment of the lineage chiefs.[80]
Akan values and philosophy are apparent in the proverbs of the Akan (see
figure 7.1).[81]

CONCLUSION

Contrary to the imperial narrative of the democratization project, there are
African histories of political community and democracy, autonomous of the
orthodox Western neoliberal notion. This chapter has highlighted the specificity of African political history and systems in the nineteenth century. It illustrates culturally and historically specific notions and forms of political community and democracy, documenting elaborate and diverse rule-based systems
of governance characterized by complex systems of claims and obligations;
restraints on political authority; collective decision making and the principle
of consensus; complex mechanisms to constrain and mediate tensions or internal oppositions arising from kinship, locality, age/generation, and gender; and
elaborate judicial procedures. Many of these social organizations were also
highly decentralized and largely egalitarian, containing redistributive mechanisms that thwarted tendencies to reproduce inequalities, thus limiting internal
social differentiation. Even in the centralized polities of the nineteenth century, authority was not absolute. Checks on precolonial authority existed in the
forms of both peer and popular restraint. The principle of extended kinship on
the jural-political level illustrates that social order does not necessarily depend
on the existence of "states" or "statesmen." The kin-ordered principle also
persisted within highly centralized polities in the tensions between centralized
authority in all its forms and clan organization.

Such history/ies contribute to the radical endeavor of "expropriating the
expropriators." They illustrate the measure of the dominance exercised by
an imperialist mode of knowledge. But while necessary, the reclaiming of
indigenous history/ies is not itself sufficient. As Taiwo argues, the iteration of
what Africans have done will never be sufficient.[82] Until the ghost of Hegel is
exorcised, "until *it is taken for granted* that Africa is part of History, that the
study of anything cannot be complete unless it encompasses this significant
part of the world," those engaged in social inquiry will continue the travesty of

silencing and negating Africa—and humanity will be dispossessed of Africa's challenge to knowledge.

NOTES

I would like to thank Muhammed Ağcan, Antony Anghie, B. S. Chimni, Siba Grovogui, Branwen Gruffydd Jones, Sandra Halperin, Sankaran Krishna, Mustapha Pasha, Julian Saurin, Burak Ülman, and an anonymous reviewer as well as participants of the panel at the *African Studies Association UK Biennial Conference: Debating Africa* (London, 2004), where an earlier version of this chapter was presented, for their insightful comments and suggestions.

1. Ranajit Guha, *History at the Limit of World-History* (New York: Columbia University Press, 2002), 5.

2. Guha, *History at the Limit of World-History*, 2–5.

3. Georg W. F. Hegel, *The Philosophy of History* (New York: Dover, 1956), 91, 99, appendix 1.

4. Hegel, *The Philosophy of History* , 1.

5. Olufemi Taiwo, "Exorcising Hegel's Ghost: Africa's Challenge to Philosophy," *African Studies Quarterly* 1, no. 4 (1998), <http://www.africa.ufl.edu/asq/v1/4/2.htm> (accessed August 15, 2005).

6. Guha, *History at the Limit of World-History*, 8.

7. Sophie Bessis, *Western Supremacy: The Triumph of an Idea?* (London: Zed Books, 2003), 12–13.

8. Charles W. Mills, *The Racial Contract* (Ithaca, N.Y.: Cornell University Press, 1999).

9. Taiwo, "Exorcising Hegel's Ghost."

10. Partha Chatterjee, "Response to Taylor's 'Modes of Civil Society,'" *Public Culture* 3, no. 1 (1990): 119–20. See also Mahmood Mamdani, *Citizen and Subject: Contemporary Africa and the Legacy of Late Colonialism* (Princeton, N.J.: Princeton University Press, 1996), 12.

11. Taiwo, "Exorcising Hegel's Ghost."

12. Taiwo, "Exorcising Hegel's Ghost."

13. The global project of "democratization" is a major (though rarely recognized) component of the imperialism of our time. This chapter is concerned to counter imperial historiography through retrieving the real histories of political community in Africa. Elsewhere, I have provided a more extensive account of the (discursive and nondiscursive) imperial nature of the democratization project. See Alison J. Ayers, "Demystifying Democratization: The Global Constitution of Neo-Liberal Polities in Africa," *Third World Quarterly* 27, no. 3: 321–38.

14. Dickson Eyoh, "African Perspectives on Democracy and the Dilemmas of Post-colonial Intellectuals," *Africa Today* 45, no. 3–4 (1998): 286.

15. Guha, *History at the Limit of World-History*, 4.

16. Alassane D. Ouattara, "The Political Dimensions of Economic Reforms— Conditions for Successful Adjustment," Keynote Address by Mr. Alassane D. Ouattara, deputy managing director, International Monetary Fund, June 9, 1999, <http://www. imf.org/external/np/speeches/1999/061099.htm> (accessed August 16, 2005).

17. Cited in Gordon Crawford, *Promoting Democracy, Human Rights and Good Governance through Development Aid: A Comparative Study of the Policies of Four Northern Donors* (Leeds: Centre for Democratisation Studies, Working Papers on Democratisation, no. 1, 1996), 15–19; Canadian International Development Agency, *Government of Canada Policy for CIDA on Human Rights, Democratization and Good Governance* (1996), <http://www.acdicida.gc.ca/cida/OpenDocument.htm> (accessed June 13, 2001); Organization for Economic Cooperation and Development (OECD) Development Advisory Committee, *Participatory Development and Good Governance, Development Co-operation Guidelines Series* (Paris: OECD, 1995), 1, 6 (emphasis added).

18. See Bhikhu Parekh, "The Cultural Particularity of Liberal Democracy," *Political Studies* 40 (special issue, 1992); and John Gray, *Liberalism*, 2nd ed. (Buckingham: Open University Press, 1995), and *Post-Liberalism: Studies in Political Thought* (London: Routledge, 1993).

19. Taiwo, "Exorcising Hegel's Ghost."

20. Mamdani, *Citizen and Subject*, 8, 12, 13, 295.

21. Mamdani, *Citizen and Subject*, 9–16.

22. See Eric R. Wolf, *Europe and the People without History* (Berkeley: University of California Press, 1997), 76.

23. Taiwo, "Exorcising Hegel's Ghost"; see also Krishna, chapter 4 in this volume.

24. Jan Vansina, "Once upon a Time: Oral Traditions as History in Africa," in *Historical Studies Today*, ed. F. Gilbert and S. R. Graubard (New York: Norton, 1972), 426, 431, cited in Ronald R. Atkinson, *The Roots of Ethnicity: The Origins of the Acholi of Uganda before 1800* (Philadelphia: University of Pennsylvania Press, 1994), 19.

25. Walter D. Mignolo, *The Darker Side of the Renaissance: Literacy, Territoriality, and Colonization* (Ann Arbor: University of Michigan Press, 1995), 127 (emphasis added), cited in Guha, *History at the Limit of World-History*, 8.

26. Taiwo, "Exorcising Hegel's Ghost."

27. Guha, *History at the Limit of World-History*, 10.

28. Wolf, *Europe and the People without History*, 100.

29. See, for example, Robin Horton, "Stateless Societies in the History of West Africa," in *History of West Africa*, vol. 1, ed. J. F. A. Ajayyi and Michael Crowder (London: Longman, 1971), and Simon Simonse, *Kings of Disaster: Dualism, Centralism, and the Scapegoat King in Southeastern Sudan* (Leiden: Brill, 1992), 1.

30. Ifi Amadiume, *Re-inventing Africa: Matriarchy, Religion, and Culture* (London: Zed Books, 1997), 16.

31. Mamdani, *Citizen and Subject*, 41.

32. John Davis, "Foreword," in *Nuer Prophets: A History of Prophecy from the Upper Nile in the Nineteenth and Twentieth Centuries*, by Douglas H. Johnson (Oxford: Clarendon Press, 1994), paraphrasing Ernest Gellner, v.

33. Wolf, *Europe and the People without History*, 92.

34. Mamdani, *Citizen and Subject*, 41.

35. Wolf, *Europe and the People without History*, 94–96.

36. See, for example, Charles P. P. Emudong, "The Iteso: A Segmentary Society under Colonial Administration, 1897–1927" (Kampala: University of Makerere, MA thesis, 1974), 1–15, and J. B. Webster, "Usuku: The Homeland of the Iteso," in *The Iteso during the Asonya*, ed. J. B. Webster (Nairobi: East African Educational Publishers, 1973), xxi–xxii, 7.

37. It is important not to conflate "precolonial" African notions of land tenure, concerned primarily with land use, with the "property rights" of modern capitalism, concerned primarily with private ownership. Archie Mafeje, *Kingdoms of the Great Lakes Region: Ethnography of African Social Formations* (Kampala: Fountain Publishers, 1998), 55–56, 90; Oduc David, "Customary Land Law and Economic Development of Uganda with Special Reference to Teso" (Kampala: University of Makerere, BL thesis, 1987).

38. Emudong, *The Iteso*, 16–22.

39. Emudong, *The Iteso*, 23–26.

40. Webster, "Usuku."

41. N. Egimu-Okuda, "Social-Political Organisation of the Etem Igetoma," in Webster, *The Iteso*, 169–70; see also D. H. Okalany, "Judicial Procedures and Legal Principles of the Asonya," in Webster, *The Iteso*, 129–42.

42. Emudong, *The Iteso*, 31.

43. Webster, "Usuku," 78.

44. Webster, "Usuku," 79.

45. Emudong, *The Iteso*, 35–36.

46. Webster, "Usuku," 78–79.

47. Grace Akello, *Iteso Thought Patterns in Tales* (Dar es Salaam: Dar es Salaam University Press, 1981), 104–5.

48. Akello, *Iteso Thought Patterns in Tales*, 79.

49. Emudong, *The Iteso*, 50.

50. Okalany, "Judicial Procedures and Legal Principles of the Asonya," 142.

51. G. K. Nukunya, *Tradition and Change in Ghana* (Accra: Ghana Universities Press, 1992), 75.

52. Nukunya, *Tradition and Change in Ghana*, 75.

53. Wolf, *Europe and the People without History*, 230.

54. The following account draws mainly on Nukunya, *Tradition and Change in Ghana*, 54–92.

55. Meyer Fortes, "The Political System of the Tallensi of the Northern Territories of the Gold Coast," in *African Political Systems*, ed. Meyer Fortes and Edward E. Evans-Pritchard (London: Oxford University Press, 1940).

56. Meyer Fortes, *Religion, Morality and the Person* (Cambridge: Cambridge University Press, 1987), 264, cited in Amadiume, *Reinventing Africa*, 32.

57. Amadiume, *Reinventing Africa*, 29–37.

58. Mamdani, *Citizen and Subject*, 41–42.

59. Wolf, *Europe and the People without History*, 80–81.

60. Mafeje, *Kingdoms of the Great Lakes Region*, 11.

61. Mafeje, *Kingdoms of the Great Lakes Region*, 25–26, 51–52, 57, 93.

62. Bill Freund, *The Making of Contemporary Africa: The Development of African Society since 1800* (Basingstoke: Palgrave, 1998), 28; Mafeje, *Kingdoms of the Great Lakes Region*, 26.

63. Mafeje, *Kingdoms of the Great Lakes Region*, 13, 86.

64. Mamdani, *Citizen and Subject*, 42, 51–52.

65. Mamdani, *Citizen and Subject*, 52.

66. This account draws on Mamdani, *Citizen and Subject*, 38–42.

67. Mafeje, *Kingdoms of the Great Lakes Region*, 90.

68. Mamdani, *Citizen and Subject*, 42.

69. Mamdani, *Citizen and Subject*, 43–47.

70. Naomi Chazan, "The Asante Case," in *The Early State in African Perspective*, ed. S. N. Eisenstadt, Michel Abitbol, and Naomi Chazan (Leiden: Brill, 1988), cited in Basil Davidson, *The Black Man's Burden: Africa and the Curse of the Nation-State* (London: James Currey, 1992), 56.

71. Ernest E. Obeng, *Ancient Ashanti Chieftaincy* (Tema: Ghana Publishing Corporation, 1986), 2.

72. Obeng, *Ancient Ashanti Chieftaincy*, 7–8.

73. Obeng, *Ancient Ashanti Chieftaincy*, 10–12, 30.

74. Obeng, *Ancient Ashanti Chieftaincy*, 35.

75. Interviews with Osei Kwadwo, historian at *Asantehene*'s Palace, and *Akyeamehene* (chief linguist) of the *Asantewaa* (Queen Mother), Kumasi, November 20, 1998.

76. Osei Kwadwo, *An Outline of Asante History* (Kumasi: O. Kwadwo Enterprise, 1994), 47–54.

77. Robert S. Rattray, *Ashanti Law and Constitution* (Oxford: Clarendon Press, 1929), in Mamdani, *Citizen and Subject*, 47.

78. Rattray, *Ashanti Law and Constitution*, in Davidson, *The Black Man's Burden*, 61.

79. Rattray, *Ashanti Law and Constitution*, in Mamdani, *Citizen and Subject*, 47.

80. Ogyeabuor Barima Adu Gyiamfi, *Kuntanasehene*, personal communication, November 15, 1998.

81. From Nana Osee Yaw Bonsu, *The Wit of Akans* (Kumasi: n.p., 1994).

82. Taiwo, "Exorcising Hegel's Ghost."

Chapter Eight

Mind, Body, and Gut! Elements of a Postcolonial Human Rights Discourse

Siba N'Zatioula Grovogui

NO GENETIC SUPERIORITY

The discourse of human rights has become increasingly attractive to activists and policymakers who view it as a deterrent against the proliferation of political violence. But the ambition to set universal standards for practices runs up against skepticism about the validity of the very idea of "human" rights. Even as French revolutionaries proclaimed the Declaration of the Universal Rights of Men and Citizens, Jeremy Bentham derided the underlying notions of natural rights as "simple . . . rhetorical nonsense, nonsense built upon stilts."[1] Today, skepticism about the idea of human rights comes from two distinct but often convergent sources: a cultural relativism that poses as guardian of communal autonomy or authenticity and a historical-philosophical rejection of the inherent and exclusive universality of Western conceptions of human rights.[2] Taking the latter position, Amartya Sen has argued that proponents of the universality of human rights mistakenly insist on the primacy of "specific classes of . . . rights" (particularly civil and political rights) over supposedly "economic, cultural, and social rights." This distinction unnecessarily excludes significant conceptions of human rights from the purview of desirable and enforceable human rights.[3] Worse, advocates of human rights frequently link the possibility and admissibility of human rights to Western political systems, social institutions, and constitutional orders or their likenesses.[4]

Other Western defenders of human rights stress the European origin of the most prevalent norms. Anthony Pagden, for instance, has argued that the concept of human rights "is a development of the older notion of natural rights" that found its present form in "the European struggle to legitimate its overseas empires." The decisions by French and American revolutionaries to encode conceptions of natural rights as constitutional provisions helped to further this goal.[5] Pagden concludes therefore that the institutions of human rights cannot be disentangled from the "particular kind of political system" (i.e., liberal democracy) and ideologies (ranging from theology to post-Enlightenment humanism and rationalism) that actualized "the Greek and Roman idea of a common law for all humanity."[6] Pagden then urges human rights advocates to champion "an essentially Western European understanding of the human" as the basis for international morality.[7]

This call and its base mysticism have resulted in dubious ethical propositions and political hubris. Thus, for instance, Michael Ignatieff envisages a (Western) right of Western intervention in the former European expanses as a mechanism of diffusion of Western standards of freedom throughout the world.[8] The argument, as proposed by Ignatieff, is built on a supposed pragmatic ground: to enhance the ability of individuals to resist an unjust state.[9] This pragmatism has broad appeal among human rights activists and policymakers in that it conforms to a specific political agenda and justifies Western intervention elsewhere.[10] The argument and the pragmatism are dismissive of the possibility of valid regional values and ideas of human and political community outside of Western visions of human subjectivity. Accordingly, Ignatieff castigates human rights activists for being overambitious and counterproductive by not acceding to the idea of limiting the scope of human rights to the defensible individual rights, which are directly connected to political agency, and thus to effectively reestablishing the balance between the rights of states and the rights of citizens.[11] Like Pagden, Ignatieff is credible when he proposes that "when individuals have defensible rights, they are less likely to be abused." But the desire to limit human rights to individual civil and political rights at the expense of other classes of rights calls into question Ignatieff's commitment to international morality and justice.

This chapter does not dispute that Western institutions are the primary reference for human rights theorists and advocates. Nor does it discount approaches to human rights that identify the historical points at which "natural rights" become "rights of nations" and later "human rights." The chapter takes it for granted that the revolutions in America and France encoded historical conceptions of political subjectivity, personal liberties, and political freedom. The established legislation—the American Declaration of Independence and Bill of Rights and the French Declaration of the Rights of Man and

Citizens—contributed to opening the possibility for the universalization of the concept of human rights. This possibility was confirmed by the 1948 Universal Declaration of Human Rights. Finally, I do not wish to diminish the appeal of certain human rights norms in political contestations such as occurred, for instance, in Eastern Europe before and after the fall of communism[12] or in Latin America on the collapse of authoritarianism.[13]

I *do* dispute three central premises underlying Pagden's and Ignatieff's arguments. The first is that a valid theory of human rights must necessarily concede the Western origination of the concept and the ontological primacy of related Western institutions. The second contestable point is that the possibility of universalization of human rights resides in affirming the sufficiency of the classes of "rights" enacted by the American and French revolutions and liberal democracies generally. The final point is that culture, tradition, and practice provide Western states and their constituencies with the legitimacy and authority to determine the extent of human rights violations and thus to define the form of intervention required in any context to rectify the conditions of abuses.

Related arguments are at once theoretical, pragmatic, and ethical. I will limit myself here to ethical ones, although these too are implicit. My argument begins with the view that the a priori designation of Western powers as legitimate enforcers of human rights is in itself problematic. The instrumental uses of the rhetoric of human rights by "Europe" and to multiple and contradictory ends during the era of imperialism and beyond, which is conceded by Pagden, suggest that there do not exist historically uniform Western traditions, cultures, and institutions.[14] This absence in turn affects the ability of the West to credibly project itself as the legitimate enforcer of human rights. In fact, this absence of consistency and uniformity on the part of Western states has greatly contributed to muting the receptivity of any Western rhetoric of human rights in the former colonial world. It is one of the causes of non-Western resistance to the universality of the classes of human rights conveniently recalled at moments of crisis. Finally, in the pragmatic instance, it is not far fetched to imagine that the cultural, economic, and social rights of individuals and communities would be less likely to be abused if the right to defend them was constitutively incorporated in the foreign policy rationales of hegemonic states. The related arguments are outside the purview of this chapter.

Against these views, I hold that the idea of ennobling human existence through authoritative ethical categories is not foreign to other regions and their cultures—even if the categories themselves are not expressed in the English language or formulated philosophically and legally as human rights. I argue that non-Europeans too have historically and contingently appealed to higher moral orders beyond the available sociopolitical imaginaries as standards by which to measure social acts and political relations. These appeals were founded on broader classes of moral codes and multiple formulations of ethics that sought to ennoble human existence through enforceable standards akin to human rights. These moral codes and their ethical expressions constitute alternative enunciations of what may be called human rights precepts or institutes. They may be the basis of a theory or postcolonial perspectives on human rights. To this end—and consistent with Sen's desire for some theory of alternative enunciations of human rights[15]—I propose a brief sketch of constitutional developments during the Haitian Revolution. My key proposition is that developments in Haiti not only expanded "the claimed domain of human rights" for the enslaved but also introduced equally enforceable notions of human rights. These domains of rights may be outside the concerns and political agendas of many human rights theorists and activists, but they are coeval to Western practices and institutions.

The Haitian Revolution does not appear as unique in character and historic importance. In many regards, it is an integral part of a genealogy of modernity. This simple fact has been ignored by theorists and historians of thought. The reasons for omission are at times straightforward. Any thoughts about historical dynamics are necessarily more uniform and less diverse than the processes that they explain. Without due familiarity with revolutionary Haitian symbols of liberty and antislavery discourses of freedom, it is nearly impossible for any thought to fully grasp the contributions of self-actualized slaves to the development of human rights. On reflection, however, one is led to accept that Haitian revolutionaries must have believed that human beings possessed inherent faculties and capacities deserving of constitutional protection. They too explored the manners and purposes for which specific moral precepts must be assembled as institutions of human rights in the context of their struggles to enact liberty, freedom, and political justice. By examining events in revolutionary Haiti, one is able to endorse a universalist position while underscoring the specificity of human rights institutions. Indeed, even if they are held to be universal, the contexts and processes of institutionalization emerged from regional and cultural contexts that stress specific dimensions of human faculties and capacities as a matter of utility and pragmatism. From my perspective, the realization of universally agreeable institutions of human rights must necessarily invite reconciling diverse positions born of ideological (or cultural) contestations and political confrontations. This is the only insurance today against the different disguises implicit in universalist and relativist positions on human rights: neoimperialist arguments disguised as moral concern and resistance to transparency and accountability in the guise of communal autonomy and authenticity.

CULTURES OF PROTECTED FACULTIES

This chapter began with the proposition that there has existed worldwide historical convergences in the human drive to institute elemental ethical principles intended to ennoble human existence. In the English language, such elemental principles might be called institutes. I use the term "human rights institute" therefore as a separate entity from human rights institutions, without prejudice to parallel linguistic formulations elsewhere. According to the *Oxford English Dictionary*, for instance, institutes are "a collection of precepts, a design or purpose"[16] regardless of their origins and/or domains of application. I assume, for instance, that the notion that "human beings" possess faculties—or certain "inherent biological capabilities," "powers of the mind," and "natural aptitudes"[17]—has existed across regions, religions, cultures, ideologies, and politics. This concern must have given rise to a multiplicity of precepts about human existence. I call the related precepts, provisionally and only for the purpose of communication, human rights institutes. They attained in any society around the globe that developed a number of precepts bearing on human faculties. Such precepts would be informed by the lived experiences or circumstances of the involved entities, and their appellation would conform to local lexicons and intellectual and moral resources.

"Europe," Pagden has shown, identified such precepts as natural rights in conjunction with developments in natural law.[18] Related developments are particular to the European trajectory and, in this manner, are unique to it. So too are the institutions of human rights defended by Europe today particular to it—although not their present meanings, which are derived from their global iterations and applications. Again, according to the *Oxford English Dictionary*, institutions are significant social practices firmly associated with a thing and a precept, or institute. Institutions are the outcome of historical processes that either established prior precepts as operative forms through specific instruments or ordained exogenous practices to fill an institutional void.[19] In either case, the process of institutionalization of, say, "human rights" is one of political and/or ideological determination of the meanings of precepts within specific sociopolitical contexts. In actuality, the institutionalization of human rights injects the generalized precepts of human rights with the passion of the powerful, the prejudice of ideology, and, by the fiat of reason, the interests of a class of people. Human rights institutions reflect thus particular economies of will, values, and interests reflecting inequalities among political subjects and entities.

Thus, it may be said that the institutions of Europe are unique to its history and cultural resources. But it cannot be ascertained prima facie that these processes and resources have no historical or moral equivalencies elsewhere.

In France, for instance, Enlightenment-era *philosophes* frequently founded their own understandings and anthologies (some would say genealogies) of natural rights on the principle that there existed parallel sentiments across the globe. Hence, Denis Diderot held that non-Europeans or "natives" understood the concept of natural right and that there was "almost no one who would not be convinced inside himself that the thing is obviously known to him."[20] The *philosophes* understood that non-Europeans too held out the prospect of ennobling human existence and that, for this reason, might relate to French institutions. This is to say that, although not always formulated philosophically as human rights, non-European imaginaries of society, agency, and ethics are valid grounds for envisaging precepts and institutions of human rights. The latter may therefore be accessible to thought through intellectual inquiry.

In sum, although human rights institutes may be related to human rights institutions, their trajectories are not identical. As such, a useful and compelling approach to human rights must distinguish between two separate spheres and trajectories of human rights discourses. Human rights institutes emerge concomitantly across regions and cultures as the products of localized imaginations of the essential needs, faculties, and capacities of persons long before their incorporation as legal instruments through political or ideological processes. They comprise ideas and/or institutes reflecting the aspirations of epic communal and individual struggles for justice, equality, and decency that must find (imperfect) linguistic representation. These aspirations are then subjected to political and ideological agendas during the course of the embodiment of institutes as institutions. It follows then that moral institutes and ethical codes that may be translated as "human rights" are neither necessarily Western nor inevitably relative.

Human rights institutions, on the other hand, are necessarily and contingently tied to particular political and ideological agendas or to the pursuit of a specific political order. This does not mean that they may never have universal applications. As studies of the French and American revolutions show, localized events may nonetheless tap into or initiate generalized views of the human condition. These particular events produced the American Bill of Rights and the French Declaration of the Rights of Man and Citizen.[21] Disagreements emerge only when theorists and advocates ignore the contingent histories of their particular human rights institutions and thus cast doubt on the possibility that other equally local human struggles were inspired by broader moral and political concerns.

Like revolutionary events in France and the United States, for instance, the Haitian Revolution aspired to emancipate human beings from political serfdom. As Michel-Rolph Trouillot has shown, late eighteenth-century revolutionaries in France, the United States, and Haiti uniformly held slavery as metaphor of human indignity and thus determined to implement instruments that would end it. From this convergence, one may read that, by necessity, modern political struggles referred to a moral commonplace: the need to protect the faculties and capacities that define human existence away from the metaphorical slavery. Such a conclusion would be hasty. Moral differences manifested themselves from the outset because of divergent political and cultural contexts in the three localities concerned. In Europe and in America, the word "slavery" was "accessible to a large public" for whom it "stood for a number of evils" or "whatever was wrong with European rule in Europe and elsewhere."[22] Yet most eighteenth-century French and American revolutionaries gave different weight and signification to *the actual* system of slavery (or the enslavement of Africans in the New World) even as they likened their own lot—or the absence of freedom—to enslavement or the institution of slavery. The fact that many of the Western revolutionaries were directly involved in the actual evil of slavery partly explained their ambivalence. It remains that they enacted juridico-political regimes and political systems that upheld slavery. They also continued the practices of imperialism and colonialism that disavowed the freedom of others.[23] Specifically, American and French revolutionaries formulated constitutional norms that, although based on compelling moral precepts, institutionally construed the word "slavery" to mean impositions or limitations on the individual liberties and freedoms of particular human entities, excluding the actual slaves.

To the extent that one is required to maintain the boundaries between the theory of language and the language of theory, the previous commentaries are not an indictment of political theory. They are to suggest, however, that a theory of human rights must demarcate the political discourses of revolutionaries from the available political thought—or philosophical ideas and ethical concepts bearing on human rights. The relevancy of such ideas and concepts to discourse must be judged by their applications to historical and cultural contexts. These applications are themselves partly mediated by the intentions and actions of revolutionaries that produced specific idioms, linguistic practices, or language games. These language games created casts and classes of persons with assigned roles and, for this reason, attributed to them in time and space bundles of capacities that defined their existence and their understanding of themselves. These language games also stripped others of the capacity to define the terms under which their own situations can be described.[24]

It would not be exaggerated to say that the subject of the Universal Declaration of Man and Citizen was not Man or human beings in the broader sense of the term. Nor was the subject of the Bill of Rights persons in their biological capacities and mental faculties. Just as full citizenship was to be granted only to "natural members" of the Three Estates and not others, the right-bearing

American individual was not the biological or natural person but a proper-tied, race- and class-based person aspiring to dominate others. There is no belaboring the point that the promoters of the inalienable rights of the individual reconciled them both metaphorically and actually with the enslavement of other persons. According to Michel-Rolph Trouillot, the French and American revolutions developed linguistic techniques and peculiar constructs of the ideas of Man and Reason and historical consciousness and agency that accentuated self-referentiality and the repression of the other.[25] Indeed, the concerns about enslavement and the related discourses of freedom and individual liberties pertained to the self. Few sought to enlarge the ethical propositions contained in the narratives of emancipation for their application to the slaves, the colonized, and the displaced natives. These linguistic techniques of the Western revolutionaries and their base morality or Reason "exacerbated the fundamental ambiguity that dominated the encounter between ontological discourse and colonial practice."[26] They spoke of Man and Reason even as "men (Europeans) were conquering, killing, dominating, and enslaving other beings thought to be equally human, if only by some."[27] These events were not merely ethical lapses. They reflect comparatively on the moral character of the French and American revolutions.

THE END OF ENSLAVEMENT

Occurring a mere twenty years after the French Revolution and 200 miles from the shore of the United States, the Haitian Revolution properly belongs to the genealogy of modern conceptions of constitutional power, popular sovereignty, and entitlements for the citizenry. First, the Haitian Revolution was fought to end political absolutism and a related form of sovereignty. Jefferson's and the American Declaration of Independence literally dethroned an absentee sovereign, King George III. Toussaint L'Ouverture and, on his death, Dessalines and Henry Christophe did likewise by seizing the opportunity of the French Revolution to rebuke their former masters, whether monarch, French revolutionaries, or counterrevolutionaries. Besides their rebuke of the absentee King, the Americans beheaded native American sovereigns (including King Philip), just as the French had done with Louis XVI and Marie Antoinette, to mark their rupture from the past. Haitian revolutionaries would not resort to such "barbarism" but signified the barbarism of enslavement through language. Thus, Boisrond Tonnerre, a formally educated mulatto, marked the rupture between the past and the present by stating that the independence act required "the skin of a white man for parchment, his skull for a desk, his blood for ink, and a bayonet for a pen."[28] This musing had deeper symbolic appeal than the contained figurative violence. Haitian revolutionaries hoped to deracialize political agency (by stripping it symbolically of its "white skin"), to debunk post-Enlightenment ontology (by figuratively flattening "the skull" that contained it), to rewrite their own history by uprooting racial oppression (where needed by spilling "white blood"), and to replace the violence of modernity represented by the bayonet (by converting it into a "pen").

In other respects, the postrevolution Haitian constitution affirms the freedom of religion (arts. 50–52) and equal access to property (art. 6). So too does it assert that "the house of every citizen is an inviolable sanctuary," only to be entered "in the case of fire, a flood, [or in the event of] a plea" (General Dispositions, arts. 6 and 7). It also affirms marriage and divorce (General Dispositions, arts. 14 and 15).[29] In these and other regards, the Haitian Revolution was integral to modern political debates on the moral quality of modern existence and the need to separate the public and private spheres of life. Like the other revolutions, the slave revolution delineated the legislative provinces of governors from the domains of decisions of the governed. Haitian slaves too realized the advisability of binding norms that protected the faculties and capacities of human beings. By assuming themselves to be human, Haitian slaves challenged reigning notions of humanity, of Man and Reason, or their access to human faculties and capacities.

Still, the Haitian Revolution was not ordinary. It was in some ways a direct response to events in France and the United States. As Sidney W. Mintz has noted, it "was, above all, the only revolution of those first three—American, French, and Haitian—that freed the slaves."[30] Not only did the imperial constitution ban all references to gradations of skin color (art. 14), it also abolished "titles, advantages and privileges other than those necessarily resulting from the regard and compensation for services rendered for liberty and independence" (art. 3). The Haitian constitution also granted equal rights to children born out of wedlock (General Dispositions, art. 16), adopted marriage and divorce laws favorable to women, and granted equal access to property to *anciens libres* (the formerly free) and *nouveaux libres* (freed slaves). Further, in recognition of the universality of goodwill, the Haitian Revolution rendered "homage to the friends of liberty, to the philanthropists of countries, as a sign of proof of divine goodness ... which provided us with the opportunity to break our chains and to constitute ourselves as free, civilized, and independent people" (General Dispositions). Now self-proclaimed blacks after independence, the former slaves recognized the equal dignity of "all mortals," including "white women who have naturalized," "their present and future children," and "Germans and Poles who have been naturalized by the Government" (art. 13).

There have been many commentaries questioning the philosophical depth of the ideas held by the former slaves. The prejudice comes partly as a result of the fact that few of the Haitian revolutionaries had any formal education, and "none could appeal directly to friends, college chums, or political allies in Europe."[31] But they were among the first to realize the connections between political violence on the one hand and modern political thoughts and systems on the other. They rose up against "being someone else's property . . . being flogged . . . being denied a family or the right to testify in court . . . being raped, tortured, murdered, or sold."[32] Mintz is unquestionably among the most sympathetic to the Haitian Revolution and its causes. But one is compelled to disagree with his judgment that the central issues of the Haitians were "less stirring issues" than those that presented themselves to the French and American revolutions.[33] As I show later, the enslaved Haitian envisaged institutions that anticipated modern-day conventions on the abolition of torture, the protection of refugees and displaced persons, and the reunification of families. They also initiated protection for women (whether married or unmarried) and children (whether "legitimate" or not). In fact, their perspectives in these regards anticipated current international debates on the subjects.

The Haitian Revolution and constitution are not without controversies. Whereas it too had been inspired by the desire and precepts of freedom, justice, equality, and decency, the Haitian constitutional provisions were drafted by historical agents with different relations to state, society, and economy. As a result, they envisaged liberty differently. The result is that social conflicts remained beyond the revolution. The most significant lines of contention opposed former slaves of African descent "who felt liberty meant securing racial equality" to large planters (*grands blancs*) and *gens de couleur or affranchis* "who identified liberty with having a lot of land for themselves."[34] Both groups sought to keep the state at bay but meant separate things by it. Whereas the *affranchis* and planters aspired to a state that did not interfere with elemental freedoms of religion and speech and property rights, the former slaves (led by Christophe) sought to limit the sovereign power of the state as a way of preserving the integrity of the person, encompassing the human body, mind, and soul, hence the objections to torture and other forms of physical molestation, to interference with familial peace, and to being sold or held as property.

It is widely recognized today that the struggle against slavery and the foundation of the Haitian state must be matters of separate concerns. The construction of the state has suffered serious setbacks over time because of internal dissension and external intervention, principally by the United States. These setbacks resulted first and foremost from domestic resistance to the implementation of the economic clauses of the constitution. In the first instance, the Haitian Revolution put forth a view of human needs and natural faculties and capacities that aimed to ensure humane existence to all persons—former slaves, or those without prior political affiliation, and freemen, or citizens whose political status preceded the revolution.[35] Related arguments bore on the plantation, which was the primary site of production, and association between workers (mostly former slaves) and planters (formerly privileged). Considering it to be a "manufacture," the former slaves envisaged a system of solidarity that eliminated titles—"No white person . . . shall set foot on this territory as a master"—and joined together the planters and the workers.[36]

The aim was not to disrupt the economy but to allow the former slaves to enjoy the benefices of the economy: "The colony being essentially agricultural, it cannot suffer the smallest disruption in the operation of its plantations" (title VI, art. 14).[37] The constitution encouraged Haitians to be productive for the duration of their natural lives in order to deserve their moral status as "good father . . . good son . . . good husband . . . and good soldier." Concurrently, the constitution mandated good management by posing the threat of loss of citizenship "as a result of insolvency and bankruptcy" (arts. 8 and 9). These constitutional dispositions granted equal access to all to the resources necessary to their subsistence. The related arrangements did away with prior political and economic covenants that had endangered the capacity of enslaved persons to lead a humane existence. But they also ran afoul of the titles and privileges of the *affranchis* (or free people of color) and white Frenchmen—but not French women who had been granted equal citizenship and certainly not Germans and Poles of any gender.

The reactions of the formerly privileged manifest themselves even in today's Haiti.[38] It is the stuff of the crisis of the Haitian state, a topic that lies beyond the scope of this chapter. It suffices to add that U.S. interventions accentuated social tensions there between the former slaves of African descent (or those who spearheaded the revolution) and the *affranchis* (those whose interests were affected by the drive of former slaves to full equality). Over the decades, successive coalitions of *affranchis* aligned themselves with and benefited from interventions by American capital and states.[39] These interventions aggravated local conflicts and helped derail the revolutionary project: to guarantee individual liberty as freedom from slavery and equality as protection from racial and economic discrimination.[40]

A HERMENEUTIC OF RIGHTS

Theorists still have difficulty considering that "illiterate black slaves" could produce universal notions of rights. According to Mintz, many today are unable or unwilling to imagine Haitian revolutionaries on par with such "intellectual giants" as William Jefferson or the Abbé de Sieyès.[41] Hence, it is generally noted that the American and French revolutions endowed particular historical subjects with specific faculties and capacities that they thought to be essential to "good government" and the "good life." It is also known that revolutionaries on both the European and the American continent imagined "rights" as instruments to guaranteeing such faculties and capacities. Specifically, it is held that French revolutionaries envisaged the *citizen* as a distinct entity with essential endowments and, thus, entitled to fundamental rights. It is also generally acknowledged that American colonists imagined the *individual* as independent and in an antagonist relation to the sovereign, and the constitution confirmed this by modeling individual rights on sovereignty—God given or natural and, at any rate, inviolable by the state and other citizens.

Hannah Arendt, for instance, upholds the primary role played by the American Revolution in laying the foundation of freedom on the distinction between political and social questions.[42] The related arguments are aimed at the French Revolution, whose descent into violence is attributed by Arendt to the invasion of politics by moral sentiments and economic matters. She thus attributes the success of the American Revolution to the fact that it wisely relegated social questions to separate domains—of legislation, for instance, as opposed to constitutional debates. Sibylle Fischer has appropriately deduced from Arendt's arguments that she presents slavery as a social question against the position of the colonists themselves who considered slavery a political question.[43] Significantly, Arendt's views lead to equivocation on the implication of the colonists' refusal to grant freedom to slaves. This equivocation is surprising because Arendt had earlier argued for the primacy of the "right to have rights" or "the right to belong to some kind of community."[44] Then, according to Seyla Benhabib, Arendt located the origins of totalitarianism in the distant European scramble for Africa, particularly in the accompanying "racial extermination policies."[45] To take the argument further, totalitarianism as the "heart of darkness" originated in hearts of Enlightened Europe in slavery and what followed it.

Arendt is not alone in her equivocation toward the rights of others, particularly those conquered and dominated by Europe. Isaiah Berlin too maintains that absolute freedom is best defined as negative liberty, or "the area within which a man can act unobstructed by others."[46] Berlin understands this form of liberty to be the sphere of action over oneself, body, and mind, "when the individual is sovereign."[47] Berlin contrasts negative liberty with positive liberty, or the right to be "one's own master" and to be self-directed in choosing and pursuing one's own goals. Thus construed, positive freedom does not merely offer absolute immunities but also presupposes agency and conditions, such that some individuals might be at liberty but lack the requisite necessities, including education, training, skills, and tools. Generations of scholars and politicians have justified slavery and colonialism on the basis of this distinction by assuming that slaves and the colonized lacked both agency (Reason) and the means (science) to be free.[48]

In fact, modern slavery was founded on a political rationality and rationalization of economic processes. Slavery and the plantation economy entailed "a radical rationalization of labor processes, an utter disregard for traditions, and a degree of instrumentalization of human life" that had not previously been seen in the colonies or by the slaves themselves in their places of origination.[49] To the slaves at least, slavery and the plantation economy were at once political, social, and moral questions in a revolutionary age. They responded as other revolutionaries would and did by drawing on their own human condition. Reading the Haitian constitution, one notes that Haitian revolutionaries were inspired by the insights of the first two revolutions: that citizens should be accorded faculties of self-governance and that individuals rights could not be curtailed by the state. But one is struck by their rejection of the moral foundations of the attendant rights as enunciated by French and American revolutionaries. For instance, the Haitians rejected the idea that *privileges* of citizenship could be envisaged for whimsically defined active, laboring, and virtuous members of society. One is also impressed by the form of human subjectivity ascertained by the Haitian revolutionaries and their understanding of the forms and range of human bondage, oppression, and suffering.

The former slaves better understood what it meant to be a *person*, a biological entity, whose existence could not be predicated on the strictures of any political system. Before the duty-bearing citizen and the rights-bearing individual, one was first and foremost a person—an entity with faculties without the protection of which life itself was without meaning. Thus, where the American stressed *life*, *liberty*, and the *pursuit of happiness* as the teleology of the revolution and the French emphasized *liberty*, *equality*, and *fraternity*, the enslaved sought to institutionalize the most basic of immunities. These can be viewed either positively as the right to the integrity of the body (including the gut), the mind, and the soul, or spirit or negatively as freedom from *oppression*, *exploitation*, and *suffering*.

When the landscapes and fragmentary but concordant facts of the Haitian Revolution are put together in the form of a theory of human rights, it becomes clear that so-called economic and social rights are not, as currently believed, a second generation of rights. They can be traced from the Haitian Revolution and anticolonial struggles against political systems and economic forms that deprived persons of the means to sustain life. Then as now, the existence of the privation—and the context—was ostensibly not the cause of revolution. In other words, the politics of human rights concerned the types of privation and political and economic systems that prevented persons from attaining their humanity. To the slave, the plantation economy, as mode of production, caused privations of body, mind, and soul. The plantation not only authorized physical molestation, interference with family, and starvation and torture but also permitted human beings to be sold and exchanged as one would things. The economic system was thus as objectionable as the political system when it resulted in dehumanization. They belong properly to the authoritative lexicon and repertoire of universal rights on the basis of their coevalness with civil and political ones.[50]

CONCLUSION

The events and motivations that generated Western conceptions of human rights are not without parallels elsewhere. The institutes (or precepts) and institutions of human rights are scattered across regions (most recently in the colonial worlds) and idioms (including those of anticolonialism) as a result of contingent events. These precepts and idioms continue to reside in the consciousness and memories of untold numbers as receptacles for the proposition that human beings possess faculties and capacities that need protection if life itself is to be ennobled. To reiterate an earlier point, these simple facts are often lost on human rights theorists and advocates. The political cause of neglect and/or erasure is the post–Cold War advent of a certain *realism or political pragmatism* that instrumentalizes human rights on behalf of political and ideological agendas. When the purpose of theory is to craft "defensible" norms of human rights as a basis for Western intervention in wayward states, then the necessity arises to teleologically insist on existing Western legislation and institutions of human rights and to affix them with determinate meanings.[51] This is not to say that existing institutions and instruments of human rights do not contingently have determinate meanings. It is to say that strictly legal and political arguments advanced in defense of interventions are not good substitutes for a reflection on the human condition. The latter requires attention to the existential conditions of persons everywhere as well as consideration of their multiple conceptions of political subjectivity and rationality. It also requires that theorists accommodate the multiple temporal and spatial motivations and articulations and iterations of the central moral precepts on which life may be founded.

Reading Pagden's and Ignatieff's arguments, one is struck by their elaborations on Western jurisprudence and their silence on the contributions of others to moral progress. For instance, Ignatieff envisages breaking the monopoly of the state on the conduct of international affairs and therefore the need to trace the fine line between the rights of states and those of citizens.[52] This impulse is commendable in view of the spread of political violence by states against their own citizens and others. Anticolonialists envisage a similar line between the capacity to intervene and the authority to intervene. Like their Western counterparts, anticolonialists and postcolonial theorists maintain even today that just as the postcolonial state may lose its sovereign privileges when it is unwilling and unable to protect some or all of its citizens, hegemonic states too lost their moral authority—and thus the right to intervene elsewhere—when they have consistently promoted political and economic regimes that deprive millions of the basic amenities of life.

If, as Ignatieff claims, Western states that are hypocritical in their adoption and monitoring of human rights do not lose the right to use force to defend them,[53] then it may be equally morally consistent to posit the following: that Third World states that are hypocritical in their implementation of Western norms of human rights do not lose the right to use force to maintain the domestic order if in fact they promote other classes of human rights. This is not a position that I would defend. I make the inference to highlight the disturbing logics that are attained through a peculiar sort of moral and methodological instrumentalism. It necessarily gives the authority to a few states and their societies to define human rights and promote a select class of institutions in combination with other declared or undeclared goals, including imperialism.[54] This sort of instrumentalism not only perpetuates the fallacious assumption that the "righteous sovereign" is necessarily a composite of Western states but also assumes that Third World states, mostly of the former Western colonial provinces, that do not adhere to Western precepts of human rights are morally deficient and in need of institutional reformation, involving the curtailment of their sovereignty.

By contrast, it is possible to close the gaps between "the given" (or the proclaimed reality of human rights) and "the real" (the heterogeneity and productive ambiguities of discourses and practices of human rights) without creating the expectation that any single entity monopolizes human aspirations and that any one method will completely reveal the complexity of human rights institutes and institutions. Again, the latter obey temporal and spatial motivations that are reflected in their articulations and iterations. But by revisiting the scenes of modern revolutions and anticolonial struggles, it is possible to obtain insights into diverse cultures of human rights and the precepts or institutes that inspired them. In the event, one is impressed that, in times of political crises, human rights institutes are derived from scattered ideas, facts, and practices. These are instrumentally assembled during political experimentation to respond to temporal and spatial conditions in conformity with existing fears, visions, desires, and fantasies.[55] In short, broader understandings of the value, extent, and forms of specific classes of human rights might be gained from visiting moral and intellectual landscapes of heterogeneous ideas, facts, and practices.[56]

From this perspective, the moral status of classes of human rights does not depend on their point of origination. This means that the non-Western origination of the idea that human rights necessarily encompass entitlements because of economic, social, and cultural needs does not inherently confer on them a lesser moral status. Nor does it signify a lesser concern among non-Western entities for the common good or a weaker sense of the common human past. In fact, it may be ascertained that Haitians too understood their ethical injunctions or commands as bearing on the aspiration of citizens, individuals, and persons everywhere to a higher moral order. They projected these injunctions and commands as immutable imperatives transcending time and space. In sum, Haitian revolutionaries and anticolonialists everywhere recognized the existence of "essential" human faculties and capacities and, as result, made the moral choice to protect them as a means to ennobling human existence. Like French and American revolutionaries, Haitians too designed their moral or ethical precepts with the purpose of bettering the lot of similarly situated persons and collectives everywhere. Their distinctive precepts and institutions of human rights were responses to the common human condition and, as such, belong equally to the collective human inheritance.

NOTES

1. John Bowing, ed., *The Works of Jeremy Bentham*, vol. 2 (New York: Russell & Russell, 1962), cited by Amartya Sen, "Elements of a Theory of Human Rights," *Philosophy and Public Affairs* 32, no. 4 (2004): 316.

2. Although the "universalist versus relativist" debate has attracted the attention of institutionalists and others, I take the view that this debate has distracted from productive consideration of the utility, instrumentalization, and appeal of the idea of global standards of governance across regions and political and cultural systems.

3. Sen, "Elements of a Theory of Human Rights," 316.

4. Sen, "Elements of a Theory of Human Rights."

5. Anthony Pagden, "Human Rights, Natural Rights, and Europe's Imperial Legacy," *Political Theory* 31, no. 2 (2003): 171.

6. Pagden, "Human Rights," 171.

7. Pagden, "Human Rights," 171.

8. Michael Ignatieff, *Human Rights as Politics and Idolatry* (Princeton, N.J.: Princeton University Press, 2001), passim.

9. Ignatieff, *Human Rights as Politics and Idolatry*.

10. See also Michael Ignatieff, "American Empire: The Burden," *New York Times Magazine*, January 5, 2003, 22.

11. Ignatieff, *Human Rights as Politics and Idolatry*.

12. Daniel C. Thomas, *The Helsinki Effect: International Norms, Human Rights, and the Demise of Communism* (Princeton, N.J.: Princeton University Press, 2001);

Joshua Cohen, ed., *For Love of Country: Debating the Limits of Patriotism* (Boston: Beacon Press, 1996); Adam Watson, *The Evolution of International Society: A Comparative Historical Analysis* (London: Routledge, 1992); Thomas M. Callaghy, Ronald Kassimir, and Robert Latham, eds., *Intervention and Transnationalism in Africa: Global-Local Networks of Power* (Cambridge: Cambridge University Press, 2001); Martha Finnemore, *National Interests in International Society* (Ithaca, N.Y.: Cornell University Press, 1996); Ignatieff, *Human Rights as Politics and Idolatry*.

13. Edward A. Kolodziej, *A Force Profonde: The Power, Politics, and Promise of Human Rights* (Philadelphia: University of Pennsylvania Press, 2003); Margaret E. Keck and Kathryn Sikkink, *Activists beyond Borders: Advocacy Networks in International Politics* (Ithaca, N.Y.: Cornell University Press, 1998).

14. Pagden, "Human Rights," 171–72 and passim.

15. Sen, "Elements of a Theory of Human Rights."

16. *Oxford English Dictionary* (Oxford: Oxford University Press, 1971), 1452.

17. *Oxford English Dictionary*, 948.

18. Pagden, "Human Rights."

19. *Oxford English Dictionary*, 1452.

20. Denis Diderot and Jean Le Rond d'Alembert, eds., *Encyclopédie ou Dictionnaire Raisonné des Sciences, Arts, et des Metiers* (Paris: Chez Briasson, 1755), 115–16.

21. Louis Henkins, *The Age of Rights* (New York: Columbia University Press, 1990).

22. Michel-Rolph Trouillot, *Silencing the Past: Power and the Production of History* (Boston: Beacon Press, 1995), 85 and passim.

23. Trouillot, *Silencing the Past*.

24. Trouillot, *Silencing the Past*, 23 and passim.

25. See Trouillot, *Silencing the Past*, and Sibylle Fischer, *Modernity Disavowed: Haiti and the Cultures of Slavery in the Age of Revolution* (Durham, N.C.: Duke University Press, 2004), 22 and passim.

26. Trouillot, *Silencing the Past*, 78.

27. Trouillot, *Silencing the Past*, 75.

28. Fischer, *Modernity Disavowed*, 201.

29. For the full text and commentaries on the imperial constitution, see Fischer, *Modernity Disavowed*, app. A, 227–81.

30. Sidney W. Mintz, "Can Haiti Change?," *Foreign Affairs* 74, no. 1 (1995): 73–86, 77.

31. Mintz, "Can Haiti Change?," 78.

32. Mintz, "Can Haiti Change?," 77–78.

33. Mintz, "Can Haiti Change?," 78.

34. Fischer, *Modernity Disavowed*, 37.

35. Trouillot, *Silencing the Past*; David P. Geggus, ed., *The Impact of the Haitian Revolution in the Atlantic World* (Columbia: University of South Carolina Press, 2001); Doris Y. Kadish, ed, *Slavery in the Caribbean Francophone World* (Athens: University of Georgia Press, 2000).

36. Fischer, *Modernity Disavowed*, 267.

37. Fischer, *Modernity Disavowed*, 267.

38. Mintz, "Can Haiti Change?," passim.

39. Trouillot, *Silencing the Past*.

40. Fischer, *Modernity Disavowed*, 267 and passim.

41. Mintz, "Can Haiti Change?"

42. Hannah Arendt, *On Revolution* (Harmondsworth: Penguin, 1963).

43. Fischer, *Modernity Disavowed*, 7–9.

44. Hannah Arendt, *The Origins of Totalitarianism* (New York: Harcourt Brace Jovanovich, 1968), chap. 9.

45. Seyla Benhabib, *The Rights of Others: Aliens, Residents, and Citizens* (Cambridge: Cambridge University Press, 2004), 52.

46. Isaiah Berlin, *Four Essays on Liberty* (London: Oxford University Press, 1969), chap 3.

47. Berlin, *Four Essays on Liberty*.

48. Robert H. Jackson, *Quasi-States: Sovereignty, International Relations and the Third World* (Cambridge: Cambridge University Press, 1990), 26–31.

49. Fischer, *Modernity Disavowed*, 12.

50. Sen, "Elements of a Theory of Human Rights," 316.

51. Ignatieff, *Human Rights as Politics and Idolatry*.

52. Ignatieff, *Human Rights as Politics and Idolatry*.

53. Ignatieff, *Human Rights as Politics and Idolatry*.

54. Ignatieff, "American Empire," passim.

55. Fischer, *Modernity Disavowed*, 20.

56. Fischer, *Modernity Disavowed*, 2.

Chapter Nine

Retrieving "Other" Visions of the Future: Sri Aurobindo and the Ideal of Human Unity

B. S. Chimni

The visions of the future of world order that find a place in contemporary writings and scholarship are essentially those advanced by Western thinkers (from Kant to Held). The work of non-Western thinkers and visionaries hardly finds a mention in them. The writings of Sri Aurobindo (1872–1950) are a good example of an integral vision of the future of global society that has received little attention. Based on a coherent, albeit contestable, theory of the evolution of human society, Sri Aurobindo argues that the ideal of human unity will be inevitably realized. But if human unity is to contribute to individual and collective growth of nations and peoples, it must have spiritualism at its foundations.

This chapter retrieves, in an effort to "decolonize international relations," Sri Aurobindo's vision of the future world order, drawing on his "philosophical" writings and his analysis of international relations and organizations in the period 1915–1950. His vision is significant for "decolonizing international relations" for many reasons. First, his vision of human unity that is inclusive of the "Other" was shaped by his active participation in anti-imperial struggle. Second, he is among the few thinkers who reflected on the different forms a world state could assume and the ideal world state from the standpoint of humanity.[1] Third, he advanced an integrated understanding of material and spiritual transformation of humankind; his brand of thinking contains a unique understanding on which to build a just world order. The latter view contrasts with that of Kant, whose basic idea was that "even without any inner, moral

197

improvement, man will improve his outward legal conduct. In the end, a moral attitude will come to prevail."[2]

Equally, Sri Aurobindo departed from the *Vedanta*[3] idea, the basis of his thought, that "the empirical world and finite individuals are illusory."[4] As the philosopher Mohanty points out, Sri Aurobindo "most definitely rejects Samkara's Advaita" and "regards the world as real and incorporates an evolutionary theory of reality into his conception of reality (Brahman manifests himself in progressively evolving forms of reality) and finds a place for history of mankind within the Advaita, and proposes a new kind of yoga adapted not to the goal of an individual's own liberation, but to the (collective) goal of elevating mankind to a higher form of consciousness ('supermind')."[5] In short, he was concerned with the limits of reason rather than its rejection.

In attempting to *critically* retrieve Sri Aurobindo's vision of future world society and state, I will proceed in the following way.

First, I offer a brief sketch of the life of Sri Aurobindo and its intimate links with colonialism. For Sri Aurobindo's writings cannot be understood or given meaning outside the colonial encounter; colonialism profoundly shaped his life and times.

Second, I sketch Sri Aurobindo's theory of the evolution of human society. He identified the distinct psychological stages through which human society has evolved, namely, symbolic, typal or conventional, individualist, and subjective. The essential point Sri Aurobindo makes is that the current subjective age must eschew "objective egoism" if it is not to continue on the path of strife, domination, and destruction.

Third, I briefly look at Sri Aurobindo's critique of the modern state, democracy, and law. The reasons for his dissatisfaction help clarify his vision of the future world state, international law, and global democracy. Sri Aurobindo was critical of both socialist and bourgeois democracy; while the former destroyed the conditions in which individual life flourishes, the latter did not facilitate participatory politics. He also anticipated and critiqued the realist theory of international relations inasmuch as it denies the relevance of moral considerations to the external policies of a state. These critiques were advanced to stress the point that a democratic state should create the normative and institutional conditions that facilitate the inner transformation of individuals and human collectives.

Fourth, I touch on his discussion of the possible political forms of human unity. His preference was for a loose confederation of humankind that preserved the diversity of peoples and nations as against a centralized world state that would encourage uniformity. From this standpoint, Sri Aurobindo saw the League of Nations and United Nations as welcome steps in the direction of the emergence of a democratic world state, albeit he was critical of both from the viewpoint of egalitarian politics and the absence in the international community of any understanding of the need for spiritual human unity to accompany what he termed "mechanical unity."

Fifth, I outline Sri Aurobindo's vision of the economics, politics, and international relations of a future spiritual society, both domestic and global. While what are on offer are mere glimpses, even these allow an insight into the thinking of Sri Aurobindo on crucial social and political issues underlying the emergence of a world state.

Sixth, I look at the critical problem of the strategy to be followed to establish a just world order and a democratic world state. I suggest that one reason the Sri Aurobindo "model" has not caught the imagination of the world is because, unlike Marx, he did not articulate an elaborate theory of social change. He increasingly came to focus more on the spiritual quest of the individual than on collective struggle to bring about social transformation. I argue instead that the inner transformation that Sri Aurobindo stresses can inter alia be brought about through participating in ethical collective struggles for a just world order; the very process of collective struggle for the material transformation of the world contributes, when conducted in the matrix of nonviolent and ethical politics, to the spiritual development of individuals who partake in it.

Before proceeding, I wish to clarify that my thesis is not about *any* marriage of materialism with religion but about transcending these binary opposites. The concept of spiritualism as deployed by Sri Aurobindo helps us to do so, as it is rooted in philosophical reflections about the essential unity of all phenomena, both material and spiritual.[6] I borrow from the philosophy of Sri Aurobindo to explore the dialectic between external and inner transformation to bring about a just world order; the idea of inner or spiritual change cannot any longer be ignored by social movements.

THE LIFE OF SRI AUROBINDO

Sri Aurobindo, born Aurobindo Ghose, is considered among the key architects of modern India. Before the arrival of Gandhi from South Africa to lead the freedom struggle, Sri Aurobindo was "a powerful influence in the nationalist upsurge which stirred the country."[7] Indeed, he "anticipated the ideals and programme of the struggle which under Gandhiji's guidance took a practical shape and culminated in Independence."[8]

Sri Aurobindo spent fourteen of "his formative years" in England and had a very "anglicized upbringing."[9] His father, Krishna Dhan Ghose, was "an avowed Anglophile."[10] He therefore sent the young Aurobindo to England, where, from the age of seven to twelve, he was in Manchester under the care of Reverend William H. Drewett.[11] During this time, he was baptized as a Christian, and his full name read Aurobindo Ackroyd Ghose (on his return to India he dropped Ackroyd from his name).[12] Later he went to St. Paul's school in London, where he was "kept wholly isolated from India."[13] Sri Aurobindo's "working life" is usually divided into three phases. The first phase began with his admission to the University of Cambridge in 1889 and ended in 1905. In this period, "he was mainly engaged in study, teaching, experimenting and thinking." The second period, from 1905 to 1910, "was short and stormy, but extraordinarily important in the history of India. He was not the sole or the most prominent leader of the nationalist movement, but he was its most eloquent spokesman."[14]

In this second phase of his working life, he embraced political extremism after criticizing the moderate congress leadership for indulging in "a little too much talk about the blessings of British rule."[15] He helped "organize secret societies" but was also "to elaborate a programme of massive passive resistance against the partition of Bengal in 1905 revealing the possibilities of a broader movement."[16] In 1908, he was implicated in what is known as the Alipore bomb case, which led to his "lone incarceration in Alipore jail for nearly a year."[17] He came out of jail "a changed man."[18]

Thus began the third and final phase of his life. He left Calcutta in 1910 and settled in Pondicherry, a French settlement, and began his long quest for spiritual realization. According to Tara Chand, "The circumstances of his flight and subsequent life has given rise to speculation of not altogether complimentary nature."[19] The historian Sarkar is more forthcoming when he states that religion became "a royal road for an honorable retreat."[20] The next forty years, in which he undertook his spiritual journey, have been described as "sterile from the point of view of history,"[21] the reason being that hereafter his impact on the freedom struggle "was negligible."[22] I have no intention to join issue with historians as to whether religion did become for Sri Aurobindo "a royal road for honorable retreat," for it is not central to the concerns of this chapter. However, it needs to be said that his turn to spiritualism could perhaps also be seen as the manifestation of Sri Aurobindo's belief that "the Indian struggle for independence was essentially an expression of the urge of the spirit for self-realization" and that it would not come about through external changes alone.[23]

My concern is more with his major works *The Human Cycle*, *The Ideal of Human Unity*, *The Life Divine*, and *War and Self-Determination*, written in Pondicherry, in which he articulated a particular vision of the future world order.[24] These are works of high philosophy articulating an evolutionary view of human society and can therefore be read more as philosophical tracts than as religious texts.[25] I turn to Sri Aurobindo to stress the importance of spiritual change in bringing about a just world order because he addressed in a systematic way the ideal of human unity and, examined from this perspective, developments in international relations.

However, before I proceed further, I must attend to one other possible criticism; that is, given Sri Aurobindo's Western upbringing and education, would it not be a travesty of sorts to see him as articulating "Other" visions of the future? Is not his vision in some ways dirtied or adulterated by the Western vision? In response, it may be said that the uniqueness of Sri Aurobindo's vision is precisely the fact that it does not—a matter worthy of consideration by those seeking to "decolonize international relations"—completely reject its "Other," an expected feature of a certain stereotypical understanding of what "Other" visions should be. What is significant is that this result is achieved amidst a colonial experience that would in the normal course spawn (and often did engender) a more exclusivist vision. As Nandy perceptively points out, what is striking about Sri Aurobindo's vision is that his "response to colonialism included a cultural self-affirmation which had a greater respect for the selfhood of the 'other' and a search for a more universal model of emancipation."[26] In other words, "while the colonial system only saw him as an object, he could not see the colonizers as mere objects. As a part of his struggle for survival, the West remained for Indian victims like Aurobindo an internal human reality, in love as well as in hate, in identification as well as in counter-identification."[27] Gandhiji too understood the cognitive superiority of such a view. He recognized too that "once the hegemony of a theory of imperialism without winners and losers was established, imperialism had lost out on cognitive, in addition to ethical, grounds."[28]

SRI AUROBINDO'S EVOLUTIONARY PHILOSOPHY: A SKETCH

Sri Aurobindo's theory of evolution of human society is a theory of both individual and collective evolution. While human society assumes various collective forms over the ages, the individual soul also undergoes evolution toward becoming one with the ultimate reality. These two processes of evolution are closely interlinked, as some forms of collective life facilitate the growth of the spiritual self and others constrain it. But insofar as these two evolutionary processes can be separated (in many ways these are separate journeys), he dealt with the idea of collective evolution in his works *The Human Cycle* and *The Ideal of Human Unity* and with individual evolution in his magnum opus, *The Life Divine*.

Where collective life is concerned, Sri Aurobindo described societies over the ages either through a classification of the central psychic features or through the political form they assumed. The psychological categorization is briefly discussed in this section and the political form, albeit only in the modern era, in the next. Thereafter, I look at the alternative future political forms of human unity that Sri Aurobindo examined.

In his work *The Human Cycle*, Sri Aurobindo sets out in the very first page his particular approach to history and sociology. He critiques historical and sociological studies as overly "concentrated on the external data, laws, institutions, rites, customs, economic factors and developments, while the deeper psychological elements so important in the activities of a mental, emotional, ideative being like man have been very much neglected."[29] He obviously had Marxist ideology in view when he went further and observed the disturbing tendency to "explain everything in history and social development as much as possible by economic necessity or motive—by economy understood in its widest sense."[30]

To articulate his alternative spiritual approach, he borrowed from the German thinker Lamprecht the distinct *psychological stages* through which human society has evolved, that is, symbolic, typal or conventional, individualist, and subjective.[31] In the symbolic age, man felt "present behind himself and his life and his activities—the Divine, the Gods, the vast and deep unnameable, a hidden, living and mysterious nature of things. All his religious and social institutions, all the moments and phases of his life are to him symbols in which he seeks to express what he knows or guesses of the mystic influences that are behind his life and shape and govern or at the least intervene in its movements."[32] On the other hand, "the tendency of the conventional age of society is to fix, to arrange firmly, to formalize, to erect a system of rigid grades and hierarchies, to stereotype religion, to bind education and training to a traditional and unchangeable form, to subject thought to infallible authorities, to cast a stamp of finality on what seems to it the finished life of man."[33]

Then comes the age of individualism "as a result of the corruption and failure of the conventional, as a revolt against the reign of the petrified typal figure."[34] It is "an attempt to get back from the conventionalism of belief and practice to some solid bed-rock, no matter what, of real and tangible Truth."[35] This age "is necessarily individualistic because all the old general standards have become bankrupt and can no longer give any inner help; it is therefore the individual who has to become a discoverer, a pioneer, and to search out by his individual reason, intuition, idealism, desire, claim upon life or whatever other light he finds in himself the true law of the world and of his own being."[36] Europe was the principal site of this development, the place where individualism has "exercised its full sway."[37] It represented the "revolt of reason" and the "triumphal progress of physical science."[38] This phase sees the rejection of the society and politics of the old order.[39]

The phase of individualism is to be now replaced by subjectivism. In this age arises, first, the belief that "it is a spiritual, an inner freedom that can alone create a perfect human order"[40] and, second, the belief that the Supreme Being "is one in all, expressed in the individual and in the collectivity and only by admitting and realizing our unity with others can we entirely fulfill our true self-being."[41] Read together, these two propositions unfold a dialectic by which it is the spiritual evolution of the individual that must underlie all human unity if it is to be a unity that facilitates the equal and free development of all. It may come about slowly in the beginning, but there was no other possible solution.[42]

This subjectivism that Sri Aurobindo proposes is to be bereft of collective egoism. Turning to Germany to exemplify his point, Sri Aurobindo noted that there was in Germany a "great subjective force" that "came from her great philosophers, Kant, Hegel, Fichte, Nietzsche, from her great thinker and poet Goethe, from her great musicians, Beethoven and Wagner, and from all in the German soul and temperament which they represented."[43] However, this subjectivism was subverted by Nazism, which represented "an *objective subjectivism* which is miles apart from the true goal of the subjective age":[44]

> To show the error it is necessary to see wherein lies the true individuality of man and of the nation. It lies not in its physical, economic, even its cultural life which are only means and adjuncts, but in something deeper whose roots are not in the ego, but in a Self . . . which relates the good of each, on a footing of equality and not of strife and domination, to the good of the rest of the world.[45]

From a contemporary perspective, it is worth emphasizing here that Sri Aurobindo understood that the egoistic rendering of subjectivism was not peculiar to Nazism alone but also to Western civilization as a whole at that point in history. In this respect, Sri Aurobindo's critique of Western civilization and Nazism is similar to that offered by Aimé Césaire. Sri Aurobindo wrote,

> If a sacred egoism—and the expression did not come from Teutonic lips—is to govern international relations, then it is difficult to deny the force of the German position. The theory of inferior and decadent races was loudly proclaimed by other than German thinkers and has governed, with whatever assuaging scruples, the general practice of military domination and commercial exploitation of the weak by the strong; all that Germany has done is to attempt to give it a wider extension and more rigorous execution and apply it to European as well as to Asiatic and African peoples.[46]

Césaire likewise observed

> that it is Nazism, yes, but that before they [i.e., other Western states] were its
> victims, they were its accomplices; that they tolerated that Nazism before it
> was inflicted on them. That they absolved it, shut their eyes to it, legitimated it,
> because, until then, it had been applied only to non-European peoples.[47]

Césaire's *Discourse on Colonialism* made a "critical contribution" to our thinking about colonialism, fascism, and revolution. Kelley, for instance, notes that
"its recasting of the history of Western Civilization helps us locate the origins
of fascism within colonialism itself; hence, within the very tradition of humanism, critics believed fascism threatened."[48] Sri Aurobindo was doing likewise.

What does the Aurobindo–Césaire critique offer by way of understanding
the contemporary world? Can we use it, for instance, to grasp the relationship
between the United States and what has come to be called Old Europe? To be
sure, the United States is a liberal democracy and far from being a fascist state.
Nor has it today turned on Europe by arms as the Nazis did. Yet one cannot
but reflect on the fact that the Old Europe's unease over U.S. policies flows
not from a fundamental opposition to neocolonial exploitation of third world
peoples but represents tactical differences on how to subordinate non-European
peoples. Thus, for example, even if Iraq had not been occupied by the United
States, the existing world order was hardly just for non-European peoples.
The absence of protest against the fundamentals of the existing world order
shows that Old Europe is an integral part of the imperial dispensation. It merely
subscribes to an alternative set of policies to sustain the imperial dispensation,
a dispensation that also offers it more than what it now receives as spoils. To
put it differently, the absence of individual and collective spiritual growth in
the imperial world has meant that objective subjectivism still defines, albeit in
its liberal form, the global politics of our time.

HUMAN UNITY, MODERN STATE, AND DEMOCRACY

But the potential of human unity remains. It explains why, even in the face of
colonialism, Sri Aurobindo conceptualized human unity. On the material plane,
he clearly saw that technological developments would bring about human
unity:

> Science, commerce and rapid communications have produced a state of things
> in which the disparate masses of humanity, once living to themselves, have been
> drawn together by a process of subtle unification into a single mass which already
> has a common vital and is rapidly forming a common mental existence. . . . The
> idea of a World-State or world-union has been born not only in the speculating

forecasting mind of the thinker but in the consciousness of humanity out of the very necessity of this new common existence.[49]

These developments gave fillip to the "natural" process in which "the family, the commune, the clan or tribes, the nation, the empire are so many stages" in the "progress and constant enlargement of humankind."[50]

At the same time, he stressed "the insufficiency of human unity without a growth of the religion of humanity which can alone make it a great psychological advance in the spiritual evolution of the race."[51] The ideal of human unity could not be realized by social and political adjustments alone. What was called for was "inner change":

> It must be remembered that a greater social or political unity is not necessarily a boon in itself; it is only worth pursuing in so far as it provides a means and framework for a better, richer, more happy and puissant individual and collective life.[52]

But while social and political tinkering alone could not unite humanity, it was important, Sri Aurobindo realized, to pay attention to the political forms that evolving human society was assuming. For if humanity were to realize the idea of a just world order or a democratic world state, one needed to theorize its nature and character. It led Sri Aurobindo to critique "the State idea," as the nation-state was the political form which human unity assumed in modern times and the expedient to which the human mind had grown accustomed.[53] In his view, the modern state (both bourgeois and socialist) greatly circumscribed real democracy.

First, given the growth in state activity, there was "the call of the State to the individual to immolate himself on its altar," forgetting that "the State is a convenience, and a rather clumsy convenience, for our common development; it ought never to be made an end in itself."[54]

Second, that the role of law in modern democracies was an unhelpful one. According to Sri Aurobindo,

> Law was often in great measure a system of legalized oppression and exploitation and on its political side has had often enough plainly that stamp, though it has assumed always the solemn face of a sacrosanct order and government and justice.[55]

Third, anticipating much contemporary debate on polyarchy, Sri Aurobindo pointed out that in most modern democracies

> the sole democratic elements are public opinion, periodical elections and the power of the people to refuse re-election to those who have displeased it. The government is really in the hands of the bourgeoisie, the professional and business men, the landholders,—where such a class still exists,—strengthened by a number

of new arrivals from the working-class who very soon assimilate themselves to the political temperament and ideas of the governing classes. If a World-State were to be established on the present basis of human society, it might well try to develop its central government on this principle.[56]

Fourth, he noted that the bourgeois state was part of a bourgeois world order and had "its eye chiefly on the possession of markets, the command of new fields of wealth, the formation or conquest of colonies or dependencies which can be commercially or industrially exploited and on political aggrandizement only as a means for this more cherished object."[57]

Fifth, he lamented the fact that the deeper impulse of the bourgeois state was not subject to moral constraints. He anticipated the realist approach to international relations in noting that

> the State is an entity which, with the greatest amount of power, is the least hampered by internal scruples or external checks. It has no soul or only a rudimentary one. It is a military, political and economic force; but it is only in a slight and undeveloped degree, if at all, an intellectual and ethical being.[58]

He went on to note that "self-protection and self-expansion by the devouring of others were its dharma."[59] Consequently,

> The present arrangement of the world has been worked out by economic forces, by political diplomacies, treaties and purchases and by military violence without regard to any moral principle or any general rule of the good of mankind. It has served roughly certain ends of the World-Force in its development and helped at much cost of bloodshed, suffering, cruelty, oppression and revolt to bring humanity together.[60]

Sixth, he pointed out that there was "neither any true and enlightened consciousness of human opinion to restrain the predatory State nor any effective international law."[61] In the fashion of the realist approach, he observed,

> States and Governments yield usually to a moral pressure only so far as it does not compel them to sacrifice their vital interests.[62]

But Sri Aurobindo also perceptively discerned an incipient contrary trend. He saw the emergence of "a cosmopolitan, international sentiment," albeit admitting that this sentiment was "still rather nebulous and vaguely ideal" but "which may still accelerate the growth of formal union."[63] He was also realistic enough to see that this "cosmopolitan, international sentiment ... could not easily be so close and forcible a sentiment as national feeling" and therefore may not be able to "resist the pressure of ... old or the effective growth of new centrifugal forces."[64] Eventually, it would be the "intellectual religion of humanity" that would bring about the "unity of humankind."[65]

POSSIBLE FUTURES: POLITICAL FORMS OF HUMAN UNITY

Sri Aurobindo's critique of the modern state, both bourgeois and socialist, alerted him to the need to conceptualize the various political forms that human unity could assume. As an important leader of the national freedom struggle, he was already aware that in the history of humankind, the drive toward "vast supranational aggregates" has assumed mostly imperial forms:

> The form it took was the desire of a strong nation for mastery over others, permanent possession of their territories, subjugation of their peoples, exploitation of their resources: there was also an attempt at quasi-assimilation, an imposition of the culture of a dominant race and, in general, a system of absorption wholesale or as complete as possible. The Roman Empire was the classic example of this kind of endeavor.[66]

Given past historical trends, Sri Aurobindo posited two possibilities:

> International unification must culminate or at least is likely to culminate in one of two forms. There is likely to be either a centralized World-State or a looser world-union which may be either a close federation or a simple confederacy of the peoples for the common ends of mankind.[67]

Drawing on the lessons of history and his encounter with colonialism, Sri Aurobindo expressed his preference for the latter: "the last form is the most desirable, because it gives sufficient scope for the principle of variation which is necessary for the free play of life and the healthy progress of the race."[68] For "unity we must create, but not necessarily uniformity."[69]

He noted that uniformity "would inevitably mean the undue depression of an indispensable element in the vigor of human life and progress, the free life of the individual, the free variation of the peoples."[70] On the other hand, he perceptively recognized that "a looser confederacy might well open to the objection that it would give too ready a handle for centrifugal forces, were such to arise in new strength."[71] How was this eventuality to be prevented? Sri Aurobindo considered the possibility of "religion of humanity" acting as the balancing force:

> The saving power needed is a new psychological factor which will at once make a united life necessary to humanity and force it to respect the principle of freedom. The religion of humanity seems to be the one growing force which tends in that

direction; for it makes for the sense of human oneness, it has the idea of the race, and yet at the same time it respects the human individual and the natural human grouping.[72]

In Aurobindo's view, "a spiritual religion of humanity is the hope of the future."[73] By this, he did not mean "universal religion":

> Mankind has tried unity by that means; it has failed and deserved to fail, because there can be no universal religious system, one in mental creed and vital form. The inner spirit is indeed one, but more than any other the spiritual life insists on freedom and variation in its self-expression and means of development.[74]

What, then, did he mean by "a spiritual religion of humanity"?

> A religion of humanity means the growing realization that there is a secret Spirit, a divine Reality, in which we are all one, that humanity is its highest present vehicle on earth, that the human race and the human being are the means by which it will progressively reveal itself here.[75]

In sum, what was needed was "a spiritual oneness" leading to "a psychological oneness" that respected "free inner variation and a freely varied outer self-expression" as the basis for "a higher type of human existence."[76]

But what is the process through which political unity would come about? In Sri Aurobindo's view,

> The process by which the World-State may come starts with the creation of a central body which will at first have very limited functions, but, once created, must absorb by degrees all the different utilities of a centralized international control, as the State.[77]

It explains why, while Sri Aurobindo was extremely critical of the Covenant of the League of Nations, he saw the creation of the League as "an event of capital importance."[78] He was clear that the League of Nations was "not happy in its conception, well-inspired in its formation or destined to any considerable longevity or a supremely successful career."[79] He was in particular critical of the mandates and colonial system, which he described as "that cloak which can cover with so noble a grace the hard reality of domination and exploitation,— things now too gross in their nakedness to be present undraped to the squeamish moral sense of a modern humanity."[80] Yet he saw the creation of the League of Nations as inaugurating "a new era in the world."[81]

Unsurprisingly, then, he saw the establishment of the United Nations as a "capital event, the crucial outcome of the world-wide tendencies which Nature has set in motion for her destined purpose."[82] It was not as if the UN system was perfect. But despite the weaknesses, he warned against pessimism, for presumably the ideal world state would be established only through an incremental process.

THE SPIRITUAL SOCIETY: FURTHER REFLECTIONS

Two questions still remain. First, in contrast to bourgeois and socialist society and state, how will a spiritual society and state function? Second, how does one get from here to there? The former question is touched on in this section and the question of agency and strategy in the next. The elaboration of the meaning and content of a spiritual society may begin with Sri Aurobindo's critique of the idea of progress:

> Modern society has discovered a new principle of survival, progress, but the aim of that progress it has never discovered,—unless the aim is always more knowledge, more equipment, convenience and comfort, more enjoyment, a greater and still greater complexity of the social economy, a more and more cumbrously opulent life. But these things must lead in the end where the old led, for they are only the same thing on a larger scale; they lead in a circle, that is to say, nowhere; they do not escape from the cycle of birth, growth, decay and death, they do not really find the secret of self-prolongation by constant self-renewal which is the principle of immortality, but only seem for a moment to find it by the illusion of a series of experiments each of which ends in disappointment. That so far has been the nature of modern progress.[83]

The idea of progress is, in short, informed by an understanding that "depends ultimately on the false perception of the material as alone real and outward life as alone of importance."[84]

But Sri Aurobindo was aware that spiritualism, on the other hand, is accused of nonconcern with the "problems with which humanity is at grips." The mystic "distorts them with his alien and unverifiable light obscure to human understanding and confuses the plain practical and vital issues life puts before us."[85] His response to this charge was twofold. First, as Sri Aurobindo clarified,

> this is not the standpoint from which the true significance of the spiritual evolution in man or the value of spirituality can be judged or assessed; for its real work is not to solve human problems on the past or present mental basis, but to create a new foundation of our being and our life and knowledge.[86]

Second, knowing that any society has to meet basic human needs, he talked of the economics of a spiritualized society:

> The aim of its economics would be not to create a huge engine of production, whether of the competitive or the co-operative kind, but to give to men—not only to some but to all men each in his highest possible measure—the joy of work according to their own nature and free leisure to grow inwardly, as well as a simply rich and beautiful life for all.[87]

However, he did not detail out the political economy of a spiritual society and state. Likewise, he did not work through the international relations between spiritual states. However, he did observe that each such state

> would regard the peoples as group-souls, the Divinity concealed and to be self-discovered in its human collectivities, group-souls meant like the individual to grow according to their own nature and by that growth to help each other, to help the whole race in the one common work of humanity. And that work would be to find the divine Self in the individual and the collectivity and to realize spiritually, mentally, vitally, materially its greatest, largest, richest and deepest possibilities in the inner life of all and their outer action and nature.[88]

It perhaps needs to be said that Sri Aurobindo was not entirely unaware of the many detailed legal rules that would be needed to structure developments that led to the creation of a qualitatively new kind of society and international relations. Thus, for example, he had already anticipated the idea of humanitarian intervention, albeit not as an instrument of empire but that of common human good. Sri Aurobindo recognized that "the principal of political non-interference is likely to be much less admitted in the future than it has been in the past or is at present."[89] He went on to note,

> There is more and more possible an intervention . . . not on avowed grounds of national interest, but ostensibly on behalf of liberty, constitutionalism and democracy, or of an apposite social and political principle, on international grounds therefore and practically in the force of this idea that the internal arrangements of a country concern, under certain conditions of disorder or insufficiency, not only itself, but its neighbors and humanity at large."

STRATEGY FOR INDIVIDUAL AND COLLECTIVE LIBERATION

Sri Aurobindo did not tell us in any detail about how to get from an imperial to a just world order with a world state at the helm that facilitates individual and collective liberation. The charge of utopianism is therefore very easily laid at the door of Sri Aurobindo. For how are we to attain the eventual goal of producing a "superman" (an idea that is to be sharply distinguished from that advanced by Nietzsche)[90] who is in the final stages of a process of becoming one with the ultimate reality? While Sri Aurobindo recognized the importance of material developments, he did not see it as a major obstacle in transforming the human psyche. This explains his lack of detailed attention to mapping appropriate social structures and institutions. His emphasis was on "living within and from within."[91]

It is here that Sri Aurobindo did not do full justice to his radical social reinterpretation of Advaita Vedanta of Samskara. He therefore neglected, first, the entire domain of political economy that Marx, for example, so assiduously addressed. Sri Aurobindo ignored the fact that "institutions matter a great deal for human psychology and social relations."[92] Thus, while property relations may not automatically transform "social psychology and social relations" (as earlier generation of socialists often believed,) such transformation cannot be brought about without reforming property relations. While there will always be the exceptional individual such as Sri Aurobindo who can transcend external reality, it cannot be the assumption on which collective social transformation can be achieved.

Second, Sri Aurobindo did not fully appreciate the role of individual and collective struggle for social change in bringing about inner transformation despite the fact that he himself was in many ways shaped by his participation in the struggle for freedom. His subsequent turning away from active politics and his lifelong focus on self-realization led him to somewhat ignore the role of struggle in bringing about inner change.

I believe after Gandhi that the collective nonviolent struggle for an egalitarian and democratic world order can transform people and help connect them to a higher self within. Activities directed toward seeking social transformation help individuals and collectives to turn and grow within. Equally, the stress on inner transformation helps those participating in the struggle for a just world order keep away egoistic concerns and ensure the presence of ethical behavior in transformative politics.

I have elsewhere argued, from a Marxist perspective, that a global state is evolving that has an imperial character.[93] I have also suggested a number of ways of democratizing and reforming the emerging global state. I now contend that the agents of democratic and progressive reforms (the old and new social movements) must possess a unified understanding of material and spiritual transformation if the reforms are to be realized and, more significantly, a just world order is to be established. In social movement literature, there is posited the contrast between "a secular vision of unfolding human destiny, a programme increasingly focused on the emerging political centre" or the state ("the civic imaginary"), on the one hand and "a politics of selves" or "movements of expression" on the other.[94] The latter involves "a heightened experience of subjectivity" that represents "a new way of constituting the social world."[95] I am arguing that the two can be combined through a morally grounded politics of social movements. In other words, inner transformation can come about both through participating in nonviolent collective struggles for a just social order and by living from within. Gandhiji represented at least one synthesis of this dialectic of individual and collective liberation.

The realist philosopher Roy Bhaskar has suggested that the call for a spiritual transformation faces the challenge of "the prehistory of spirituality":

> Bhaskar says that we are at a prehistory of spirituality as spiritual seeking in the past has not always embodied collectivist struggles for human emancipation. Spiritual seekers and movements continue to face the challenge of overcoming their egoism, a narrow self-centred view of salvation, and the will to assert and here participation in mutually validating discursive argumentation is a crucial step in overcoming these.[96]

To be fair, Sri Aurobindo did recognize that "in the secular thought of mankind there are signs of an idealism which increasingly admits a spiritual element among its motives."[97] However, in his spiritual phase he did not pursue this line of thinking further so as to suggest ways of embedding it in movements for social change.

CONCLUSION

Marx and Engels, criticizing Feuerbach's concept of man, wrote that the "essence of man is no abstraction inherent in each single individual. In its reality it is the ensemble of the social relations."[98] Feuerbach, as Marx and Engels went on to point out, "resolves the essence of religion into the essence of man."[99] He therefore did not see "that the 'religious sentiment' is itself a social product, and that the abstract individual which he analyses belongs to a particular form of society."[100]

But it is perhaps equally true—and the experience of former and present socialist societies appear to endorse this—that whatever the "particular form of society," the individual is not transformed in a fundamental sense. The seeking for spiritual illumination never ceases. For spiritualism is a response to the eternal condition of humankind, to the alienation that humans feel in a lonely universe, and to the intuitive unity of being and nonbeing. The alienation cannot be overcome in any form of political society, as it is a response to an externally imposed condition that can never cease unless it is transcended through spiritual growth. Sri Aurobindo extended this understanding to the collective and thereby to the idea of human unity:

> While it is possible to construct a precarious and quite mechanical unity by political and administrative means, the unity of the human race, even if achieved, can only be secured and can only be made real if the religion of humanity, which is at present the highest active ideal of mankind, spiritualizes itself and becomes the general inner law of human life.[101]

But Sri Aurobindo, who offered a unique unified understanding of material and spiritual transformation, unfortunately did not pay the same attention to material as to spiritual transformation. This meant that there is no detailed mapping in his work of the social structures and institutions of a future just world order. Equally, Sri Aurobindo did not appreciate that at least one path to inner transformation is active participation in a collective nonviolent struggle for creating a just world order. While individuals may secure spiritual enlightenment through various forms of yoga, it is not the only way to individual and collective spiritual salvation: there is also, what one may call, the "yoga of social transformation." Be that as it may, there is little doubt that in any effort to "decolonize international relations," the Aurobindo vision of future world order needs to be retrieved and brought to bear on the contemporary discourse of international relations and law.

NOTES

1. I argue elsewhere that a global state is already in the process of being established (B. S. Chimni, "International Institutions Today: An Imperial Global State in the Making," *European Journal of International Law* 15, no. 1 [2004]: 1–37).

2. Karl Jaspers, *Philosophy and the World: Selected Essays* (Chicago: A Gateway Edition, 1963), 106.

3. The *Concise Oxford Dictionary* gives the meaning of "Vedanta" as "Hindu philosophy based on the doctrine of the Upanishads, especially in its monistic form"; "Upanishad" as "each of a series of Hindu sacred treatises written in Sanskrit and expounding the vedas"; and "Veda" as "the most ancient Hindu scriptures, in particular the Rig Veda, Sama Veda, Yajur Veda, and Atharva Veda."

4. J. N. Mohanty, *Explorations in Philosophy: Essays by J. N. Mohanty*, vol. 1, *Indian Philosophy*, ed. Bina Gupta (New Delhi: Oxford University Press, 2001), 71. Mohanty cites Samkara, the great master of nondualist philosophy: "Brahman (alone)

is real, the world is false, the finite individual is identical with (and) none other than Brahman (Brahma satyam, jaganmithya, jiva brahmava naparam)" (67).

5. Mohanty, *Explorations in Philosophy*, 67.

6. "Spirituality," according to Sri Aurobindo, "is in its essence an awakening to the inner reality of our being, to a spirit, self, soul which is other than our mind, life and body, an inner aspiration to know, to feel, to be that, to enter into contact with the greater Reality beyond and pervading the universe which inhabits also our being, to be in communion with It and union with It, and a turning, a conversion, a transformation of our whole being as a result of the aspiration, the contact, the union, a growth or waking into a new becoming or new being, a new self, a new nature" (Sri Aurobindo, *The Life Divine* [Pondicherry: Sri Aurobindo Ashram, 1970], 857).

Sri Aurobindo denied that he was a philosopher even as he confessed that he had written philosophy. For philosophy was for Sri Aurobindo not simply an intellectual exercise but also a rational narration/summation of yogic (in this case his) experiences.

7. Tara Chand, *History of the Freedom Movement in India*, vol. 3 (Delhi: Ministry of Information and Broadcasting, Government of India, 1972), 150.

8. Chand, *History of the Freedom Movement in India*, 150.

9. Chand, *History of the Freedom Movement in India*, 150; Sumit Sarkar, *Modern India* (New Delhi: Macmillan, 1983), 97; Ashis Nandy, *Exiled at Home: Comprising, At the Edge of Psychology, The Intimate Enemy*, and *Creating a Nationality* (New Delhi: Oxford University Press, 1998), 87. All the quotations are from *The Intimate Enemy*.

10. Makarand Paranjape, *Aurobindo Reader* (New Delhi: Penguin, 1999), xv.

11. Paranjape, *Aurobindo Reader*, xv.

12. Nandy, *The Intimate Enemy*, 89.

13. Chand, *History of the Freedom Movement in India*, 154.

14. Chand, *History of the Freedom Movement in India*, 153.

15. Sarkar, *Modern India*, 98.

16. For more details see Chand, *History of the Freedom Movement in India*, 167–68. For a selection of his political writings in this period, see Paranjape, *Aurobindo Reader*, 3–45.

17. Chand, *History of the Freedom Movement in India*, 152.

18. Chand, *History of the Freedom Movement in India*, 152. "During his internment in Alipur jail, he had a religious experience which caused a major change in his outlook. In a vision, he saw the Spirit of God all around him, later in the law-court, he heard a divine message" (T. M. P. Mahadevan and G. V. Saroja, *Contemporary Indian Philosophy* [New Delhi: Sterling Publishers, 1981], 163). See also Paranjape, *Aurobindo Reader*, xvii. For the story of the transformation in his own words, see Sri Aurobindo, *Tales of Prison Life* (Pondicherry: Sri Aurobindo Ashram, 1997).

19. Chand, *History of the Freedom Movement in India*, 153.

20. Sarkar, *Modern India*, 125.

21. Chand, *History of the Freedom Movement in India*, 153.

22. Chand, *History of the Freedom Movement in India*, 153.

23. Chand, *History of the Freedom Movement in India*, 156.

24. Many of these books "were written in a serial form in the pages of the monthly review, *Arya*," which Sri Aurobindo edited (Sri Aurobindo, *The Human Cycle, The Ideal of Human Unity*, and *War and Self-Determination* [Pondicherry: Sri Aurobindo Ashram, 1970], 257). *Arya* was started in 1914.

25. As Mohanty notes, "The philosophical status of Advaita Vedanta is well established.... It has its own logical and conceptual, epistemological and metaphysical basis. If philosophy is, and must be, an intellectual examination and validation of theses (however received), then Advaita Vedanta has amply demonstrated its claim to be philosophy" (Mohanty, *Explorations in Philosophy*, 107). Indeed, he argues that it is not a religion (105–13).

I do not wish to debate in this chapter on what some would term Sri Aurobindo's turn toward Hindu revivalism. Among other things, Sri Aurobindo himself emphasized that "the different world religions representing different world cultures that have found a habitation in India will remain here always, form elements of the common national life, and contribute to the evolution of the composite culture of modern India" (cited by Chand, *History of the Freedom Movement in India*, 163).

26. Nandy, *The Intimate Enemy*, 85.

27. Nandy, *The Intimate Enemy*, 87.

28. Nandy, *The Intimate Enemy*, 87.

29. Aurobindo, *The Human Cycle*, 1.

30. Aurobindo, *The Human Cycle*, 1.

31. Of course, he gave these stages his own meaning by inter alia noting the cognitive limits of these categories. He noted of the four stages that "the psychology of man and his societies is too complex, too synthetical. Nor does this theory of a psychological cycle tell us what is the inner meaning of its successive phases or the necessity of their succession or the term and end towards which they are driving (Aurobindo, *The Human Cycle*, 2).

32. Aurobindo, *The Human Cycle*, 3.

33. Aurobindo, *The Human Cycle*, 8.

34. Aurobindo, *The Human Cycle*, 11.

35. Aurobindo, *The Human Cycle*, 11.

36. Aurobindo, *The Human Cycle*, 11.

37. Aurobindo, *The Human Cycle*, 11.

38. Aurobindo, *The Human Cycle*, 12.

39. Aurobindo, *The Human Cycle*, 12–13.

40. Aurobindo, *The Human Cycle*, 206.

41. Aurobindo, *The Human Cycle*, 40–41.

42. Aurobindo, *The Human Cycle*, 207.

43. Aurobindo, *The Human Cycle*, 34–35.

44. Aurobindo, *The Human Cycle*, 46 (emphasis added).

45. Aurobindo, *The Human Cycle*, 46–47. When World War II broke out, Sri Aurobindo issued a declaration that stated, "We feel that not only is this a battle waged in just self-defense.... But that it is a defense of the civilization and its highest attained social, cultural and spiritual values, and the whole future of humanity. To this

cause our support and sympathy will be unswerving, whatever may happen. We look forward to the victory of Britain and, as the eventual result, an era of peace and union among the nations and a better and more secure world order" (Chand, *History of the Freedom Movement in India*, 154). See also Paranjape *Aurobindo Reader*, xxii.

46. Aurobindo, *The Human Cycle*, 45–46.

47. Aimé Césaire, *Discourse on Colonialism* (New York: Monthly Review Press, 2000), 36.

48. Robin D. G. Kelley, "Introduction," in Césaire, *Discourse on Colonialism*, 10.

49. Aurobindo, *The Human Cycle*, 441. He noted that "the life and movements of one affect the life of the others in a way that would have been impossible a hundred years ago" (*The Human Cycle*, 441).

50. Aurobindo, *The Human Cycle*, 267.

51. Aurobindo, *The Human Cycle*, 258.

52. Aurobindo, *The Human Cycle*, 263.

53. Aurobindo, *The Human Cycle*, 443.

54. Aurobindo, *The Human Cycle*, 443.

55. Aurobindo, *The Human Cycle*, 630.

56. Aurobindo, *The Human Cycle*, 449. See also 377.

57. Aurobindo, *The Human Cycle*, 457.

58. Aurobindo, *The Human Cycle*, 280.

59. Aurobindo, *The Human Cycle*, 280.

60. Aurobindo, *The Human Cycle*, 406.

61. Aurobindo, *The Human Cycle*, 281.

62. Aurobindo, *The Human Cycle*, 374.

63. Aurobindo, *The Human Cycle*, 550.

64. Aurobindo, *The Human Cycle*, 550.

65. Aurobindo, *The Human Cycle*, 550.

66. Aurobindo, *The Human Cycle*, 564.

67. Aurobindo, *The Human Cycle*, 551.

68. Aurobindo, *The Human Cycle*, 551.

69. Aurobindo, *The Human Cycle*, 401.

70. Aurobindo, *The Human Cycle*, 556.

71. Aurobindo, *The Human Cycle*, 556.

72. Aurobindo, *The Human Cycle*, 556.

73. Aurobindo, *The Human Cycle*, 554.

74. Aurobindo, *The Human Cycle*, 554.

75. Aurobindo, *The Human Cycle*, 554.

76. Aurobindo, *The Human Cycle*, 555.

77. Aurobindo, *The Human Cycle*, 551. The world state "may even end by abolishing national individuality and turning the divisions that it has created into mere departmental groupings, provinces and districts of the one common State" (551).

78. Aurobindo, *The Human Cycle*, 556.

79. Aurobindo, *The Human Cycle*, 556.

80. Aurobindo, *The Human Cycle*, 556.

81. Aurobindo, *The Human Cycle*, 556.

82. Aurobindo, *The Human Cycle*, 556.

83. Aurobindo, *The Human Cycle*, 210.

84. Aurobindo, *The Life Divine*, 883.

85. Aurobindo, *The Life Divine*, 883.

86. Aurobindo, *The Life Divine*, 883.

87. Aurobindo, *The Human Cycle*, 241.

88. Aurobindo, *The Human Cycle*, 242.

89. Aurobindo, *The Human Cycle*, 478.

90. As Sri Aurobindo noted, "Any attempt to heighten inordinately the mental or exaggerate inordinately the vital man,—a Nietzschean supermanhood, for example,—can only colossalise the human creature, it cannot transform or divinise him" (Aurobindo, *The Life Divine*, 722).

91. Aurobindo, *The Life Divine*, 1027.

92. Euclid Tsakalotos, "Homo Economicus, Political Economy and Socialism," *Science and Society* 68, no. 2 (2004): 139.

93. Chimni, "International Institutions Today."

94. Kevin McDonald, "Oneself as Another: From Social Movement to Experience Movement," *Current Sociology* 52, no. 4 (2004): 581, 584.

95. McDonald, "Oneself as Another," 590, 589.

96. This was suggested in a personal communication with Giri. Ananta Kumar Giri, "Knowledge and Human Liberation: Jurgen Habermas, Sri Aurobindo and Beyond," *European Journal of Social Theory* 7, no. 1 (2004): 99.

97. Aurobindo, *The Human Cycle*, 466.

98. Karl Marx and Friedrich Engels, *The German Ideology*, 3rd rev. ed. (Moscow: Progress Publishers, 1976), 616.

99. Marx and Engels, *The German Ideology*, 616.

100. Marx and Engels, *The German Ideology*, 617.

101. Aurobindo, *The Human Cycle*, 548.

Conclusion

Imperatives, Possibilities, and Limitations

Branwen Gruffydd Jones

This volume has sought to confront and begin to go beyond the Eurocentric and imperial quality of mainstream International Relations (IR) scholarship or discourse.[1] In conclusion, it is necessary to reflect on the lessons provided and the challenges faced. A useful point of departure is the major concern articulated by Saurin regarding the relationship between decolonizing knowledge and struggling against the real structures and practices of imperial international relations. In light of his concerns and the arguments elaborated in this volume, what are the imperatives and possibilities of decolonizing knowledge, and what limitations must be recognized?

DECOLONIZING KNOWLEDGE: IMPERATIVES

Saurin's reminder of the massive and violent presence of imperialism compels acknowledgment that a politically motivated concern with subaltern histories cannot be enough to decolonize IR. The weight of imperialism in structuring world order through the relentless dispossession of peoples, their histories, and their voices poses a huge contradiction when it comes to the problem of decolonizing IR. It is necessary for those dispossessed to reclaim their history, both the means of making history and the telling of history. This is why, as Saurin insists, "the central historiographical battle is a political battle over ownership of the means of production of memory and the definition of progress." Yet it is the structures and production of imperial order that must ultimately be confronted. This is why no amount of retelling the histories of the subaltern will be enough; why "however much postcolonial theorists reject the essentialisms of authenticity, as long as their chosen political contestation is to represent the people without history, the argument will be lost . . . the postcolonial yapping and nibbling at the heels of imperialism is a forlorn endeavor." It seems at first that Saurin is making two contradictory arguments. He characterizes imperialism in terms of the imposition of meaning and so concurs with Guha's radical call to expropriate the expropriators. But he warns against a metropolitan, postcolonial appropriation of the histories of the dispossessed, which gets stuck over questions of authenticity and voice, as if representing the voiceless was an end in itself. It is the contradictions of imperialism and the imperatives of making history in unwanted inherited conditions that give rise to both of these apparently conflicting positions. To reclaim the *telling* of histories arrogated by imperialism is paramount but never enough—or, rather, the telling of history presupposes reclaiming the means to make history. Decolonizing knowledge cannot be conceived in purely ideational terms. Saurin's dual concerns echo the analysis of Amílcar Cabral: the only way to reclaim authentic history is to gain possession of the means of production of history:

> In our opinion, the foundation for national liberation rests in the inalienable right of every people to have their own history, whatever formulations may be adopted at the level of international law. The objective of national liberation, is therefore, to reclaim the right, usurped by imperialist domination, namely: the liberation of the process of development of national productive forces. Therefore, national liberation takes place when, and only when, national productive forces are completely free of all kinds of foreign domination . . . [which] necessarily opens up new prospects for the cultural development of the society in question, by returning to that society all its capacity to create progress . . . if imperialist domination has the vital need to practice cultural oppression, national liberation is necessarily an act of *culture*.[2]

Central to Saurin's argument is that we live not in a postcolonial but in an imperial world order, whereas IR is falsely premised on the narrative of a decolonized world order of sovereign nation-states. To decolonize IR therefore requires "the active production of a different international social order." It might seem that Saurin is ultimately dismissing the battle of ideas as futile, given the superior organized violence of imperialism. However, he defends the need, in decolonizing knowledge, to "better explain the production of particular world orders and world organization." Here his emphasis on *method*, following Marx, becomes crucial. Marx criticized a contemplation that can offer only interpretations of the given world; rather, he pursued a form of understanding and explanation *that can help in changing the world.* He did not abandon inquiry in order *instead* to try to change the world. Thus, Saurin defends the need to decolonize knowledge in order to reveal the political economy of power, the imperial production of world order, because IR obscures and misrecognizes the basis of international order. This is the crux of his argument that decolonizing IR requires not a pale postcolonialism but an anti-imperialism.

DECOLONIZING KNOWLEDGE: POSSIBILITIES

Eurocentrism and the features of IR's colonial or imperial mentality are manifest in various forms requiring different strategies of critique. As the chapters in this volume have variously drawn attention to. the manifestations of Eurocentrism and imperial mentality include the assumption of a "useful past," an idealized narrative of Western progress and modernity that is silent on race, slavery, centuries of wars and dispossession against non-European peoples. IR scholarship is dominated by Western academics, turns to the European canon as a matter of instinct, and consistently ignores both earlier and current non-European scholarship. Central analytical categories such as sovereignty, democracy, governance, and the state are informed exclusively by a sanitized European ideal that systematically ignores forms, struggles, and discourses of social and political organization from the non-Western world.

Escaping from this Western imperial imagination requires first of all that IR discourse is situated historically. As Pasha argues, the current form or foundation of IR discourse arises from deep historical currents and tendencies. The current Western imagination has crystallized over centuries as the necessary surface of Europe's hegemonic imperial project and encounters with non-European peoples, cultures, religions, and ways of life. For five centuries, world history has been deeply fractured by practices of conquest and dispossession and the corresponding assumption of racial, cultural, religious, and civilizational hierarchy. Thus, as Krishna argues, the symbolic date of international relations is not 1648 but 1492, the historical origin of the modern global condition of alienation. The failure of IR as a modern discipline to attend to this fractured world history and its necessary ideological forms reveals its constitution as the modern *continuation* of that very hegemonic discourse and expression of alienation.

How can this deeply entrenched, alienated, and alienating mode of apprehending the world be transcended? The contributions to this volume have provided various examples of how to proceed in the quest for decolonized knowledge. First, it is necessary to reject the underlying social ontology assumed by the mainstream. IR's strategies of containment operate on the basis of an underlying ontology or model of the basic constitution of social life, time, history, and the international. The mainstream model is atomized, along various dimensions in time and space, issuing in the self-contained histories of regions and states that sever real historical relations of extended cause and conditions of possibility. It is therefore necessary to self-consciously identify a different model of social ontology, one that is more adequate and capable of revealing rather than concealing actual historical connections, revealing, in Said's words, the intertwined nature of spatially distant forms and processes of historical change and social reproduction. Only by refusing the mainstream ontology is it possible to meet Halperin's challenge of producing alternative accounts that are *unassimilable* by the mainstream. IR discourse, Saurin argues, reproduces the "illusion of the epoch"—"the mistake that the explanation of international order and organization of the world remains to be found in the examination of the nation-state and international organisation." Halperin refuses this illusion, instead directing attention to historically extended networks of relations that connect not whole countries or societies but distinct regions and classes across vast spatial distance and over time.

The need for a more adequate ontology is not an abstract analytical problem and cannot be resolved through any "purely" theoretical move. Thus, second and relatedly, decolonizing knowledge demands attention to questions of history. What kind of historical method can help reveal the actual historical connections and causal relations that constitute the international? Krishna employs what Said has described as *contrapuntal* analysis, which places standard themes and concepts of the mainstream in their wider historical context, thus exposing crucial flaws in the usually isolated rendering of such themes. This does not issue in a multiplicity of alternative and inherently contested "readings" that can only ever be ordered in priority according to one's particular, shifting perspective or standpoint. Rather, contrapuntal analysis exposes very specific forms of causal connection between spatially distant but temporally coincident processes, social forms, and conditions. It is the necessity of such connections that are systematically overlooked—or rather, as Du Bois said, *suppressed*—by the mainstream. In doing so, half or parts of a history are presented as complete and whole. This constitutes not one perspective among others but a false historical account. The broader history revealed through contrapuntal method both is more adequate and exposes the falsity of the sanitized dominant account. The power of contrapuntal method lies not only in revealing historical relations of cause and conditions of possibility ignored by analysis informed by the state-centric ontology of the mainstream but also in resituating the intellectual canon in the context of imperialism. Here Krishna foregrounds Grovogui's discussion of the intimate relationship between Grotius's scholarship and imperial practice and Mehta's examination of the integral relationship between nineteenth-century liberal thought and colonial practice. Others have produced important accounts of a similar form with regard to other figures of the Western canon of IR and international law, including Francisco de Vitoria, Hegel, Kant, and John Stuart Mill.[3]

A third strategy, employed by Anghie, Gathii, Grovogui, and Ayers, is to refuse the disciplining taboos of dominant forms of inquiry. As Krishna discusses, the continuity of the imperial imagination is secured in part by disciplining maneuvers that relegate attention to historical and empirical detail to secondary or "specialist" forms of inquiry, maintaining the heights of theoretical abstraction as the proper form of IR. This is precisely both legacy and continuation of what Saurin has termed imperialism's habitual "refusal to translate or interpret" but only impose meaning. It is the same in international law, as Anghie argues: knowledge is governed by a set of conceptual categories centered on Europe, and it is these categories that are routinely reaffirmed by conventional histories of the discipline as well as by the very doctrines of international law. In this way, the theoretical apparatus and approved modes of inquiry in both IR and international law suggest that imperialism and the detail of non-European history more broadly are "somehow incidental" to the proper disciplinary concerns.

The adequate response has to be to provide different accounts, different forms of historical knowledge, that reveal the exercise of power and, as Saurin urges, the production of world order. As Ranajit Guha has argued, such efforts cannot be framed by the same coordinates as dominant forms of knowledge: "no discourse can oppose a genuinely uncompromising critique to a ruling culture so long as its ideological parameters are the same as those of that very culture."[4] Any effort to counter the dominant forms of knowledge that legitimize international power must be separated from those forms by a "paradigmatic distance."[5] That is why the content of this volume has not been determined by the theoretical or substantive coordinates of the IR discipline as such. The quest to decolonize knowledge cannot be pursued by revisiting the endless interactions and iterations of IR's so-called great debates or by surveying once again the sins of realism, neorealism, structuralism, liberal institutionalism, constructivism, and so on.

Only by examining "other" and much longer histories—by refusing the taboos against history, context, and empirical detail, by insisting on negotiation, on two-way translation—can the constant reaffirmation of the idealized European as universal be overturned. Anghie's argument that the study of history is a central means of facilitating and furthering the reconstructive project is confirmed throughout this volume. It is precisely the widespread ignorance of world history, histories of imperialism, histories of anti-imperial struggles, and histories of nonimperial non-European social forms that enables the persistent blindness to more recent forms of imperialism and racial discourse. With a knowledge of history, the current humanitarian, apparently benign and well-intentioned international discourses and techniques of governance, development, democratization, or security are revealed as modern cloaks legitimizing imperialism's recurring "dual mandate" of civilization and commerce, freedom and the market, and human rights and property.

It was argued in the introduction that the importance of recovering marginalized (or, rather, wholly denied) histories, struggles, and scholarship is both substantive and political. The process of recovery in itself serves to counter imperialism and its effects in the realms of knowledge. As Anghie discusses, international relations, law, and order today appear to be formally deracialized and decolonized. Yet the practice of ignoring non-Western contributions to world history and non-Western practices, values, and struggles remains integral to modern Western thought. While abandoning the overtly racialized language of earlier centuries of imperialism, the imperial *attitude* remains as strong as ever. In Fanon's words, "Racism no longer dares appear without disguise."[6] The fact that, as Grovogui demonstrates, theorists still have difficulty considering that "illiterate black slaves" could produce universal notions of rights or the almost universal assumption, as Ayers relates, that Africans *have yet* to develop a democratic tradition reveals a strong continuity of imperial attitude and Western supremacy. Indeed, a book published as recently as 1992 writes apparently without embarrassment of "primitive peoples of Africa."[7]

However, the turn to history and alternative forms of social organization and the enduring imperative of anticolonial struggle remain fraught with contradictions. In light of such contradictions, it is necessary to draw out a further specific lesson from the contributions to this volume regarding the theme of universal humanity.

From the Universalism of Western Supremacy to Universal Humanity and Unity

A major element of Eurocentrism and imperial ideology is the false claim to universalism. This theme runs through many of the chapters in this volume. Central to both IR and international law over the centuries has been the projection of a partial and idealized European history to the status of universal norm and ideal according to which all aspects of human life—democracy, state form, human rights, governance, property, law, economy, religion, language, even family structure—are to be filtered and measured and forced to conform. Three forms of response have been articulated here. The first, advocated by Halperin, is a form of response widely overlooked even by critical approaches: namely, undermining the idealized norm by retelling a more adequate account of *European* history. The second is to demonstrate the complicity between concepts and doctrines that appear innocent—apparently universal, neutral, self-evident, technical, progressive, or humanitarian—and the actual practices of imperial domination, as demonstrated by Anghie with regard to the notion of "good governance" and Gathii with regard to international law relating to property in situations of conquest. Third, many of the contributions have insisted on the specificity of histories and cultures that are routinely abused through evaluation against the presumed universal standard of Europe, treated through orientalist lenses as homogeneous and unchanging caricature, or simply denied altogether.

However, none of these latter responses amounts to the celebration of essential particulars. All reject the false universalization of Western standards but simultaneously eschew the dichotomous reaction of universal/Western = bad, particular/local/non-Western = good. They do not "drop anchor in nativism," as Krishna puts it, or discount that which is valuable in European culture. Rather, the various accounts in this volume (and many other anticolonial, anti-imperialist, and anticapitalist struggles) suggest values of an alternative universalism or unity, rooted in a broader conception of humanity. This is most explicit in Chimni's discussion of Sri Aurobindo's thought. This broader form or possibility of universalism is not a question of standardization or assimilation, nor does it claim European or any other origin. Actual histories and diverse forms of community and social organization embody varied particular manifestations of universal human qualities. As Grovogui, Ayers, and Chimni demonstrate in different ways here, notions of humanity and the nature and faculties of human being and existence are found in all cultures and societies. Moreover, such ideas are often revealed in sharper relief, especially in the context of struggles for progressive change. It is no coincidence that the various alternative, nonhegemonic or counterhegemonic norms, discourses, and practices are often more open, more accommodating, and more expansive than the false universals of liberal capitalist imperialism, as demonstrated in Ayers's analysis of nineteenth-century African political systems, Grovogui's discussion of the ideas articulated in the Haitian Revolution, and Chimni's critical analysis of Sri Aurobindo's writings on human unity and universal emancipation. However, there is nothing inherent in this; non-European or precolonial norms and practices are not necessarily more progressive than dominant or subsequent liberal forms. This is why it is important to discriminate between various possible forms of anticolonial/imperial struggle, critique, and alternatives, which can take progressive or regressive forms.

A broader vision therefore critically judges all histories, Western or non-Western, on their own merits and in terms of the human condition as such. The anticolonial response ought not to privilege the non-Western as a matter of principle—to do so simply mirrors in reverse the logic of imperial value. So Grovogui acknowledges that the Haitian Revolution was not unique but part of a broader genealogy of modernity alongside the French and American revolutions. However, the problem is that the Haitian Revolution has been ignored and Western history elevated as originary and universal. In countering this legacy, it is necessary to transcend such logic altogether and to approach *all* histories, values, practices, and institutions with an equally critical method.

Such an approach has been demonstrated in many anticolonial struggles. As Grovogui relates, whereas the ideals articulated in the French and American revolutions applied only to restricted categories of subjects, the ideals espoused by the Haitian revolutionaries were deliberately expansive, rooted in the human condition as such and therefore embracing both former slave owners and former slaves, peoples of all color and nationality, born in or out of wedlock, propertied and propertyless. The anticolonial struggles in the Portuguese colonial territories in Africa also embodied expansive values rooted in humanity as such. Again, such values were brought into relief through the experience of struggle for liberation. During the Mozambican independence struggle, an important debate took place over the nature of the enemy and the form of postcolonial society to be constructed.[8] The debate was won in favor of the more expansive concept rooted in the human condition; thereafter, the struggle was characterized in imperial rather than racial terms. Thus, Samora Machel declared, "Our war is a war of national liberation against Portuguese colonialism, against imperialism and against the exploitation of man by man" and not "a war against the Portuguese people."[9] Agostinho Neto similarly affirmed,

In our countries we are not making a racial war. Our objective is not to fight against the white man solely because he is white. It is that we fight against those who support the colonial regime . . . all those who in any manner show their desire not to cooperate with the colonial regime must not be despised or treated as enemies . . . in the same way . . . on the international plane. There we do not seek support only in the countries of Africa south of the Sahara, called Black Africa, where the skin of the inhabitants is darker; but we also go to look for the aid of countries of North Africa, where the people have a light skin. We go even further to Europe to look for the political, diplomatic and material help from countries where the majority of the population have white colour, and in other continents where the racial differences are even more evident . . . if there exists in some of our combatants the idea of a war against the white man, it is necessary that it be immediately substituted by the idea of a war against colonialism and against imperialism; a war against oppression, for the liberty and for the dignity *of all men in the world*. This idea will fortify our struggle. It will offer more guarantees and new prospectives that open up a brilliant future for all men. In a time of hatred we will have fraternity and understanding.[10]

Amílcar Cabral, speaking to an audience of black Americans in 1972, affirmed the connections and ultimate unity between the distinct struggles against colonial oppression being waged in Africa and the struggles for racial equality being waged in the United States. But he went further; he was not affirming a distinctly *black* struggle:

> Does that mean we are racists? No! We are not racists. We are fundamentally and deeply against any kind of racism. Even when people are subjected to racism we are against racism from those who have been oppressed by it. In our opinion—not from dreaming but from a deep analysis of the real conditions of the existence of mankind and of the division of societies—racism is a result of certain circumstances . . . we cannot answer racism with racism . . . we are not fighting against the Portuguese people or whites. We are fighting for the freedom of our people—to free our people and to allow them *to be able to love any kind of human being.*[11]

This demonstrates widespread evidence across centuries and continents of actual struggles that do not simply counter but seek to *transcend* the logics of imperialism, racism, exclusion, and domination. In their practice and conscious enunciation, they reveal a far broader inclusive vision, a vision of solidarity and human unity.

On what basis should anti-imperial struggles, in thought and practice, be founded, if not on some essentialist notion of non-European authenticity? These historical examples suggest an answer to that question. Progressive struggles and alternative forms of social organization have been informed by principles and values of unity and inclusion. They have also been informed by ideas about the inherently social nature of human beings in contrast to the abstract individualism espoused and produced by liberal capitalist modernity. This is seen, for example, in the institutions of Iteso society that seek to restrain individual accumulation at the expense of the society and community as a whole and promote values of hospitality over individual displays of wealth. Such institutions are the product of a culture that deliberately sustains *autonomy* through cooperation and unity. Rather than posing the individual against or above society, which as Pasha argues is so characteristic of liberal modernity and its underlying basis in capitalist exchange, or subsuming the individual to the abstract collective good of society as such, as many "actually existing" socialist societies tended to, it is possible and necessary to pursue both individual and collective fulfillment as related and inherently mutual goals—one presupposes and requires the other. This is one of the lessons of Sri Aurobindo's thought, underlined by Chimni: "activities directed toward seeking social transformation help individuals and collectives to turn and grow within." Sri Aurobindo's vision of human unity took the political form of a close federation of global cooperation through which the free variation of peoples would be secured. Similar notions can be found instantiated in living values and practices around the world. For example, Okot p'Bitek, discussing the values of Acholi society, affirms the value and necessity of "the tough struggle for realising oneself, that is, by full participation in societal life, being meaningful to one's society, contributing to the happiness of self and society by thought and deed."[12]

However, it is the massively material structures and logic of global capitalism that encroach on and undermine possible or existing alternatives and that make the quest for human unity-in-diversity at all scales both ever more important and ever more difficult. As Pasha soberly observes, "Few spaces remain 'outside' the imperium of capitalism or the modern state. The syntax of social existence is deeply conditioned by the logic of exchange and rationalities of modern power." It is in part because of the historical engagement with colonialism, for example, that caution must always be exercised before naively embracing any notion of the authentic indigenous of past or present. Ayers's account of African notions and practices of political community and democracy draws on nineteenth-century history. She makes no claims that such traditions have survived unscathed by the encounter with colonialism. As Mahmood Mamdani has demonstrated with regard to Africa and Ranajit Guha with regard to India, the effect of colonial rule was to preserve, entrench, and strengthen the undemocratic or authoritarian tendencies of precolonial institutions while deliberately inhibiting the democratic tendencies.[13] Thus today, alternative ways of thinking and organizing social life are constrained by the global hegemony of liberalism and capitalism and by the historical legacy of the rupture of colonialism. It is neither possible nor desirable to seek to return to the past, but it is possible and necessary to seek to learn, critically, from history and from superior values arising from alternative ways of organizing social life.

DECOLONIZING KNOWLEDGE: LIMITATIONS

Having defended the importance of decolonizing knowledge and explored the various possibilities demonstrated in this volume, it is necessary to acknowledge and reflect on the limitations of this project. The task of decolonizing IR has necessarily to be a collaborative, ongoing, and, as noted by Krishna, *relentless* project. This volume makes a contribution, raising certain questions, putting forth arguments and evidence, and offering possibilities and examples of alternative methods and insights. The volume makes no claim to be comprehensive—such an ambition would be impossible to realize. While the question of security, so central to the discipline, has been addressed here by

Krishna and Pasha, this area requires further extensive critique, as, for example, has been begun by Tarak Barkawi and Mark Laffey.[14] Another absence is the possibility of learning from feminist scholarship, which shares many concerns in exposing oppressive structures and social relations, revealing normally hidden intersections between race, class, and gender and reflecting on the effects of the positionality of the researcher.[15] This volume has not included scholarship from Latin America or the Caribbean despite their long and vigorous tradition of autonomous thought and critique, exposing the enduring features and structures of Eurocentrism and imperialism in its neocolonial forms. However, this project did not set out to achieve comprehensive coverage or representation. The problematic of decolonizing IR was not conceived in immediately regional or geographical terms or solely in terms of location or origin of author. Nevertheless, the international inequalities in the production and circulation of knowledge and the marginalization of scholarship from outside North America and Europe are major dimensions of the Eurocentric nature of IR and are discussed further here.

These points serve only to underline the necessarily collaborative, ongoing, unfinished, and expanding nature of the task of decolonizing IR and other areas of social inquiry. It is important to acknowledge that such efforts are by no means new and that this volume constitutes only one contribution to a far broader, evolving effort. Earlier important struggles to decolonize ideologies and structures of international relations were of course the anticolonial struggles themselves as well as the Third World campaign for nonalignment and the new international economic order.[16] The major importance of these struggles by the Third World coalition should not be overlooked despite their ultimate lack of success—floundering, as Chimni has observed, on the rocks of neocolonialism.[17] That these important campaigns and achievements of collective struggle—in spite of diversity among the states of the Third World[18]—were unable to realize significant and lasting structural change in the international order demonstrates the massive difficulties of such a task. It is easier to write about the imperatives of decolonizing IR and the lofty ambitions of emancipation and transformation than to achieve such massive goals. Nevertheless, these earlier struggles continue today in the critical and reconstructive work of the TWAIL network of scholars.[19]

This volume, then, aims at contributing to a broader collective project or set of concerns rather than attempting a comprehensive critique. However, it is worth reiterating the particular position that underlies this volume, which marks its location within a range of possible forms of critique. This project was not conceived in a manner that imposed methodological unity on the various contributors. Nevertheless, a certain consistency, a broadly shared political as well as substantive and methodological orientation, emerges from the chapters of this volume. Underlying each argument, in perhaps different ways, is some kind of commitment to providing more adequate knowledge of the world and of international relations and, in particular, a commitment to understanding and learning from history. Some forms of postcolonial and critical IR scholarship seem to leave history and the reality of international relations behind as they venture deeper into the realms of theory and text, both as object of critique and as source of alternatives. Here the focus of critique has been largely the imperial practices of international relations and the actual as opposed to mythologized history of Europe rather than the texts and theories of IR discourse (which, for once, are relegated to footnotes). Similarly, alternatives are found by turning to actual histories and scholarship from the non-Western (colonized) world. The ultimate motivation underlying each contribution here is to better understand and explain the world rather than to dwell on the failings of the IR discipline. Nor do these contributions offer alternative "readings" of familiar topics or texts; rather, they offer *more adequate* treatments of various themes central to international being in the world and the construction of international order.

The tenacity of Saurin's return to thesis eleven warns against the possibility of complacency, however. To repeat Saurin's words, "resolving the problems of historical subordination, whether material or ideational, is not exclusively (perhaps not even primarily) an intellectual or mental task but a substantive political task." All such forms of discursive critique and intellectual struggle, in the battle of ideas, are necessarily constrained or circumscribed by broader structures and social relations. Such struggles are at once vitally necessary but never enough.

The final section of this concluding reflection on the imperatives and limitations of decolonizing knowledge turns to an often-neglected dimension of the problem: the internationally structured material conditions of possibility for the production of knowledge. This is explored with particular reference to Africa, arguably the most marginalized from international circuits of knowledge exchange; but the issues discussed no doubt have broader relevance in terms of general constraints, if not in the particular detail.

AFRICA IN THE GLOBAL POLITICAL ECONOMY OF ACADEMIC INQUIRY

Eurocentrism in academic inquiry is reproduced in part by inequalities in material conditions. The international economy, as Saurin noted, produces "a profound and chronically structured distribution of scientific power." The structures and legacies of colonialism are manifest in the sphere of academic inquiry in very material as well as ideational ways. The immediate legacy of colonialism in Africa was a massive paucity in levels of formal education and literacy, especially higher education. This must be emphasized, notwithstanding the value of oral forms of knowledge. The establishment, expansion, and "Africanization" of schooling and higher education was therefore an integral part of the project of "nation building" in the postindependence years. The relationship between the state and the university was strong and controlling during the early years after independence and became far tighter and more restrictive with the rise of authoritarian rule across Africa from the 1970s.[20] This included banning books, closing publishing houses, and detention and torture of critical academics and writers and led to a significant exodus of critical scholars either to other African countries or to the West as well as a process of self-censorship among those remaining. The political oppression of African scholarship during the 1970s was then exacerbated by economic oppression from the 1980s to the present. Economic poverty is perhaps an even better means of silencing critique, removing the material conditions of possibility for critical social inquiry while simultaneously celebrating a new era of political and civil liberties.

The imposed structural adjustment programs of international financial institutions, embarked on in the 1980s and continuing under evolving terminology to the present, have had multiple implications for universities and the conduct of teaching and research in Africa. In short, and following Saurin, while continuing the neocolonial dispossession of the means of life, structural adjustment has dispossessed African scholars of the means of producing their own account of that dispossession. Just as colonial rule before it, neocolonial structural adjustment eliminates both self-provision and self-definition. The cutbacks in state spending in the higher-education sector have had very visible effects, seen in the dilapidated buildings, half-empty libraries, overcrowded lecture halls, and overworked lecturers of African public universities. The combination of salary cuts and currency devaluation has massively undercut the living conditions of academics, "to the point where self-reproduction is impossible."[21] This has prompted a flight of academics to the West or to other, more lucrative sectors of employment. Those who remain are compelled to supplement their meager salaries, moonlighting "as tutors for children of the rich and teachers in secondary schools, as taxi drivers, or even as petty traders in order to make ends meet."[22]

The combination of reduced funding and currency devaluation affected academic publishing and libraries. Zeleza has documented how the economic crisis of the 1980s produced a crisis in publishing that undermined African scholarship and increased African scholars' dependency on publishing outlets outside Africa.[23] An indigenous African publishing industry had arisen in the first few decades after independence, and strong, internationally renowned research traditions, schools of thought, and publications were established, notably in Nigeria, Tanzania, and Senegal.[24] The economic crisis of the 1980s decimated such achievements, producing a "book famine" as structural adjustment programs took their toll on African publishing industries:

> Investments and sales plummeted, printing equipment and facilities deteriorated, production and retail costs escalated, and distribution networks and outlets atrophied.... Many once renowned periodicals and journals ceased publication or were reduced in size and frequency, while many new ones often did not survive beyond Volume 1, number 1.[25]

Notable in the specific context of this book is the *African Journal of International Affairs*, established by CODESRIA in 1998, which has apparently not survived beyond volume 2, number 1&2, 1999, while the *African Journal of International Affairs and Development*, established in 1995 and published by College Press & Publishers, Nigeria, appears to be available only up until 2002. The brief online description notes sadly that the journal has not "acquired immunity from the ongoing crisis in African publishing."[26] Meanwhile, some of the long-established publications and book series of international renown, such as the *Journal of the Historical Society of Nigeria* and the Ibadan History Series, had by 1980 "practically died."[27]

The combination of budget cuts and currency devaluation drastically reduced the funds and purchasing power of university libraries. A survey of thirty-one university and research libraries in thirteen African countries, carried out in 1993, revealed that all but three had suffered a sharp drop in their subscriptions to journals since the mid-1980s.[28] This was further exacerbated by the rising prices of books and journals. It was estimated that between 1986 and 1994, the cost of journals published in North America increased by 115 percent and monographs by 55 percent.[29] Since then, there has been a further and very significant process of concentration and centralization in the northern and, increasingly, transnational academic publishing industry, with further increases in the price of academic journals.[30] A recent survey of around 6,000 journals, published by twelve academic publishers over the period 2000–2004, found considerable variation both in journal prices, ranging from £124 to £781 in 2004, and in the rate of price increase, ranging from 27 to 94 percent.[31] The prices and rate of price increase of biomedical journals are considerably higher than social science journals. Biomedical journal prices ranged from £186 to £731 in 2004; biomedical journal price increases over the period 2000–2004 ranged from 27 to 92 percent. The price increases of biomedical journals over the longer period from 1993 to 2004 are staggering, ranging from 80 to 352 percent.[32] In another study, Edlin and Rubinfield found that "the price of library subscriptions to periodicals in law, medicine, and physics and chemistry rose by 205 percent, 479 percent, and 615 percent between 1984 and 2001."[33] As Zeleza observes, "If research libraries in the North were feeling the chill, those in Africa caught pneumonia."[34] Awasom describes the context in Cameroon:

> The economic crises of the late 1980s had a suffocating effect on tertiary education in Cameroon, marked by dwindling budgetary allocations to libraries. As collection development virtually came to a standstill, libraries were close to collapse. The increasing cost of journals, books and currency weaknesses combined to place western publications beyond the reach of most African libraries. The prospects of reversing this situation currently remain dim and this is of concern not only for universities, research institutes and publishers but also for international science as a whole.[35]

On the one hand, the logic of the free market in the global economy of academic research, knowledge production, and publishing produces a growing glut of overproduction in the West, a "perverse inflation of publications . . . and mountains of papers . . . churned out to be listed and indexed rather than read,"[36] while on the other hand Africa suffers the multiple dimensions of "book hunger." University libraries in the West are forced to weed their collections of dated material to make way for the ever-increasing volume of new publications. Discarded and outdated books are then sent in charitable donations to fill the half-empty shelves of African libraries.[37]

Thus, capital's inherent tendency to concentration and centralization, increasingly manifest on an international scale, affects the production of knowledge just as it affects the production of food and clothing. That this tendency reinforces the concentration of academic production in the West and dependency relations for the rest is just another indication of the failure of decolonization and the enduring presence of imperialism.

The effects of economic crisis and structural adjustment are multiple and very material, undermining access not only to books and journals but also to computers and printing facilities, secretarial and other support services, "and even paper on which to write," all of which are exacerbated by the trials of ordinary day-to-day living and operating in structurally adjusted economies.[38] In the context of economic crisis, the reproduction of academic research has become increasingly dependent on donor funding, from bilateral donors and private philanthropic agencies such as the Carnegie Corporation, the Ford Foundation, the Rockefeller Foundation, the Friedrich Elbert Foundation, and many others.[39] The major American philanthropic foundations have provided significant funding to African universities since the 1960s with the aim of nurturing an elite of African leaders.[40] Between 1990 and 1999, the Ford Foundation grants to African universities and nongovernmental organizations totaled $52.7 million, and grants from the Rockefeller Foundation totaled $33.1 million. However, this is a small amount if compared with funds available for teaching and research in Western universities. For example, funds raised by American universities in the single year of 1997 ranged from $52.9 million raised by Iowa State University to $724.5 million raised by Johns Hopkins University.[41] Under a new initiative, "The Partnership for Higher Education in Africa," several private American philanthropic foundations have joined together to support universities in seven African countries.[42] It would be crude to suggest a direct or determining effect by the source of funding (public, private, international) on the content and quality of research, still less the approach of individual scholars. Nevertheless, the role of the large American foundations and other international private, governmental, or religious donors is not necessarily neutral.[43] As Berman observed in the 1970s, "American foundations are American foundations. As mainstays of the American establishment we would expect them to conduct programs which, if not perceived by everyone as in the best interests of the United States, at least are not antagonistic to the nation's dominant values."[44] Many such organizations seek to promote a specific agenda in line with neoliberal principles of society and economy, such as the American foundations' promotion of private philanthropy and entrepreneurship as a solution to social ills. The increasing role of private funding in African universities is central to the ongoing commodification of the African university—as elsewhere. Just as in the nineteenth century the interests of European capital were represented in Africa by philanthropic and scientific organizations, so today many international foundations funding research in Africa are ultimately promoting a specific agenda of liberal capitalist expansion and market society.

The acute dependency of African researchers on external funds inevitably increases donor influence over research agendas and engineers a shift from academic research to policy-related short-term consultancy work.[45] As critics such as Zeleza, Mkandawire, Shivji, and many others have observed, African social scientists are compelled to reproduce the changing discourse of donor priorities—from empowerment and participation to stakeholder analysis, social philanthropy, and good governance—in order to attract funding. Issa Shivji is bitterly critical of the metamorphosis of African scholars into poorly paid policy consultants and universities into entrepreneurial purveyors of commodified qualifications in the marketplace:

The public intellectual, whose vocation is to comment, protest, caricature, satirize, analyse, and publicize the life around him or her is rapidly becoming history, which history, by the way, has no historian to record. (The historian is busy taking American tourists on a tour of the Bagamoyo slave market.)[46]

Even in the arena of policy-related studies, African academics are subordinate to expatriate consultants, often performing the menial tasks of preparing reports or background papers for foreign researchers to draw on. Mkandawire thus complains, "In the dire financial straits in which most of us find ourselves, it is difficult to be selective about one's sources of income. Some have exploited our penury to reduce us to nothing more than barefoot empiricists"[47] or, in Zeleza's words, "paid native informants."[48] Bethwell Ogot cites a 1988 study by the UN Development Program that found that Tanzania paid over $200 million to 1,000 foreign consultants, a sum equivalent to a quarter of Tanzania's agro-export earnings and two-thirds of foreign aid in the form of technical assistance. This left local researchers "to scramble for the crumbs, which was less than 0.5 per cent of the total consultancy budget."[49]

The effective muting or cramping of academic production by African scholars in Africa by political and, more insidiously, economic modes of oppression and dispossession leaves the field open to the continuing domination of Western scholarship across all fields, from IR to anthropology. The very notion of "African studies" is a historically specific colonial legacy and reproduces the marginality of Africa to the study of international relations, restricting Africa's appearance largely to the subfields of international political economy or area studies or as a "case study" in security or strategic studies. The marginalization of African scholarship is noticeable among Africanists, as many have discussed and Zeleza has documented,[50] and is even worse in the field of IR. Perhaps this is because in IR, the general, *international* applicability of IR theory is simply assumed.

The effects of the economic onslaught on African universities and scholarship is more significant than simply who gets published or cited where—than, as Saurin puts it, "who tells the stories." It has implications for the possibility of critical social inquiry informing struggles to change the neocolonial structures of Africa's societies. As Shivji notes, "The 'insurrection of ideas' of the age of liberation and revolution [of the 1970s] was as important in delegitimising imperialism as the suppression of ideas and the decimation of the intellectual body has been in rehabilitating it."[51] And it reproduces, with modern efficiency, the centuries-old silencing of Africa's self-affirmation; the habit of "forgetting and detracting from the thought and acts of the people of Africa."[52] Thandika Mkandawire has remarked, "We are probably the only part of the world about which it is still legitimate to publish without reference to local scholarship,"[53] an acute frustration mirrored by Ifi Amadiume's observation, "I do not know one single case in which Africans wrote the social history of any other nation."[54]

Despite these major constraints, academic research is conducted and published by African scholars in Africa, and the various regional and continental networks such as CODESRIA, OSSREA, AAWORD, AAPS, and SAPES play a very significant role.[55] However, much of this remains in Africa, partly because of the constraints against exporting to the West but also because of the lack of interest or effort on the part of Western researchers and libraries to acquire African books and journals. In other words, because of "the habit, long fostered, of forgetting and detracting from the thought and acts of the people of Africa." Zeleza spurns the common complaint that it is hard to get hold of African publications, noting the efficiency of the African Books Collective.[56] Ignoring scholarship about Africa written by Africans is one of the simple techniques by which IR secures the removal of the subordinated from their own history, as Saurin observed. Thus, Mkandawire commented,

> If at times I sound querulous and too insistent on declaring our [African scholars] existence, it is partly because others have chosen to obliterate us either by studied silence about our existence or by declaring that we simply do not exist... we sometimes feel that the invisibility of African scholarship has gone on for so long that we are inclined to attribute it to deliberate attempts to render it invisible.[57]

This impoverished condition of the university in Africa is the result of the long history of imperialism and more immediately the neoliberal reforms imposed by the World Bank, International Monetary Fund, and Western donor governments. The conditions of universities and academics vary considerably in different parts of the world and are likely to become increasingly uneven with the entrenchment of the free market in virtually all regions and the creation of a global market in higher education under the General Agreement on Trade in Services.[58] The point of this overview of conditions in Africa is not to generalize but to highlight the significance of internationally uneven material conditions in the global political economy of social inquiry. Calls for IR to make room for alternative and dissident voices rarely pay much attention to the material conditions of possibility for such discursive expansion or dialogue, above all on the global scale. Perhaps this is precisely an indication of IR's habit of ignoring imperialism, shared even by many critical scholars.

Thus, we return finally to Saurin's concern with the real decolonization of international relations, with the struggle against the structures of imperialism as the major condition of possibility for decolonized knowledge. Amílcar Cabral and Frantz Fanon similarly emphasized the material conditions of possibility for the liberation of knowledge and culture and the inherent relationship between culture, knowledge, and anti-imperial struggle. Fanon's observation regarding the liberation of African culture can be extended to our concern with the liberation of knowledge about the international:

> No one can truly wish for the spread of African culture if he does not give practical support to the creation of the conditions necessary to the existence of that culture; in other words, to the liberation of the whole continent.[59]

No one can truly wish for the spread of non-Eurocentric IR knowledge if they do not give practical support to the conditions necessary to the existence of that knowledge, in other words, to the liberation of the whole world from imperialism.

NOTES

1. In this conclusion, I adopt Krishna's example in referring to IR discourse.

2. Amílcar Cabral, "National Liberation and Culture," in *Return to the Source: Selected Speeches of Amílcar Cabral* (London: Monthly Review Press, 1973), 43.

3. See Antony Anghie, "Francisco de Vitoria and the Colonial Origins of International Law," *Social and Legal Studies* 5, no. 3 (1996): 321–36; Susan Buck-Morss, "Hegel and Haiti," *Critical Inquiry* 26, no. 4 (2000): 821–65; Beate Jahn, "Kant, Mill, and Illiberal Legacies in International Affairs," *International Organization* 59 (winter 2005): 177–207; Beate Jahn, "Barbarian Thoughts: Imperialism in the Philosophy of John Stuart Mill," *Review of International Studies* 31, no. 3 (2005): 599–618; Bhikhu Parekh, "Liberalism and Colonialism: A Critique of Locke and Mill," in *The Decolonization of Imagination: Culture, Knowledge and Power*, ed. Jan Nederveen Pieterse and Bhikhu Parekh (London: Zed Books, 1995); and, more generally, Emmanuel Chukwudi Eze, ed., *Race and the Enlightenment: A Reader* (Oxford: Blackwell, 1997).

4. Ranajit Guha, *Dominance without Hegemony: History and Power in Colonial India* (Cambridge, Mass.: Harvard University Press, 1997), 11.

5. Guha, *Dominance without Hegemony*, 11–13.

6. Frantz Fanon, "Racism and Culture," in *Toward the African Revolution: Political Essays* (New York: Monthly Review Press, 1967), 46.

7. Adam Watson, *The Evolution of International Society: A Comparative Historical Analysis* (London: Routledge, 1992), 277, 296.

8. See Jacques Depelchin, "African Anthropology and History in the Light of the History of FRELIMO," *Contemporary Marxism* 7 (1983): 69–88, and Barry Munslow, *Mozambique: The Revolution and Its Origins* (London: Longman, 1983), 102–13.

9. Samora Machel, "White Mozambicans: A Message by the President of FRELIMO, on the day of the Mozambican Revolution, 25 August 1971," in *The African Liberation Reader: Documents of the National Liberation Movements. Volume 2: The National Liberation Movements*, ed. Aquino de Bragança and Immanuel Wallerstein (London: Zed Press, 1982), 177.

10. Agostinho Neto, "Not an Isolated Struggle: From a Message by the President of MPLA, Broadcast on 6 June 1968 on the 'Voice of the Angolan Freedom-Fighter' on Radio Tanzania," in de Bragança and Wallerstein, *The African Liberation Reader*, 172 (emphasis added).

11. Amílcar Cabral, "Connecting the Struggles: An Informal Talk with Black Americans," in *Return to the Source: Selected Speeches of Amílcar Cabral* (London: Monthly Review Press, 1973), 76–77 (emphasis added).

12. Okot p'Bitek, "Man the Unfree," in *Artist the Ruler: Essays on Art, Culture and Values* (Nairobi: East African Educational Publishers, 1986), 21.

13. Mahmood Mamdani, *Citizen and Subject: Contemporary Africa and the Legacy of Late Colonialism* (Princeton, N.J.: Princeton University Press, 1996); Guha, *Dominance without Hegemony.*

14. Tarak Barkawi and Mark Laffey, "The Postcolonial Moment in Security Studies," *Review of International Studies* 32, no. 2.

15. See, for example, Gita Chowdhry and Sheila Nair, eds., *Power, Postcolonialism and International Relations: Reading Race, Gender and Class* (London: Routledge, 2002), and the journal *Meridians: Feminism, Race, Transnationalism.*

16. A. W. Singham and Shirley Hune, *Non-Alignment in an Age of Alignments* (Westport, Conn.: Lawrence Hill, 1986); Mohammed Bedjaoui, *Towards a New International Economic Order* (New York: Holmes and Meier, 1979); Marc Williams, *Third World Cooperation: The Group of 77 in UNCTAD* (London: Pinter, 1991).

17. B. S. Chimni, "Marxism and International Law: A Contemporary Analysis," *Economic and Political Weekly,* February 6, 1999, 346.

18. Williams, *Third World Cooperation.*

19. The TWAIL vision statement reads in part, "We are a network of scholars engaged in international legal studies, and particularly interested in the challenges and opportunities facing 'third world' peoples in the new world order. We understand the historical scope and agenda of the dominant voice in international law and scholarship as having participated in, and legitimated global processes of marginalization and domination that impact on the lives and struggles of Third World peoples" (cited in James Thuo Gathii, "Alternative and Critical: The Contribution of Research and Scholarship on Developing Countries to International Legal Theory," *Harvard International Law Journal* 41 [spring 2000]: 273). See, in particular, Antony Anghie, B. S. Chimni, Karin Mickelson, and Obiora Okafor, eds., *The Third World and International Order: Law, Politics and Globalization* (Leiden: Martin Nijhoff, 2003); B. S. Chimni, "Third World Approaches to International Law: A Manifesto," in Anghie et al., *Third World and International Order;* Makau Mutua, "What Is TWAIL?" *American Society of International Law Proceedings* 94 (2000): 31–38; Balakrishnan Rajagopal, *International Law from Below: Development, Social Movements and Third World Resistance* (Cambridge: Cambridge University Press, 2003); Antony Anghie, *Imperialism, Sovereignty and the Making of International Law* (Cambridge: Cambridge University Press, 2005); and the articles in the special issue of *Osgoode Hall Law Journal,* 43 no. 1–2 (2005), on Third World approaches to international law after 9/11, edited by Obiora Okafor.

20. The following discussion draws on accounts by Paul Tiyambe Zeleza, Adebayo Olukoshi, Thandika Mkandawire, Zenebeworke Tadesse, and Issa Shivji. See Paul Tiyambe Zeleza, *Manufacturing African Studies and Crises* (Dakar: CODESRIA, 1997), and "The Politics of Historical and Social Science Research in Africa," *Journal of Southern African Studies* 28, no. 1 (2002): 9–23; Adebayo Olukoshi and Paul Tiyambe Zeleza, "Introduction: The Struggle for African Universities and Knowledges," in *African Universities in the Twenty-First Century: Liberalisation and Internationalisation,* ed. Paul Tiyambe Zeleza and Adebayo Olukoshi (Dakar:

CODESRIA, 2004); Thandika Mkandawire, "The Social Sciences in Africa: Breaking Local Barriers and Negotiating International Presence," *African Studies Review* 40, no. 2 (1997): 15–36, and "Social Sciences and Democracy: Debates in Africa," *African Sociological Review* 3, no. 1 (1999): 20–34; Zenebeworke Tadesse, "From Euphoria to Gloom? Navigating the Murky Waters of African Academic Institutions," in *Out of One, Many Africas: Reconstructing the Study and Meaning of Africa*, ed. William G. Martin and Martin O. West (Champaign: University of Illinois Press, 1999); and Issa G. Shivji, "From Neo-Liberalism to Pan-Africanism: Towards Reconstructing an Eastern African Discourse," *Pambazuka News* 200 (March 31, 2005), <http://www.pambazuka.org/index.php?issue=200> (accessed September 15, 2005), and "The Life and Times of Babu: The Age of Liberation and Revolution," *Review of African Political Economy* 95 (2003): 109–18.

21. Claude Ake, "Academic Freedom and Material Base," in *Academic Freedom in Africa*, ed. Mamadou Diouf and Mahmood Mamdani (Dakar: CODESRIA, 1994), 21.

22. Quintas Oula Obong, "Academic Dilemmas under Neo-Liberal Education Reforms: A Review of Makerere University, Uganda," in Zeleza and Olukoshi, *African Universities in the Twenty-First Century*, 109.

23. Zeleza, *Manufacturing African Studies and Crises*, 44–69.

24. Hans M. Zell, "Publishing in Africa: The Crisis and the Challenge," in *A History of Twentieth-Century African Literatures*, ed. Oyekan Owomoyela (Lincoln: University of Nebraska Press, 1993), cited in Zeleza, *Manufacturing African Studies and Crises*, 53; Tadesse, "From Euphoria to Gloom?", 147; Mohamed Mbodji and Mamadou Diouf, "Senegalese Historiography, Present Practices and Future Perspectives," in *African Historiographies: What History for Which Africa*, ed. Bogumil Jewsiewicki and David Newbury (Beverly Hills, Calif.: Sage, 1986); Paul E. Lovejoy, "Nigeria: The Ibadan School and Its Critics," in Jewsiewicki and Newbury, *African Historiographies*.

25. Zeleza, *Manufacturing African Studies and Crises*, 53–54.

26. *African Journal of International Affairs and Development*, College Press and Publishers, Nigeria, <http://72.41.110.51/policies.php?jid=173#focus> (accessed September 15, 2005).

27. Ayodeji Olukoju, "The Crisis of Research and Academic Publishing in Nigerian Universities," in *African Universities in the Twenty-First Century: Knowledge and Society*, ed. Paul Tiyambe Zeleza and Adebayo Olukoshi (Dakar: CODESRIA, 2004), 364.

28. L. A. Levey, ed., *A Profile of Research Libraries in Sub-Saharan Africa: Acquisitions, Outreach, and Infrastructure* (Washington, D.C.: American Association for the Advancement of Science, 1993), cited in Paul Tiyambe Zeleza, "Manufacturing and Consuming Knowledge: African Libraries and Publishing," *Development in Practice* 6, no. 4 (1996), 294.

29. R. Birenbaum, "Scholarly Communication under Siege," *University Affairs*, August–September 1995), 6, cited in Zeleza, "Manufacturing and Consuming Knowledge," 295.

30. See Mary H. Munroe, "Which Way Is Up? The Publishing Industry Merges Its Way into the Twenty-First Century," *Library Administration and Management* 14,

no. 2 (2000): 70–78; Mary H. Munroe, *The Academic Publishing Industry: A Story of Merger and Acquisition* (Washington, D.C.: Association of Research Libraries and Information Access Alliance, 2004), <http://www.niulib.niu.edu/publishers/> (accessed September 15, 2005); and Thomas M. Susman and David J. Carter, *Publishing Mergers: A Consumer-Based Approach to Antitrust Analysis* (Washington, D.C.: Information Access Alliance, 2003), <http://www.informationaccess.org/WhitePaperV2Final.pdf> (accessed September 15, 2005).

31. Sonya White and Claire Creaser, *Scholarly Journal Prices: Selected Trends and Comparisons* (Loughborough: Library and Information Statistics Unit, Loughborough University, 2004). Thanks to Claire Molloy for drawing this resource to my attention.

32. All statistics from White and Creaser, *Scholarly Journal Prices*.

33. Aaron Edlin and Daniel Rubinfeld, "Exclusion or Efficient Pricing? The 'Big Deal' Bundling of Academic Journals," *Antitrust Law Journal* 72, no. 1 (2004): 128–59.

34. Zeleza, "Manufacturing and Consuming Knowledge," 295.

35. Innocent Afuh Awasom, "Academic and Research Libraries in Cameroon: Current State and Future Perspectives," in Zeleza and Olukoshi, *African Universities in the Twenty-First Century*, 410–11.

36. Zeleza, *Manufacturing African Studies and Crises*, 45.

37. Zeleza found that donor-funding support to university libraries in Africa is generally not sustainable, largely provides material published in the donor country, and rarely allows the African library to select the journals and books provided by donors (Zeleza, "Manufacturing and Consuming Knowledge," 295).

38. Ayesha M. Imam and Amina Mama, "The Role of Academics in Limiting and Expanding Academic Freedom," in Diouf and Mamdani, *Academic Freedom in Africa*, 76–77; Olukoju, "The Crisis of Research and Academic Publishing in Nigerian Universities," 363. The all-encompassing and demoralizing social and individual effects of structural adjustment for academic staff and students are described brilliantly in two short stories, "Professor's Focal Adjustment" and "Permutations of Triple Zero," by Nigerian writer F. Odun Balogun in *Adjusted Lives: Stories of Structural Adjustments* (Trenton, N.J.: Africa World Press, 1995).

39. Zeleza, *Manufacturing African Studies and Crises*, 36–39; Shivji, "The Life and Times of Babu," 114; Mkandawire, "The Social Sciences in Africa," 29.

40. For an analysis of foundation funding to African universities and Africanist scholarship in the United States from the 1950s to the 1970s, see Edward H. Berman, "American Philanthropy and African Education: Toward an Analysis," *African Studies Review* 20, no. 1 (1977): 71–85, and Inderjeet Parmar, "American Foundations and the Development of International Knowledge Networks," *Global Networks: A Journal of Transnational Affairs* 2, no. 1 (2002): 22–24.

41. Zeleza, "The Politics of Historical and Social Science Research," 13–14.

42. In 2000, the Carnegie Corporation and the Ford, Rockefeller, and MacArthur foundations pledged $100 million to fund higher education in Africa. In 2005, the William and Flora Hewlett Foundation and the Andrew W. Mellon Foundation joined the partnership, and the six foundations have pledged $200 million to support universities in Ghana, Kenya, Mozambique, Nigeria, South Africa, Tanzania, and

Uganda over the next five years. See Partnership for Higher Education in Africa, *African Universities: Stories of Change* (New York: 2005).

43. Parmar, "American Foundations and the Development of International Knowledge Networks"; Berman, "American Philanthropy and African Education." This is a very significant issue that can be only pointed to rather than addressed here.

44. Berman, "American Philanthropy and African Education," 73.

45. Ebrima Sall, "African Scholars: Too Poor to Be Free," *UNESCO Courier* 54 (November 2001), <http://www.unesco.org/courier/2001_11/uk/doss15.htm> (accessed September 15, 2005).

46. Shivji, "From Neo-Liberalism to Pan-Africanism."

47. Mkandawire, "The Social Sciences in Africa," 29.

48. Paul Tiyambe Zeleza, "Neo-Liberalism and Academic Freedom," in Zeleza and Olukoshi, *African Universities in the Twenty-First Century*, 48; see also Shivji, "The Life and Times of Babu," 114–15.

49. Ogot, Bethwell Allan, "Lessons of Experience: Higher Education Policy of the World Bank in Africa" in *The Challenges of History and Leadership in Africa: the Essays of Bethwell Allan Ogot*, ed. Toyin Falola and E. S. Atieno Odhiambo (Trenton, NJ: Africa World Press, 2002).

50. Mahmood Mamdani, "A Glimpse at African Studies, Made in USA," *CODESRIA Bulletin* 2 (1990): 7–11; Mamdani, "A Critique of the State and Civil Society Paradigm in Africanist Studies," in *African Studies in Social Movements and Democracy*, ed. Mahmood Mamdani and Ernest Wamba-dia-Wamba (Dakar: CODESRIA, 1995); Jacques Depelchin, *Silences in African History: Between the Syndromes of Discovery and Abolition* (Dar es Salaam: Mkuki na Nyoyta Publishers, 2005); Zeleza, *Manufacturing African Studies and Crises*, 44–69. Zeleza examined five leading Africanist journals over the period 1982–1992 and found that of the 1,361 articles published, only 15 percent were written by African authors based in Africa.

51. Shivji, "The Life and Times of Babu," 112.

52. William Edward Burghardt Du Bois, *The World and Africa: An Inquiry into the Part Which Africa Has Played in World History* (1946; reprint, New York: International Publishers, 1996), 2.

53. Mkandawire, "The Social Sciences in Africa," 29.

54. Ifi Amadiume, *Re-Inventing Africa: Matriarchy, Religion, and Culture* (London: Zed Books, 1997), 5.

55. The Council for the Development of Social Science Research in Africa, Organization for Social Science Research in Eastern and Southern Africa, Association for African Women on Research and Development, African Association of Political Science, Southern Africa Political and Economic Series Trust.

56. Zeleza, *Manufacturing African Studies and Crises*, 86.

57. Mkandawire, "The Social Sciences in Africa," 16.

58. Christoph Scherrer, "GATS: Long-Term Strategy for the Commodification of Education," *Review of International Political Economy* 12, no. 3 (2005): 484–510; Tadesse, "From Euphoria to Gloom?"

59. Frantz Fanon, *The Wretched of the Earth* (Harmondsworth: Penguin, 1967), 189.

Bibliography

Abaza, Mona, and Georg Stauth. "Occidental Reason, Orientalism, Islamic Fundamentalism: A Critique." Pp. 209–30 in *Globalization, Knowledge and Society*, edited by Martin Albrow and Elizabeth King. London: Sage, 1990.

Abu-Lughod, Janet L. *Before European Hegemony: The World System A.D. 1250–1350*. New York: Oxford University Press, 1989.

Agamben, Giorgio. "On Security and Terror." *Frankfurter Allgemeine Zeitung*, translated by Soenke Zehle, September 20, 2001. <http://www.egs.edu/faculty/giorgioagamben.html> (accessed August 22, 2005).

Agence France-Press. "US Forces Demolish Iraq Homes." March 3, 2003. <http://www.news.com.au/common/story_page/0,4057,7942137% 5E1702,00.html> (accessed March 4, 2004).

Ahmad, Aijaz. *In Theory: Classes, Nations, Literatures*. London: Verso, 1992.

Ake, Claude. "Academic Freedom and Material Base." Pp. 17–25 in *Academic Freedom in Africa*, edited by Mamadou Diouf and Mahmood Mamdani. Dakar: CODESRIA, 1994.

Akello, Grace. *Iteso Thought Patterns in Tales*. Dar es Salaam: Dar es Salaam University Press, 1981.

Al-Azmeh, Aziz. *Islams and Modernities*. London: Verso, 1993.

Alessandrini, Anthony, ed. *Frantz Fanon: Critical Perspectives*. New York: Routledge, 1999.

Alford, William P. "Exporting the Pursuit of Happiness." *Harvard Law Review* 113, no. 7 (2000): 1677–715.

Alva, J. Jorge Klor de. "The Postcolonization of the (Latin) American Experience: A Reconsideration of 'Colonialism,' 'Postcolonialism,' and 'Mestizaje.'" Pp. 241–77 in *After Colonialism: Imperial Histories and Postcolonial Displacements*, edited by Gyan Prakash. Princeton, N.J.: Princeton University Press, 1995.

Alvarez, José E. "Hegemonic International Law Revisited." *American Journal of International Law* 97 (2003): 873–88.

Amadiume, Ifi. *Re-inventing Africa: Matriarchy, Religion, and Culture*. London: Zed Books, 1997.

Anderson, Benedict. *Imagined Communities: Reflections on the Origin and Spread of Nationalism*. London: Verso, 1991.

Ando, Nisuke. *Surrender, Occupation, and Private Property in International Law: An Evaluation of US Practice in Japan*. Oxford: Clarendon Press, 1991.

Anghie, Antony. "Francisco de Vitoria and the Colonial Origins of International Law." *Social and Legal Studies* 5, no. 3 (1996): 321–36.

———. "Universality and the Concept of Governance in International Law." Pp. 20–40 in *Legitimate Governance in Africa: International and Domestic Legal Perspectives*, edited by Edward Kofi Quashigah and Obiora Chinedu Okafor. The Hague: Kluwer Law International, 1999.

———. "Civilization and Commerce: The Concept of Governance in Historical Perspective." *Villanova Law Review* 45, no. 5 (2000): 887–911.

———. *Imperialism, Sovereignty and the Making of International Law*. Cambridge: Cambridge University Press, 2005.

Anghie, Antony, B. S. Chimni, Karin Mickelson, and Obiora Okafor, eds. *The Third World and International Order: Law, Politics and Globalization*. Leiden: Martin Nijhoff, 2003.

Appiah, Kwame Anthony. "Is the Post- in Postmodernism the Post- in Postcolonial?" Pp. 55–71 in *Contemporary Postcolonial Theory: A Reader*, edited by Padmini Mongia. London: Arnold, 1996.

Archer, Margaret, Roy Bhaskar, Andrew Collier, Tony Lawson, and Alan Norrie, eds. *Critical Realism: Essential Readings*. London: Routledge, 1998.

Arendt, Hannah. *On Revolution*. Harmondsworth: Penguin, 1963.

———. *The Origins of Totalitarianism*. New York: Harcourt Brace Jovanovich, 1968.

Asad, Talal. *Anthropology and the Colonial Encounter*. London: Ithaca Press, 1975.

———. *Genealogies of Religion: Discipline and Reasons of Power in Christianity and Islam*. Baltimore: The Johns Hopkins University Press, 1993.

Ashley, Richard K. "Three Modes of Economism." *International Studies Quarterly* 27, no. 4 (1983): 463–96.

———. "The Poverty of Neo-Realism." *International Organization* 38, no. 2 (1984): 225–86.

Atkinson, Ronald R. *The Roots of Ethnicity: The Origins of the Acholi of Uganda before 1800*. Philadelphia: University of Pennsylvania Press, 1994.

Aurobindo, Sri. *The Human Cycle, The Ideal of Human Unity, War and Self-Determination*. Pondicherry: Sri Aurobindo Ashram, 1970.

———. *The Life Divine*. Pondicherry: Sri Aurobindo Ashram, 1970.

———. *Tales of Prison Life*. 4th ed. Pondicherry: Sri Aurobindo Ashram, 1997.

Awasom, Innocent Afuh. "Academic and Research Libraries in Cameroon: Current State and Future Perspectives." Pp. 409–20 in *African Universities in the Twenty-First Century: Knowledge and Society*, edited by Paul Tiyambe Zeleza and Adebayo Olukoshi. Dakar: CODESRIA, 2004.

Ayers, Alison J. "Demystifying Democratization: The Global Constitution of Neo-Liberal Polities in Africa." *Third World Quarterly* 27, no. 3: 321–38.

Ayubi, Nazih. *Political Islam: Religion and Politics in the Arab World*. London: Routledge, 1991.

Bairoch, Paul. "Europe's Gross National Product 1800–1975." *Journal of European Economic History* 5, no. 2 (1976): 273–340.

———. "The Main Trends in National Income Disparities since the Industrial Revolution." Pp. 3–17 in *Disparities in Economic Development since the Industrial Revolution*, edited by Paul Bairoch and Maurice Lévy-Leboyer. London: Macmillan, 1981.

———. *Economics and World History: Myths and Paradoxes*. London: Harvester, 1993.

Balogun, F. Odun. *Adjusted Lives: Stories of Structural Adjustments*. Trenton, N.J.: Africa World Press, 1995.

Banerjee, Neela. "A Retired Shell Executive Seen as Likely Head of Production." *New York Times*, April 2, 2003, B12.

Barkawi, Tarak, and Mark Laffey. "The Postcolonial Moment in Security Studies." *Review of International Studies* 32, no. 2.

Bartlett, Robert. *The Making of Europe: Conquest, Colonization and Cultural Change, 950–1350*. Princeton, N.J.: Princeton University Press, 1993.

Barya, John-Jean B. "The New Political Conditionalities of Aid: An Independent View from Africa." *IDS Bulletin* 24, no. 1 (1993): 16–23.

Baxi, Upendra. "'The War on Terror' and the 'War of Terror': Nomadic Multitudes, Aggressive Incumbents, and the 'New' International Law." *Osgoode Hall Law Journal* 43, no. 1/2 (2005): 7–43.

Bedjaoui, Mohammed. *Towards a New International Economic Order*. New York: Holmes and Meier, 1979.

Bell, Gertrude. *The Desert and the Sown*. London: Heinemann, 1907.

Benhabib, Seyla. "Unholy Wars." *Constellations: An International Journal of Critical and Democratic Theory* 9, no. 1 (2002): 34–45.

———. *The Rights of Others: Aliens, Residents, and Citizens*. Cambridge: Cambridge University Press, 2004.

Benvenisti, Eyal, and Eyal Zamir. "Private Claims to Property Rights in the Future Israeli-Palestinian Settlement." *American Journal of International Law* 89 (1995): 295–340.

Berlin, Isaiah. *Four Essays on Liberty*. London: Oxford University Press, 1969.

Berman, Edward H. "American Philanthropy and African Education: Toward an Analysis." *African Studies Review* 20, no. 1 (1977): 71–85.

Bessis, Sophie. *Western Supremacy: The Triumph of an Idea?* Translated by P. Camiller. London: Zed Books, 2003.

Bhuta, Nehal. "A Global State of Exception? The United States and World Order." *Constellations: An International Journal of Critical and Democratic Theory* 10, no. 3 (2003): 371–91.

Bigo, Didier. "Security and Immigration: Toward a Critique of the Governmentality of Unease." *Alternatives: Global, Local, Political* 27 (2002): 63–92.

Bilgin, Pinar, and Adam David Morton. "From 'Rogue' to 'Failed' States? The Fallacy of Short-Termism." *Politics* 24, no. 3 (2004): 169–80.

Birdsall, Nancy. "Life Is Unfair: Inequality in the World." *Foreign Policy* 111 (summer 1998): 76–93.

Birenbaum, R. "Scholarly Communication under Siege." *University Affairs*, August–September 1995, 6.

Blair, Tony. "Speech on the London Bombings Delivered at the Labour Party National Conference." BBC, July 9, 2005. <http://news.bbc .co.uk/1/hi/uk/4689363.stm> (accessed August 5, 2005).

Blaut, James M. *The Colonizer's Model of the World: Geographical Diffusionism and Eurocentric History*. London: Guilford Press, 1993.

Blum, Vanessa. "After the War, a Time to Pay: How JAG Lawyers Settle Foreign Claims over Non-Combat Damage." *Legal Times*, April 21, 2003, 1.

Bonsu, Nana Osee Yaw. *The Wit of Akans*. Kumasi: n. p., 1994.

Bowing, John, ed. *The Works of Jeremy Bentham.* Vol. 2. New York: Russell & Russell, 1962.

Bozeman, Adda B. *Politics and Culture in International History: From the Ancient Near East to the Opening of the Modern Age*. 2nd ed. New Brunswick, N.J.: Transaction, 1994.

Bradley, Curtis A. "The Charming Betsy Canon and Separation of Powers: Rethinking the Interpretive Role of International Law." *Georgetown Law Journal* 86 (1998): 479–537.

Braudel, Fernand. *The Mediterranean and the Mediterranean World in the Age of Philip II*. New York: Collins, 1972.

Bravin, Jess, and Chip Cummins. "US Offers Concessions to U.N. in Bid to Lift Sanctions on Iraq." *Wall Street Journal*, May 9, 2003, A1.

Brown, Chris. *Understanding International Relations*. 2nd ed. Basingstoke: Palgrave, 2001.

Brown, Chris, Terry Nardin, and Nicholas Rengger, eds. *International Relations in Political Thought: Texts from the Ancient Greeks to the First World War*. Cambridge: Cambridge University Press, 2002.

Buck-Morss, Susan. "Hegel and Haiti." *Critical Inquiry* 26, no. 4 (2000): 821–65.

Burchill, Scott. "Introduction." Pp. 1–28 in *Theories of International Relations*, edited by Scott Burchill, Richard Devetak, Andrew Linklater, Matthew Paterson, Christian Reus-Smit, and Jacqui True. 2nd ed. Basingstoke: Palgrave, 2001.

Buzan, Barry, and Ole Wæver. *Liberalism and Security: The Contradictions of the Liberal Leviathan*. Copenhagen: Copenhagen Peace Research Institute, Working Paper, April 1998. <http://www.cianet.org/wps/bub02> (accessed August 22, 2005).

Cabral, Amílcar. "Connecting the Struggles: An Informal Talk with Black Americans." Pp. 75–92 in *Return to the Source: Selected Speeches of Amílcar Cabral.* London: Monthly Review Press, 1973.

———. "National Liberation and Culture." Pp. 39–56 in *Return to the Source: Selected Speeches of Amílcar Cabral.* London: Monthly Review Press, 1973.

Callaghy, Thomas M., Ronald Kassimir, and Robert Latham, eds. *Intervention and Transnationalism in Africa: Global-Local Networks of Power.* Cambridge: Cambridge University Press, 2001.

Cameron, Rondo. "The Industrial Revolution: A Misnomer." Pp. 367–76 in *Wirtschaftskrafte und Wirtschaftwege: Festschrift für Hermann Kellenbenz,* vol. 5, edited by Jurgen Schneider. Stuttgart: Komission bei Klett-Cotta, 1981.

———. "A New View of European Industrialization." *Economic History Review* 38, no. 1 (1985): 1–23.

Campbell, David. *Writing Security: United States Foreign Policy and the Politics of Identity.* Minneapolis: University of Minnesota Press, 1998.

Canadian International Development Agency. *Government of Canada Policy for CIDA on Human Rights, Democratization and Good Governance.* 1996. <http://www.acdicida.gc.ca/cida/OpenDocument.htm> (accessed June 13, 2001).

Cerna, Christina M. "Universal Democracy: An International Legal Right or the Pipe Dream of the West?" *New York University Journal of International Law and Politics* 27 (winter 1995): 289–329.

Césaire, Aimé. *Discourse on Colonialism.* (With an introduction by Robin D. G. Kelley). New York: Monthly Review Press, 2000.

Chakrabarty, Dipesh. "Postcoloniality and the Artifice of History: Who Speaks for 'Indian' Pasts?" *Representations* 37 (1992): 1–26.

———. "Postcoloniality and the Artifice of History: Who Speaks for 'Indian' Pasts?" Pp. 263–93 in *A Subaltern Studies Reader 1986–1995,* edited by Ranajit Guha. Minneapolis: University of Minnesota Press, 1997.

———. *Provincializing Europe: Postcolonial Thought and Historical Difference.* Princeton, N.J.: Princeton University Press, 2000.

Chand, Tara. *History of the Freedom Movement in India.* Vol. 3. Delhi: Ministry of Information and Broadcasting, Government of India, 1972.

Channing, Edward. *The Jeffersonian System, 1801–1811.* New York: Cooper Square, 1968.

Chatterjee, Partha. "Response to Taylor's 'Modes of Civil Society.' " *Public Culture* 3, no. 1 (1990): 119–32.

Chazan, Naomi. "The Asante Case." Pp. 60–97 in *The Early State in African Perspective,* edited by S. N. Eisenstadt, Michel Abitbol, and Naomi Chazan. Leiden: Brill, 1988.

Checkel, Jeffrey. "The Constructivist Turn in International Relations Theory." *World Politics* 50, no. 1 (1998): 324–48.

Cheyfitz, Eric. *The Poetics of Imperialism: Translation and Colonization from The Tempest to Tarzan.* Philadelphia: University of Pennsylvania Press, 1991.

Chimni, B. S. "Marxism and International Law: A Contemporary Analysis." *Economic and Political Weekly*, February 6, 1999, 337–49.

———. "Third World Approaches to International Law: A Manifesto." Pp. 47–73 in *The Third World and International Order: Law, Politics and Globalization*, edited by Antony Anghie, B. S. Chimni, Karin Mickelson, and Obiora Okafor. Leiden: Martin Nijhoff, 2003.

———. "International Institutions Today: An Imperial Global State in the Making." *European Journal of International Law* 15, no. 1 (2004): 1–39.

Chirot, Daniel. *Social Change in the Twentieth Century*. New York: Harcourt Brace Jovanovich, 1977.

Chowdhry, Gita, and Sheila Nair, eds. *Power, Postcolonialism and International Relations: Reading Race, Gender and Class*. London: Routledge, 2002.

Clark, Colin. *The Conditions of Economic Progress*. 3rd ed. London: Macmillan, 1957.

Cohen, Joshua, ed. *For Love of Country: Debating the Limits of Patriotism*. Boston: Beacon Press, 1996.

Collier, Andrew. *Critical Realism: An Introduction to the Philosophy of Roy Bhaskar*. London: Verso, 1994.

Commission on Global Governance. *Our Global Neighborhood: The Report of the Commission on Global Governance*. New York: Oxford University Press, 1995.

Conrad, Joseph. *Heart of Darkness*. 1925. Reprint, Harmondsworth: Penguin, 1995.

Cooper, Frederick. "Conflict and Connection: Rethinking African History." *American Historical Review* 99, no. 5 (1994): 1516–45.

Cowell, Alan. "Faith-Hate on Rise in UK." *New York Times*, August 3, 2005. <http://www.iht.com/articles/2005/08/03/news/London. php> (accessed August 10, 2005).

Cox, Robert W. "Gramsci, Hegemony and International Relations: An Essay in Method." *Millennium: Journal of International Studies* 12, no. 2 (1983): 162–75.

Crafts, Nicholas F. R. "British Economic Growth, 1700–1813: A Review of the Evidence." *Economic History Review* 36 (1983): 177–99.

Crawford, Gordon. *Promoting Democracy, Human Rights and Good Governance through Development Aid: A Comparative Study of the Policies of Four Northern Donors*. Working Papers on Democratisation, no. 1. Leeds: Centre for Democratisation Studies, 1996.

Crawford, Robert M. A., and Darryl S. L. Jarvis, eds. *International Relations—Still an American Social Science? Toward Diversity in International Thought*. New York: State University of New York Press, 2001.

Crenshaw, Kimberlé, Neil Gotanda, Garry Peller, and Kendall Thomas, eds. *Critical Race Theory: The Key Writings That Formed the Movement*. New York: New Press, 1995.

Crock, Stan, Paul Magnusson, Lee Walczak, and Frederik Balfour. "The Doctrine of Digital War." *Business Week*, April 7, 2003. <http://www. businessweek.com/magazine/content/03_14/b3827601 .htm> (accessed October 13, 2005).

Cummins, Chip. "State-Run Oil Company Is Being Weighed for Iraq." *Wall Street Journal*, January 7, 2004, A1.

Daniel, Norman. *Islam and the West: The Making of an Image*. Edinburgh: The University Press, 1966.

Daniszewski, John, and Geoffrey Mohan. "Looters Bring Baghdad New Havoc." *Los Angeles Times*, April 11, 2003, A1.

Darby, Philip. "Pursuing the Political: A Postcolonial Rethinking of Relations International." *Millennium: Journal of International Studies* 33, no. 1 (2004): 1–32.

———, ed. *At the Edge of International Relations: Postcolonialism, Gender and Dependency*. London: Pinter, 1997.

David, Oduc. "Customary Land Law and Economic Development of Uganda with Special Reference to Teso." BL thesis, University of Makerere, Kampala, 1987.

Davidson, Basil. *The Black Man's Burden: Africa and the Curse of the Nation-State*. London: James Currey, 1992.

Davis, John. "Foreword." P. v in *Nuer Prophets: A History of Prophecy from the Upper Nile in the Nineteenth and Twentieth Centuries*, edited by Douglas H. Johnson. Oxford: Clarendon Press, 1994.

Defoe, Daniel. *The Life and Adventures of Robinson Crusoe*. Harmondsworth: Penguin, 1965.

Depelchin, Jacques. "African Anthropology and History in the Light of the History of FRELIMO." *Contemporary Marxism* 7 (1983): 69–88.

———. *Silences in African History: Between the Syndromes of Discovery and Abolition*. Dar es Salaam: Mkuki na Nyoyta, 2005.

Derian, James Der. *On Diplomacy: A Genealogy of Western Estrangement*. Oxford: Basil Blackwell, 1987.

Diaz, Bernal. *The Conquest of New Spain*. Harmondsworth: Penguin, 1963.

Diderot, Denis, and Jean Le Rond d'Alembert, eds. *Encyclopédie ou Dictionnaire Raisonné des Sciences, Arts, et des Metiers*. Paris: Chez Briasson, 1755.

Dillon, Michael. *Politics of Security: Towards a Political Philosophy of Continental Thought*. New York: Routledge, 1996.

Dirlik, Arif. *The Post Colonial Aura: Third World Criticism in the Age of Global Capitalism*. Boulder, Colo.: Westview Press, 1997.

Dowling, William. *Jameson, Althusser, Marx: An Introduction to the Political Unconscious*. Ithaca, N.Y.: Cornell University Press, 1984.

Doyle, Michael. "Kant, Liberal Legacies, and Foreign Affairs." *Philosophy and Public Affairs* 12, no. 2–3 (1983): 205–35, 323–53.

Du Bois, William Edward Burghardt. *The World and Africa: An Inquiry into the Part Which Africa Has Played in World History*. 1946. Reprint, New York: International Publishers, 1996.

Edlin, Aaron, and Daniel Rubinfeld. "Exclusion or Efficient Pricing? The 'Big Deal' Bundling of Academic Journals." *Antitrust Law Journal* 72, no. 1 (2004): 128–59.

Edwards, Jim. "Rebuilding Iraq's Judicial System from the Ground Up." *New Jersey Law Journal*, October 27, 2003. <http://www.law.com/jsp/article.jsp?id=1066605424932> (accessed August 15, 2005).

Egimu-Okuda, N. "Social-Political Organisation of the Etem Igetoma." Pp. 167–74 in *The Iteso during the Asonya*, edited by J. B. Webster. Nairobi: East African Educational Publishers, 1973.

Emudong, Charles P. P. "The Iteso: A Segmentary Society under Colonial Administration, 1897–1927." MA thesis, University of Makerere, Kampala, 1974.

Esposito, John L., ed. *Voices of Resurgent Islam.* New York: Oxford University Press, 1983.

Eviatar, Dephne. "Free-Market Iraq? Not So Fast." *New York Times*, January 10, 2004, 9.

Eyoh, Dickson. "African Perspectives on Democracy and the Dilemmas of Postcolonial Intellectuals." *Africa Today* 45, no. 3–4 (1998): 281–306.

Eze, Emmanuel Chukwudi, ed. *Race and the Enlightenment: A Reader.* Oxford: Black-well, 1997.

Fabian, Johannes. *Time and the Other: How Anthropology Makes Its Object.* New York: Columbia University Press, 1983.

Falk, Richard A. *On Humane Governance: Toward a New Global Politics.* University Park: Pennsylvania State University Press, 1995.

Fanon, Frantz. "Racism and Culture." Pp. 39–54 in *Toward the African Revolution: Political Essays.* New York: Monthly Review Press, 1967.

———. *The Wretched of the Earth.* Harmondsworth: Penguin, 1967.

———. *Black Skin, White Masks.* London: Pluto Press, 1986.

Feilchenfeld, Ernst H. *The International Economic Law of Belligerent Occupation.* Washington, D.C.: Carnegie Endowment for International Peace, 1942.

Feldstein, Martin. "Refocusing the IMF." *Foreign Affairs* 77, no. 2 (1998): 20–33.

Fenwick, Charles G. *Wardship in International Law.* Washington, D.C.: U.S. Govern-ment Printing Office, 1919.

Finnemore, Martha. *National Interests in International Society.* Ithaca, N.Y.: Cornell University Press, 1996.

Fischer, Sibylle. *Modernity Disavowed: Haiti and the Cultures of Slavery in the Age of Revolution.* Durham, N.C.: Duke University Press, 2004.

Fores, Michael. "The Myth of a British Industrial Revolution." *History* 66, no. 217 (1981): 181–98.

Fortes, Meyer. "The Political System of the Tallensi of the Northern Territories of the Gold Coast." Pp. 239–70 in *African Political Systems,* edited by Meyer Fortes and Edward E. Evans-Pritchard. London: Oxford University Press, 1940.

———. *Religion, Morality and the Person.* Cambridge: Cambridge University Press, 1987.

Foucault, Michel. *Power/Knowledge: Selected Interviews and Other Writings 1972–1977.* Edited by Colin Gordon. New York: Pantheon, 1980.

Fox, Gregory H. "The Right to Political Participation in International Law." *Yale Jour-nal of International Law* 17 (1992): 539–607.

Franck, Thomas M. "The Emerging Right to Democratic Governance." *American Jour-nal of International Law* 86, no. 1 (1992): 46–91.

Freund, Bill. *The Making of Contemporary Africa: The Development of African Society since 1800.* 2nd ed. Basingstoke: Palgrave, 1998.

Friedman, Thomas L. *The World Is Flat: A Brief History of the Twenty-First Century.* New York: Farrar, Straus and Giroux, 2005.

Fromkin, David. *A Peace to End All Peace: The Fall of the Ottoman Empire and the Creation of the Modern Middle East*. London: Deutsch, 1989.

Fukuyama, Francis. *The End of History and the Last Man*. New York: Free Press, 1992.

Furedi, Frank. *The New Ideology of Imperialism: Renewing the Moral Imperative*. London: Pluto Press, 1994.

———. *The Silent War: Imperialism and the Changing Perceptions of Race*. London: Pluto, 1998.

Furet, Françoise. *Penser la Révolution Française*. Paris: Gallimard, 1978.

Furnivall, John S. *Progress and Welfare in Southeast Asia: A Comparison of Colonial Policy and Practice*. New York: Institute of Pacific Relations, 1941.

Furtado, Celso. *The Economic Growth of Brazil*. Berkeley: University of California Press, 1965.

Gardam, Judith G., and Michelle J. Jarvis. *Women, Armed Conflict and International Law*. The Hague: Kluwer Law International, 2001.

Gathii, James Thuo. "International Law and Eurocentricity." *European Journal of International Law* 9, no. 1 (1998): 184–211.

———. "Good Governance as a Counter-Insurgency Agenda to Oppositional and Transformative Social Projects in International Law." *Buffalo Human Rights Law Review* 5 (1999): 107–74.

———. "The Limits of the New International Rule of Law on Good Governance." Pp. 207–31 in *Legitimate Governance in Africa: International and Domestic Legal Perspectives*, edited by Edward Kofi Quashigah and Obiora Chinedu Okafor. The Hague: Kluwer Law International, 1999.

———. "Alternative and Critical: The Contribution of Research and Scholarship on Developing Countries to International Legal Theory." *Harvard International Law Journal* 41 (2000): 263–75.

———. "Geographical Hegelianism in Territorial Disputes Involving Non-European Land Relations: An Analysis of the Case concerning Kasikili/Sedudu Island (Botswana/Namibia)." *Leiden Journal of International Law* 15, no. 3 (2002): 581–622.

———. "Assessing Claims of a New Doctrine of Pre-Emptive War under the Doctrine of Sources." *Osgoode Hall Law Journal* 43, no. 1/2 (2005): 67–103.

Geggus, David P., ed. *The Impact of the Haitian Revolution in the Atlantic World*. Columbia: University of South Carolina Press, 2001.

Gerson, Allan. "Peace Building: The Private Sector's Role." *American Journal of International Law* 95, no. 1 (2001): 102–19.

Gilroy, Paul. *The Black Atlantic: Modernity and Double Consciousness*. Cambridge, Mass.: Harvard University Press, 1993.

———. *Small Acts*. London: Serpent's Tail, 1993.

Giri, Ananta Kumar. "Knowledge and Human Liberation: Jurgen Habermas, Sri Aurobindo and Beyond." *European Journal of Social Theory* 7, no. 1 (2004): 85–103.

Goldstein, Robert J. *Political Repression in Nineteenth Century Europe*. London: Croom Helm, 1982.

Goodman, Davis P. "The Need for Fundamental Change in the Law of Belligerent Occupation." *Stanford Law Review* 37 (1985): 1573–608.

Gough, Kathleen. "Anthropology and Imperialism." *Current Anthropology* 9, no. 5 (1968): 403–7.

Gramsci, Antonio. *Selections from the Prison Notebooks*. Translated and edited by Quintin Hoare and Geoffrey Nowell Smith. London: Lawrence and Wishart, 1971.

Gray, John. *Post-Liberalism: Studies in Political Thought*. London: Routledge, 1993.

———. *Liberalism*. 2nd ed. Buckingham: Open University Press, 1995.

Gregory, Derek. *The Colonial Present: Afghanistan, Palestine, Iraq*. Malden, Mass.: Blackwell, 2004.

Grovogui, Siba N'Zatioula. *Sovereigns, Quasi Sovereigns, and Africans: Race and Self-Determination in International Law*. Minneapolis: University of Minnesota Press, 1996.

———. "Regimes of Sovereignty: International Morality and the African Condition." *European Journal of International Relations* 8, no. 3 (2002): 315–38.

Guha, Ranajit. *A Rule of Property for Bengal: An Essay on the Idea of Permanent Settlement*. 1963. Reprint, Durham, N.C.: Duke University Press, 1996.

———. *Dominance without Hegemony: History and Power in Colonial India*. Cambridge, Mass.: Harvard University Press, 1997.

———. *History at the Limit of World-History*. New York: Columbia University Press, 2002.

———, ed. *Subaltern Studies*. New Delhi: Oxford University Press, 1982.

———, ed. *A Subaltern Studies Reader 1986–1995*. Minneapolis: University of Minnesota Press, 1997.

Halliday, Fred. "'Orientalism' and Its Critics." *British Journal of Middle Eastern Studies* 20 (1993): 145–63.

Halperin, Sandra. *In the Mirror of the Third World: Capitalist Development in Modern Europe*. Ithaca, N.Y.: Cornell University Press, 1997.

Harvey, David. *The New Imperialism*. Oxford: Oxford University Press, 2003.

"Hate Crimes against U.K. Muslims Soar." *CBC News*, August, 3 2005. <http://www.cbc.ca/story/world/national/2005/08/03racism050803.html?print> (accessed September 9, 2005).

Hegel, Georg W. F. *The Philosophy of History*. Translated by J. Sibree with an introduction by C. J. Friedrich. New York: Dover, 1956.

———. *Lectures on the Philosophy of World History. Introduction*. Translated by H. B. Nisbet. Cambridge: Cambridge University Press, 1975.

Henkins, Louis. *The Age of Rights*. New York: Columbia University Press, 1990.

Higgins, Andrew. "Contract Cops: As It Wields Power Abroad, US Outsources Law and Order Work." *Wall Street Journal*, February 2, 2004, A1.

Higgott, Richard, and Jim Richardson, eds. *International Relations: Global and Australian Perspectives on an Evolving Discipline*. Canberra: Australian National University, 1992.

Hinsley, F. H. *Power and the Pursuit of Peace: Theory and Practice in the History of Relations between States*. Cambridge: Cambridge University Press, 1963.

Hoffman, Stanley. "International Relations: An American Social Science." *Daedalus* 106 (1977): 41–59.

Horton, Robin. "Stateless Societies in the History of West Africa." Pp. 78–119 in *History of West Africa*, vol. 1, edited by J. F. A. Ajayi and Michael Crowder. London: Longman, 1971.

Howell, Sally, and Andrew Shryock. "Cracking Down on Diaspora: Arab Detroit and America's 'War on Terror.' " *Anthropological Quarterly* 76, no. 3 (2003): 443–62.

Hulme, Peter, and Ludmilla Jordanova, eds. *The Enlightenment and Its Shadows*. London: Routledge, 1990.

Huntington, Samuel P. *The Clash of Civilizations and the Remaking of World Order*. New York: Simon and Schuster, 1997.

Hurd, Elizabeth Shakman. "The Political Authority of Secularism in International Relations." *European Journal of International Relations* 10, no. 2 (2004): 235–62.

Hutchings, Kimberly. *International Political Theory: Rethinking Ethics in a Global Era*. London: Sage, 1999.

Huysmans, Jef. "Minding Expectations: The Politics of Insecurity and Liberal Democracy." *Contemporary Political Theory* 3, no. 3 (2004): 321–41.

Hymes, Dell H., ed. *Reinventing Anthropology*. New York: Random House, 1972.

Ignatieff, Michael. *Human Rights as Politics and Idolatry*. Princeton, N.J.: Princeton University Press, 2001.

———. "American Empire: The Burden." *New York Times Magazine*, January 5, 2003, 22.

Imam, Ayesha M., and Amina Mama. "The Role of Academics in Limiting and Expanding Academic Freedom." Pp. 73–107 in *Academic Freedom in Africa*, edited by Mamadou Diouf and Mahmood Mamdani. Dakar: CODESRIA, 1994.

Inayatullah, Naeem, and David L. Blaney. *International Relations and the Problem of Difference*. London: Routledge, 2004.

Jackson, Robert H. *Quasi-States: Sovereignty, International Relations, and the Third World*. Cambridge: Cambridge University Press, 1990.

Jahn, Beate. *The Cultural Construction of International Relations: The Invention of the State of Nature*. Basingstoke: Palgrave, 2000.

———. "Barbarian Thoughts: Imperialism in the Philosophy of John Stuart Mill." *Review of International Studies* 31, no. 3 (2005): 599–618.

———. "Kant, Mill, and Illiberal Legacies in International Affairs." *International Organization* 59 (winter 2005): 177–207.

James, C. L. R. *American Civilisation*. 1950. Reprint, Oxford: Blackwell, 1993.

———. *At the Rendezvous of Victory*. London: Allison and Busby, 1984.

Jameson, Frederic. *The Political Unconscious: Narrative as a Socially Symbolic Act*. Ithaca, N.Y.: Cornell University Press, 1981.

Jaspers, Karl. *Philosophy and the World : Selected Essays*. Chicago: A Gateway Edition, 1963.

Jay, Stewart. "The Status of the Law of Nations in Early American Law." *Vanderbilt Law Review* 42 (1989): 819–49.

Jørgensen, Knud E. "Continental IR Theory: The Best Kept Secret." *European Journal of International Relations* 6, no. 1 (2000): 9–42.

Kadish, Doris Y., ed. *Slavery in the Caribbean Francophone World*. Athens: University of Georgia Press, 2000.

Kant, Immanuel. "Perpetual Peace." Pp. 107–43 in *Perpetual Peace and Other Essays*. Translated by Ted Humphrey. Cambridge: Hackett, 1983.

Kapur, Devesh. "The IMF: A Cure or a Curse?" *Foreign Policy* 111 (summer 1998): 114–29.

Keck, Margaret E., and Kathryn Sikkink. *Activists beyond Borders: Advocacy Networks in International Politics*. Ithaca, N.Y.: Cornell University Press, 1998.

Keebel, Edna. "Immigration, Civil Liberties and National/Homeland Security." *International Journal* 60, no. 2 (2005): 359–72.

Keene, Edward. *Beyond the Anarchical Society: Grotius, Colonialism and Order in World Politics*. Cambridge: Cambridge University Press, 2002.

Kiernan, Victor G. *Poets, Politics and the People*. Edited by Harvey J. Kaye. London: Verso, 1989.

King, Neil, Jr. "Bush Officials Draft Broad Plan for Free-Market Economy in Iraq." *Wall Street Journal*, May 1, 2003, A1.

Knutsen, Torbjörn L. *A History of International Relations Theory: An Introduction*. Manchester: Manchester University Press, 1992.

Kolodziej, Edward A. *A Force Profonde: The Power, Politics, and Promise of Human Rights*. Philadelphia: University of Pennsylvania Press, 2003.

Krippendorf, Ekkehart. "The Dominance of American Approaches in International Relations." *Millennium: Journal of International Studies* 16, no. 2 (1987): 207–14.

Krisch, Nico. "Weak as Constraint, Strong as Tool: The Place of International Law in US Foreign Policy." Pp. 41–70 in *Unilateralism and US Foreign Policy: International Perspectives*, edited by David M. Malone and Yuen Foong Khong. Boulder, Colo.: Lynne Rienner, 2003.

Kuhn, Thomas S. *The Structure of Scientific Revolutions*. 2nd ed. Chicago: University of Chicago Press, 1970.

Kwadwo, Osei. *An Outline of Asante History*. Kumasi: O. Kwadwo Enterprise, 1994.

Landes, David. *The Unbound Prometheus*. Cambridge: Cambridge University Press, 1969.

Lapid, Yosef, and Friedrich Kratochwil, eds. *The Return of Culture and Identity in IR Theory*. Boulder, Colo.: Lynne Rienner, 1997.

Lepore, Jill. *The Name of War: King Philip's War and the Origins of American Identity*. New York: Knopf, 1998.

Levey, L. A., ed. *A Profile of Research Libraries in Sub-Saharan Africa: Acquisitions, Outreach, and Infrastructure*. Washington, D.C.: American Association for the Advancement of Science, 1993.

Levy, Carl. "The European Union after 9/11: The Demise of a Liberal Democratic Asylum Regime." *Government and Opposition* 40, no. 1 (2005): 26–59.

Lewis, Bernard. "The Return of Islam." *Commentary* January (1976): 39–49.

———. *The Muslim Discovery of Europe*. New York: Norton, 1982.

———. "The Roots of Muslim Rage." *Atlantic Monthly* 266, no. 3 (1990): 47–60.

————. *What Went Wrong? Western Impact and Middle East Response*. New York: Oxford University Press, 2002.

Lewis, W. Arthur. *Growth and Fluctuation, 1870–1913*. London: George Allen & Unwin, 1978.

Lindley, Mark F. *The Acquisition and Government of Backward Territory in International Law: Being a Treatise on the Law and Practice Relating to Colonial Expansion*. London: Longmans, Green and Co., 1926. Reprint, New York: Negro Universities Press, 1969.

Ling, L. H. M. *Postcolonial International Relations: Conquest and Desire between Asia and the West*. Basingstoke: Palgrave, 2002.

Linklater, Andrew. *The Transformation of Political Community: Ethical Foundations of the Post-Westphalian Era*. Cambridge: Polity Press, 1998.

Lobel, Jules. "The Limits of Constitutional Power: Conflicts between Foreign Policy and International Law." *Virginia Law Review* 71 (1985): 1071–180.

Loomba, Ania. *Colonialism-Postcolonialism*. London: Routledge, 1998.

López, Carlos Scott. "Reformulating Native Title in Mabo's Wake: Aboriginal Sovereignty and Reconciliation in Post-Centenary Australia." *Tulsa Journal of Comparative and International Law* 11 (2003): 21–110.

Louis, William Roger, and Ronald Robinson. "The Imperialism of Decolonisation." Pp. 49–79 in *The Decolonisation Reader*, edited by James Le Seuer. London: Routledge, 2001.

Lovejoy, Paul E. "Nigeria: The Ibadan School and Its Critics." Pp. 207–14 in *African Historiographies: What History for Which Africa*, edited by Bogumil Jewsiewicki and David Newbury. Beverly Hills, Calif.: Sage, 1986.

Lugard, Lord Frederick J. D. *The Dual Mandate in British Tropical Africa*. 1922. Reprint, London: Frank Cass, 1965.

Machel, Samora. "White Mozambicans: A Message by the President of FRELIMO, on the Day of the Mozambican Revolution, 25 August 1971." P. 177 in *The African Liberation Reader: Documents of the National Liberation Movements. Volume 2: The National Liberation Movements*, edited by Aquino de Bragança and Immanuel Wallerstein. London: Zed Books, 1982.

MacIver, Robert. *The Modern State*. London: Oxford University Press, 1932.

Macmillan, Margaret. *Paris, 1919*. New York: Random House, 2003.

MacQuarrie, Brian. "For Iraqis, a Struggle to Recoup Loss." *Boston Globe*, August 6, 2003, A1.

Maddison, Angus. "A Comparison of Levels of GDP Per Capita in Developed and Developing Countries, 1700–1980." *Journal of Economic History* 43 (1983): 27–41.

————. "Measuring European Growth: The Core and the Periphery." Pp. 82–118 in *Growth and Stagnation in the Mediterranean World in the 19th and 20th Centuries*, edited by Erik Aerts and Nuno Valério. Leuven: University of Leuven Press, 1989.

————. *The World Economy in the 20th Century*. Paris: Development Center of the Organization for Economic Cooperation and Development, 1989.

Mafeje, Archie. *Kingdoms of the Great Lakes Region: Ethnography of African Social Formations*. Kampala: Fountain Publishers, 1998.

Mahadevan, T. M. P., and G. V. Saroja. *Contemporary Indian Philosophy*. New Delhi: Sterling Publishers, 1981.

Mamdani, Mahmood. "A Glimpse at African Studies, Made in USA." *CODESRIA Bulletin* 2 (1990): 7–11.

———. "A Critique of the State and Civil Society Paradigm in Africanist Studies." Pp. 602–16 in *African Studies in Social Movements and Democracy*, edited by Mahmood Mamdani and Ernest Wamba-dia-Wamba. Dakar: CODESRIA, 1995.

———. *Citizen and Subject: Contemporary Africa and the Legacy of Late Colonialism*. Princeton, N.J.: Princeton University Press, 1996.

———. *Good Muslim, Bad Muslim: America, the Cold War, and the Roots of Terror*. New York: Pantheon Books, 2004.

Mann, F. A. "Enemy Property and the Paris Peace Treaties." *Law Quarterly Review* 64 (1948): 492–518.

Marcus, Maxine. "Humanitarian Intervention without Borders: Belligerent Occupation or Colonization." *Houston Journal of International Law* 25 (2003): 99–139.

Marx, Karl. "The Eighteenth Brumaire of Louis Bonaparte." Pp. 143–249 in *Surveys from Exile: Political Writings*. Vol. 2. 1869. Reprint, Harmondsworth: Penguin, 1992.

Marx, Karl, and Friedrich Engels. *The German Ideology*. London: Lawrence and Wishart, 1968.

———. *The German Ideology*. 3rd rev. ed. Moscow: Progress Publishers, 1976.

Mayer, Arno J. *The Persistence of the Old Regime: Europe to the Great War*. New York: Pantheon Books, 1981.

Mbodji, Mohamed, and Mamadou Diouf. "Senegalese Historiography, Present Practices and Future Perspectives." Pp. 207–14 in *African Historiographies: What History for Which Africa*, edited by Bogumil Jewsiewicki and David Newbury. Beverly Hills, Calif.: Sage, 1986.

McClintock, Anne. *Imperial Leather: Race, Sexuality and Gender in the Colonial Contest*. London: Routledge, 1995.

McDonald, Kevin. "Oneself as Another: From Social Movement to Experience Movement." *Current Sociology* 52, no. 4 (2004): 575–93.

McGurk, Brett H. "Revisiting the Law of Nation-Building: Iraq in Transition." *Virginia Journal of International Law* 45 (2005): 451–64.

McNeill, William H. *The Rise of the West: A History of the Human Community*. New York: New American Library, 1963.

Mearsheimer, John J. "Back to the Future: Instability in Europe after the Cold War." *International Security* 15, no. 1 (1990): 5–56.

Mehta, Uday Singh. *Liberalism and Empire: A Study in Nineteenth-Century British Liberal Thought*. Chicago: University of Chicago Press, 1999.

Memmi, Albert. *The Colonizer and the Colonized*. London: Souvenir Press, 1965.

Menocal, Maria Rosa. *Ornament of the World: How Muslims, Jews, and Christians Created a Culture of Tolerance in Medieval Spain*. Boston: Little, Brown, 2002.

Meron, Theodor. "Applicability of Multilateral Conventions to Occupied Territories." *American Journal of International Law* 72, no. 3 (1978): 542–57.

Mesquita, Bruce Bueno de. *The War Trap*. New Haven, Conn.: Yale University Press, 1981.

Mignolo, Walter D. *The Darker Side of the Renaissance: Literacy, Territoriality, and Colonization*. Ann Arbor: University of Michigan Press, 1995.

Mills, Charles W. *The Racial Contract*. Ithaca, N.Y.: Cornell University Press, 1999.

Mintz, Sidney W. "Can Haiti Change?" *Foreign Affairs* 74, no. 1 (1995): 73–86.

Mitchell, Timothy. *Colonising Egypt*. Berkeley: University of California Press, 1988.

Mkandawire, Thandika. "The Social Sciences in Africa: Breaking Local Barriers and Negotiating International Presence." *African Studies Review* 40, no. 2 (1997): 15–36.

———. "Social Sciences and Democracy: Debates in Africa." *African Sociological Review* 3, no. 1 (1999): 20–34.

Mohanty, J. N. *Indian Philosophy*. Edited by Bina Gupta. Vol. 1 of *Explorations in Philosophy: Essays by J. N. Mohanty*. New Delhi: Oxford University Press, 2001.

Moore, John Bassett. *International Law and Some Current Illusions and Other Essays*. London: Macmillan, 1924.

Moore, Barrington, Jr. *Social Origins of Dictatorship and Democracy: Lord and Peasant in the Making of the Modern World*. Boston: Beacon Press, 1966.

Munroe, Mary H. "Which Way Is Up? The Publishing Industry Merges Its Way into the Twenty-First Century." *Library Administration and Management* 14, no. 2 (2000): 70–78.

———. *The Academic Publishing Industry: A Story of Merger and Acquisition*. Association of Research Libraries and Information Access Alliance, 2004. <http://www.niulib.niu.edu/publishers/> (accessed September 15, 2005).

Munslow, Barry. *Mozambique: The Revolution and Its Origins*. London: Longman, 1983.

Mutua, Makau. "What Is TWAIL?" *American Society of International Law Proceedings* 94 (2000): 31–38.

Nandy, Ashis. *The Intimate Enemy: Loss and Recovery of Self under Colonialism*. Delhi: Oxford University Press, 1983.

———. *Exiled at Home: Comprising, At the Edge of Psychology, The Intimate Enemy, Creating a Nationality*. New Delhi: Oxford University Press, 1998.

Nederveen Pieterse, Jan, and Bhikhu Parekh. "Shifting Imaginaries: Decolonisation, Internal Decolonisation, Post-Coloniality." Pp. 1–19 in *The Decolonization of Imagination: Culture, Knowledge and Power*, edited by Jan Nederveen Pieterse and Bhikhu Parekh. London: Zed Books, 1995.

Neto, Agostinho. "Not an Isolated Struggle: From a message by the President of MPLA, broadcast on 6 June 1968 on the 'Voice of the Angolan Freedom-Fighter' on Radio Tanzania." Pp. 171–72 in *The African Liberation Reader: Documents of the National Liberation Movements. Volume 2: The National Liberation Movements*, edited by Aquino de Bragança and Immanuel Wallerstein. London: Zed Books, 1982.

Neufeld, Mark. *The Restructuring of International Relations Theory*. Cambridge: Cambridge University Press, 1995.

Nietschmann, Bernard. "The Third World War." *Cultural Survival Quarterly* 11, no. 3 (1987): 1–16.

Normand, Roger, and Chris af Jochnick. "The Legitimation of Violence: A Critical Analysis of the Gulf War." *Harvard International Law Journal* 35 (1994): 387–416.

North, Douglass C. *Structure and Change in Economic History.* New York: Norton, 1981.

Nukunya, G. K. *Tradition and Change in Ghana.* Accra: Ghana Universities Press, 1992.

Nussbaum, Arthur. *A Concise History of the Law of Nations.* 2nd rev. ed. New York: Macmillan, 1954.

Obeng, Ernest E. *Ancient Ashanti Chieftaincy.* Tema: Ghana Publishing, 1986.

Obong, Quintas Oula. "Academic Dilemmas under Neo-Liberal Education Reforms: A Review of Makerere University, Uganda." Pp. 108–25 in *African Universities in the Twenty-First Century: Liberalisation and Internationalisation,* edited by Paul Tiyambe Zeleza and Adebayo Olukoshi. Dakar: CODESRIA, 2004.

Ogg, Frederick A. *Economic Development of Modern Europe.* New York: Macmillan, 1930.

Ogot, Bethwell Allan. "Lessons of Experience: Higher Education Policy of the World Bank in Africa" in *The Challenges of History and Leadership in Africa: the Essays of Bethwell Allan Ogot,* ed. Toyin Falola and E. S. Atieno Odhiambo. Trenton, NJ: Africa World Press, 2002.

Okalany, D. H. "Juridical Procedures and Legal Principles of the Asonya." Pp. 129–42 in *The Iteso during the Asonya,* edited by J. B. Webster. Nairobi: East African Educational Publishers, 1973.

Olukoju, Ayodeji. "The Crisis of Research and Academic Publishing in Nigerian Universities." Pp. 363–75 in *African Universities in the Twenty-First Century: Knowledge and Society,* edited by Paul Tiyambe Zeleza and Adebayo Olukoshi. Dakar: CODESRIA, 2004.

Olukoshi, Adebayo, and Paul Tiyambe Zeleza. "Introduction: The Struggle for African Universities and Knowledges." Pp. 1–18 in *African Universities in the Twenty-First Century: Liberalisation and Internationalisation,* edited by Paul Tiyambe Zeleza and Adebayo Olukoshi. Dakar: CODESRIA, 2004.

Oppenheim, Lassa. *International Law: A Treatise. Vol. 1: Peace.* 4th ed. Edited by Arnold McNair. London: Longmans, 1928.

Organization for Economic Cooperation and Development, Development Advisory Committee. *Participatory Development and Good Governance, Development Cooperation Guidelines Series.* Paris: Organization for Economic Cooperation and Development, 1995.

Ouattara, Alassane D. "The Political Dimensions of Economic Reforms—Conditions for Successful Adjustment." Keynote Address by Mr. Alassane D. Ouattara, deputy managing director, International Monetary Fund, June 9, 1999. <http://www.imf.org/external/np/speeches/1999/061099.htm> (accessed August 16, 2005).

p'Bitek, Okot. "Man the Unfree." Pp. 19–24 in *Artist the Ruler: Essays on Art, Culture and Values*. Nairobi: East African Educational Publishers, 1986.

Pagden, Anthony. "Human Rights, Natural Rights, and Europe's Imperial Legacy." *Political Theory* 31, no. 2 (2003): 171–99.

Paolini, Albert J. *Navigating Modernity: Postcolonialism, Identity, and International Relations*. Boulder, Colo.: Lynne Rienner, 1999.

Paranjape, Makarand. *Aurobindo Reader*. New Delhi: Penguin, 1999.

Parekh, Bhikhu. "The Cultural Particularity of Liberal Democracy." *Political Studies* 40 (special issue, 1992): 160–75.

———. "Liberalism and Colonialism: A Critique of Locke and Mill." Pp. 81–98 in *The Decolonization of Imagination: Culture, Knowledge and Power*, edited by Jan Nederveen Pieterse and Bhikhu Parekh. London: Zed Books, 1995.

Parmar, Inderjeet. "American Foundations and the Development of International Knowledge Networks." *Global Networks: A Journal of Transnational Affairs* 2, no. 1 (2002): 13–30.

Partnership for Higher Education in Africa. *African Universities: Stories of Change*. New York: Partnership for Higher Education in Africa, 2005.

Pasha, Mustapha Kamal. "Islam, 'Soft' Orientalism and Hegemony: A Gramscian Rereading." *Critical Review of International Social and Political Philosophy* 8, no. 4 (2005): 543–58.

Phillipson, Coleman. *The Effect of War on Contracts and on Trading Associations in Territories of the Belligerent*. London: Stevens & Haynes, 1909.

Prakash, Gyan. "Subaltern Studies as Postcolonial Criticism." *American Historical Review* 99, no. 5 (1994): 1475–90.

Quashigah, Edward Kofi, and Obiora Chinedu Okafor, eds. *Legitimate Governance in Africa: International and Domestic Legal Perspectives*. The Hague: Kluwer Law International, 1999.

Rajagopal, Balakrishnan. *International Law from Below: Development, Social Movements and Third World Resistance*. Cambridge: Cambridge University Press, 2003.

Rattray, Robert S. *Ashanti Law and Constitution*. Oxford: Clarendon Press, 1929.

Reif, Linda C. "Building Democratic Institutions: The Role of National Human Rights Institutions in Good Governance and Human Rights Protection." *Harvard Human Rights Journal* 13 (2000): 1–69.

Reus-Smit, Christian, ed. *The Politics of International Law*. Cambridge: Cambridge University Press, 2004.

Robbins, Bruce. "The East Is a Career: Edward Said and the Logics of Professionalism." Pp. 48–73 in *Edward Said: A Critical Reader*, edited by Michael Sprinker. Oxford: Blackwell, 1992.

Roberts, Susan, Anna Secor, and Matthew Sparke. "Neoliberal Geopolitics." *Antipode: A Radical Journal of Geography* 35, no. 5 (2003): 886–97.

Roy, Arundhati. *An Ordinary Person's Guide to Empire*. Cambridge, Mass.: South End Press, 2004.

Rummel, Rudolph J. *Power Kills: Democracy as a Method of Non-Violence*. New Brunswick, N.J.: Transaction, 1997.

Safranski, Rudiger. *Martin Heidegger: Between Good and Evil.* Translated by Ewald Osers. Cambridge, Mass.: Harvard University Press, 1998.

Said, Edward W. *Orientalism.* London: Vintage, 1978.

———. *Culture and Imperialism.* London: Vintage, 1994.

———. "Secular Interpretation, the Geographical Element and the Methodology of Imperialism." Pp. 21–39 in *After Colonialism: Imperial Histories and Postcolonial Displacements,* edited by Gyan Prakash. Princeton, N.J.: Princeton University Press, 1995.

Sall, Ebrima. "African Scholars: Too Poor to Be Free." *UNESCO Courier* 54, November 2001. <http://www.unesco.org/courier/2001_11/uk/doss15.htm> (accessed September 15, 2005).

Salvatore, Armando. "Beyond Orientalism? Max Weber and the Displacement of 'Essentialism' in the Study of Islam." *Arabica Revue d'Etudes Arabes* 43 (1996): 412–33.

Sarkar, Sumit. *Modern India.* New Delhi: Macmillan, 1983.

Scheffer, David J. "Beyond Occupation Law." *American Journal of International Law* 97, no. 4 (2003): 842–60.

Scherrer, Christoph. "GATS: Long-Term Strategy for the Commodification of Education." *Review of International Political Economy* 12, no. 3 (2005): 484–510.

Schmitt, Carl. *On the Concept of the Political.* Translated by George Schwab. Chicago: University of Chicago Press, 1996.

Schwenk, Edmund H. "Legislative Power of the Military Occupant under Article 43, Hague Regulations." *Yale Law Journal* 54 (1945): 393–416.

Sen, Amartya. "Elements of a Theory of Human Rights." *Philosophy and Public Affairs* 32, no. 4 (2004): 315–56.

Shapiro, Michael J. *Violent Cartographies: Mapping Cultures of War.* Minneapolis: University of Minnesota Press, 1997.

———. "Samuel Huntington's Moral Geography." *Theory and Event* 4 (1999). <http://muse.jhu.edu/journals/theory_and_event/> (accessed September 15, 2005).

Sherwood, Bob. "Legal Reconstruction: Investors Want Reassurance over Iraq's Framework of Commercial Law." *Financial Times,* November 3, 2003, 14.

Shihata, Ibrahim F. I. "Democracy and Development." *International and Comparative Law Quarterly* 46 (1997): 635–43.

Shivji, Issa G. "The Life and Times of Babu: The Age of Liberation and Revolution." *Review of African Political Economy* 95 (2003): 109–18.

———. "From Neo-Liberalism to Pan-Africanism: Towards Reconstructing an Eastern African Discourse." *Pambazuka News* 200, March 31, 2005. <http://www.pambazuka.org/index.php?issue=200> (accessed September 15, 2005).

Simonse, Simon. *Kings of Disaster: Dualism, Centralism, and the Scapegoat King in Southeastern Sudan.* Leiden: Brill, 1992.

Singer, J. David, ed. *The Correlates of War.* Vols. 1 and 2. New York: Free Press, 1979.

Singham, A. W., and Shirley Hune. *Non-Alignment in an Age of Alignments.* Westport, Conn.: Lawrence Hill, 1986.

Sinha, Mrinalini. *Colonial Masculinity: The "Manly" Englishman and the "Effeminate Bengali" in the Late Nineteenth Century*. Manchester: Manchester University Press, 1995.

Slater, Mark B. "Passports, Mobility and Security: How Smart Can the Border Be?" *International Studies Perspectives* 5, no. 1 (2004): 71–91.

Slaughter, Anne-Marie. "International Law and International Relations Theory: A Dual Agenda." *American Journal of International Law* 87, no. 2 (1993): 205–39.

Smith, Steve. "The Self-Images of a Discipline: A Genealogy of International Relations Theory." Pp. 1–37 in *International Relations Theory Today*, edited by Ken Booth and Steve Smith. Cambridge: Polity Press, 1995.

———. "The Discipline of International Relations: Still an American Social Science?" *British Journal of Politics and International Relations* 2, no. 3 (2000): 374–402.

———. "The United States and the Discipline of International Relations: 'Hegemonic Country, Hegemonic Discipline.' " Pp. 67–85 in *International Relations and the New Inequality*, edited by Mustapha Kamal Pasha and Craig N. Murphy. Malden, Mass.: Blackwell, 2002.

Smith, Thomas W. "The New Law of War: Legitimizing Hi-Tech and Infrastructural Violence." *International Studies Quarterly* 46, no. 3 (2002): 355–74.

Snow, Alpheus H. *The Question of Aborigines in the Law and Practice of Nations*. New York: G. P. Putnam's Sons, 1921.

Sommerich, Otto C. "A Brief against Confiscation." *Law and Contemporary Problems* 11 (1845): 152–65.

Steele, Jonathan. "US Decree Strips Thousands of Their Jobs." *The Guardian*, August 30, 2003, 16.

Steiner, Henry J. "Political Participation as a Human Right." *Harvard Human Rights Yearbook* 1 (spring 1988): 77–134.

Stokes, Eric. *English Utilitarians in India*. Oxford: Clarendon Press, 1959.

Susman, Thomas M., and David J. Carter. *Publishing Mergers: A Consumer-Based Approach to Antitrust Analysis*. Washington, D.C.: Information Access Alliance, 2003. <http://www. informationaccess.org/WhitePaperV2Final.pdf> (accessed September 15, 2005).

Tadesse, Zenebeworke. "From Euphoria to Gloom? Navigating the Murky Waters of African Academic Institutions." Pp. 145–54 in *Out of One, Many Africas: Reconstructing the Study and Meaning of Africa*, edited by William G. Martin and Martin O. West. Champaign: University of Illinois Press, 1999.

Taiwo, Olufemi. "Exorcising Hegel's Ghost: Africa's Challenge to Philosophy." *African Studies Quarterly* 1, no. 4 (1998). <http://www.africa.ufl.edu/asq/v1/4/2.htm> (accessed August 15, 2005).

Teschke, Benno. *The Myth of 1648: Class, Geopolitics and the Making of Modern International Relations*. London: Verso, 2003.

Thies, Cameron G. "Progress, History and Identity in International Relations Theory: The Case of the Idealist-Realist Debate." *European Journal of International Relations* 8, no. 2 (2002): 147–85.

Thiong'o, Ngũgĩ wa. *Decolonising the Mind: The Politics of Language in African Literature*. London: James Currey and Heinemann, 1986.

Thomas, Daniel C. *The Helsinki Effect: International Norms, Human Rights, and the Demise of Communism*. Princeton, N.J.: Princeton University Press, 2001.

Tickner, Arlene. "Seeing IR Differently: Notes from the Third World." *Millennium: Journal of International Studies* 32, no. 2 (2003): 295–324.

Treaty of Amity, Commerce, and Navigation November 19, 1794, US-GB, 8 Stat. 116 (1794). <http://www.yale.edu/lawweb/avalon/diplomacy/brit/jay.htm> (accessed March 28, 2004).

Trouillot, Michel-Rolph. *Silencing the Past: Power and the Production of History*. Boston: Beacon Press, 1995.

Tsakalotos, Euclid. "Homo Economicus, Political Economy and Socialism." *Science and Society* 68, no. 2 (2004): 137–60.

United Nations. "Humanitarian Appeal for Iraq: Revised Inter-Agency Appeal 1 April–31 December." 2003. <http://www.reliefweb.int/appeals/2003/files/irq03flash2.pdf> (accessed March 29, 2004).

United Nations Development Program. *Human Development Report 1992: Global Dimensions of Human Development*. New York: United Nations Development Program, 1992.

———. *Human Development Report 2005. International Cooperation at a Crossroads: Aid, Trade and Security in an Unequal World*. New York: United Nations Development Program, 2005.

United States Government. *The National Security Strategy of the United States of America*. Washington, D.C.: The White House, 2002. <http://www.whitehouse.gov/nsc/nss.pdf> (accessed October 13, 2005).

Vansina, Jan. "Once upon a Time: Oral Traditions as History in Africa." Pp. 413–36 in *Historical Studies Today*, edited by Felix Gilbert and Stephen R. Graubard. New York: Norton, 1972.

various authors. "Colloquium. International Law, Human Rights, and LatCrit Theory." *University of Miami Inter-American Law Review* 28 (1997): 177–302.

various authors. "Symposium. Critical Race Theory and International Law: Convergence and Divergence." *Villanova Law Review* 45, no. 5 (2000): 827–1220.

Vasquez, John A. *The Power of Power Politics: From Classical Realism to Neotraditionalism*. Cambridge: Cambridge University Press, 1998.

Victoria, Franciscus de. *De Indis Et Ivre Belli Relectione (1557)*. Edited by Ernest Nys and translated by John Pawley Bate. Washington, D.C.: Carnegie Institute of Washington, 1917.

Viswanathan, Gauri. *Masks of Conquest: Literary Study and British Rule in India*. New York: Columbia University Press, 1989.

Wade, Robert. "The Coming Fight over Capital Flows." *Foreign Policy* 113 (winter 1998): 41–54.

Wæver, Ole. "The Sociology of a Not so International Discipline: American and European Developments in International Relations." *International Organization* 52 (1998): 687–727.

Walker, R. B. J. *Inside/Outside: International Relations as Political Theory*. Cambridge: Cambridge University Press, 1993.

Wallerstein, Immanuel. *The Modern World System I*. New York: Academic Press, 1974.

Watson, Adam. *The Evolution of International Society: A Comparative Historical Analysis*. London: Routledge, 1992.

Weber, Eugen. *Peasants into Frenchmen: The Modernization of Rural France 1870–1914*. Stanford, Calif.: Stanford University Press, 1976.

Webster, J. B. "Usuku: The Homeland of the Iteso." Pp. xvii–80 in *The Iteso during the Asonya*, edited by J. B. Webster. Nairobi: East African Educational Publishers, 1973.

Wendt, Alexander. *Social Theory of International Politics*. Cambridge: Cambridge University Press, 1999.

Westlake, John. *Chapters on the Principles of International Law*. Cambridge: Cambridge University Press, 1894.

White, Sonya, and Claire Creaser. *Scholarly Journal Prices: Selected Trends and Comparisons*. Loughborough: Loughborough University, Library and Information Statistics Unit, 2004.

Wickramasinghe, Nira. "From Human Rights to Good Governance: The Aid Regime in the 1990s." Pp. 305–26 in *The New World Order: Sovereignty, Human Rights and the Self-Determination of Peoples*, edited by Mortimer Sellers. Oxford: Berg, 1996.

Williams, Howard. *International Relations in Political Thought*. Milton Keynes: Open University Press, 1992.

Williams, Marc. *Third World Cooperation: The Group of 77 in UNCTAD*. London: Pinter, 1991.

Williams, Patrick, and Laura Chrisman, eds. *Colonial Discourse and Post-Colonial Theory*. London: Harvester Wheatsheaf, 1993.

Wolf, Eric R. *Europe and the People without History*. Berkeley: University of California Press, 1997.

———. *Pathways of Power: Building an Anthropology of the Modern World*. Berkeley: University of California Press, 2001.

World Bank. *Development and Human Rights: The Role of the World Bank*. Washington, D.C.: International Bank for Reconstruction and Development/World Bank, 1998. <http://www.worldbank.org/html/extdr/rights/> (accessed September 2, 2005).

Wyn Jones, Richard, ed. *Critical Theory and World Politics*. Boulder, Colo.: Lynne Rienner, 2001.

Zaretsky, Eli. "Trauma and Dereification: September 11 and the Problem of Ontological Security." *Constellations: An International Journal of Critical and Democratic Theory* 9, no. 1 (2002): 98–105.

Zeleza, Paul Tiyambe. "Manufacturing and Consuming Knowledge: African Libraries and Publishing." *Development in Practice* 6, no. 4 (1996): 293–303.

———. *Manufacturing African Studies and Crises*. Dakar: CODESRIA, 1997.

———. "The Politics of Historical and Social Science Research in Africa." *Journal of Southern African Studies* 28, no. 1 (2002): 9–23.

————. "Neo-Liberalism and Academic Freedom." Pp. 42–68 in *African Universities in the Twenty-First Century: Liberalisation and Internationalisation*, edited by Paul Tiyambe Zeleza and Adebayo Olukoshi. Dakar: CODESRIA, 2004.

Zell, Hans M. "Publishing in Africa: The Crisis and the Challenge." Pp. 369–87 in *A History of Twentieth-Century African Literatures*, edited by Oyekan Owomoyela. Lincoln: University of Nebraska Press, 1993.

Žižek, Slavoj. "Multiculturalism, or, the Cultural Logic of Multinational Capitalism." *New Left Review* 225 (September–October 1997): 28–51.

Index

abstraction, 3, 10, 30, 34, 89–106, 212, 223
Abu-Lughod, Janet, 47, 59
Abyssinian expedition, 92
Acholi society, 228
Adorno, Theodor W., 12
Afghanistan, 146
Africa, 59, 89, 91, 111; and Berlin Conference, 121–24; British colonial occupation of, 11, 27; conditions of academic research in, 16, 230–37; European acquisition of territory, 132, 138–39; Great Lakes region of, 167; Grotius in, 95–98; imperial historiography of, 155–60, 224; Portuguese colonial territories, independence struggle, 226–27; and postcolonial studies, 36; scholarship from, 1–2; scramble for, 122, 159, 190. See also East Africa
Africanist scholarship, 14, 235
African political systems, 13–14, 160–74, 225, 228
AIDS, 94

Akello, Grace, 164
alienation, 15, 91, 94–95, 105, 212, 221
Amadiume, Ifi, 160, 167, 235
America, 48, 185. See also North America
American Bill of Rights, 180, 184–85
American Empire, 28
American philanthropic foundations, 233–34
American Revolution, 14, 49, 180–81, 184, 188, 189–90, 226
American revolutionaries, 180, 184–85, 190–91
American unilateralism, 11, 146
Amerindians, 99–100, 118–19. See also Native Americans
Andalusia, 46, 48
Anderson, Benedict, 98
Ando, Nisuke, 143
Anghie, Antony, 8, 11, 16, 99, 109–26, 223–35
anthropology, 2, 90, 105, 235
anticolonial struggles, 12–13, 15, 191, 193, 224–26, 229

Antoinette, Marie, 186
Appiah, Kwame Anthony, 36
area studies, 4, 67, 235
Arendt, Hannah, 190
Asante polity, 92, 170–73
Asia, 46, 59, 89, 96, 111, 115, 123
Aurobindo, Sri. *See* Sri Aurobindo
Australia, 5, 35
Austria, 55–56
Austro-Hungarian Empire, 54
authenticity, 15, 35, 37, 69, 179, 182,
    220, 227
Awasom, Innocent, 233
Ayers, Alison, 8, 13–14, 15, 99, 155–74,
    223–25, 228

Balkans, 54
Barkawi, Tarak, 229
Bartlett, Robert, 46
Baxi, Upendra, 135
Beethoven, Ludwig van, 203
Belgium, 54, 56, 92
Bell, Gertrude, 27
Bengal, 101–3, 121, 200
Benhabib, Seyla, 190
Bentham, Jeremy, 101, 103, 179
Berlin, Isaiah, 190
Berlin Conference. *See* Africa
Berman, Edward, 234
Bessis, Sophie, 26, 29, 34
Bhaskar, Roy, 212
Bismarck, Otto von, 122
Blair, Tony, 145
Blaut, James, 26, 29, 59
Bodin, Jean, 3
bourgeoisie, 52, 205
bourgeois state, 53, 205–7, 209
Brazil, 51
Britain, 51–54, 56–57, 92, 100, 102, 123,
    136
British Crown, 121, 136
British Empire, 137, 200
British Raj, 92, 100–102
British South Africa Company, 121

Buganda Kingdom, 168–69
Bunyoro Kingdom, 169–70
Burke, Edmund, 101, 103–5
Burma, 92

Cabral, Amílcar, 12, 220, 227, 236
Cameroon, 233
Canada, 35, 92, 158
capitalism, 9, 28–29, 32, 58, 68, 77, 81,
    228
capitalist accumulation, 77
capitalist development, 59
capitalist economy, 78
capitalist exchange, 67–68, 227
capitalist modernity, 78, 227
Caribbean, 27, 229
Carolingian Empire, 29
Central Europe, 52
Césaire, Aimé, 203–4
Chakrabarty, Dipesh, 113
Chamberlain, Joseph, 122–23,
Chand, Tara, 200
Cheyfitz, Eric, 35–36,
Chimni, B. S., 15, 16, 197–213, 225,
    227, 229
China, 47–50, 59, 92, 120, 123,
Christendom, 71, 78
Christianity, 99, 133
Christophe, Henry, 186, 188
"civilization," 1, 7–8, 66, 68, 70, 94,
    98–99, 110, 116–126, 133, 143, 156,
    224. *See also* Western civilization
civilizing mission, 46, 103, 111, 116,
    124, 158
civil liberties, 57, 73–74, 146, 231
civil society, 72, 74, 79, 81, 125
Clark, Colin, 51
class / classes, 27, 44–45, 51–57, 59, 80,
    102, 104, 169, 185, 205–6, 222, 229
Coalitional Provisional Authority,
    141–46
CODESRIA, 232, 235
Colombia, 51
Columbus, Christopher, 36, 48, 94, 118

common sense. *See* Westphalian
  imaginary
Concert of Europe, 91
conditionalities, 115
Conrad, Joseph, 27
contrapuntal analysis, 10, 44, 90–106,
  222–23
Counter Terrorism Committee, 135
Crimean War, 92
critical realism, 27

decolonization, 3, 7, 26, 28, 38, 111,
  123–24, 233
Defoe, Daniel, 27
democracy, 7, 13, 44, 125, 204–6, 221,
  224; African, 13–14, 157–174, 228;
  bourgeois, 198; in Europe, 52, 55–57;
  free market, 143; liberal, 4–5, 13–14,
  57, 180–81, 204; promotion of, 114,
  125; socialist, 198
democratization, 7, 50, 51, 55–57, 144,
  157–59, 173, 224
Denmark, 56
Dessalines, Jean-Jacques, 186
development, 7, 9, 34, 44, 53, 114–15,
  125, 224; capitalist, 44, 58–59;
  dependent, 51, 53, 59; of Europe,
  50–55; in Sri Aurobindo's thought,
  199, 203–8; sustainable, 143
development institutions, 115
Diaz, Bernal, 27
Diderot, Denis, 184
dispossession, 3, 11, 25, 32–36, 89–90,
  94, 99, 119, 131–52, 219, 221, 231,
  235
Disraeli, Benjamin, 33
division of intellectual labor, 4–5, 27
dualistic economies, 53–54, 59
dual mandate, 122–23, 224
Du Bois, W. E. B., 1–2, 222
Dutch East India Company, 96–98, 121

East Africa, 27, 167
Eastern Europe, 35, 181

East India Company, 100–102, 121
Ebola virus, 94
egalitarianism, 14, 163–64, 173, 199
Egypt, 92
emancipation, 12, 38, 186, 201, 212,
  225, 229
Engels, Friedrich, 212
England, 49, 52, 101, 103, 123, 136,
  199
English Revolution, 52
Enlightenment, 3, 4, 14, 33–34, 49–50,
  58, 74, 156, 184, 187
equality, 11, 24, 33, 55, 71, 184, 188–89,
  203
equality, racial, 227
Eurocentrism, 5–9, 12–13, 33–34, 43,
  58, 110, 156–60, 221, 224, 230
European expansion, 10, 14, 44–48, 50,
  57, 59, 116, 119, 139
Eyoh, Dickson, 157

"failed states," 68
Fanon, Frantz, 6, 12, 224, 236
feminisim, 5, 6, 229
Feuerbach, Ludwig Andreas, 212
Fichte, Johann Gottlieb, 203
first world war. *See* World War I
Fischer, Sibylle, 190
Fortes, Meyer, 166–67
Foucault, Michel, 90–91, 104
Fox, Gregory, 117
France, 47, 51–54, 56, 92, 122–23, 180,
  184, 187
French Declaration of the Universal
  Rights of Men and Citizens, 179–81,
  184–85
French Revolution, 14, 49, 52, 55, 104,
  179–81, 184–86, 189–91

Gandhi, Mahatma, 12, 199, 201, 211–12
Gathii, James, 8, 11, 16, 99, 121,
  131–47, 223, 225
gender relations, 71, 94, 161, 166–67,
  173

General Agreement on Trade in Services, 236
genocide, 4, 89, 93, 105
Germany, 11, 51, 54, 56, 92, 122, 143–45, 203
Ghana, 159, 161, 164–67, 170–73
globalization, 23, 58, 72, 115–16, 123
Goethe, Johann Wolfgang von, 203
"good governance," 7, 9, 11, 109–26, 158, 225, 234
Gramsci, Antonio, 12, 72
Greece, 46, 51, 56
Grotius, Hugo, 3, 95–98, 222
Grovogui, Siba, 3, 8, 14, 96–98, 179–94, 222–26
Guha, Ranajit, 29, 31, 34, 36, 38, 155, 220, 223, 228

Habermas, Jürgen, 12
Habsburg Empire, 28
Hague Convention Respecting the Laws and Customs of War on Land, 132
Hague Regulations, 134, 140–41, 143–44
Haitian constitution, 187–89, 191
Haitian Revolution, 182, 184, 186–94
Halperin, Sandra, 8, 10, 14, 43–60, 66, 77, 158, 222, 229
Hamilton, Alexander, 132
Hegel, Georg Wilhelm Friedrich, 3, 12, 15, 34, 94, 155–59, 173, 203, 223
hegemony, 33, 57–58, 68–70, 72, 74, 76, 79, 228
Heidegger, Martin, 90, 93
historiography, 23, 28, 34, 38; imperialist, 13, 35–36, 155, 157, 159–60; nationalist, 44, 47; Western, 45, 47, 50
Hobbes, Thomas, 3, 35, 73, 161
Horkheimer, Max, 12
hospitality, 70, 72, 164, 227
House of Lords, 57, 136
humanitarian intervention, 210

humanitarianism, 11, 37, 121–26, 134–35, 139, 224–25
human nature, 69, 225
human needs, 188, 210
human rights, 7, 13–15, 33, 111, 114–17, 124, 135, 147, 158, 179–94, 224
human unity, 13, 15, 197–213, 224–28
Hume, David, 101, 104, 156
Hundred Years' Peace, 90–91
Huntington, Samuel, 37
Hussein, Saddam, 140, 144, 147; regime of, 141, 143

identity, 38, 65, 71–72
Ignatieff, Michael, 180–81, 192–93
IMF. *See* International Monetary Fund
Imperial East Africa Company, 121
India, 15, 48, 91–92, 100–105, 121, 199–200, 228
Indian Revolt of 1857, 92
industrial revolution, 49–53, 59
inequality, 4, 9–10, 33, 52, 90, 105, 116, 161, 173, 183; in knowledge production, 13, 16, 229–37
intellectual division of labor. *See* division of intellectual labor
International Convention on the Elimination of All Forms of Racial Discrimination, 111
International Covenant on Civil and Political Rights, 111
international law, 3, 4, 8, 9, 11, 16, 28, 66, 95–98, 109–30, 131–52, 198, 224; human rights, 109, 114–17; positivist, 31, 119–20
International Monetary Fund (IMF), 114–16, 158, 236
international society, 3, 4, 7
Iraq, 11, 131–32, 139–47, 204
Ireland, 54
Islam, 8–9, 47, 58, 65–82; rejectionist, 80; resurgent, 70, 80
Islamic civilization, 50, 67, 76
Islamic cultural zones, 9, 73–82

Islamic empires, 58
Islamic thought, 58
Islamophobia, 73
Italy, 11, 31, 51, 54, 92, 122, 143–45
Iteso society, 162–64, 227

Jamaica, 92
James, C. L. R., 27
Jameson, Frederic, 93–94
Japan, 11, 29, 143–45
Jefferson, William, 186, 189
just war, 95, 119

Kant, Immanuel, 3, 12, 13, 15, 35, 156,
    197, 203, 223
Kelley, Robin D. G., 204
Keynes, John Maynard, 101
Korea, 116
Krishna, Sankaran, 10–11, 72, 89–106,
    109, 121, 221–23, 225, 228–29

Laffey, Mark, 229
Lamprecht, Karl Gottfried, 202
Latin America, 52, 59, 95, 181, 229
laws of war, 132–34
League of Nations, 24, 39, 111, 124,
    198, 208
legal personality, 119–20
Lenin, Vladimir Ilyich, 28, 35
liberal tolerance, 9, 69–70, 73
liberalism, 5, 6, 9, 11, 65–82, 228;
    liberalism and colonialism, 75, 80,
    102–5. *See also* democracy
Lindley, M. F., 123
Locke, John, 35,
Louis, William Roger, 31
L'Ouverture, Toussaint, 186
Lugard, Lord Frederick, 122

Macaulay, Thomas Babington, 101, 103
Machel, Samora, 226
Machiavelli, Niccolò, 3, 35
Mafeje, Archie, 168
Mamdani, Mahmood, 35, 158–59, 228

mandate system, 124
Maoris, wars against, 92
Marx, Karl, 12, 27–31, 38, 101, 199,
    211–12, 220–21
Marxism, 6, 27, 34, 202, 211
Mayer, Arno, 52
Mehta, Uday Singh, 103–4, 222–23
Mesquita, Bueno de, 93
method, 8, 25, 26–28, 38, 113, 159,
    220–21
Mexico, 51, 99–100,
Middle East, 46–47, 49–50, 59, 96, 142
Mignolo, Walter, 98–100
Mill, James, 101, 103
Mill, John Stuart, 101, 103–4, 223
Mintz, Sidney W., 187–89
Mkandawire, Thandika, 234–36
mode of production, 13, 160, 162,
    167–68, 191
modernization, 7, 71, 73, 76, 80
modernity, 4, 8–9, 43–60, 65–82, 95,
    182, 187, 221, 226–27
Mohanty, J. N., 198
Moore, Barrington, 52
Moore, John Basset, 133–34
Morrison, Toni, 95
Mozambique, 226
multinational corporations, 132

Nandy, Ashis, 201
nationalism, 24, 30–31, 117
nation-state, 23, 28, 30, 53, 68, 80, 94,
    96, 98, 105, 205, 220, 222
Native Americans, 136–38
natural law, 118–19, 183
natural rights, 179–80, 183–84
Nazism, 144, 203–4
Nederveen Pieterse, Jan, 26
neocolonialism, 7, 9–10, 24, 32, 35,
    158–59, 204, 229, 231
neoliberal economic policies, 115
neoliberal values, 145, 158–59
neorealism, 65, 223
Netherlands, 56, 96

Neto, Agostinho, 226
Nietschmann, Bernard, 93
Nietzsche, Friedrich, 203, 211
Nigeria, 232
North America, 35, 36, 78, 229, 232
Nukunya, Kwame, 165

Ogot, Bethwell, 235
Okalany, D. H., 164
ontology, 44, 58, 67, 72, 156, 187,
    221–22
oral history, 99, 159, 231
orientalism, 9, 33, 38, 65, 70–71, 75–76,
    79–80
Ottoman Empire, 47
Ouattara, Alassane, 158

Pagden, Anthony, 180–81, 183, 192
Palestine, 47
Parekh, Bhikhu, 26
Pasha, Mustapha Kamal, 8–9, 15, 65–82,
    94, 146, 221, 227–29
p'Bitek, Okot, 228
pedagogy, 90, 105–6
Permanent Settlement, 101–3
Persia, 92
plantation economy, 189, 191–92
Portugal, 54, 56, 92
Portuguese Empire, 96, 226
postcolonialism / postcolonial studies, 6,
    7, 25, 29, 36, 38, 113, 193, 220–21
post-Westphalian order, 66, 77
private property, 11, 94, 131–47, 167,
    169
privatization, 115, 142–43, 146
progress, 7, 8, 9, 15, 34, 46–47, 50,
    57–58, 67, 71, 76, 78, 209
property, 36, 91, 95, 99, 119, 124, 166,
    187–88, 225. *See also* private
    property
property relations, 11, 168, 211
property rights, 11, 46, 97, 119, 188
Prussia, 46
Punjab, conquest of, 92

race, 2, 10, 89–108, 109–26, 186, 221,
    229
racial categories, 120
racial extermination policies, 190
racial oppression/discrimination, 111,
    187, 189
racism, 2, 4, 10, 11, 30, 59, 73, 76, 94,
    105, 110–11, 156, 224, 227
realism, 6, 65, 198, 206, 223
reciprocity, 14, 47, 173
refugees, 94, 188
Ricardo, David, 101
rights, 4, 38, 96, 116, 171, 224. *See also*
    human rights; natural rights; property
    rights
Robbins, Bruce, 33
Robinson, Ronald, 31
Roman Empire, 28
Rousseau, Jean-Jacques, 3, 14
rule of law, 114, 123, 125, 145–46, 158
Rummell, Rudy, 93
Russia, 54, 56

Said, Edward, 1, 2, 3, 30, 33, 91, 222
Sarkar, Sumit, 200
Sartre, Jean-Paul, 37
Saurin, Julian, 7, 23–42, 69, 219–23,
    230–31, 235–36
Schmitt, Carl, 73
second world war. *See* World War II
secularization, 69–72, 77–78, 96
secularism, 9, 67–68, 70–71, 78
securitization, 9, 65–66, 69–82
security, 3, 7, 74–78, 96, 224, 228–29
Security Council, 140–43
self-determination, 24, 28, 143
Sen, Amartya, 179, 182
Senegal, 232
Shivji, Issa, 10, 234–35
Sieyès, Abbé de, 189
Singer, David, 92–93
slavery, 1, 4, 90, 93, 94–95, 122, 184–91,
    221
slaves, 182, 186–89, 191

slave trade, 3, 4
Smith, Adam, 101, 104
socialism, 57
solidarity, 161, 189, 227
South Africa, 14, 35, 92, 136, 168, 199
sovereign power, 92
sovereignty, 3–4, 7, 28, 66, 73–78, 80,
    89–106, 109–26, 136, 143, 147, 186,
    190, 193, 221
Spain, 47–48, 54–55, 56, 92, 96, 98–100,
    123, 136–38
Spanish crown, 137–38
Spanish Empire, 96, 118–19
Sri Aurobindo, 15, 197–213, 225
state-centrism, 30, 93
Stokes, Eric, 110
structural adjustment, 115, 231–33
subaltern studies, 7, 29
supremacism / supremacy, 25–27,
    29–30, 32–35, 65, 224
surveillance, 73
Sweden, 56, 158
Switzerland, 56

Taiwo, Olufemi, 156–57, 173
Tallensi society, 164–67
Tanzania, 232, 235
terra nullius, 139
territoriality, 96
terrorism, 94, 105, 135
Thailand, 116
Thiong'o, Ngũgĩ wa, 27
Thirty Years' War, 95
Thucydides, 3, 35
Tonnerre, Boisrond, 186
Toynbee, Arnold, 50
Trouillot, Michel-Rolph, 184, 186
Turkey, 35
TWAIL, 16, 112, 229

Uganda, 159, 161–64, 168–70
United Kingdom, 35, 133, 141

United Nations, 25, 111, 135, 141–42,
    198, 208–9
United States, 27, 35, 72, 131–37,
    140–41, 146, 184, 186–88, 204, 227,
    234
Universal Declaration of Human Rights,
    181
universalism, 66, 68–69, 73, 76, 158,
    182, 224–28
universality, 33–34, 68–69, 73, 79, 97,
    111, 156–58, 179, 181, 187
U.S. State Department, 141
U.S. Supreme Court, 132, 136–38
U.S. Treasury Department, 142

Vansina, Jan, 159
Vitoria, Francisco de, 117–20, 123–24,
    223
voting, 55–57

Wagner, Richard, 203
warfare, 134
War on Terror, 112, 135
Weber, Eugen, 98
Western civilization, 8, 11, 15, 68,
    71–73, 76–78, 203–4
Westlake, John, 121, 123–24
Westphalia, 3, 4, 9, 67, 78
Westphalian imaginary ("Westphalian
    common sense"), 3, 68, 75
Wickramasinghe, Nira, 117
Wilson, Woodrow, 24
Wolf, Eric, 29
Wolfensohn, James, 124
World Bank, 114–16, 124, 236
World War I, 2, 24, 51–52, 55–57, 95
World War II, 51, 57, 95

xenophobia, 66, 69

Zeleza, Paul Tiyambe, 231–36
Žižek, Slavoj, 65

About the Contributors

Antony Anghie is the Samuel D. Thurman Professor of Law at the S. J. Quinney School of Law. He received his LL.B and B.A. degrees from Monash University, Australia, and his S.J.D. from Harvard Law School. He teaches contracts and subjects in the international law curriculum. He has written on various aspects of international law, including the history of international law, globalization, international organizations, and human rights. He is the author most recently of *Imperialism, Sovereignty and the Making of International Law* (2005). He is a member of the Third World Approaches to International Law network of scholars.

Alison J. Ayers is assistant professor of global political economy in the Department of Political Science, Simon Fraser University, Canada. She previously worked at the University of Sussex and the University of Southampton in the United Kingdom and has ten years of program and research experience in Sudan, Kenya, Uganda, Tanzania, Ghana, Mali, and Bolivia with a range of organizations, including the United Nations, nongovernmental organizations, grassroots organizations, and the Sudan People's Liberation Movement. Recent publications include "Demystifying Democratisation: The Global Constitution of Neo-Liberal Polities in Africa," *Third World Quarterly* (2006) and, with Tony Evans, "In the Service of Power: The Global Political Economy of Citizenship and Human Rights," *Citizenship Studies* (2006).

B. S. Chimni is the vice-chancellor of the West Bengal National University of Juridical Sciences, Kolkata. He is on leave from Jawaharlal Nehru University, New Delhi, where he taught international law in the School of International Studies for nearly two decades. He is part of and committed to the Third World Approaches to International Law project. His areas of research interest are international legal theory, international trade law, and international refugee law. He is one of the general editors of the *Asian Yearbook of International Law*.

James Thuo Gathii is associate professor of law at Albany Law School in New York, where he teaches public international law, international business transactions, international organizations, and business organizations. He completed his LL.B.(Hons.) at the University of Nairobi and his S.J.D. from Harvard Law School. He has published extensively in international law, international intellectual property and trade law, and the political economy of reform in sub-Saharan Africa. He is a member of the Third World Approaches to International Law network of scholars.

Siba N'Zatioula Grovogui is professor at The Johns Hopkins University, where he teaches international relations theory and international law. He is author of *Sovereigns, Quasi Sovereigns, and Africans: Race and Self-Determination in International Law* (1996), *Beyond Eurocentrism and Anarchy* (2006), and articles that seek to illuminate the position of "Africa" in the international order, its "past" and "future" in light of recent scholarship in the fields of hermeneutics, ethnography, and historiography.

Branwen Gruffydd Jones is lecturer in the School of Politics and International Studies, University of Leeds. Her teaching and research interests include the global political economy of poverty with particular reference to Africa, theories and histories of imperialism, colonialism and neocolonialism, and questions of method in social inquiry. She is author of *Explaining Global Poverty: A Critical Realist Approach* (2006).

Sandra Halperin is professor of International relations in the Department of Politics and International Relations, Royal Holloway, University of London. She is the author of *In the Mirror of the Third World: Capitalist Development in Modern Europe* (1997), *Global Civil Society and Its Limits* (coedited with Gordon Laxer, 2003), *War and Social Change in Modern Europe: The Great Transformation Revisited* (2004), and articles on contemporary Middle East politics, nationalism, ethnic conflict, state building, historical sociology, and global development.

Sankaran Krishna is professor of international relations at the University of Hawai'i. His research and teaching has centered on nationalism, ethnic identity and conflict, identity politics, and postcolonial studies. He is author of *Postcolonial Insecurities: India, Sri Lanka and the Question of Nationhood* (2000).

Mustapha Kamal Pasha is chair in international relations at the University of Aberdeen. His recent publications include *International Relations and the New Inequality* (coedited with Craig Murphy, 2002) and *Colonial Political Economy: State-Building and Underdevelopment in the Punjab* (1998). He has published widely on postorientalist Islam and international relations, globalization, hegemony, and critical security studies. Currently, he is a member of the Nominating Committee of the International Studies Association (2006–2009) and has served as program director of the 2001 ISA Annual Convention in Chicago.

Julian Saurin teaches international relations and development studies at the University of Sussex. His research interests focus on the history of imperialism with special reference to the formation of the modern state system. He has a particular interest in Ottoman and Middle Eastern history. Additionally, he works on questions of global political economy and global environmental change.

Printed in Great Britain
by Amazon.co.uk, Ltd.,
Marston Gate.